Social Networking Spaces

*From Facebook to Twitter and
Everything In Between*

A Step-by-Step Introduction to Social Networks
for Beginners and Everyone Else

Todd Kelsey

Apress®

Social Networking Spaces: From Facebook to Twitter and Everything In Between

ISBN-13 (pbk): 978-1-4302-2596-6

ISBN-13 (electronic): 978-1-4302-2597-3

Printed and bound in the United States of America 9 8 7 6 5 4 3 2 1

President and Publisher: Paul Manning
Lead Editor: Michelle Lowman
Technical Reviewer: Alexandra Constantin
Editorial Board: Clay Andres, Steve Anglin, Mark Beckner, Ewan Buckingham, Tony Campbell, Gary Cornell, Jonathan Gennick, Michelle Lowman, Matthew Moodie, Jeffrey Pepper, Frank Pohlmann, Ben Renow-Clarke, Dominic Shakeshaft, Matt Wade, Tom Welsh
Coordinating Editor: Jim Markham
Copy Editors: Tiffany Taylor, K. Stence, Tracy Brown Collins
Compositor: Mary Sudul
Indexer: Potomac Indexers
Artist: April Milne
Cover Designer: Anna Ishchenko

Distributed to the book trade worldwide by Springer-Verlag New York, Inc., 233 Spring Street, 6th Floor, New York, NY 10013. Phone 1-800-SPRINGER, fax 201-348-4505, e-mail orders-ny@springer-sbm.com, or visit http://www.springeronline.com.

For information on translations, please e-mail info@apress.com, or visit http://www.apress.com.

Apress and friends of ED books may be purchased in bulk for academic, corporate, or promotional use. eBook versions and licenses are also available for most titles. For more information, reference our Special Bulk Sales–eBook Licensing web page at http://www.apress.com/info/bulksales.

To my brother, Mark

Thanks for living life so fully. What an inspiration!

Contents at a Glance

Contents

About the Author

 **Todd Kelsey**, PhD (ABD) is an author and educator whose publishing credits include several books written to help people learn more about technology. He has appeared on television as a featured expert and has worked with a wide variety of corporations and nonprofit organizations. He is the founder of Communications for the World (CFTW), a nonprofit organization whose mission is to develop free learning materials in different languages, and his research has included work in social media; delivering content in different languages; sustainability; and helping people to capture, preserve, and share their life stories. He is currently seeking a permanent home, at or near a college or university, for CFTW and the Digital Archaeology Institute. For more information, see www.cftw.com and www.digitalarchaeology.org

About the Technical Reviewer

 **Alexandra Constantin** is a writer, editor, and 3D artist who lives with her husband and daughter in the Chicago area. Her background includes architecture and working in the advertising industry in Europe and the U.S. In addition to tech-editing *Social Networking Spaces*, she created the 3D characters that appear throughout the book and in the appendixes. Her design/3D portfolio can be found at www.cgadvertising.com. She is seeking a remote position where she can be a creative director and/or work on 3D character or toy design.

Acknowledgments

A special thanks to the following people, and to all who helped out in various ways during the writing of this book:

To Mom and Dad, for being there.

@Apress: to Michelle, Leo, Dominic, and any others in the future at Apress or elsewhere who agree to either shave their head or dye their hair (red, green, or blue, of course) when this book sells 50,000 copies (don't look so glum, it's for a good cause!); to Michelle Lowman, for taking this book on; to Clay Andres, for introducing me to Apress; to Dominic Shakeshaft, for taking a risk on a higher page count; to Lisa Lau and Leo Cuellar, for their help in marketing and publicity; to James Markham, for gathering together all the pieces; to the "Three Musketeers," the copyeditors who so carefully went through the entire manuscript—Tiffany Taylor, Katie Stence, and Tracy Brown Collins; to the production artists, additional editors, and all other staff—it's a group effort, and I greatly appreciate your help, and thanks for putting up with me!

To all the readers of this book: the thought of helping you inspired me to really care about this book and provided energy.

To Alexandra, for the helpful tech editing, for bringing Maya into the world, for all the wonderful 3D images.

To Chuck, for choosing life, taking pictures, and inspiring me to do the same; to Chris, for hospitality and friendship; to Rachael, for adventures to American Science and Surplus and other tomfoolery.

To the "pre-reviewers" who agreed to read through the early, much loopier drafts of chapters and provided valuable feedback (and helped me to tone down the personal commentary): David Partain, Nina Gribble, Kelly Turner, Laura Needs, Bob Langworthy, Mia Ruth, Christie Chu, Ehren Von Lehen, Lydia Moorman, Jamie Reiner, Loren Baird, Paul Heidebrecht.

To each and every person who agreed to have their picture or blog or site used in the book: Todd Tomlinson, Catherine Sigmar, Anselm Hook, Dancing Ink, and all the others. To sfskz and China—may the love increase between our countries, and may your blog on www.sina.com be in the top 10 someday.

To Peter Gabriel, for caring enough about the world to do something about it, and for having a wonderful magical studio. I hope I see it again someday!

To DG, for playing along with the Sunflower Club, for sharing stories, and for all the many hours you've been putting into shepherding creative works. May VDT do well, may the zoning be peaceful, and may you end up with a groovy solar/wind house!

To Dorothy Raymond, for passing along your dearly beloved 1969 van, for taking care of it from the day you picked it up in 1970 until the day you saw it off on its way to Illinois, for sharing stories about your adventures for me to put on the 2069.us blog, for the great pictures—I promise to take care of the van, and here's hoping that both the van and myself make it to the hundredth anniversary of Woodstock in 2069!

To Paul Allen, for acquiring Hendrix's guitar from the Italian collector. Can I borrow it in 2069, if I live that long, and play the National Anthem at Woodstock?

To BG and WB, for the inspiration from your hard work and generosity.

To my housemates Mark, Adam, Josiah, who put up with my late nights working on this book, and our neighbor Bob, for helping out with some plumbing crises.

To each of the helpful contacts at various companies who answered questions, including Jennifer Nielsen at Ning and Ann FitzGibbons at Meetup. To Phil Rosedale, Brian Semper, Phil Freeman, and Jessica Ornitz, for fun and frolic on Second Life.

To the helpful folks at Google—Karen Wickre, Jason Freidenfelds, Chris Dale, Siobhan Quinn, as well as the courageous engineers of the Data Liberation Front—a toast to cage-free data! And a special thanks to Franz Och and the multilingual team for making very helpful tools for crossing the language gap.

To Jeremy Hahn, for sacrificing your time and making use of your Jedi talents to help CFTW and bring about the Life Story Suitcase and other projects. Carpe diem!

To the Knight Foundation—Gary Kebbel, Jose Zamora, and the others—for triggering a sense of "the local" in me. Thanks for bringing about the News Challenge contest and for all the countless hours you spend going through entries—the process helped me to refine ideas that I hope will come about in my future research.

To Todd, Catherine, Cecilia, Dan, Stuart, Scott, and other CFTW advisors, for guidance and patience. To Dr. Nick Patel, M.D., for daydreaming with CFTW, for moral support for big ideas, and for the work you do in the developing world. To Brent Oxley, for taking a risk on free learning at CFTW.

To Annalisa Roger, for pursuing dotgreen; may it come to pass, and grow into something wonderful.

To Dr. Alex Tabibi, M.D., for allowing something to be done with Green.org, Wind.com, and Solar.com—may the present efforts bear fruit, reward you for risk, and make the world better. To Griffin DeLuce, for putting up with me in our early conversations, and for the great RGB logo.

To Dr. Broadhead, Dr. Stolley, Dr. Snapper, and Dr. Pulliam—thanks for helping me to get into the final stretch of the PhD. Look out, here comes Dr. Fun! (I hope!)

To Dr. Hein, for allowing me to barge in and help you make a blog.

To SJ, NN, MLJ, WB and all the other staff and volunteers in the OLPC and Sugar Labs community, for bringing educational opportunity to kids who otherwise might not have it.

To Ed Bice, Rich Gibson, Anselm, Siko, and Amber, for working to bring the world closer together.

To Howie, for opening doors and patiently helping successive projects come about.

To Ben, Jim, Andrew, Rachel, Jon, Karl, Jamesie, Rick, Josh, Neal, and all the other folks from the music crowd I've ever come across who've given me a heritage of joy. To Marko, for late night idiot checks, for keeping me out of trouble on the road, for stories about NIN, and for being the first urban sunflower grower.

To Jeff and Margaret, for a vision of the future.

To KP, T-roh, Chloe, Joy, Mark, Scott, Shannon, Aaron (and your special friend), Jeff, Angie, and the Labradoodle—for a wonderful time in Da UP that really sustained me. (Jeff/Angie —keep on singing, and please record—holy cow.)

To Molly, for having the courage to act.

To "Courtney and the Regulars" @ Cadillac Ranch, for making a few Friday nights sweeter.

To all my Facebook friends, who've provided feedback and encouragement on thoughts, creative expression, and ideas. To Zack Jackson, for your wonderful talents as a game developer and the risk you took in making the Mantis game.

To all the members of the Sunflower Club, past, present, and future, for joining in the fun—and a special thanks to Mrs. Neal, a.k.a. Mother Nature, and Dr. Hein, for gardening advice.

To all the people at Cradle.org and Adoption Learning Partners, including Ivy, Merrilee, Julie, Joan, Noreen, Marianne, Judy, Tasha, Barbara, and everyone else, for helping to connect kids with new homes.

To Chad Mezera, Kristen Wilkerson, and the rest of the staff at WVU, for making a good academic program that's helping people to develop marketable skills.

To Tan Le at Emotiv and Andrew Junker at Brainfingers, for inspiration on Thinkwriter. Thanks for making the world a better place.

To Oprah, and everyone at Harpo: thanks for surprising people. I believe this book could be helpful to many of the people in your audience, and all author proceeds are going to CFTW, a nonprofit organization. If you read the book and agree, please consider getting in touch, and giving the book some exposure, either on the show, or in a video or article on the site.

(And to all the other people who I inadvertently forgot to mention, please accept my apology. Let's put your name in the Acknowledgements section at www.snspaces.com!)

Introduction

This book is a how-to guide, a tour of social networks like Facebook, Twitter, Blogger, LinkedIn, and others. It's appropriate for beginners and anyone else who'd like to get a sense of what you can do on various social networks. I've tried to make the book as friendly as possible and easy to read, and I hope you enjoy it.

Most of the book contains step-by-step instructions for specific things you can try. My goal is that by the end of the book, you gain a good understanding of what you can do in today's social networks.

There are also some sections written in a blog style, where I share personal examples as an attempt to provide some inspiration. I hope that when you see what I share, maybe you'll think back to kindergarten and how much fun show-and-tell can be.

Life Stories

I hope you'll discover how much fun it can be to take pictures, gather stories, and use social networks to share your adventures with friends and family. At some point, I discovered this for myself, and I've also seen this "aha!" moment with friends and in classes I've taught. I'm convinced that in the end, for many people, this can be one of the most meaningful and satisfying things to do on social networks, so I'm interested in helping people explore this area.

This *life story* theme is introduced in Chapter 1 and appears throughout the book. It's related to *personal digital archaeology*, a concept that is also discussed in Chapter 1 and on www.digitalarchaeology.org. Chapter 1 also introduces the Life Story Suitcase, a tool for backing up material that has been placed on social networks. The tool can also be used to gather, preserve, and share stories.

Facebook/Twitter

Chapters 2–5 explore Facebook, which is a great way to stay in touch with friends, family, and relatives. After Facebook comes Twitter, and how to make short messages called *tweets* on Twitter.com or with a mobile device.

I show how some social networks can be connected to make it easier to share news and other information. For example, I relate how when I get back from the gym, I sit down and tweet how many minutes I spent on the elliptical machine. Because of the connections you can make between Twitter and Facebook, this message goes on my Twitter page, to my followers, and also to my friends and acquaintances on Facebook.

Blogger

In Chapters 8 and 9, you can try making a blog on Blogger.com. A blog is a simple, easy, and very popular way to share thoughts, either privately or publicly. You'll discover how Blogger.com is a great tool for blogging.

Flickr

Chapter 10 introduces Flickr, a site with millions of users that is based almost entirely around pictures. You can go and browse, or start an account of your own. If you enjoy taking pictures, this site is for you! It's nice because you end up having visitors who like checking out pictures, and you can get feedback and encouragement. There are a lot of fascinating pictures on Flickr, and the people are also interesting. In Chapter 10, you meet Chuck Isdale, a friend and Flickr enthusiast who inspired this chapter.

YouTube

I hope you enjoy relaxing and taking a look at YouTube in Chapter 11. YouTube has videos that will make you laugh. And if you like, you can spend part of your day at YouTube EDU, where you can learn new things for free.

LinkedIn

As part of your tour, I *highly* recommend checking out LinkedIn in Chapters 12 and 13. In my opinion, LinkedIn is a *very* important site, which can help anyone to build a career network and find work. You learn about the power of referrals on LinkedIn, which can be very helpful to you and also allow you to help others.

MySpace

In Chapter 14, you can learn about MySpace, who uses it, and how it is well-suited for musicians, bands, and sharing music or the spoken word (such as poetry, stories, or interviews of friends and family members). Like the other chapters, the MySpace chapter has examples you can follow to try things out. Because this chapter has an audio theme, I provide access to some files you can use (in case you don't have a recording of a band, or an interview—yet).

Meetup, Ning, and Second Life

In the "Alternative Social Spaces" section, Chapters 15–17 introduce you to various sites that millions of people enjoy, which you may want to check out.

Meetup is a really interesting site that provides useful tools for meeting up with people who have similar interests.

Ning is a great resource for finding niche social networks that are focused on a particular topic, and it also allows you to easily make your very own online community.

Second Life is fun and worth trying at least once. It's a fascinating phenomenon in modern history: a 3D social network and an entire virtual world you can explore. You can create your own avatar (3D person) and make it look however you like, and do things like socialize, attend concerts, or even dance at a nightclub.

As part of your tour of social networks, I recommend trying virtual tourism on Second Life, ideally with one or more friends, going on an adventure, and taking pictures, so that you can have something unique and memorable to add to a digital photo album on Facebook (or for printing and adding to a traditional, non-digital photo album).

I show how you can visit famous places from the real world that have been re-created in Second Life, such as a popular re-creation of downtown Dublin, Ireland. And you see how several places that have been classified by the United Nations as World Heritage sites in real life are also on Second Life and explorable in 3D, such as architectural treasures. It's interesting stuff, both entertaining and educational, providing adventures that are worth going on for individuals, friends, families, or as part of a class.

Going Global

Chapter 18, the last chapter, is one of my favorites. It starts with some introductory comments about social networks in various parts of the world and provides a few links to explore, including one that leads to a fascinating map of what networks are popular in which countries.

I like this chapter because it showcases exciting technology from Google that is easy enough for anyone to use. Google's language tools can help you to communicate with someone who speaks a different language. (Computer translation isn't as good as human translation, but it's the next best thing, and it's like having your own personal interpreter.)

The likelihood of people from various countries and language groups connecting on social networks is increasing. And it's nice to know how easy it is to access these tools, which can enable conversations that otherwise wouldn't be possible. Thanks, Google!

Kahonua/RGB

Appendix A is an invitation to consider and give feedback on a set of ideas, including Kahonua, a set of 3D characters that appear at the beginning and end of some chapters. *Kahonua* is a word that means "globe of the earth" in Hawaiian. It's a concept for encouraging young minds in math and science through a set of stories, as well as some projects that can be done at home or at school, such as growing sunflowers. (To see how much impact something as simple as growing sunflowers can have on a young mind, see the earliest post on the blog at http://walter.sunflowerclub.net, by Walter Bender, who wound up as a professor at MIT.)

Related to Kahonua, RGB is a suggested method of assigning colors to causes. It's a simple way to pursue a balanced approach for making the world better—red (health), green (environment), blue (community). Appendix A includes a short visual presentation (also at http://tinyurl.com/aboutrgb), which explains how digital colors are a mix of red, green, and blue, and how the Sunflower Club came about.

The Sunflower Club is mentioned in the book and used as an example, especially in the Facebook chapters. It's open to all, no green thumb required, and is an opportunity to have fun growing ridiculously tall sunflowers. Members share the seeds and can trace their sunflowers on a "sunflower family tree" that goes back to the original blog at http://sunflowerreport.blogspot.com. The main site is at www.sunflowerclub.net.

The RGB presentation then relates some additional influences, such as a project called One Laptop Per Child, and how these influences led to the RGB concept.

CFTW

Communications for the World is a nonprofit organization I started during my PhD study at Illinois Institute of Technology. All author proceeds from this book are being donated to CFTW, whose mission is ultimately to develop free learning materials in various languages. Appendix B shares a series of project ideas that CFTW is considering, and you're invited to explore them further, to share your thoughts, and to get involved if you like. Some ideas are quite serious, and others are less so, such as the funvelope, a decidedly low-tech idea for a parallelogram-shaped envelope (which I hope can provide enjoyment, revenue to support CFTW's mission, and employment opportunities).

    I invite you to check out Appendixes A and B and share any thoughts you have. If any of it sounds interesting, both appendixes represent opportunities to get involved and learn more about social networks at the same time.

www.snspaces.com

There is a companion website for the book, www.snspaces.com, where you can ask questions, see full-color versions of every picture in the book, and post links. All are welcome at www.snspaces.com, whether you're a reader or just dropping by to visit.

Ultimately, what I tried to do with this book is to think of how to make it *fun*.

I've found that time and time again, with students from various backgrounds and all age experience levels, fun can make a difference in helping people learn. So, when I finish my PhD, I'm going to call myself Dr. Fun!

I hope you enjoy the tour. Remember, when you're out exploring social networks, don't worry about breaking anything, and click everything!

–Todd Kelsey, a.k.a. Dr. Fun
Chicago, Illinois
http://www.digitalarchaeology.org

CHAPTER 1

■ ■ ■

Carpe Diem! Capture, Preserve, and Share Your Adventures on Social Networks

In this chapter:

- How you can use social networks to capture, preserve, and share your stories
- Introducing the life story suitcase and personal digital archaeology

Come and visit the Social Networking Spaces companion web site at www.snspaces.com, where you can find more tips and updates and have an opportunity to share your thoughts or ask questions.

In Living Color: You can visit www.snspaces.com/pics to see full-color versions of all the pictures from this chapter.

Introduction

This chapter introduces the concept of using social networks to capture and share your life story. The rest of the book focuses on various social networks and the kinds of things you can do with them.

I invite you to glance through this chapter, go read the parts of the book you're most interested in, and then come back and read this chapter again.

I placed this chapter first because the experience of writing this book has strengthened my interest in helping people to capture, preserve, and share their stories. For me, of the many online activities I've tried over the years, the simple act of gathering and sharing pictures and stories has been one of the most important and meaningful things I've done. In this chapter I attempt to introduce this idea by expressing myself and sharing something of my own experience.

Disclaimer: Feedback, Participation Desired

You see that throughout the book that I add personal commentary and expression. This is especially true in this chapter; so, if you're looking for a more straightforward style or want to dive right in, you may wish to skip ahead to Chapter 2.

If you like the way this chapter and book are written, I'd love to hear from you. And if you don't like the style, I'd also love to hear from you!

My goal with this book is to inspire you to explore and to express yourself. I want to make it helpful, personal, friendly, and welcoming, to the point that you feel comfortable exploring the various social networks. This includes the companion site at snspaces.com, where you can ask questions and share your thoughts.

In the spirit of social networking, I also see this book as the beginning of a conversation in which you're welcome to participate. I'm beginning the conversation by introducing you to various social networks and the idea of gathering your adventures together so you can share them with others.

I shared drafts of the chapters with a number of people, listened to what they had to say, and took their feedback into account when revising the drafts. To me, a book is an ongoing effort. There's always room for improvement: in some cases, the improvement may take place on the companion site, but there are always future editions, too.

In short, I'm actively interested in any thoughts you have about the book and how it could be improved.

Sharing Stories from Your Life on Social Networks

Social networks provide a wonderful way to gather pictures and thoughts and then share them with people, either privately or publicly. For example, I really enjoyed putting this picture on Facebook:

It's a picture of the Hammondsport High School Girls' Basketball Team, 1917. My Grandma Kelsey is on the far left. I think she was pretty spunky to play basketball in 1917. (See how a bit of fun can make a picture come alive? In my opinion, this is a good reason to try taking some fun pictures of your own in the here and now, so future generations can see all sides of you.)

There's a lot to be said for digitizing things in order to make it easier to share them. (Digitizing = making things digital.) This means doing things like scanning pictures, using a digital camera with video capability to interview a relative, and so on. It can feel good to do this: to start putting it together. At least for me, it feels very meaningful; and as you read this chapter and book, I want to encourage you as much as possible to think about this concept: capture, preserve, and share.

But no one would be interested …

Wrong.

It's simple. Wouldn't it be interesting if you had even a single page of your great-grandparent's thoughts—say, written on their birthday, describing what they were going through at the time? Or a single page from a single day about what their life was like, what they did, what they enjoyed?

If the answer is yes, then maybe *you're* the great-grandparent, or will be.

What I mean is, you should never assume no one would be interested in your life; in fact, there's strong evidence to suggest that many people would be interested. Even if you don't think your life is interesting, there are people right now who think it is, and there's a good likelihood that there will be more such people in the future.

The other thing I want to mention is that people go through seasons: sometimes the seasons are good, sometimes the seasons are bad, sometimes they're dark, and sometimes they're joyful. I know something about my ancestors, but not a whole lot. But I'm interested in the good, bad, the ugly, and the beautiful. For example, my grandparents lived through the Great Depression. Grandpa Kelsey's first wife died, but he got married again. I'm interested in every part of that story, and I wish I had more pictures, letters, and so on to tell me more.

I believe that when you capture, preserve, and share *your* story, there's bound to be someone, somewhere, who *will* be interested and find some meaning in it (and quite possibly, find some strength in it).

Dr. Fun's Prescription: Capture, Preserve, and Share

Sometimes I go by the name "Dr. Fun." It won't be official until the Illinois Institute of Technology grants me a Ph.D; but in the meantime, sometimes it's a role I play in the classroom or outdoors. For example, here's me, Dr. Fun, wearing my Dr. Fun hat, playing bocce ball with some friends. (Having fun with Dr. Fun!)

I think living life in person can be fun: connecting with people, building meaningful significant relationships. I think this the greatest kind of fun: making history and going on adventures with people where you're doing something to enjoy the world, or make it better, and maybe inspire people.

And I think the story of what you do, whatever you do, is worth capturing. When you start capturing stories, it can be a lot of fun to look back at an experience and then to share it, as privately or publicly as you like. You can capture your life as you live it and *make history*. Carpe diem.

Preserve

Sometimes you're the only one who has a copy of something: a picture, a letter, an article. I think it makes a lot of sense to *back things up*. Sometimes this means making things digital and then sharing them on sites like Facebook, where suddenly everyone in the family has a copy.

Backing things up can mean digitizing, as in scanning a picture. But it can also mean *de-digitizing*. De-digitizing involves taking something that is digital and preserving it by printing it out. What happens if your computer crashes? What happens if the device you use to access your life stories breaks? Digitizing is about preserving things (and making it easier to share them). De-digitizing is also about preservation.

You probably have an awful lot of stuff in digital form these days, and if you're not careful, you may lose it: formats can become obsolete. Ever heard of VHS videocassettes? Not too long ago, most people didn't have iPods; they used CDs or cassettes. I know, that's so twentieth century, but a lot of people have cassettes in boxes somewhere, and in some cases, some interesting stuff is locked away on that media. If you wanted to access something that was recorded on an obsolete format, you'd need to translate it. And in the future, when formats change, there will be a need to translate again. There's a continual need for methods of converting pictures, video, voice, and so on, from older to newer formats, so that this personal media can be available going into the future.

It doesn't matter whether what you're talking about is in digital form, or pre-digital form. The point is, if something is important, it's a good idea to think about backing it up and preserving it in a way that can live into the future.

Bad News: Social Networks Aren't Eternal or All Powerful

You may take it for granted that a given company that runs a social network or web site will be around forever, but you should be skeptical in direct proportion to how precious your life media is to you. And I want to convince you that your life media is precious. Therefore, I think it's worth not taking these things for granted. Ever hear of an early social network called Geocities? A lot of people were on Geocities, but it eventually disappeared.

You can reasonably make the comparison between lost civilizations and social networks. Modern social networks are like digital civilizations, but there are many reasons the *digital artifacts* could get lost or buried:

- Companies go out of business.

- Businesses can change their rules or start charging for things that used to be free.

- Businesses have computers that can get hacked. There's no such thing as a computer connected to the Internet that is 100 percent secure. Did you happen to catch in the news how Google was hacked, along with several other large corporations?

- Sometimes people pass on unexpectedly, and they may not tell everyone about their online accounts.

- Sometimes bad things happen: Mother Nature, Father Time, our neighbors, or our neighboring countries may do unexpected things.

It makes sense to think about digitizing and also de-digitizing. It's good to put stuff up on social networks, but it's also good to pull everything from anywhere you have it online, anything that is important to you, to make sure you have some cool stuff to share with your great-grandchildren.

And when you take things off a given social network, after you've preserved it, you don't need to keep it hidden: you can also *share* it elsewhere.

Good News: Personal Digital Archaeology

Capture, preserve, and share. This is the invitation of personal digital archaeology.

To *preserve*, learn how to digitize and de-digitize, and have fun with it. It's certainly been fun for me, and the greatest part can be when you have stories gathered together that you can *share*, and get peoples' reaction. It may be pictures, written thoughts, a video or audio recording of a conversation or event, or anything else.

Capturing can also be fun. As in, capturing the here and now. For extra credit, watch the movie *Dead Poet's Society* and practice the principle of carpe diem (and bring a digital camera). Finally, gather stories from the people you love while they're still alive. Please do it. I'm fairly certain you'll be glad you did.

For better or worse, people tend to wait until someone has passed on before celebrating their life, and it seems to me that it's worth learning about the people you love while they're still alive. I want to invite you to consider that peoples' lives are worth *celebrating* while they're still alive. For me, because older generations aren't getting any younger, I think it's *especially* important to think about getting their life stories while you still can. This can be a lot of fun: the capturing part, the preserving part, and the sharing part. The whole nine yards. I've experienced this personally. I've seen it in classes I've taught. I hope you discover this, too, if you haven't already.

I don't claim to have all the answers, but after some experiences I've had, I'm increasingly convinced that placing more value on getting to know people and their stories is a mindset, and I believe this mindset of *gathering* can be a good balance to what you typically do. You can substitute the word *gather* for *capture*. (What do *you* think? Share your thoughts on www.snspaces.com.)

Our society tends to think in the moment, in a kind of individualistic day-to-day frenzy. Advertising feeds the cycle: advertising is necessary to sell products to have companies to employ people. But things seem to have gotten a little out of hand, because the strongest advertisements appeal to our self interest; and when people act on this self interest, it seems to turn them inward, and they live in the instant of gratification. Click it, buy it, use it, throw it away.

It feels like the more value you place on *interacting* with people, the more you develop a mindset of gathering, preserving, and sharing stories. And social networks provide a good environment for this.

Social Network Roadmap: Back It Up, or Capture, Preserve, and Share

Here are a few notes about how backing up your digital life and capturing life stories relates to the social networks mentioned in the book. This is meant to be like a blog entry, where I'm sharing my thoughts freely, to provide an example of the kind of thing you can do on social networks. Don't ever feel like you have to be formal or an expert to share your thoughts! It's also meant to show the conversational nature of social networks. If you see anything in this section that you want to respond to, by all means do! Make a blog post, and share the link on www.snspaces.com, or find the Social Networking Spaces Facebook page (see Part II for more about Facebook) and share your thoughts there.

Facebook

In my opinion, Facebook is an excellent gathering point for collecting stories and digital artifacts and sharing them online. You can set privacy restrictions however you want, and the social context helps with motivation to get stuff on the computer and share it. On the other hand, I think it's important not to take it for granted that your digital life will be safe on Facebook for eternity, so back it up at the very least, or gather it into your life story suitcase, with existing or emerging tools.

Facebook is a lot of fun, but you also have to keep it on a leash. One of the nice things about Facebook is that by rolling your mouse over your News Feed, you can hide the comments of someone who is posting a little too much for your comfort. The more friends you have, the more stuff you see in your News Feed (whenever one of your friends posts something), so there may be times when you want to shut someone off. It's like putting someone on mute. And it can help you manage your Facebook experience so you can concentrate on what is important: like getting your pictures up there.

Twitter

I don't have a strong opinion about Twitter either way as regards capturing your life story. If Twitter becomes a part of your life, and you like tweeting, and you end up posting stuff, then I'd say, yeah, at the very least, back it up; and ditto, if it's a part of your life, it can and should be a source of material for gathering, so gather it up! You may also enjoy the discussion in Chapter 6 about how you can connect Twitter to Facebook, so that whenever you post something on Twitter, it also shows up on your Facebook News Feed. This can be a good thing, but it can also be a bad thing: some people may like hearing from you, and some people may not like reading every tweet you make.

If a person follows you on Twitter, that's one thing; but if you connect your Twitter to Facebook and then overload your News Feed and annoy your friends, they may hide you. So, treat your friends as you would like to be treated. I like show-and-tell so much that my own preference is to share whatever comes to mind, and if a person hides me on their Facebook News Feed, then so be it. But I had the twenty-first century experience of being de-friended on Facebook, and one of the things this means is that you can't tag someone in a picture.

I was about to tag one of my heroes in a picture, and I found they weren't on my friend list anymore. And I had this feeling like, hmmm: I wonder if it's because I said something that offended, or if I posted too much and they got overloaded. And sure enough, when I asked (in a Facebook message, of course), they said, "no offense, too much posting. Want me to hide you?" I think we'll re-connect. I don't think I'll drastically change my habits, but I may limit the quantity of postings. I need to take some of my own medicine (see Chapter 15 on Meetup) and get out and have more in-person contact.

Blogs/Blogger/Google Tools

Blogs are cool. I like how the South Korean 3D social network Cyworld became incredibly popular, and then there was a trend of returning to what they liked most: writing a blog. I think it's insightful: 3D is fun, but if you have to pick one thing, nothing beats self-expression (and if you like, enabling comments so it becomes a conversation). What's funny to me about blogs is that, with all the expertise I have on open source content-management systems, I still find it easier to use Blogger (See Chapters 8 and 9) sometimes: it's better to get the thoughts down and sharable than to wade in technical details.

I don't want to scare any Google employees too much, but I'd like to mention that Google Sites, and even Google Docs, could be considered blog-like tools: they're free, easy to use, and allow you to put stuff down and share. In my opinion, as I've helped various people to explore how to put their thoughts online, the easier a tool is to use, the more likely it is to get used: anything that lowers the barrier through being easy to use, is good. The point is to capture your stories: it's better to get something down, in my opinion, and refine it later, than to be concerned about it being too sophisticated.

I'm also influenced by having dreams of fancy looking web sites; there's nothing wrong with that, but sometimes I've ended up not writing things on the web sites I've wanted to create, because of getting bogged down in the technical details. I think it's funny, and perhaps insightful, that here I am, pursuing a Ph.D in Technical Communication, and my dissertation is on advanced web site systems such as Drupal, and yet over the course of time, I've gravitated more and more toward tools like the ones Google provides, such as Blogger, Google Sites, and Google Docs.

This is because they're easier and less time consuming to use. It's not that I've given up on sophistication or design (I've taught web design classes); it's that I've realized that for me, sometimes I'd rather have a nice, easy-to-use tool to get some material up on the Web, rather than have it not get up at all. For this reason, I recommend seriously considering Blogger and Google Sites for starting out and prototyping. You may find that they're OK as a medium- or long-term solution for your blog or web site.

Is a blog a social network? No, but it's a social tool; and in a way, it's a simplified form of social network, because you can enable comments, and suddenly it becomes a conversation. That is ultimately why blogs are so popular. Yes, they're popular because of what people write, but they're also popular because they're social. It's about community and conversation. And remember, a blog can also be private if you want.

Is Google Documents a social network? Not technically; but again, it's a social tool. Google Documents enables people to remotely collaborate on a document. For example, you can sign on to Gmail, click Documents, and discover that you have a free alternative to Microsoft Office sitting right in your Gmail account, and then you may start jotting down some thoughts about a life story or a memory. You can then use the collaborative feature to invite a relative to jot down some additional thoughts. Super cool, super easy, and social. Then, you can invite others privately to read it; or if you want to go public, you can always publish it as a web page. The fascinating thing to me is that as I got comfortable with Google Documents, I discovered that it's the easiest way on the planet to make a web page, and the quickest.

■ **Tip** Google has introduced a new tool called Google Buzz, which is specifically designed to integrate within Gmail and allow you to easily connect to various social networks. At the time of writing, the jury isn't out yet on Google Buzz, as far as whether it will be popular. For some basic information and to share your thoughts, see www.snspaces.com.

Sometimes I put something in a Google Document and then publish it, and because the address is so long, I use www.tinyurl.com to make it shorter (see Chapter 6 for more about URL shorteners). Because the things I typically put on Google Documents are things I'd like to share, I sometimes place a link to a Google Document in Twitter, or Facebook. For instance, one time I wrote a poem that caused me to start profusely weeping: I felt a mixture of release and hope at the thought that people could someday possibly overcome their differences (http://tinyurl.com/1000years), and Google Documents + www.tinyurl.com + Twitter + Facebook allowed me to share this little poem. Over time, I started to see how getting comfortable with tools like Google Documents and Blogger and www.tinyurl.com gave me the tools I needed for playing show and tell. And these experiences had a direct impact on my desire to write this book.

Is Google Sites a social network? No, but if you read the director's cut of my Ph.D dissertation (see www.snspaces.com), one of the other funny things is that even though I work professionally with open source content-management systems, and even though they're wonderful alternatives to commercial systems that may be out of the reach of many people (or a company that has limited revenues because of something like say—oh, a recession, for example), and even though they're powerful enough to drive sites like FedEx.com or Change.gov, sometimes you need a simple hassle-free solution, and Google Sites is that solution.

During the writing of this book, I had a few experiences where Google Sites was the perfect answer to what someone needed. They didn't need an open source content-management system like Drupal or Joomla, they needed something that worked, was easy, and was cheap (try free!). The limitations didn't bother them. So no, Google Documents and Google Sites aren't social networks, but Gmail is a social network in a way: a lot of people have Gmail addresses, and Google has all kinds of powerful free tools online that you can get to with your Gmail account.

Google's goal is to get more people online for longer periods of time, which can be good and bad. But Google is sustainable because of advertising. And sometimes it's helpful the way you may go into Google.com or look in Gmail, and see an ad that happens to relate to something you're interested in (because you've been talking with people about it in Gmail or on Google Talk).

If you're extremely cautious about privacy, there's no need to be on the Internet. And if you're a dissident or protester in a country with a politically repressive regime, then yeah, it's probably not a good idea to spend a lot of time using tools on the Internet to express yourself, words that could conceivably be traced back to you, because Google and other companies are at the mercy of your government. So think carefully about what you do, depending on your situation.

Otherwise, for most people in the world, Google isn't out to get you. It's anonymously analyzing data, and my humble opinion is that the risk is worth the reward. I definitely think it's a good idea to back up your data from any Google service, and I particularly appreciate the Data Liberation Front project at Google: a bunch of engineers who are making it easier to do exactly that. Google has always been pretty good about providing ways to get stuff off Google. And their spirit of exportability is in exact alignment with the idea of a life story suitcase. So my opinion is, use Google's great, easy-to-use, free tools, and also back your stuff up.

Flickr

My friend Chuck is a Flickr fanatic. If you like taking pictures, there are some nice opportunities to share them in Flickr. For more, see Chapter 10. I think it's definitely worth exploring. In regards to your life story, pictures are probably a big part of your story (or can be, if you get a digital camera or a reasonable camera phone—carpe diem!). And Chuck says some people also think of Flickr as a tool for backing things up. It gives you a place to store your photos. It's another place for them to exist if, for example, your home burns down.

And that brings up a good question. Why should you pull anything off social networks, if you had to upload the content from your computer anyway and it's all still there? And I guess the answer is that if you keep track of everything and know where all your stuff is, OK. But you may put stuff on a social network that doesn't exist anywhere else. Say you upload a picture, but then you add a caption. Pictures are nice, but captions make them come alive, because they give context. Simple test: look at any pictures you have from a great-grandparent. Wouldn't it be nice to have some explanation of what was going on in the photo? Consider gathering whatever you put online, no matter where your stuff is. Learn how to gather, capture, and preserve it, because it's worth preserving. And share it however you like.

YouTube

For many, YouTube is like a television channel. From a life-story perspective, even if you don't put anything on YouTube, you may like to see a few videos that you enjoyed years ago, as a kind of time capsule—things you can share later, something that was popular back in the day. As far as a place to post video, YouTube thrives because people are sharing things publicly, and it's entirely user-created. It can definitely be fun to share stuff on YouTube and see who comes by to watch it. (If you search for "Todd Kelsey" on YouTube, you come across the "Dr. Fun Mantis Report" video. I put it up for grins and never thought I'd have 500 people view such an obscure thing, but it was fun. I had a digital camera that shoots video, and I asked a friend to film me, because it occurred to me, eh, maybe I can put this on YouTube.) After you try it, you get more comfortable with it; and at least in my experience, the social context of

Facebook or YouTube provides motivation to continue making things and increases the chances that you're going to capture something. I do it in part because I want to see if I can make people smile or laugh. I'd also like to mention that you can share videos *privately* on YouTube, although it seems like it's a little easier to do this on Facebook.

So try it. Get a camera or camera phone or Flip Video, and get comfortable with it. Then, if something occurs to you, you can try it. I make no apology for having the agenda of encouraging you to get comfortable, because the easier it is for you to do this, the more likely you are to try something like interviewing a relative or getting a friend to interview you. Again, I urge you to do the simple test: how cool would it be to have a picture or web page of a great-grandparent? Or how cool would it be to have even a minute of film of your great-grandparent, even if they were doing something like baking cookies, but especially if they were telling a story? If you do think it would be interesting, think of yourself as the great-grandparent. Get a device if you can, or bug your library to get some, and get some of your life story online (including any relatives you have).

Do it. I can almost guarantee you'll be glad you did. It doesn't all have to be a Hollywood happy story either. Good memories are nice, but I personally believe it should be the whole nine yards: the good, the bad, and the ugly. And partly the reason I choose to emphasize this throughout the book is the great satisfaction I've had when I have been able to capture something or recover something. I didn't always feel this way, but I do know. So I'm encouraging you to consider this, especially in the context of video. It's relatively easy with a device like a Flip Video to start asking someone questions. I'm convinced that if you make the effort, you'll be glad you did, even if you don't put it on YouTube (it's a little easier to control privacy with videos on Facebook, and they can still be shared with family; see Part II for more).

Ning

Open source content-management systems are great tools for doing any number of things, and the more you need to customize a web site, the more they come in handy. Open source systems such as Drupal and Joomla can be used to create your own social network. But Ning is a pretty powerful, free, and easy-to-use web site. No muss, no fuss, and it allows you to get up and running in no time. I'm increasingly likely to put www.snspaces.com on Ning, or at least a part of it, because I'd like www.snspaces.com to be multilingual—and no one, not even Facebook, has touched the way open source content-management systems can make a truly multilingual web site (if you're interested in such things, see Chapter 18). But even as I dream of www.snspaces.com being multilingual, and even though I know that Drupal or Joomla would be great tools for going multilingual, it still takes time, and that's part of the thing that makes me laugh: it's all about sustainability.

Ning, like Blogger/Google Docs/Google Sites, is very *sustainable*. Even though you can't customize as much as you can with an open source CMS or a completely manually built web site, in the end you may find that for cost or other reasons, you can have a reasonably good look and feel; and not having to worry about anything else frees you up to concentrate on what matters most: the content. Then, when you get going, you'll be in a better position to know at what point it makes sense to consider going to something more powerful.

Dr. Fun's two cents' worth on sustainability is to start with the simple free tools, and prototype; you may find that the prototype becomes home. As my friend Chuck Isdale says, start small, and grow organically. In terms of social networking, Ning is great for that. See Chapter 16.

Second Life

I'm intrigued with the idea of having a birthday party or a family event of some kind in a 3D virtual world such as Second Life, as you'll see in Chapter 17. Families go on vacations sometimes, but these days it can be hard to get everyone together in one place, especially if you're on the other side of the planet. Whenever possible, families should make every effort to spend time together, in person, especially to allow younger generations to spend time with older generations.

But when there's no alternative, technology can provide a way to close distance, and I think virtual 3D stuff may be fun, especially as it grows more sophisticated. As you'll see in Chapter 17, some nifty things are out there in Second Life, like world heritage sites. Dr. Fun's recipe for family adventure is to get a relative on Second Life who lives far away, and try visiting the Louvre together, and take a picture next to a painting. Then, maybe fly to the top of the Louvre and take a picture there. And maybe a few of you will wind up with pictures from Second Life in your photo albums next to "real" pictures of your family. Wouldn't it be amusing to visit the Louvre both in real life and in Second Life, take pictures of both, and *de-digitize* the pictures?

MySpace

MySpace is very popular, although not quite as popular as Facebook. Don't be shocked if one buys the other, or one disappears. My guess is that Facebook isn't likely to disappear; at the moment, Facebook is trending up, while MySpace isn't attracting quite as many users. But it's a huge network, and YouTube and MySpace are extremely popular with teens.

If you're a teen reading this book, I urge you to ask for a Flip Video for Christmas or your birthday and go have fun with it. If you want an easy way to make mom or dad or a grandparent very happy, make a video of yourself doing whatever you like to do. If you're paying enough attention between texting and adjusting your iPod and talking on your phone and tweeting, then I think you should take the same test: ask yourself, why should I bother capturing my life? I'm too busy living it. I'd say: think about how cool it would be to have something from your great-grandparents, like a video of them. Wouldn't that be cool, possibly even vaguely interesting? (Just make sure not to put anything risky on there. That can come back to burn you. Look at the help section for parents and see what can happen if you put risky stuff on MySpace.)

But MySpace isn't just for teens. If you have a band or are an artist, it can be a good tool for you. See Chapter 14 for more. In my opinion, if you like exploring, and if you're promoting something, try MySpace. Either way, if MySpace is part of your life, make sure to look into backing it up. Because (like other sites), things can change, and MySpace could go away someday, or change, or be hacked; or someone may hack into your account and cause everything to be gone. So back it up. And it wouldn't hurt to gather your digital life on MySpace and throw it in your life story suitcase.

Meetup

I really like Meetup, because I think it's cool and fun and important to meet people in person. If I had to pick only one social network, which would it be? I'd answer: the original social network. That is, hanging out locally with people who have similar interests. In terms of your life story, Meetup is probably my favorite.

Meetup is a great tool for living your life: making *history*, and getting to know people who have similar interests (such as interests you haven't explored because you're watching too much TV or spending too much time on Facebook). You could even expand the catchphrase and agree that a good word to a friend may be something like: "Live your life, and as you do: capture, preserve, and share it." Carpe diem.

(Again, if you need some inspiration along these lines to help you in your journey through social networks, I recommend the movie *Dead Poet's Society*. I recommend watching it and then trying to live it, in the context of living fully and making the effort to capture some of those efforts, in video, or pictures, or writing. Then, work to preserve the story for future generations, as well as share it with others in the here and how. If you want some extra inspiration, come on www.snspaces.com and look for the story of Dr. McClatchey, a professor I had who was a great inspiration to me, and the person I think of when I hear the phrase "oh captain, my captain" from the movie.)

Part of what I'm trying to get across is the strong opportunity I believe you have, whether within your family or your local community, to discover the treasure of all the stories that are there. I believe it's treasure; I've seen people discover it in classes I've taught, and I hope you'll consider seeking some of it and helping other people to gather their stories.

After you're off and running living your life, with a little help from Meetup (or your local civic organization, or church, or mosque, or synagogue, or temple, or ping-pong league, or whatever), I recommend that you consider getting a camera or Flip Video and having some fun capturing things. There's a little thing called *collective heritage*, which my friend Sophia Liu and others are interested in: capturing, preserving, and sharing the heritage of a *community*. And that's cool. (See www.sophiabliu.com and look for the "grassroots heritage blog.")

A good definition of *community* is any group you find yourself in. There can be something special in capturing, preserving, and sharing the experiences of a group, even if it's within that group. So, I definitely recommend checking out Meetup.

The Story of Personal Digital Archaeology

The main reason I started thinking about digital archaeology is that I inherited an old computer from my Grandpa Miller when he passed away. Here it is:

The picture shows an "antique" Atari 800XL that my grandpa left me, with a whopping 64K of RAM. (A recent computer, by comparison, would have more like 2,000,000K, which would be 2 gigabytes of memory.) This computer is what inspired www.digitalarchaeology.org.

When I inherited this computer, I suddenly found myself in the situation of wondering how in the world I was going to figure out how to get it running, check and see if any of my grandpa's writing was on it, and recover any of his writing from the old 5 ¼-inch disks that came with the computer.

I though, wait a minute, this computer is an antique! I had always associated computers with the future: advanced technology, science fiction, and so on. I never thought about the fact that they were starting to become *antiques*. (One definition of antique: 25+ years old.)

Then I thought, that means there's such thing as digital antiquity—and my mind started doing flip flops. I realized (climbing outside of my cocoon) that if I was in this situation, there were a lot of other people in this situation at one time or another, and it would be helpful if resources were available to help people navigate this kind of thing. What if you have a VHS tape of a wedding, and you want to put in on a DVD? What if you find some kind of media disk or tape, and you have no idea what it is? What if I'm an antique myself and have audiocassettes lying around in the garage, and I want to put them on a CD? And so on.

In 2005, I wrote a booklet that was up on Amazon.com for a while before I decided to do a second edition, and it appears in its entirety at www.digitalarchaeology.org. As social networks started getting more popular, the mission of the Digital Archaeology Institute became more clear: to help people gather, preserve, and share their life stories, including helping people who are trying to recover digital artifacts. I want to connect with existing resources: computer museums, digital scrap bookers, and the like. And I want to create new resources. With this book, I'm making it official, casting the die so to speak, and hoping it will be helpful.

Conversation and Community

From my perspective, no one tool can take care of every issue. For example, there's no software program to take an old VHS videocassette and convert it to video that can play on an iPod. It takes physical equipment, and knowledge. If you ever run into a more obscure situation like I did (my grandpa's antique computer), it may take very specialized equipment and knowledge. The answer is conversation and community.

The conversation hasn't been defined: it's more of an open invitation to anyone who would like to participate, even if it's just to ask a question.

The Digital Archaeology Institute has a space where people can ask questions and access free learning material on how to do some of this stuff: gathering, preserving, and sharing their stories. A second edition of the original Personal Digital Archaeology booklet from www.digitalarchaeology.org is underway, which will be updated and expanded (and, I hope, will benefit from your feedback: please visit www.snspaces.com or www.digitalarchaeology.org if you're interested in participating).

I figure the best way to develop the conversation is to start by *doing*. For me, this means going into boxes and finding things that I'd like to digitize somehow. It also means continuing to capture some stories from what's happening in my life right now, like the ones that I share in this book and on Facebook. Then, I intend to explain how I did things: what tools I used, and so on. If this sounds interesting, please join me!

In some ways, it seems like the digital archaeology theme, or *personal* digital archaeology, if you prefer, is more about recovering things, perhaps digitizing old pictures, or recovering things from obsolete formats. There has been some discussion about making a Digital Archaeology lab, where you can send in your stuff and figure out how to capture it or translate it into a new format. People are already doing this kind of thing. Because I'm something of a geek, I'm particularly looking forward to making a directory of computer museums, for example.

This experience of having to recover things (like my grandfather's writing, locked up in older computer disks) leads naturally to the question: now that I've got it in the latest format, how do I make sure it will be around for a while?

The answer is both a community and a conversation, and part of the fun will be to see what happens when this book comes out, to learn what people are doing. I already know of some resources out there: web sites, software applications, and the like. It will be fun to build a collection of links together and explore them and write about them. So, feel free to check out and see what's up at www.snspaces.com and www.digitalarchaeology.org.

My personal philosophy is that the learning material should be free, and ideally the tools to do it, whether online or not, because I don't want there to be any barriers. Making the learning material free is straightforward: it's easy to put that on the Web and relatively easy to make it sustainable, especially if people participate in the conversation: some people ask questions, or say "wouldn't it be nice to have such and such?" and then others step up to the plate and write tutorials.

And that brings us to the life story suitcase.

The Life Story Suitcase

The Life Story Suitcase is a concept for helping people to gather their life stories. As you explore social networks, I want to invite you to consider the following:

> *Capture, preserve and share: you may want to try capturing and preserving some of your life stories and those of your family, and sharing them on social networks (privately or publicly).*

Or

> *Back up: as you spend time on social networks, you may want to consider backing up some of your life media.*

The simple test is, would you miss *anything* if you lost *everything* from _____? (Fill in the blank: Facebook, Gmail, Blogger, Twitter, Picasa, Flickr, AOL, Yahoo, and so on.) For example, would you miss anything if you lost everything from Facebook?

If you aren't on Facebook yet, you may not think so; but I invite you to consider coming back and reading this chapter again in a year, and ask yourself the question again.

If you would miss anything, then by all means, consider this question, read this chapter, and participate in the conversation by visiting www.snspaces.com. Good tools already exist, and tools are being created to address this issue.

In some cases, you may have original copies, but what if it's the *only* copy? That's one of the nice things about digitizing: it makes it easy to make as many copies as you like. The point is, the more copies you have, the better, because more people can enjoy it, and because it's safer that way. For example, my aunt took a number of pictures that the family only had a single copy of, put them up on Snapfish.com, used the site to make a really nice hard-cover book, and gave everyone a copy. Suddenly, one photo album became 15 or 20 books, along with comments. This involved *digitizing* (getting the material scanned) and *de*-digitizing (getting several books printed out). And somewhere along the way, comments were added, and these recollections are important, too.

This book my aunt put together is representative of the kind of thing you can do on social networks. When you get some material up there, you can share it with everyone, and they can each get a copy if they like (by copying the pictures and comments to their own computer). You may find that in a social context, it can be a nice opportunity for people to come by and add their recollection, and that's where it gets even more fun. One of the things social networks excel at is collaboration; they provide an excellent opportunity for family and friends to gather stories, and everyone can add their own thoughts. Entire communities can do this: it can be a shared heritage.

The Story of Lifestorysuitcase.com

While writing this book, I found myself shocked into the realization that there was a need for information and tools to make sense of what was going on with social networks. Whereas some people may be motivated to back up their stuff, others may be convinced to think about gathering their material from social networks as a matter of preservation and continuity, protecting what is precious for future generations and for immediate fun: show and tell.

You've got all this stuff floating around out there, and you may want to back it up or put it all together and share it. How the heck do you do it?

I scratched the surface and found a number of tools starting to appear, in some cases free, in other cases for a price. Back up Twitter, back up Facebook, back up Gmail, and so on. I think it makes sense to gather links and thoughts about such things, but I also thought it would be fun to try to create something new: a tool that can make it easier to gather stuff from various social networks and pull it down to your computer. A virtual life story suitcase. Then, maybe have a function to put the stuff you've gathered online, on Facebook, on Twitter, wherever you like, and maybe also in a special place that's focused on life stories. To review, people are developing some tools, but in their present form, most of the focus is on backing things up, and I think there's a need for more.

To me, when people think about building new things, especially something like software, it's nice to base it on the real task and to think broadly about it. The definition of a life story suitcase is loose. You could call it a different name, but I like the idea of a suitcase, because it implies adventure. Not just memories, but taking the suitcase with you and putting stuff in it. When I go on a trip, one of the things I enjoy is getting gifts and bringing something special back for people. I think pictures and thoughts can be a nice gift. So the suitcase concept works for me.

I started asking around among the programmers I'm acquainted with, the coding wizards who can turn dreams into screens and clickable things, and I started the conversation. I guess with this chapter I'm hoping to start a community, or at least to join an existing community (and conversation).

I like the idea of looking at what's out there, seeing what's needed, and building it. I like the idea of making information available for free, but I also like the idea of providing employment for people. We're going to try to make a few premium things that people will pay for after they try the free stuff, so see what happens.

Meet CFTW

The life story suitcase is a CFTW project. As part of my Ph.D research, I started the nonprofit organization CFTW (Communication for the World).

All proceeds from this book, and from projects like the life story suitcase, are donated to CFTW. In general, the mission is to simply explore how to make the world better, especially with free learning material.

You can find out more about the organization and the proposed projects in Appendix B.

Meet MakeAByte

Jeremy Hahn kindly volunteered to help develop the life story suitcase prototype. He has a company called MakeAByte, where they do programming for all the latest social applications as well as just about any other kind of web application. Jeremy is also working on a cool thing called hosted infrastructure, which can be very helpful for a small or medium-sized and enterprise businesses. The software can help a small business and medium business to be secure and save money. See http://makeabyte.com and http://hostabyte.com.

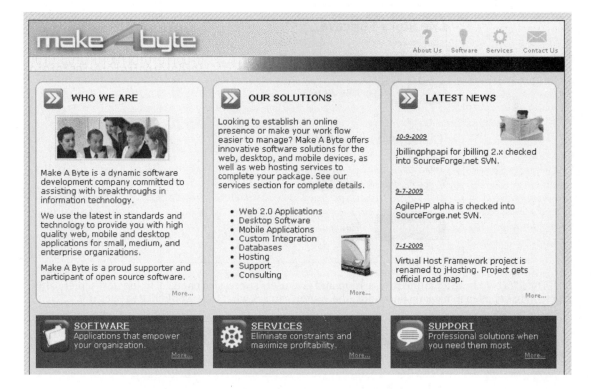

Life Story Suitcase: A Sneak Peek

This section has some ideas and thoughts about what the life story suitcase can be. It's an excerpt of what's known as a *user interface design* or *user experience* document, which is a fancy name for a document that shares ideas about what a web site could look like and how it works. By the time this book comes out, you'll be able to see a live prototype of what resulted at www.lifestorysuitcase.com.

A Visual Tour

Capture, Preserve, Share is the general paradigm of digital archaeology, and as we were working on developing an interface and thinking how the Life Story Suitcase could work, it seemed natural to follow this capture—preserve—share pattern.

What follows is a series of images that represent early thought for the life story suitcase. The prototype is available at www.lifestorysuitcase.com. You're welcome to look through these pages, to visit the prototype, and to share your thoughts. It's an open invitation to participate in something new.

Capture

Capture is the aspect of backing up. I kind of like the word *capture*, maybe even on a button.

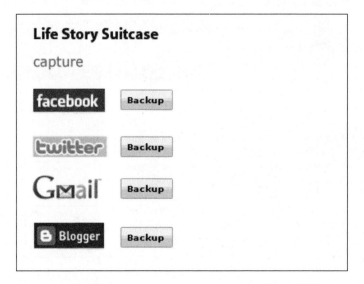

The idea is to have a natural progression and give users successive choices. In the next screen, after a person has chosen to back up Facebook, the system can ask what they would like to back up.

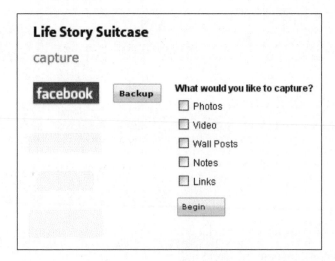

Preserve

In the Preserve section, the concept is to have a place where you can browse the media you capture from various networks and think of ways that it can be accessed, and even combined, to create new stories.

The next screen presents a view of one way the media could be access and organized, based on the original network the material was gathered from.

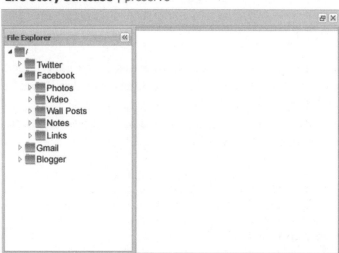

Then it would probably be good to have a view for general categories of media types.

Share

In the Share section, the idea is to find ways to help people take items they've gathered or scanned into their computer and share them. For example, you may have posted a picture on Facebook and can use the tool to back it up. Then, if you decide you want to put it on Blogger too, a share tool could make this easier.

There may be potential to make this a kind of *media migration* tool. For example, maybe you choose an online source and an online destination, and click: now your pictures from Facebook are copied directly to Picasa web albums. The main idea is to share, or upload media to the life story network; but given the flexibility of the underlying system (known in technical terms as APIs), there could also be a way to upload back to your social network.

■ **Note** Feedback is welcome from anyone, especially if you have no experience but are interested in the concept: for example, what features you'd like to see, questions you have, and so on. If you happen to be a developer, please know that the plan is to have an open API where modules can be written so that you can add new functions and connect the life story suitcase to other things. (It would also be nice to make it available in other languages.)

The next screen is a concept for a sharing scenario, where you could move social media files around from one network to another, download, upload, and so on. One question is whether there's a need for an online space specifically for stories. Is there? That's part of the conversation.

Thanks for taking the time to browse through this section. It would be great to hear any thoughts you may have. Don't feel as if you need any particular experience. Please visit www.lifestorysuitcase.com, check out the prototype, and let us know what you think.

2069.us

This section looks at a personal example of a blog project that represents the life story theme. Sometimes I like to think of stories as *adventures*. ("Go on adventures, gather your adventures.") To me, that sounds even more fun. And 2069.us is meant to be an adventure.

One of the first combined projects of the Digital Archaeology Institute will be a life-long blog at www.2069.us. It's meant to be an example of creating, gathering, and sharing an ongoing story. I hope it will inspire some people to try making a blog. (To learn how to make a blog, see Chapters 8 and 9.)

The blog will be about my dream, as a musician, to live long enough to play at the one-hundredth anniversary of the Woodstock music festival in 2069. I thought it would be nice to have something to take pictures of and discuss in relation to this dream.

As an example of the kind of show-and-tell you can do with a blog, here's a picture of the van I'm planning to drive to Woodstock in 2069:

This will be one of the pictures I put in the blog. (Guess what color it is? Check the blog to find out, or let's hang out sometime between now and 2069, and you can go for a ride.)

In a blog, you can tell a *story*. (Hint, hint. Have I got you interested yet? See Chapters 8 and 9 to learn how to make your own blog.)

This 1969 VW van was previously owned by a kind lady named Dorothy, who was the original purchaser. She's 85 now but sharp as a tack and friendly, and she has some good stories, which I'll be interviewing her about and putting on 2069.us as part of the story. I'm planning to fix up the van, like I need to fix myself up. I'll grow into the future with the van and take care of it, and take care of myself, and talk about the things I need to do to the van and in my own life, to keep on going. It's basically meant to be a blog about sustainability and pursuing dreams.

One of the purposes of the project is also to inspire the readers of this book to try blogging.

You may be wondering, what about stories you'd like to capture but not share except with close friends or family? As you'll see in Chapters 8 and 9, it's possible to make a blog private; and based on my experience, Blogger is a simple, easy way to get started. For example, I helped my mom to start a Blogger blog, so she could have a place to type in some thoughts that she'd written on paper; it's set to private, so it's only be for family to see. Another option for ease of use and privacy is to investigate the Facebook feature known as notes (See Chapters 2 through 5). When you type a note in Facebook, it's easy to set the privacy on it so it only goes to the people you want it to. Some people may prefer this over a blog, because it's very easy to invite people to view something in Facebook.

The idea is, one thing you can do on a blog, or on Facebook, or on just about any other social network, is to interview people, including your family members, relatives, and even yourself. It's a great way to gather stories.

For example, if you like music, depending on the age of the person you're interviewing, you may ask them if they remember Woodstock or hearing about it. Or you can ask them if they've ever been to any concerts they enjoyed.

Part of the reason I'm setting the goal of living until 2069 is because I'm interested in experimenting with how I can encourage other people to set the goal of sustainable health. I believe that one of the other values of social networks can be for mutual encouragement for helping each other reach our goals.

My point here is to invite you into considering setting goals of your own, whatever they may be, and maybe blogging about them. I know that at least in one case, another person mentioned in this book e-mailed me one time and said, "I really appreciated your messages on Twitter about getting on the elliptical, because I need to do that, too." I do think that sometimes mutual encouragement about positive goals can be a good thing.

The Importance of Sharing Your Stories

Here is an example of a story that gave me some inspiration.

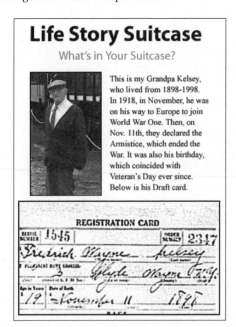

I invite you to consider the impact Grandpa Kelsey's life had on me and to consider how you can live your life in a way that can inspire others. The things you do in life, the way you treat people, the influence on people, the story of that influence … all these things can be an inspiration for future generations. No matter what the story is, it can inspire. For example, my grandpa Kelsey inspired me. I don't know a lot about his life: he was a simple farmer who had a bowl of oatmeal every day, and he blew my mind by living to 99. Pretty cool stuff, and knowing a few things about him helped me in my own life. If I can, I want to live to be 100.

In these next pictures you see the influence of another grandfather, and it may make more sense to you now that you've learned about the story of digital archaeology and the 2069.us blog. Another invitation is to consider taking pictures of yourself and your family members, from past and present, and comparing them. Maybe have a bit of fun when you take the pictures, as I did here. (For more examples of having fun with pictures, see Chapter 10.)

I was pretty excited about recovering the picture on the left. When I was in high school, my Grandfather Miller had a sense of fun and indulged me when I asked him to put on a tie-dye shirt and take a picture with the guitar. When he passed away, I inherited his computer, and this is what got me thinking about digital archaeology: the idea of helping people recover digital artifacts.

On the right is me, about the same time as the picture of my grandpa. I have a dream of playing Jimi Hendrix's version of the National Anthem at the one-hundredth anniversary of Woodstock, and I'm hoping to convince Paul Allen (co-founder of Microsoft) to agree to let me use Hendrix's original guitar, which is owned by the Experience Music Project museum in Seattle.

If you like the 2069 idea, I invite you to check out the blog sometime at `www.2069.us`. As you read the rest of the book, I invite you to consider your dreams and goals, to make new ones, and to experiment with ways of capturing, preserving, and sharing your adventures.

Conclusion

Dear Reader,

Thank you for reading this chapter.

Here are a few of my favorite things that appear on social networks, which I pulled out of my own treasure chest to share. I hope they will inspire you to engage in some digital archaeology of your own. If you have any questions about how I put them together, please feel free to ask:

- *Backstage Passes:* Some pictures of backstage passes I put up from my past life as a rock 'n' roll musician: `http://tinyurl.com/bkstagepasses`. (On `www.sunflowerclub.net`, there's the only picture I have of me actually *wearing* a backstage pass, at an event where I was trying to slip Al Gore some sunflower seeds and convince him to join the Sunflower Club. If you like, look at the backstage passes and try to tell which backstage pass I proudly wore when I met Mr. Gore.)

- *Flying Dutchman:* A blog post with a music video for a song I wrote about a legendary Huey pilot in Vietnam. The style of music was influenced by Jimi Hendrix, along with some comments and a poem Hendrix wrote. That's me on vocals, guitar, and flute: `http://tinyurl.com/flyingdutchmanvid`.

You can also look on `www.snspaces.com` at my page for links to these and some of the other music videos and songs that are up on the Web, and which I'll be adding, as I put my money where my mouth, get my life story online, and explain the technical details.

I wish you the best as you explore various social networks and as you read the rest of the book, I invite you to consider how you can use them to gather and share your adventures.

Regards,

–Todd

snspaces.com

Life Story Suitcase

Capture, Preserve and Share

Come and visit the Social Networking Spaces companion web site at www.snspaces.com, where you can find more tips and updates and have an opportunity to share your thoughts or ask questions.

In Living Color: You can visit www.snspaces.com/pics to see full-color versions of all the pictures from this chapter.

CHAPTER 2

■ ■ ■

What the Heck Is Facebook?

In This Chapter:

- Introduction: Gives some general background on what Facebook is and a few things that it does.

- Understanding Facebook: Provides a visual tour and some brief explanations of some of the common things that people enjoy doing in Facebook.

- Facebook applications: Introduces Facebook applications, which are free programs you can install on Facebook to try new things.

snspaces.com

Come and visit the Social Networking Spaces companion web site at www.snspaces.com, where you can find more tips and updates and have an opportunity to share your thoughts or ask questions.

In Living Color: You can visit www.snspaces.com/pics to see full-color versions of all the pictures from this chapter.

Introduction

This chapter is meant to be a friendly visual tour, introducing you to some of the features of Facebook. So don't worry about trying to follow along in Facebook unless you want to (or if you get inspired and want to have some fun). If you're new to the world of Facebook, you may enjoy just reading along to get acquainted with the kinds of things you can do. In Chapter 3, I'll launch into step-by-step instructions on how to create an account and explore. If you already know some of the basics, but wonder why you should bother with Facebook, try skipping to the "Why Facebook?" section.

I first heard about Facebook from students in a class I was teaching who were on it. After we connected as friends, I thought, "OK, people are telling each other about what they ate for lunch or where they went on vacation." I thought "no big deal," and yawned. I pretty much ignored Facebook, and I'd get annoyed when someone sent me a message on Facebook and I'd get an e-mail. Then I'd have to log on to Facebook to respond.

25

Over time, though, I started to connect with people who I had gone to college with, because they'd see that I was on Facebook, and they'd invite me to be on their Friends list. I began to enjoy posting pictures to share with them from places such as Kodak's online gallery, Picasa Web Albums, and so forth. Later, I started posting more and more pictures directly to Facebook (and I shared links to the photos with people who weren't on Facebook).

Then, I started learning how to do some other things on Facebook, like updating my status or playing a game of Scrabble online with a friend, and I enjoyed it even more. After many people started using it, Facebook gradually went from "yawn" to being *fun*.

My own personal perspective is that aside from all the other features, at its root Facebook is a great way for people to capture, preserve, and share their life story (see Chapters 1 and 4). Plus, it's a nice way to keep in touch, especially when people live far away.

HOW SOME FOLKS USE FACEBOOK

My biggest thing is to reconnect with my high school friends. I moved to Chicago from Arizona after high school and lost track of many of my former classmates simply due to the distance. Facebook helps to shrink those miles down. Some of them I talk with daily while sharing what is going on in my career and in our family through pictures. —David

Facebook Friends

According to Wikipedia, Facebook is "a social networking website … users can join networks organized by city, workplace, school, and region. People can also add friends and send them messages, and update their personal profiles to notify friends about themselves" (see http://en.wikipedia.org/wiki/Facebook).

Facebook basically started as a way to go online and join a group of people with something in common and then exchange information with each other. It began with college students, branched out to high school students, and then allowed anyone age 13 or older to join.

Part of the reason Facebook took off in the school environment is because Facebook is inherently *social*. For example, it provides a way to make a list of friends. So, you can sign in and see who is on someone's list of friends, and you can invite people to be your friends. It basically provides a framework to organize what people do anyway—they like to keep a circle of friends. As shown in Figure 2-1, part of the appeal for college and high school students (and everyone else) is being able to say, "Look at my circle of friends."

Figure 2-1. The Facebook Friends panel, which displays on your Facebook Profile page. The Friends panel shows some of your friends and the number of friends in your social network.

It's no mistake that Facebook resembles a school yearbook. In a yearbook, you see pictures of your friends and their names, and it's a record of what people have done at school. Then, people write messages on each other's yearbook when the yearbook comes out.

The same thing happens on Facebook. You could legitimately say that in a way, it's like a yearbook for you and all your friends. But in this case, you and your friends decide what goes into the yearbook, and it's not so much a book as a place.

Status

If you're a student now, or remember what it was like, you know how important status can be sometimes; for better or worse, you end up seeking social status. There's a bit of that at work in social networks ("Look at how many friends I have!"), but the irony is that status is now a message.

People enjoy expressing themselves to different degrees; and although it's not the same amount of fun for everyone, it can be fun to express yourself by telling others what you're up to. That's one of the core elements of Facebook. You might update your status with a picture, by saying something you're doing, or by giving a link to an article you've just read (see Figure 2-2).

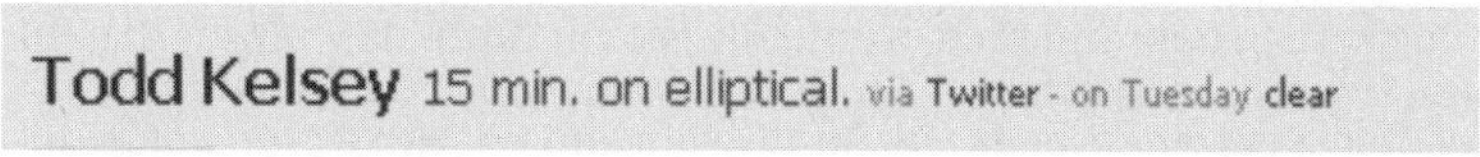

Todd Kelsey 15 min. on elliptical. via Twitter - on Tuesday clear

Figure 2-2. This happened to be my Facebook status message at the time I was writing this section. It appears at the top of the Facebook profile, and is one of the many ways on Facebook to share what's going on. I'm just indicating, as a form of keeping myself accountable, that I spent 15 minutes on the elliptical machine.

It may be safe to say that fun is the engine that drives Facebook. At this point, however, Facebook has gone far beyond being an online equivalent to a school yearbook. At the time of writing, there are 350 million people on Facebook. It's become a nation unto itself, with an economy, media attention, and everything else that goes along with any phenomena.

Chat

I talked with an unnamed editor at an unnamed publishing company who confessed to me, "All I want to do is just log on to Facebook and see the cat pictures, but I don't, because I don't want to get hit with chat messages from 20 people at once."

Chat is another popular feature of Facebook, otherwise known as *instant messaging*. It functions very similar to other instant messaging programs such as Google Chat, Yahoo Instant Messenger, MSN Messenger, and AOL Instant Messenger. In this case, you're connected to anyone who is on your friend list. Figure 2-3 shows that you can turn this feature off, if you just want to log on and see the cat pictures.

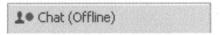

Figure 2-3. *To turn off chat: At the bottom right-hand corner of Facebook, click Options at the top of the Chat window, and then choose the Go Offline option. When and if you want to turn it back on, just click the Chat bar again.*

There's a lot more than chat to Facebook. The easiest way to think of it is that when you get together with family and friends, there are things you typically do: tell each other what you've been up to, share pictures, or play games. Facebook is basically a place where you can do those same kind of things, but online.

Why Facebook?

The easy answer is that if you're a business, you can't afford to ignore Facebook, simply because people are spending so much time on it. Even if you don't have an active presence on Facebook (try searching for the phrase "social media marketing" on Amazon.com), you probably will at least want to consider advertising on Facebook (see Chapter 5).

If you're an individual, then it's up to you. People got along just fine before Facebook, and people can get along just fine without it. But because so many people are on it, you may at least enjoy trying it, if for no other reason than to have an easy way to log on once in awhile and see what's happening with your friends or family members. Chances are that some of them have begun to upload pictures into photo albums in Facebook and to capture other parts of their life as well.

Keeping in Touch, Catching Up, and Show-and-Tell

One of the most common things people use Facebook for is simply keeping in touch. For me, it started with reconnecting with friends from college, and went on to including connecting with family members. I began reconnecting with people and then eventually got comfortable with sharing things on Facebook such as pictures and important experiences I'm going through. By reconnecting with friends from the past and by connecting to current friends and family, you end up with a group of people with whom it's convenient to go on and say, "What's up?"

My other favorite is show-and-tell. It's a great deal of fun to share pictures of the latest adventure or pose a question. As you'll see, when you go on Facebook and make a post, your friends or family may comment, and then it can turn into a conversation if you like. In short, Facebook offers an easy way to make a conversation piece—pictures, comments, thoughts, and questions all can turn into conversations.

Life Stories

In my opinion, one of the coolest things you can do on Facebook is share your life story through pictures (see Figure 2-4).

Figure 2-4. *If you'd like to see an example of someone sharing their life story, you're welcome to add me as a friend on Facebook (search for* tekelsey@gmail.com*) and check out my photos (on my Profile page under the Photos tab). You'll find that one part of my life I like sharing is my interest in growing sunflowers— ridiculously tall sunflowers.*

Career Networking

It also makes sense to maintain a network of friends on Facebook as a matter of maintaining your career or finding a job. LinkedIn is generally known as the most important site to be a part of for job and career networking (see Chapter 12). As shown in Figure 2-5, Facebook is increasingly being used by businesses as well.

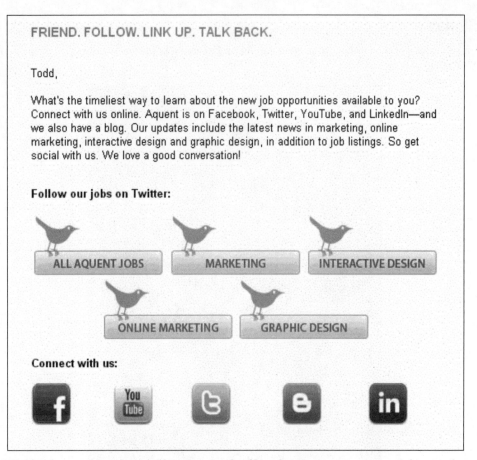

Figure 2-5. *This excerpt from an e-mail is an example of how businesses are using social networks to connect with potential employees. For example, connecting with Aquent on Facebook or Twitter provides an opportunity for graphic designers and other creative talent to find out about job opportunities and learn about other resources that Aquent provides. (See* www.aquent.com *for more information.)*

As a general principle, it's good to have some tools at your disposal to help get the word out if you're looking for work. In fact, some people choose to have more than one Facebook account—one for colleagues at work and other companies and one for closer personal friends and family. With Facebook's privacy controls, you can control what you share with whom, so if you want to keep things simple and only have a single Facebook account you can share a particular set of pictures *only* with the people you want (see Figure 2-6).

My Photos - Misc. Me

Photo 10 of 11 | Back to Album | My Photos   Previous Next

Gosh why do they have to make computers so difficult.   From your album:
                                                                          "Misc. Me"

Figure 2-6. You may wish to limit who can see certain pictures, such as if you were having a bad hair day. One solution is to use Facebook's privacy feature to make an album or picture available only to certain people. Another option some choose is to keep two separate Facebook accounts, one for business and one personal.

Have Fun, but Don't Burn Out

My personal recommendation is to make whatever you do on Facebook meaningful and worthwhile. In a recent ad hoc poll on a major news web site, 75 percent of the people responded "yes" when asked, "Are you tired of social networking?"

Don't feel that you need to do *everything* that people are doing. Try it out, have fun, ride the boat down the river, or get off if you like. But pilot the boat yourself; don't let the river pilot you or take you somewhere you don't really want to go.

Now that you've got some basic knowledge, let's take a look at what is going on in Facebook!

Understanding Facebook

This section is a visual tour of some of the things you can do in Facebook, based primarily on my own experience, FWIW (For What It's Worth).

■ **Tip** If you're new to the world of Facebook, especially if you feel intimidated at all, you may find it helpful to just read along and get acquainted with the kinds of things you can do (without feeling any pressure to try things). In Chapter 3, I'll launch into detailed, step-by-step instructions. At the same time, you won't hurt anything by exploring—that's a great way to learn. If the mood takes you and you see something you'd like to try, go for it!

Writing on the Wall

The Wall is another place to explore on your profile or someone else's profile. What the Wall does is to gather whatever a person has been up to. It's kind of like a roundup or summary of news.

If you've posted a picture, joined a group, or made some comments, they'll show up on the Wall. To fine tune, some people choose to have some things show up while other things remain hidden.

As you're getting to know your friends, you can go to their Wall and explore what they've been up to. Another way to think of it is like a time capsule. Figure 2-7 shows just a few entries, but when you actually go on Facebook, you can keep scrolling to see more. When you're on your own Profile page, you also notice at the very top that the Wall asks you, "What's on your mind?" You can type in a thought, a comment, a link, or a variety of other things. In other words, the Wall keeps track of things automatically so you can post whatever you want to it.

■ **Tip** To get to the Wall, go to the Profile link at the top of the Facebook screen, and then choose the Wall tab. Alternatively, whenever you're on Facebook and click someone's name, you go directly to their Profile page and right to their Wall.

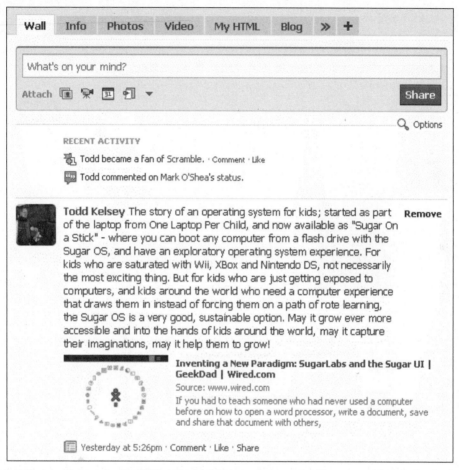

Figure 2-7. *A few entries on the Wall. If you're looking at your own Wall, you can click "What's on your mind?", type something in, and click Share, and it appears on your Wall as well as on your friends' News Feeds (see the section "News Feeds").*

At first, I didn't do anything with my own Wall. I just uploaded pictures and created photo albums. Then, I found that I enjoyed sharing links too, so I'd sign in to Facebook, go to my Wall, type in a comment or two, and paste a link to a news article I'd read or an interesting web page I'd just visited.

In Figure 2-8, you see another Wall where a friend posted a picture of his daughter; you also see that a couple of people have commented on the picture.

Figure 2-8. A picture posted to the Wall, and some comments. When you're looking at a friend's Wall, you can type a thought and click the Share button, and your note appears on their Wall.

There are a variety of ways to comment. That's part of what makes Facebook fun. When you see peoples' comments, you can type something in, but you can also click the Like link, and Facebook says, "so and so likes this."

Photos

What has always been the most fun for me is sharing photos. Figure 2-9 shows the upper-left corner of a typical Facebook Profile page, arranged with the tabs. Adding your own photos to your Facebook page is as easy as clicking the Photos tab.

Figure 2-9. Click the Photos tab to see photos.

Figure 2-10 shows what you see when you click your own Photos tab or a friend's.

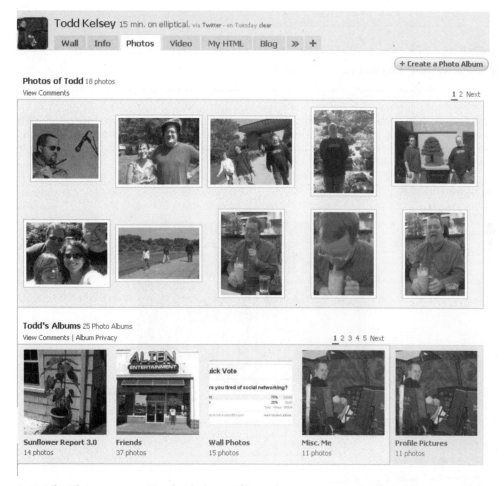

Figure 2-10. The Photos area on Facebook shows photos that a person is in, albums they've created, and their profile picture(s).

The following sections can be found within Photos:

- *Photos of you*: The top section consists of pictures that a person appears in (for example, Photos of Todd). These are pictures that people have taken of you, in which you've been tagged. As you start making friends on Facebook, people will mark pictures they've taken of you, and those photos show up in the top section—you can also tag your own pictures. It's just another way for people to share pictures.

- *Your albums*: The bottom of the Photos area shows any photo albums a person has created.

- *Profile pictures*: At lower right in the Photos area, you can see a person's profile pictures. People often have more than one profile picture and have fun switching them on occasion and using new ones.

■ **Note** When you try Facebook for the first time, feel free to invite me as a friend and to explore my Photos tab. You can search for me on Facebook using `tekelsey@gmail.com`.

Another nice thing about having photos on Facebook is that it can be a social experience. When you share your pictures with your family and friends, they have an opportunity to comment on them. For example, Figure 2-11 shows my grandmother and her high school basketball team from 1917. A friend has commented on the picture.

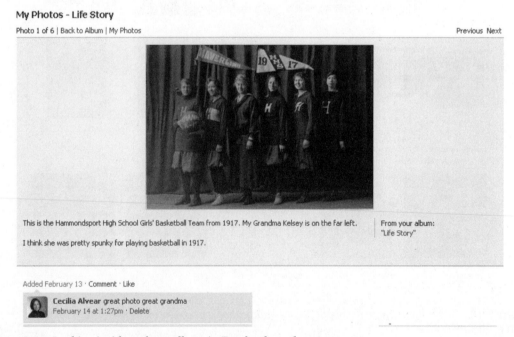

Figure 2-11. Looking inside a photo album in Facebook, and a comment

■ **Note** Facebook has a variety of ways to control the privacy of pictures. You can make photos viewable by everyone or only by your friends or specific groups of friends. Another nice thing is that if you upload pictures to Facebook, a link is provided if you want to share the pictures with people who aren't on the web site.

Profile

The profile is an area where you can fill out as much or as little as you like, to share basic information about yourself with your friends. Getting to your own profile is as easy as clicking the Profile link at the top of the Facebook screen (see Figure 2-12).

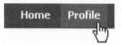

Figure 2-12. The Profile link is one of the main links on Facebook.

Clicking the Info tab on your profile (or on your Friends' profiles) is the way to get some details. You see in Chapter 3 that Facebook guides you through the process of filling out your profile as part of the sign-up process, but you can always come back and change things. As Figure 2-13 reflects, sometimes it's fun to add new things and update information.

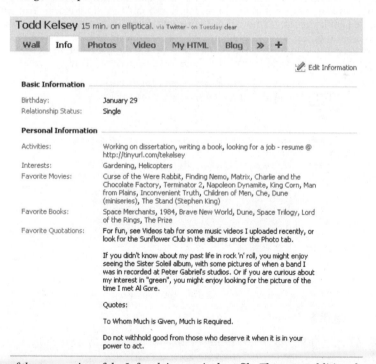

Figure 2-13. A view of the top portion of the Info tab in a typical profile. There are additional sections, depending on what a person has filled out, including favorite music, where a person lives, and their e-mail address.

Swimming in the Stream: News Feed

The News Feed in Facebook is where things can get really interesting. It's one of the things that is completely your own—a stream of all your friends' activity, accessible from the Home link at the top of the Facebook screen (see Figure 2-14).

Figure 2-14. *Going home to go swimming in the stream*

Basically, when you add friends, whatever they have shared on Facebook appears in your News Feed on your Home page. Another way to think of it is like a series of magazines. Everyone who has a Facebook page is like a mini-magazine publisher. Reading the stream is like browsing through all the latest articles that everyone has published. Then, if you want to focus on an individual person, you can click their name and look at their Wall.

You can also think of it like watching a news show on television; a news show is made up of little segments that tell different stories about a variety of people. So when you log in to Facebook and view your Home page, the News Feed gives you a live update of what people are up to, with the most recent news first.

If you're new to Facebook and not quite sure what to make of it, the best thing to do is to try adding friends when you sign up, and then click the Home link to see what kinds of things you come across.

It may be helpful to think of the Facebook News Feed as a stream, as if you're living along the same river as your friends and each day people put messages in boats that float along. You can pick them out, look at them, and see what they say. You can put your own boat in the water with a picture, a thought, or something you enjoyed reading, and others can pick it up and look at it.

Figures 2-15 to 2-19 are samples of what people post on Facebook, taken from a snapshot of my News Feed at the time of writing. What appears in your News Feed depends entirely on what people post.

Figure 2-15. *Some friends post what they're doing or how they're spending their day. Cory, who makes artisan soaps, is posting a link to a festival she's going to attend. Zack is providing an update about his profile icon, which people have been commenting about.*

Anselm Hook these folks are looking for ways to intersect dance and technology … any of you geniuses have any ideas?
http://www.zataomm.org/
58 minutes ago · Comment · Like

 Jim Cooper Baby Teeth tonight in Boston @ the Middle East :
http://www.last.fm/venue/9022145
✩ **Concerts at The Middle East Upstairs, Cambridge — Last.fm**
Source: www.last.fm
Listings and tickets for 61 events at The Middle East Upstairs, Cambridge, United States. The Middle East Restaurant and Nightclub consists of three live-music performance rooms, two family-style restaurants …

about an hour ago · Comment · Like · Share

Figure 2-16. Anselm is posting a link and asking a question. Jim is posting a link about a gig his band Baby Teeth is playing.

 E. John Walford has been exchanging some thought with Matthew Huggins about New Media, empty content, and the restlessness of our generation. Under today's date, 8/5/09, the 28th anniversary of my coming to the States, I have added a short reflection on these themes, see: http://nowonlyconnect.blogspot.com/

 **Only Connect**
Source: nowonlyconnect.blogspot.com
The Blog of John Walford, British-born, but long resident in The United States. I am an art historian, currently studying satire in Netherlandish art, an amateur photographer, and occasional writer, who …

about an hour ago · Comment · Like · Share

👍 Matthew Huggins likes this.

Write a comment…

 Karen Fulghum Sear sees the light. Not the "step into the bright light" but the light-at-the-end-of-the-tunnel.
about an hour ago · Comment · Like

 Melanie Pahl
 **Deal of the day: historic hotel, Lufthansa's fall Europe sale, winter Paris river cruise by Denver O**
Source: www.examiner.com
Photo courtesy of: Uniworld Cruise Lines City of eternal light-
Paris, France.
about an hour ago · Comment · Like · Share

Figure 2-17. Dr. Walford posted a comment about his art blog. Karen is commenting about something she's going through. My cousin Melanie Pahl is Denver Outdoor Travel correspondent for examiner.com and is posting a link about an article she just wrote.

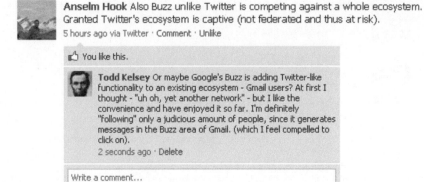

Anselm Hook Also Buzz unlike Twitter is competing against a whole ecosystem. Granted Twitter's ecosystem is captive (not federated and thus at risk).

5 hours ago via Twitter · Comment · Unlike

👍 You like this.

Todd Kelsey Or maybe Google's Buzz is adding Twitter-like functionality to an existing ecosystem - Gmail users? At first I thought - "uh oh, yet another network" - but I like the convenience and have enjoyed it so far. I'm definitely "following" only a judicious amount of people, since it generates messages in the Buzz area of Gmail. (which I feel compelled to click on).

2 seconds ago · Delete

Write a comment...

Figure 2-18. More thoughts, including a comment by me, and an example of what happens when someone clicks the Like link. Depending on how you have Facebook settings adjusted (Notifications), when you comment on something, you may get a Facebook message and/or e-mail every time someone else comments on the same post. Sometimes, people click the Like link to tell the person they're interested yet limit the amount of messages they have to deal with.

Mark Moskovitz Really liking this ad: http://www.youtube.com /watch?v=U_0C-J8dtu4

Vincent : 30
Source: www.youtube.com
http://www.americansforthearts.org/public_awareness We are very excited about our current television ads as well, which are part of the latest phase of "The Arts. Ask For More" PSA campaign! Created in ...

🎞 3 hours ago · Comment · Like · Share

Figure 2-19. This is Mark posting a link for a YouTube video on his Wall. A little thumbnail image appears with a summary, so you can click to watch the video.

Hide and Seek with the "Hide" Function

The hide function may be one of the most important things to learn on Facebook. As you add friends, some post more than others, and you may not want to have to read through all of the posts. You may still want to remain friends with someone but not have their posts show up in your News Feed.

Remember, you can always roll your mouse over one of their posts and click the Hide button, as shown here.

Anselm Hook rt @Urbanverse 2020 Tech That Will Change Our Lives: solar, augmented and virtual reality. Ray Kurzweil http://bit.ly/771PSQ #trends

12 minutes ago · Comment · Like

Hide

If you want to add someone back, click Home and then News Feed.

Then, look for the Edit Options function, and click it; scroll all the way to the bottom of the News Feed if you need to.

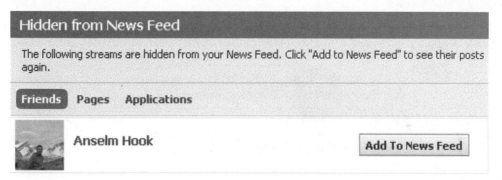

Next, find the friend you hid, and click the Add To News Feed button to unhide them so you start seeing their posts again.

Finally, click the Close button when you're done. That's it! Definitely useful.

■ **Note** You may see a different screen than the previous one. Sometimes, some Facebook features aren't consistently available to all users, especially when the site is in the midst of a redesign. According to *Economist* magazine, as of February 2010, Facebook has 400 million users, and when they're rolling things out it may take some time.

Facebook Applications

Facebook applications are like computer programs, except you add them to your Facebook account and use them online. Most of them are free and range from utilities to help keep track of birthdays to games you can play with other people. There are thousands of applications in every available category. The following is a look at a couple of representative examples.

Games

Scrabble was probably the first Facebook application that I added, because I heard about it and I thought it would be great to be able to play Scrabble on the Internet with friends and family. When you want to add an application, search for it by name, or browse applications to find something you'd like to try. There's also a lot of cross-pollination. If you like an application, you can share it with a friend and invite them to try it (see Figure 2-20).

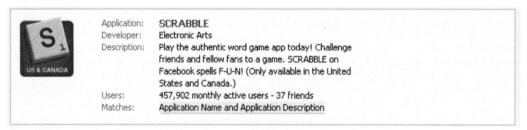

Figure 2-20. Scrabble on Facebook is awesome. It's so popular that sometimes it runs slowly because so many people are playing it.

Figure 2-21 shows what happens when you click the Home link at the top of the screen in Facebook. If you have an application installed, like Scrabble, it shows up on the left side of your Home page.

Figure 2-21. When you click the Home link at the top of the screen on the left side, you have a number of choices. If you've installed an application like Scrabble, it shows up in the list.

It used to be that to play Scrabble with someone over the Internet, you had to install the game on your computer as shown in Figure 2-22 and then hope your Internet connection wasn't too wacky in order to connect with the other person. When it worked, it was awesome because you could play Scrabble with someone on the other side of the country.

Figure 2-22. After clicking the Start menu in Windows a list of applications appears, kind of like the list of applications in Facebook.

Now, with the advent of Facebook and the free online version of Scrabble, you can connect with friends and family and play online (see Figure 2-23).

Figure 2-23. A screenshot of the online version of Scrabble on Facebook, where mom is kicking the pants off the other player (me), who is posing as Abraham Lincoln.

Scrabble is a great deal of fun, and it helps to keep the brain cells active and build new brain cells; plus, like Pedro's promise in the movie *Napoleon Dynamite*, it will make all your dreams come true. Did I say it was fun? It also happens to be a great example of *intergenerational gaming*, a game that an older generation will probably be familiar with and can play with their children (and grandchildren).

More and more software is being developed to be used entirely online. If you look carefully at how things are going, many more people are spending a lot of time on Facebook. It's not too different from having a mini operating system on the Internet.

Groups

Groups are another way to enjoy Facebook. They provide a way to connect with people who have common interests. Sometimes people join groups as a joke. In fact, some groups are quite silly. When you join, an announcement shows up on your stream and on your Profile page. If it's a silly group, it may give someone a laugh, and perhaps they'll join too! In many cases, people join groups and actively participate in them. Groups provide a common area for discussion, pictures, and the latest news. Facebook also makes it very easy to create your own group.

Joining a group is as simple as someone inviting you to join, or searching for it on Facebook by typing the name in the search area at the top of the screen. If you like sunflowers or gardening, or if you'd like to practice joining a group, you're welcome to join the Sunflower Club. Figure 2-24 shows a search for "A Sunflower Club."

Figure 2-24. Just like applications, you can search for a group you want to join. Just type what you're looking for, and press the Enter or Return key on your keyboard.

Whether you're searching for groups or browsing them, when the entries show up you can either click a name to check it out or click Join Group to join it (see Figure 2-25).

Figure 2-25. A group summary appears when you're browsing or searching for groups.

Some groups are private, and you have to ask to join; others are completely open, and you can click Join Group. (You can also click the group name if it's a public group, and visit.)

The group's Home page is the center of activity. When you join a group, new group activity appears in your stream when you're looking at your Facebook page (under the Home link). You can also click the Home link at the top of the Facebook screen and look along the left side for the Groups link, as shown in Figure 2-26.

Figure 2-26. The Groups link shows you a list of groups that you belong to.

If you want to try the Group feature, feel free to search for "A Sunflower Club" using the search function at the top of the Facebook screen. Feel free to join the group (see Figure 2-27) and try some of these things.

Figure 2-27. Click the Join button to join a group.

■ **Note** It's a shame that it costs so much to print in color—the picture of the sunflower is such a gem. But if you like, you can see it as well as all the other pictures from this chapter in full color, by visiting `www.snspaces.com/pics`.

When you visit a group, if you haven't joined yet, you can't make posts; but after you join, you can click the Wall tab. Just like on your own Wall or your friends' Walls, you can do the following:

- Post a message by clicking Write Something, typing a message, and clicking the Share button
- Attach a link, picture, or video by clicking one of the small icons beneath Write Something, loading what you want, and then clicking the Share button

Figures 2-28 to 2-31 show many of the things you can do when you're part of a group.

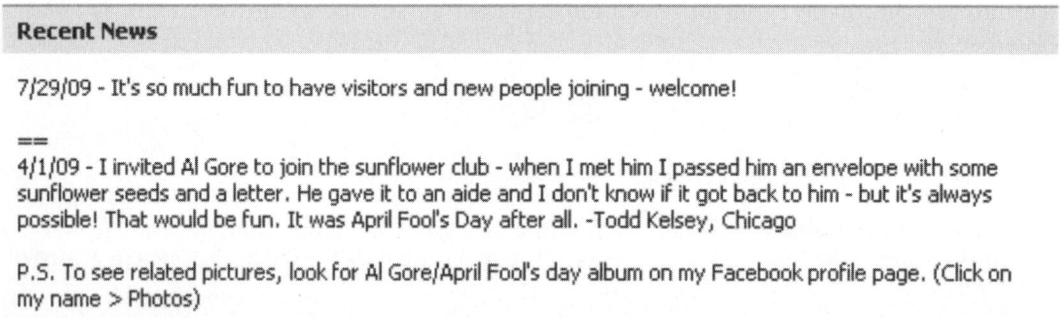

Recent News

7/29/09 - It's so much fun to have visitors and new people joining - welcome!

==

4/1/09 - I invited Al Gore to join the sunflower club - when I met him I passed him an envelope with some sunflower seeds and a letter. He gave it to an aide and I don't know if it got back to him - but it's always possible! That would be fun. It was April Fool's Day after all. -Todd Kelsey, Chicago

P.S. To see related pictures, look for Al Gore/April Fool's day album on my Facebook profile page. (Click on my name > Photos)

Figure 2-28. Under the Info tab, the Recent News area is a place for posting and reading the latest group news. This is in addition to anything people post under the Wall tab.

Members

Displaying 8 of 208 members   See All

Shanuka Maduwantha | Tracey Walsh Caraballo | Maureen Gale Mrenna | Ruvini Tharanga Vithana Arachchi | Nichole Humbles Clausen | Prasith Premachandra | Melissa Ferguson | Edna E Heatherington

Figure 2-29. Each group page randomly displays some of the members, and you can click the See All link to see all the members or search for people.

Figure 2-30. The Discussions area (under the Discussions tab) is a nice feature of groups, where people can start new topics, add to existing topics, or exchange information or comments.

Figure 2-31. Photos are another nice feature of groups. Any member can upload photos directly or add photos from any of their own photo albums. In the case of this group, people have added a lot of photos of sunflowers; it's become a collection of sunflower pictures from around the world. You can see photos by looking for the Photos panel on the left side of the group page or by clicking the Photos tab at the top of the group page.

Groups are a pretty cool Facebook feature/application. You may want to try starting out by joining a group, and then at some point maybe you'd like to create your own! There's more about groups in Chapter 3.

Links

Another basic, useful feature on Facebook is Links. Links is an official built-in Facebook application. It helps you to manage links that you'd like to share on Facebook and gives you a way to see your friends' links. The application keeps track of your links and makes a collection of them.

Figure 2-32 is an example of a link with introductory comments, which I posted on my Wall.

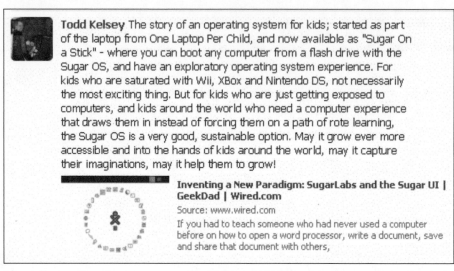

Figure 2-32. When you post a link, sometimes it shows up with a thumbnail image along with the title of an article that appears on the web page you're sharing. A person can click the title to access the link.

The Links application also has a panel that appears on your Facebook Profile page, which keeps track of links you post. People share a variety of links on Facebook, such as news articles, tutorials, and even recipes (see Figure 2-33).

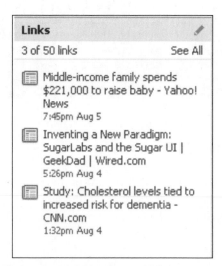

Figure 2-33. The Links panel keeps track of links you post. Both you and your visitors can check out the panel and can click the See All link to browse through them.

Never fear, you learn how to post links in the next chapter!

Q/A

Q: Do you necessarily need to spend an hour on Facebook every day?
A: No.

Q: Would it be good for some people to *limit* themselves to an hour a day on Facebook?
A: Probably, especially if they're forgetting to feed the dog, play with their kids, or make the day romantic for their spouse. My personal recommendation is to stay away from Farmville (a popular game that takes up a lot of time). Instead, reread the chapter on Meetup, and consider building time in your day for participating in the oldest social network (that is, hanging out in person with people).

Q: Might it be fun to spend some time each week playing show and tell, posting some pictures, and looking at Facebook to see what's going on in the lives of your friends and relatives?
A: I think it would be time well spent.

Q: What's the difference between the Top News and the Most Recent news?
A: When you log in to Facebook, you see your News Feed, and by default, it shows the Top News. Facebook keeps track of what all your friends have posted recently over the last day or so, and you can go back into older posts, chronologically. You can also click on the Most Recent link, to see your friends' posts as soon as something is placed up. Their posts appear on your News Feed eventually, but the Most Recent link is more immediate, a bit more like Twitter.

Q: I like this book, but there are only four chapters about Facebook. Where can I read more?
A: If you liked this book, and this chapter or section, keep your eyes open for an entire book from CFTW Press about Facebook. If you want to keep posted about the book's progress, go on Facebook and search for (and join) the Social Networking Spaces Group, or search for (and become a fan of) the Social Networking Spaces Facebook page. I'll post messages once in a while to both. Just as with this book, all author proceeds will be donated to CFTW (see the Introduction to this book). Don't worry if you don't know how to join a group or become a fan; you can learn how by reading Chapters 3 through 5.

Q: Wait, I have another question! Where can I ask it?
A: On `www.snspaces.com`.

Conclusion

Dear Reader,

Thank you for flying Facebook Airlines. In this chapter, you've gone on a whirlwind visual tour of some of the features of Facebook, and I hope I've satisfied some of your curiosity as well as introduced you to new things that you may like to try. Please fasten your seatbelts. You're now approaching the next chapter, where you have an opportunity to join Facebook and try some things with step-by-step instructions.

Regards,

–Todd

P.S. If you've read Chapter 1, you may already know that the Life Story Suitcase is an experimental tool for gathering all your life media from Facebook, Blogger, and so on. If you like, when you've had a chance to start a Facebook account, you're welcome to come by `www.lifestorysuitcase.com` and tell us how good or bad the experiment is.

snspaces.com

Come and visit the Social Networking Spaces companion web site at www.snspaces.com, where you can find more tips and updates and have an opportunity to share your thoughts or ask questions.

In Living Color: You can visit www.snspaces.com/pics to see full-color versions of all the pictures from this chapter.

CHAPTER 3

Getting Started with Facebook

In This Chapter:

- A step-by-step guide for joining Facebook
- Adding and changing your profile picture
- Exploring and joining Facebook groups
- Trying free Facebook applications: free software you can run on Facebook— games, utilities, gift-giving applications, and more

snspaces.com

Come and visit the Social Networking Spaces companion web site at www.snspaces.com, where you can find more tips and updates and have an opportunity to share your thoughts or ask questions.

In Living Color: You can visit www.snspaces.com/pics to see full-color versions of all the pictures from this chapter.

Introduction

The best way to explore Facebook is to join up and start exploring. Don't worry about needing any special knowledge—remember that 400,000,000 people all started out in the same position as you.

As for me, after I signed up and connected with a few friends, other people saw that I had joined and began inviting me to be their friend. Soon, I started seeing more of what people do on Facebook, by logging in and reading the summary of other people's activities. Simply by checking out Facebook once in a while, you can learn a lot by watching what other people do.

And don't worry if you can't think of anyone to invite to be your friend. If you like, you've got one to begin with: me! (When you're on Facebook, to find me, search for tekelsey@gmail.com—I often have Abraham Lincoln as my profile icon.)

The chapter shows you how Facebook can check your web mail contacts during the signup process (Gmail, Hotmail, Yahoo, and so on), to see if anyone you know is on Facebook; and you learn how to search for friends by name. (You can also enter peoples' e-mail addresses when you're searching.) You also explore Facebook groups, one of the many ways you can try new things, make new friends, and find people with similar interests.

> *"I see Fbk as one tool among others that can open dialog between people, not a substitute for in-person networking, but more like a useful linking mechanism for staying in touch, out of which to trigger more substantial and direct contact."*
> —Dr. John Walford

Joining

Joining Facebook is a straightforward process: just visit `www.facebook.com`. If you happen to have them, assembling the following things helps a bit:

- If you have a Gmail, AOL, and/or Yahoo web mail account, and you assemble the login information, Facebook can check to see if any of your friends are on Facebook and show you a list so you can see if you'd like to add any of them. This chapter looks at how this works.

- During the signup process (see Figure 3-1), you can add a profile picture—any picture will do. If you'd like a picture to use for practice, you can visit `www.cftw.com/snspaces`—I uploaded a pic and left instructions on how to download it. (You can always add/change your profile picture later.)

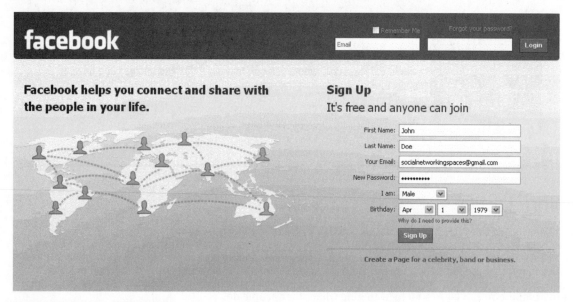

Figure 3-1. Joining Facebook

Enter your name, your e-mail address, and a password that you'd like to use with Facebook (see Figure 3-2). Technically, you don't need to enter your real birthday, and you can decide on your profile whether to share the year, but Facebook needs to know that you're over 13.

Figure 3-2. Facebook signup screen

In the window shown in Figure 3-3, you can enter your e-mail information, if you have Gmail, Yahoo, or AOL, including your e-mail password—Facebook doesn't store the password, but it can automatically check for friends. Click Find Friends, or click "Skip this step."

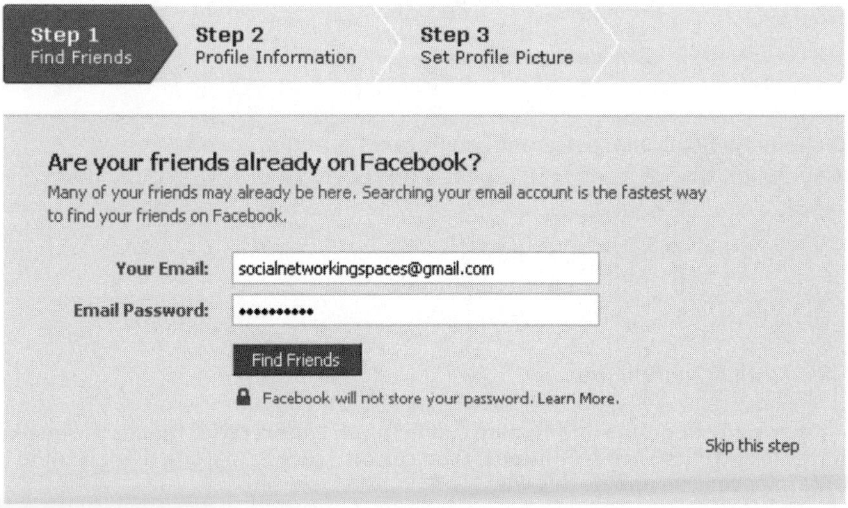

Figure 3-3. Step 1: finding friends

If you choose to have Facebook check your web mail, it shows a list of people who are on Facebook (see Figure 3-4). You can check them individually, or click Select All Friends and then click Add as Friends, or click Skip.

Figure 3-4. Adding friends

After you get through one web mail account, you can try another e-mail account or file, or click Skip (see Figure 3-5).

Figure 3-5. Friend request confirmation

Filling out some of your profile information can help you connect with friends. If you like, do so as shown in Figure 3-6, and click Save & Continue. (You can also click Skip if you don't want to do it now—like other profile info, you can update this later.)

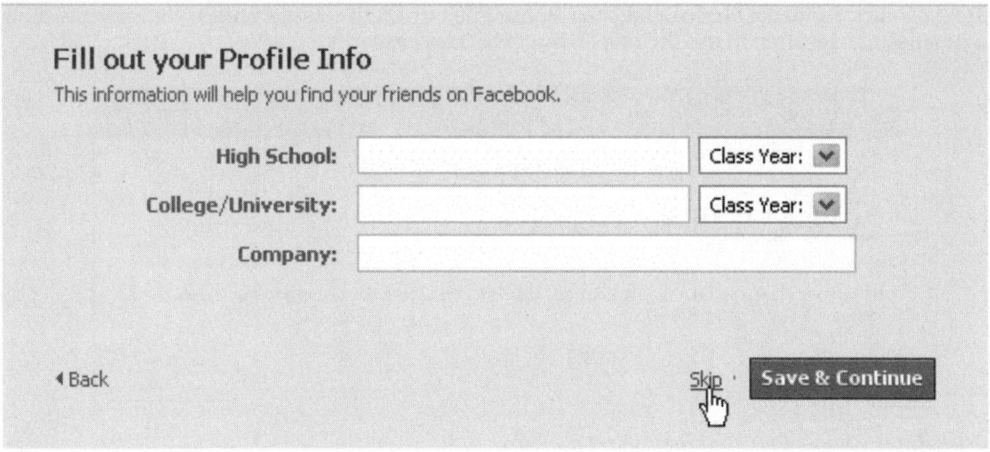

Fill out your Profile Info
This information will help you find your friends on Facebook.
High School:
Class Year:
College/University:
Class Year:
Company:
Back
Skip
Save & Continue

Figure 3-6. *Filling out basic profile info*

If you have a picture of yourself—or a picture of anything else you like, for that matter—the screen in Figure 3-7 gives you an opportunity to add it to your profile. You can have multiple profile pictures, and it's common for people to change them regularly for variety and fun. To try this, click Upload a Photo.

Step 1
Find Friends
Step 2
Profile Information
Step 3
Set Profile Picture
Set your profile picture
Upload a Photo
From your computer
OR
Take a Photo
With your webcam
Back
Skip
Save & Continue

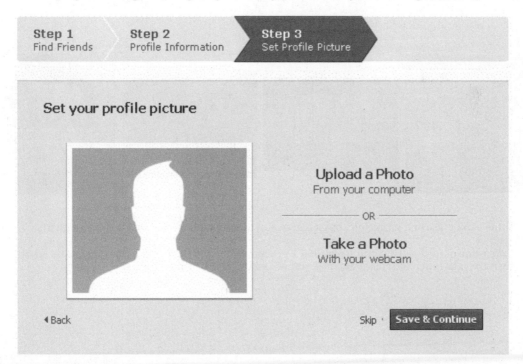

Figure 3-7. *Step 3: seting your profile picture*

After you click Upload a Photo, click the Choose File button to select a photo (see Figure 3-8). If you need a practice file, feel free to use the one at www.cftw.com/snspaces.

Figure 3-8. Click Choose File, and then select a picture.

■ **Note** In Facebook, people use profile pics ranging anything from a picture of themselves, to their cat, their children, a famous person—I've seen just about everything.

Some people use one profile pic, but it can be fun to switch pictures. Many people regularly change their pic.

Here's one of my favorite profile pics that I've seen. It's very simple, but it has nice colors (go to www.snspaces.com to see the color version if you're looking at the printed form of the book).

When you've uploaded your profile picture, click Save & Continue. As you can see in Figure 3-9, a profile picture doesn't have to be just a face, or a small image—it can be a larger picture. It appears larger when someone is looking at your profile, and a small thumbnail version appears along with your activity on Facebook. (You can edit what Facebook shows as a thumbnail—see the tip in the "Changing Your Profile Picture" section in this chapter.)

Figure 3-9. Setting the profile picture

Filling Out Your Profile

After you enter basic information in the earlier screens, Facebook gives you an opportunity to fill out your profile (see Figure 3-10). As with other aspects of the signup process, you can come back and change things later, but I recommend putting in a few pieces of information now.

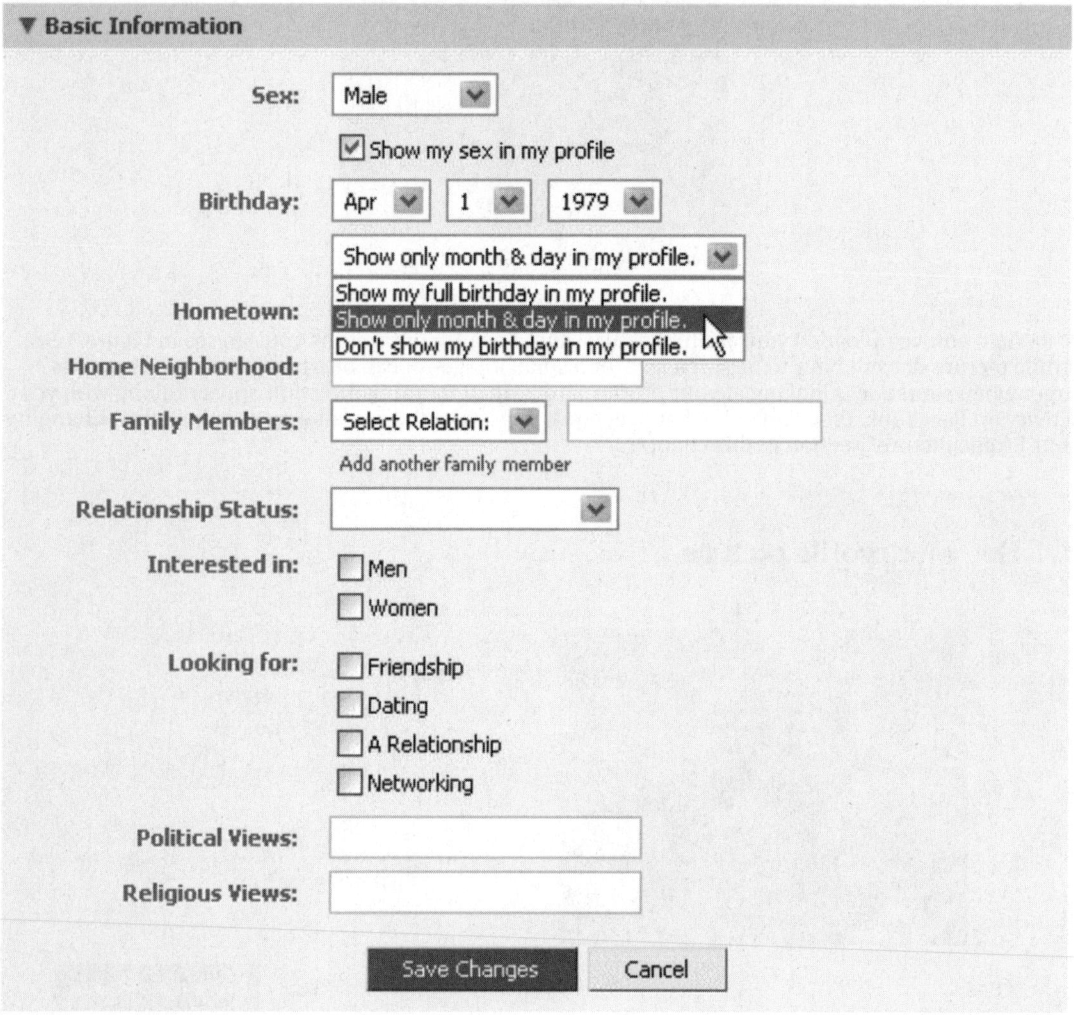

▼ Basic Information

Sex:	Male ▾
	☑ Show my sex in my profile
Birthday:	Apr ▾ 1 ▾ 1979 ▾
	Show only month & day in my profile. ▾
	Show my full birthday in my profile.
Hometown:	Show only month & day in my profile.
	Don't show my birthday in my profile.
Home Neighborhood:	
Family Members:	Select Relation: ▾
	Add another family member
Relationship Status:	▾
Interested in:	☐ Men
	☐ Women
Looking for:	☐ Friendship
	☐ Dating
	☐ A Relationship
	☐ Networking
Political Views:	
Religious Views:	

[Save Changes]   [Cancel]

Figure 3-10. Basic profile information

You don't have to check any of the boxes, fill out any of the information, or put your views, but you have the freedom to do so. If you prefer to keep your age private, you can click the drop-down menu as shown in Figure 3-10 and choose "Show only month & day in my profile." Then people can at least wish you a happy birthday.

Continue filling out the information as desired. In some areas, when you begin typing, Facebook may suggest options; you can click them, as shown in Figure 3-11.

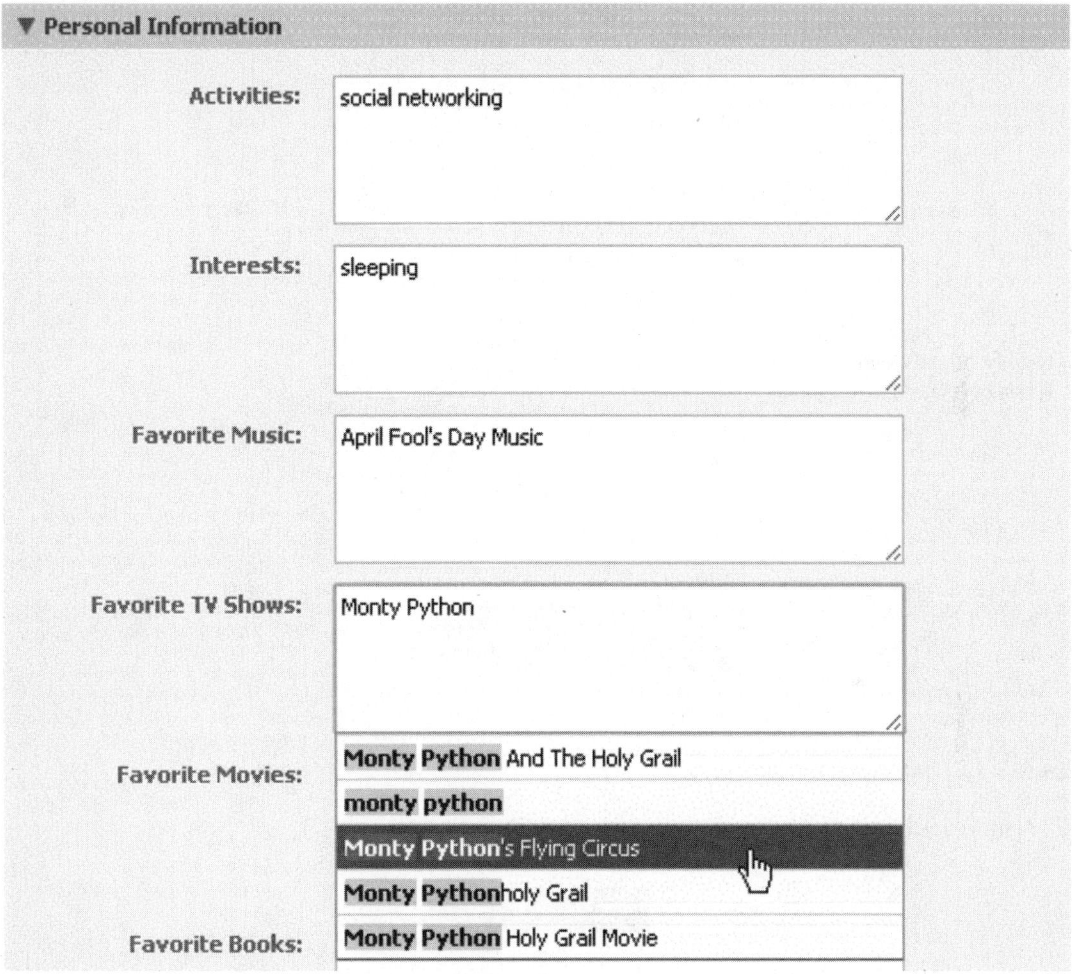

▼ **Personal Information**

Activities:	social networking
Interests:	sleeping
Favorite Music:	April Fool's Day Music
Favorite TV Shows:	Monty Python
Favorite Movies:	**Monty Python** And The Holy Grail
	monty python
	Monty Python's Flying Circus
	Monty Pythonholy Grail
Favorite Books:	**Monty Python** Holy Grail Movie

Figure 3-11. Personal information

When you're done filling out what you like on each screen, click the Save Changes button, shown in Figure 3-12.

Figure 3-12. Click Save Changes on each screen when you finish.

Contact information appears on another optional screen (see Figure 3-13). As with other areas of Facebook, you can adjust your privacy settings later.

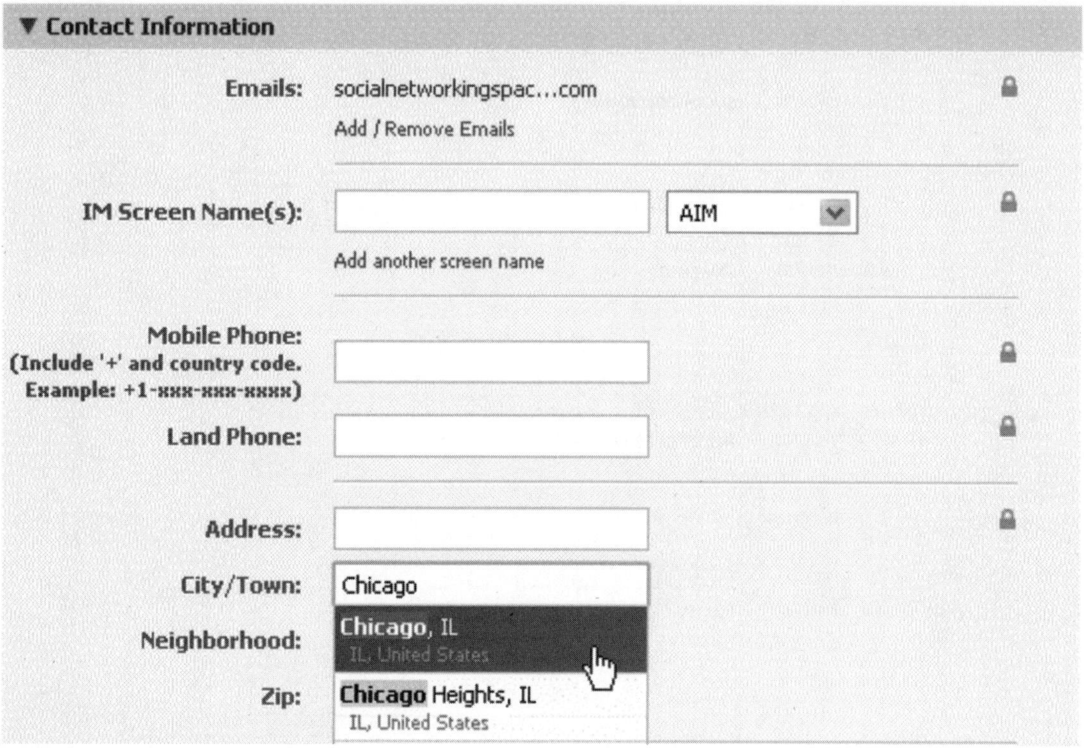

▼ Contact Information

Emails:	socialnetworkingspac...com
	Add / Remove Emails
IM Screen Name(s):	[ ] AIM ▾
	Add another screen name
Mobile Phone: (Include '+' and country code. Example: +1-xxx-xxx-xxxx)	[ ]
Land Phone:	[ ]
Address:	[ ]
City/Town:	Chicago
Neighborhood:	**Chicago**, IL IL, United States
Zip:	**Chicago** Heights, IL IL, United States

Figure 3-13. Contact information

Again, click Save Changes when you're done (see Figure 3-14).

Figure 3-14. Save Changes

Don't be afraid of Figure 3-15. It isn't a job application. It's a way to share more information about yourself and to update friends and family members about what you've been up to. If you'd like to add information about more than one employer, click Add Another Job. When you're finished, click Save Changes.

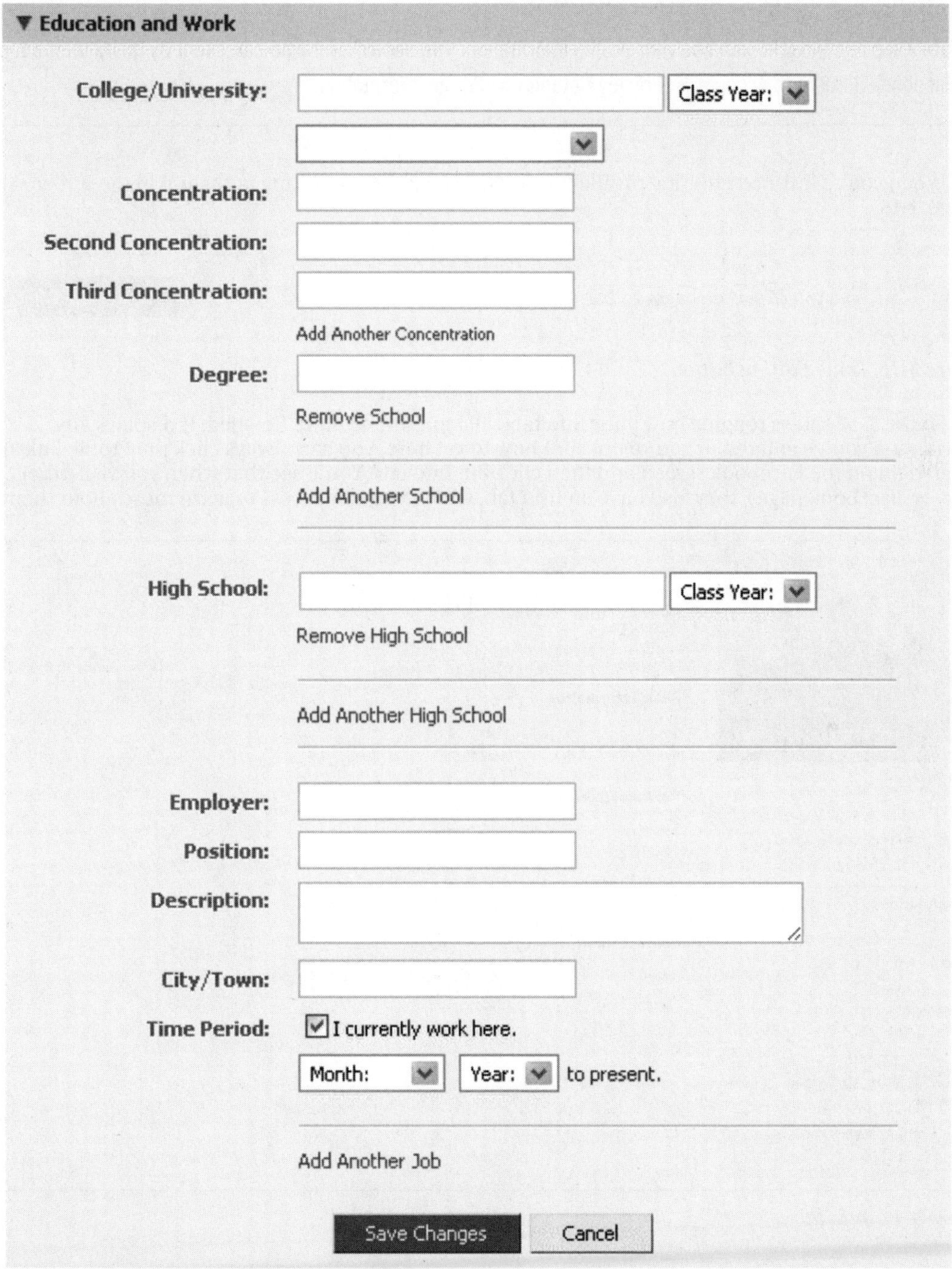

▼ Education and Work

College/University: [_____] | Class Year: ▾ |

[_____ ▾]

Concentration: [_____]

Second Concentration: [_____]

Third Concentration: [_____]

Add Another Concentration

Degree: [_____]

Remove School

Add Another School

High School: [_____] | Class Year: ▾ |

Remove High School

Add Another High School

Employer: [_____]

Position: [_____]

Description: [_____]

City/Town: [_____]

Time Period: ☑ I currently work here.

[Month: ▾] [Year: ▾] to present.

Add Another Job

[Save Changes] [Cancel]

Figure 3-15. Education and work info

■ **Note** Keep in mind who can see your profile information. You can control who can see it by going (at the top of the Facebook Screen) to Account ➤ Privacy Settings ➤ Profile Information.

When you're finished entering profile information, click Done Editing at the top of the screen (see Figure 3-16).

Figure 3-16. Done Editing button

Figure 3-17 shows roughly how your Info tab will look when you're finished. It displays any information you've entered. If you're not sure how to get here, you can always click the Profile link at upper-right on the Facebook screen and then click the Info tab. You'll see that when you visit other peoples' Facebook pages, they also have an Info tab, which you can access to learn more about them.

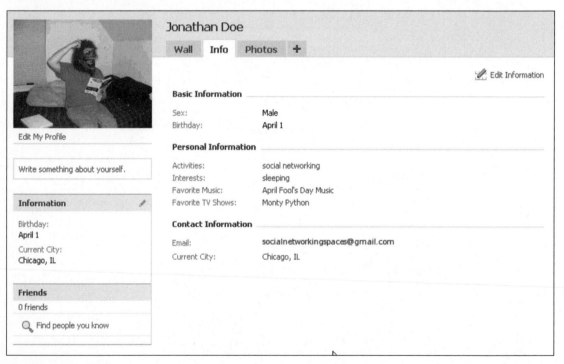

Figure 3-17. Info tab

Searching for Friends

After you're signed up for Facebook, one of the things you may like to do is search for friends. The most direct way is probably to gather up e-mail addresses and paste them one by one into the search box—but you can also type in peoples' names. (Just be aware there may be more than one person with the same name!)

Go to the upper part of the Facebook screen, as shown in Figure 3-18, type a name, and press the Enter key on your keyboard.

Figure 3-18. Searching Facebook

When you find who you're looking for, click Add as Friend (see Figure 3-19). If your friend is using a silly picture of their cat for their profile icon, it may be hard to tell who is who; but they may have a network listed, a location where they live, or other distinguishing characteristics.

Figure 3-19. Add as Friend. If you see a link on a search result that says "mutual friends," you can click it to see who they are, to help determine whether you have the right person.

After you click Add as Friend, it may be nice to click "Add a personal message," as shown in Figure 3-20.

Figure 3-20. Add a personal message.

After you're finished adding the message, click Send Request (see Figure 3-21).

Figure 3-21. Send Request.

When you're adding someone as a friend, on the final screen you may have to go through a security check; this is simply Facebook making sure you're human. (Lots of spammers and hackers out there would love to scan through all of Facebook and have a computer automatically try to add people as friends.) But gosh, the random security phrases that come up are sometimes funny, as you can see in Figure 3-22. "Mildred Maggots" sounds like the name of a garbage patch doll or a heavy metal band.

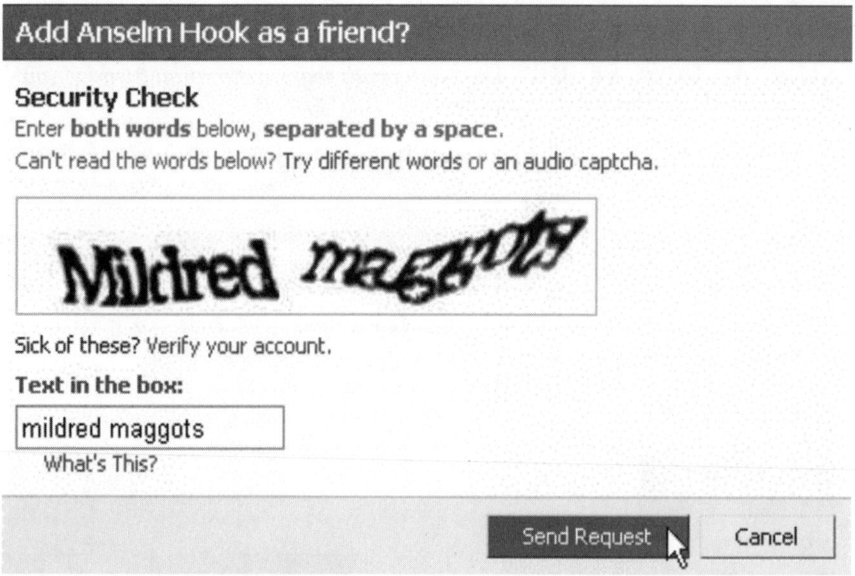

Figure 3-22. Security check

Exploring Friends' Profiles and Photos

When you have friends on Facebook, it's fun to explore their Facebook pages. (Don't feel bad if you don't have any friends yet. If you're waiting to hear back from people or aren't sure where to start, you *do* have a friend already—feel free to add me if you need some practice. Search for me at the top of the Facebook screen by entering my name; or if you're not sure which Todd Kelsey to add because I have a silly profile icon, search using the e-mail address tekelsey@gmail.com. I'll be sure to confirm you as a friend so you can get started having some fun! And don't worry if you de-friend me later—it won't hurt my feelings.)

To get started, click the Profile link at the top of the Facebook screen, and scroll down to the Friends section on the left (see Figure 3-23). To explore someone's profile, click their name or picture. If you don't see the friend you're looking for in the immediate list, click the See All button.

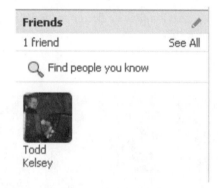

Figure 3-23. Scroll down to the Friends panel.

You can also see peoples' profiles by first clicking the Home link at the top of the screen to look at what people have been posting to their Walls. (Remember, the Home tab shows the News Feed, a stream of everyone's activity—see Chapter 2.) Then, you can click anyone's name to be brought to their Wall (see Figure 3-24). Just as you have your own profile, you can click the tabs at the top of their profile—Wall, Info, Photos, and so on.

Figure 3-24. When you click a friend's name in Facebook, your friend's profile looks something like this, with things they've posted recently and tabs at the top that they want you to explore.

Leaving a Message on Someone's Wall

When you're out and about on Facebook, one of the things you may enjoy doing is leaving a message on someone's Wall. This is a message that anyone coming by will also see—anyone who can see your friend's Wall can read the message (as if you actually did write on someone's wall in their home). When you leave a message, you can leave more than text; you don't need to, but if you like you can attach a picture, video, or link—just about anything (see Figure 3-25).

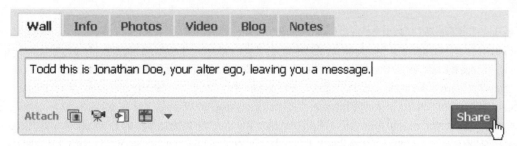

Figure 3-25. You can just type something in and click Share.

After you click Share, your message appears on your friend's Wall (which is accessed by the Wall tab, as shown in Figure 3-26). I wonder what is on their Info tab, or the Photos tab—or any of the other tabs people may have on their profile? Maybe you should click the tabs and find out!

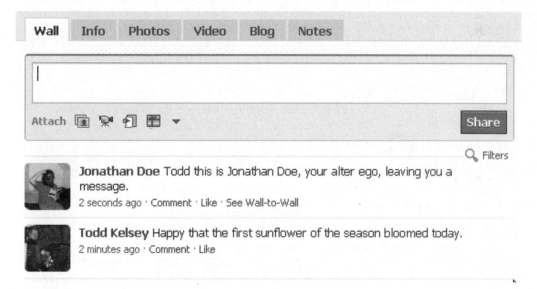

Figure 3-26. Wall tab

■ **Tip** You may explore someone's profile and then wonder how to find out what the latest is since the last time you checked. If you go on Facebook regularly and click the Home link at the top of the screen, you can see what people are posting, such as pictures or activity. (See Chapter 2 to learn about the News Feed.) And if you want to make sure you catch up on all the latest, go to the person's profile and look at their Wall—then you can scroll down, and click the Older posts link, and so on, until you're all caught up.

■ **Tip** Don't feel like you have to log on to Facebook all the time. You can if you want, and Mark Zuckerberg and all the employees and investors of Facebook would be happy if you did—but there's no need to. My suggestion is, try logging on once a week. In the meantime, you may get e-mails from people sending you messages on Facebook— you can either leave those alone until you log in, or you can go onto Facebook and turn off Facebook messages (Account ➤ Account Settings ➤ Notifications ➤ Click corresponding Email check box ➤ scroll down ➤ click Save Changes). If you turn off Facebook e-mail notifications, then you may still wish to sign on to Facebook and click the Messages icon at the top of the screen (directly to the right of the Facebook logo),to see what people are sending you.

Leaving a Link on a Friend's Wall

It can be fun to leave a link on your friend's Wall. If you add a link to your own Wall, they may see it in their News Feed (see Chapter 2), but adding a link (or a photo, or whatever) to a person's Wall is more direct.

To do so, go to a person's profile, click the Wall tab if you're not already there, type your message, and click the Link icon (see Figure 3-27). (You may also want to go and select and copy the link into memory so you can paste it—if you need a tutorial on how to do that, *first* check and see if there are any tutorials at www.snspaces.com; if not, e-mail me, and I'll put one up.)

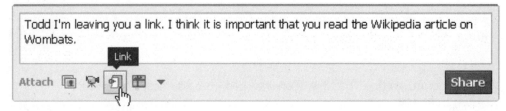

Figure 3-27. Clicking the Link icon

Paste in your link, and click Attach, as shown in Figure 3-28.

> Todd I'm leaving you a link. I think it is important that you read the Wikipedia article on Wombats.
>
> 🔗 **Link**   ✕
>
> http://en.wikipedia.org/wiki/Wombats   **Attach**
>
>   Share

Figure 3-28. Attach button

The link is attached, and it shows a preview of the article and perhaps a picture from the web page. Depending on the type of web page, if there's more than one picture on it, you may be able to click the little left- and right-facing triangles to choose a thumbnail—or if you don't want a thumbnail image to appear, you can click the No Thumbnail check box. When you're finished, click the Share button.

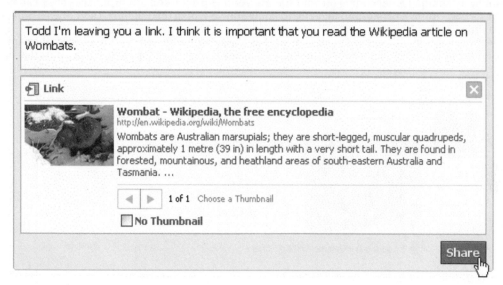

Figure 3-29. Clicking the Share button

After you've shared your link, it appears on the person's Wall (see Figure 3-30).

Figure 3-30. The link appears!

Exploring and Commenting on Pictures

Another thing that's a great deal of fun is to look at peoples' pictures and comment on them. You may not necessarily want to comment on every single picture you visit (because doing so may generate an e-mail for every comment, depending on your friends' settings); but if something strikes you, it can be a nice way to say "hi" to a person and to let them know you've visited (like sighing a sort of Welcome book at their little Facebook home).

One way to get into a person's pictures is to click their Photos tab and explore pictures they appear in or photo albums they've created. Another way is to look at their Wall (or pictures they post that appear in your stream when you sign in); you can click the name of the photo album to go take a closer look (see Figure 3-31).

Figure 3-31. If someone posts a photo, you can click the photo album name.

When you click a photo album name, the album opens, as shown in Figure 3-32. You can click photos, click the link at the top (for example, Todd's Profile, as shown in Figure 3-33) to go back to your friend's profile, or click the link beneath that one to go back to their general photo area (for example, Back to Todd Kelsey's Photos).

Figure 3-32. *A Photo album on Facebook*

Figure 3-33. *The Profile link takes you back to a person's profile (or back to Kansas, if you're not there anymore).*

Clicking a picture, as shown in Figure 3-34, takes you right to that individual picture.

Todd Kelsey It was nice to come out and see the first bloom of the season.

Sunflower Report 3.0

7 hours ago · Comment · Like · Share

Figure 3-34. *Click a picture to take a closer look at someone's photo album.*

When you're looking at a picture, you can click the Previous and Next links (at the top in Figure 3-35) to look through other pictures in the album.

Todd Kelsey's Photos - Sunflower Report 3.0

Photo 15 of 15 | Back to Album | Todd's Photos | Todd's Profile   Previous Next

It was nice to come out and see the first bloom of the season.

■ Uploaded via Facebook Mobile.

From the album:
"Sunflower Report 3.0" by Todd Kelsey

Figure 3-35. *Browsing with the Previous and Next links*

■ **Tip** In Facebook, anything that's blue is clickable. Remember *Willy Wonka and the Chocolate Factory*? The original production is my favorite. There's a scene in a room where everything is lickable or edible. You may like to try thinking like a child, and explore things on the Facebook screen. Try clicking something blue—you can't hurt anything! If you're feeling timid, I wish you joy, courage (and fun) in the face of technology.

■ **Note** *Friending*: Did you catch that I used the word *friend* as a verb? Welcome to the twenty-first century. If it makes you feel more comfortable, use the traditional prefix, and befriend people instead of friending them.

Another very interesting and fun thing you can do is scroll down below a picture, click "Write a comment," and type in a comment, as shown in Figure 3-36. Try it: Type in a message, and click the Comment button, as shown in Figure 3-37. Comment away!

Figure 3-36. The "Write a comment" area

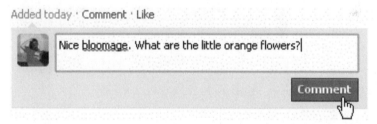

Figure 3-37. Comment button

Your comment appears below the picture in the album and also appears on the person's Wall. (And depending on how you have your settings adjusted in Account ➤ Privacy Settings, when you comment on someone's photo, the fact that you commented may appear on your Home page—so if you're on Aunt Bertha's page commenting about how loud Uncle Felix snores, Uncle Felix may see that you made a comment on Aunt Bertha's page.) The point is, Facebook is like a big ice cream social, or cross pollination—when you post something, it invites further comment and becomes a social gathering, in effect (see Figure 3-38).

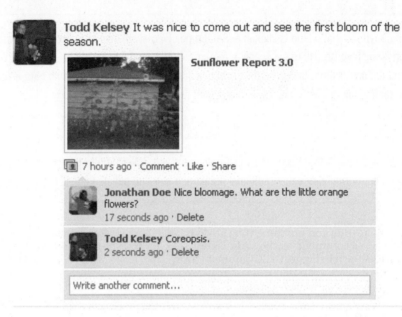

Figure 3-38. *Care to comment?*

When you comment or ask a question, it may get answered, and it appears both in the stream of posts, as in Figure 3-28, as well as below the picture, as you see in Figure 3-39.

Figure 3-39. *Comments on pictures appear in photo albums, below the pictures.*

Exploring Friends' Pages and Becoming a Fan

One other thing worth mentioning is looking at what your friends are fans of—maybe you'd like to check out what all the hubbub is about (or use the search box at the top of the Facebook screen to find your favorite band or movie star and become a fan of them).

Click someone's Info tab, as shown in Figure 3-40.

Figure 3-40. Info tab

To check on fandom, scroll down to the person's Pages section. Pages can be about anything (and you can create your own page if you like—see Chapter 5). By all means, check out all the pages shown in Figure 3-41! To check out the pages, click their titles. What the heck is Gerbil Liberation Front, you ask? I guess you'll have to go on Facebook and find out (see Figure 3-42).

Figure 3-41. Some pages I'm a fan of

Figure 3-42. The top of a Facebook page. Click Become a Fan.

If you like, try friending me, looking at my pages under the Info tab, and clicking one of the pages I'm a fan of, like dotGreen (see Figure 3-43). (It's pretty cool: a nonprofit organization whose dream is to propose, apply for, and manage .green so that people and organizations can have URLs like www.website.green. You can learn more at www.dotgreen.org or by visiting the Facebook page or group.)

Figure 3-43. When you look at someone's profile and see something they're a fan of, you can click it to explore what they're interested in.

Pages can have Info, Photos, and Video tabs, just like people's pages. To become a fan, click Become a Fan, as shown in Figure 3-44—and the page is added to your Info tab.

Figure 3-44. Click the Become a Fan button, and the badge appears on your Profile page.

■ **Tip** If you want to "un-fan" yourself from a page, you can visit that page, scroll down, and click the Remove link.

Another way to search for pages/causes/stars/whatever is to type the name into the search box at the top of Facebook, as shown in Figure 3-45.

Figure 3-45. The search box at the top of Facebook

When you search on Facebook, you get a list of results. If you want to explore the page, click the title (such as Social Networking Spaces in Figure 3-46); or if you know you want to become a fan, click the Become a Fan link at right in the search results.

Figure 3-46. Facebook pages appear in search results.

Posts and Privacy

When you post on someone's Wall, that person controls who can see the post; so who can see your posts depends on your friends' settings. If you want to send someone a private message and be sure it's private, you can send them a direct message by clicking the Send Message link on their profile, beneath their profile picture (see Figure 3-47).

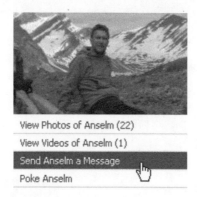

Figure 3-47. You can click someone's name, visit their profile, and send them a message.

Post Privacy

You can control who sees your posts—either making them viewable only by certain people, or hiding them from others. To adjust post privacy, type in a message, click the little lock icon next to the Share button, and choose Customize, as shown in Figure 3-48.

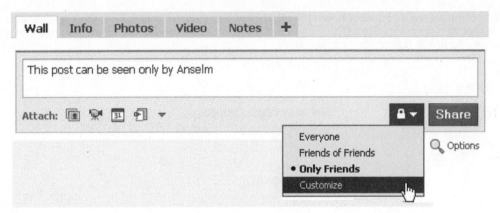

Figure 3-48. The little lock icon is the key to privacy for posts.

Then, select your desired setting. For example, to make the post viewable by only one person, click the "These people" drop-down menu, and choose Specific People, as shown in Figure 3-49.

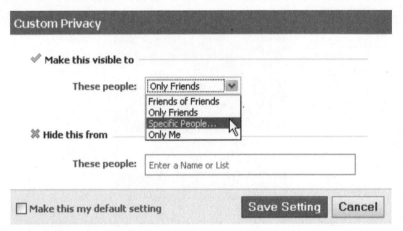

Figure 3-49. "These people" drop-down menu

■ **Note** At some point, it may come in handy to learn how to make a list of friends, so you can use custom privacy settings for posts and other material on Facebook and have an easy way to send them to specific people. You could use a list of friends in this example, so your post would go to that list. To make a list of friends, click Home at the top of the Facebook screen, then click the Friends link on the left side of your Home page, and on the Friends page, click the Create a List button. (Remember, you can ask questions on www.snspaces.com if you search Facebook help and search www.snspaces.com and don't find an answer.)

You can then begin typing in someone's name; the name pops up, and you can select (see Figure 3-50). You can also type in the name of a list, as mentioned in the preceding Note.

Figure 3-50. Selecting a friend

After you've selected who you want to be able to view the post, click Save Setting (see Figure 3-51).

Figure 3-51. Remember to click the Save Setting button.

Before you share your message, if you want to make sure it's going to the right place, you can roll the mouse pointer over the lock icon to verify your settings (see Figure 3-52).

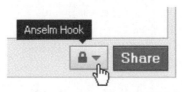

Figure 3-52. Not every post on Facebook has to be to everyone. When you're about to make a post that you only want to share with one person, or exclude from people, you can make sure by rolling over and clicking the lock icon.

After you click Share, you can verify the privacy settings for a post by clicking the little lock icon—but after you post something, you can't edit its settings. However, remember that you can always roll over your post and click the Remove button (see Figure 3-53).

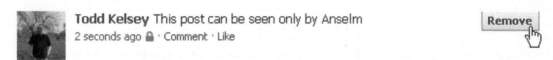

Figure 3-53. It's nice to know you can roll over a post and click Remove. This comes in handy if you have second thoughts about what you put up, or if there's a typo. You can always select the text of a post, copy it, remove the post, fix it, and post it again.

Personally, the most common reason I use the post privacy feature is if I post something but don't want all my friends to see it. If it's something that I want to keep private from some people, I click the lock and hide the post from those people.

I haven't yet created friends lists to send messages or direct posts to, but I like the idea and plan to use it. Generally, for better or worse, I post to whoever is on my friends list.

Controlling Who Sees Your Friends' Wall Posts

This feature is helpful to understand Wall posts. To review, when you post to someone else's Wall, the audience is determined by that person's settings. So, to control who can see posts on your Wall that are made by your friends, go to your Wall, and click Options, as shown in Figure 3-54.

Figure 3-54. *The handy Options link*

Then, click Settings (see Figure 3-55).

Figure 3-55. *The Settings link*

Scroll down to the relevant section, as shown in Figure 3-56.

Stories Posted by Friends

Posting Ability: ☐ Friends may post to my Wall

Who can see posts made   🔒 **Friends of Friends** ▼
by friends?

Figure 3-56. *A sample section where you can adjust settings*

I happen to have "Friends may post to my Wall" unchecked, and currently I have things set so friends of friends can see posts made to my Wall. Allowing friends of friends to see posts is nice, because if your friend posts to your Wall, their friends can see a message in their News Feed that your friend has made a post; the friend's friends can click to see it, and, depending on your privacy settings, they can see your Wall. This can be a way to get to know people.

Another approach that I may switch to is to check the "Friends may post to my Wall" box, because some people seem to like leaving Wall messages (kind of like a semi-public "hey what's up" that may begin a conversation others can join in); then, I may change the settings of who can see posts to a customized list.

Don't be alarmed if privacy seems complicated. You'll start to come across situations where you may remember this section of the book and want to come back and dig in. Also, I recommend clicking around to explore—like trying out different privacy settings by clicking the things I'm describing in this section, as well as exploring the Account ➤ Privacy Settings area, to see if your settings are the way you want them to be.

If you're following this example and want to change who can see posts made by friends, you can choose Everyone (that is, anyone on Facebook who visits your profile), Friends of Friends (friends, and their friends too), Only Friends, or Customize (which may be a series of friends you specify, or a list), as shown in Figure 3-57.

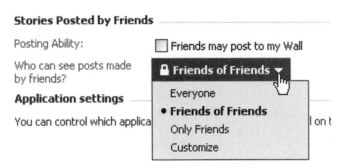

Figure 3-57. Setting things so friends of friends can see

Exploring Groups

At this point, it would probably be a good idea to go outside and take a walk, to take your eyes off the screen. Or if you have kids or friends who can think with a childlike imagination, try making a non-electronic Facebook, with pictures and glue (does anyone remember glue?). Try scrapbooking.

Pretend you've lost electricity; pretend you're living in a pre-Facebook, precomputer world. In short, *step away from the computer.*

```
::gets up from the computer::
```

If you weren't aware—in electronic communication these days—with instant messaging, or Facebook postings, or in the middle of a book—when you put two colons at the beginning and end of an action phrase, it means you're "doing" the action. For example, if I type

```
::laughing::
```

it means I'm laughing. But I'm going to get up from the computer to set a good example for readers who are faithfully working through the book, sitting at their computer, dazed from the enchantment of Facebook. So, I'll type

```
::gets up from the computer::
::drinks some iced tea, takes a break::
::comes back to computer::
```

When you're out and about exploring Facebook, wrapping action statements in :: can be a way to have a bit of fun. For example, if you're bored by what I'm saying, you can say

```
::yawn::
```

And then I'll get back to the task at hand. Which is exploring groups.

Groups are very cool. They allow you to join a group of people of like mind and heart, who have something in common. It's very easy to create a group, and there are a lot of groups on Facebook—everything from commonly held interests, to complete jokes, to fandom (try searching for "peanut butter"). You name it, there's probably a group. (Of course, only one magical group on Facebook can make all your dreams come true: the group called A Sunflower Club, of course.)

To search for a group on whatever topic, go to the search box at the top of Facebook, type the name (see Figure 3-58), and press Enter.

Figure 3-58. *When you join the Sunflower Club, you will suddenly be filled with energy, and your day will go better.*

When you search for a group, a list of results comes up, as shown in Figure 3-59. Each entry has some basic information. If you know you want to join the group already, you can click Join Group.

Figure 3-59. *When you find a group you'd like to try, click Join Group.*

Clicking the group title after searching for groups, as shown in Figure 3-60, takes you to the group page.

Figure 3-60. *Click a group title to go to the group's page.*

■ **Tip** You can also go to your friends' profiles to see what groups they're a member of. And when a person joins a group, it may show up in your News Feed.

When you explore a group page, as shown in Figure 3-61, you can scroll down to view whatever is there; and if you like it, you can click Join. If you really like the group or think of someone who would like to have all their dreams come true, you can also click the Share link.

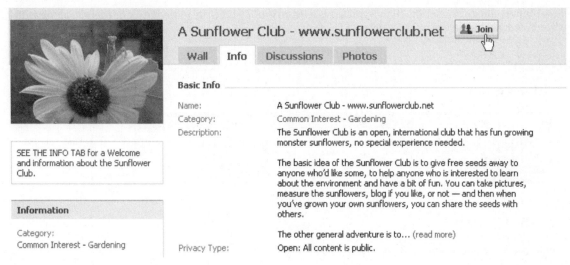

Figure 3-61. The Join button on the group page is another way to join.

After you've joined a group, you can click the Home link at the top of the Facebook screen and then look to the left and click the Groups link (see Figure 3-62).

Figure 3-62. Groups link on your Home page

When you do, one of the things you see is a list of groups recently joined by your friends, along with your own groups on the right (see Figure 3-63).

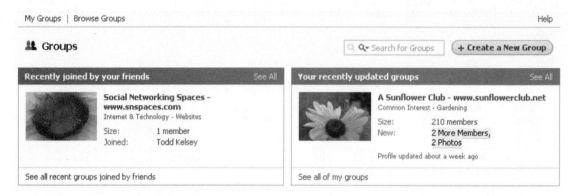

Figure 3-63. Recently joined, recently updated groups

Tips and Tricks

Here are some additional things you may like to try.

Sharing a Link

Sharing a link on your own profile is like sharing a link on someone else's Wall. But in this case, the Links application keeps track of it and collects all the links in a list on your page so that you and your friends can view the list.

Share a link on your own page by clicking the Profile link at the top of Facebook (see Figure 3-68).

Figure 3-64. Profile link

Next, click your Wall tab (see Figure 3-65).

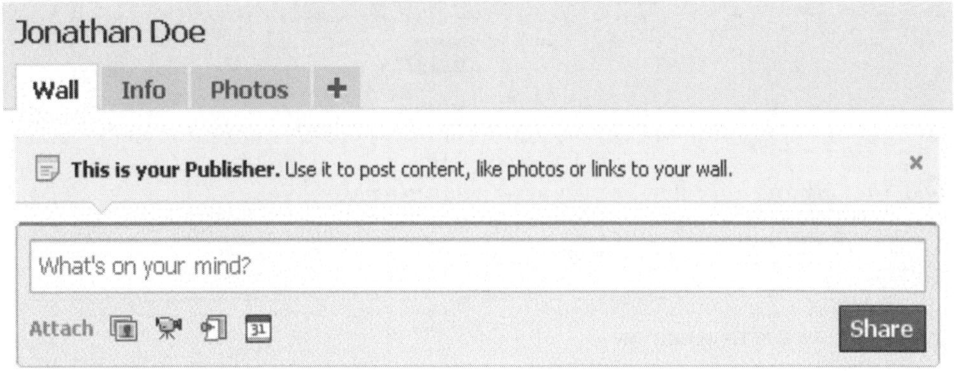
Jonathan Doe
Wall
Info
Photos
+
This is your Publisher. Use it to post content, like photos or links to your wall.
What's on your mind?
Attach
Share

Figure 3-65. Wall tab

Type in a message if you like (see Figure 3-66).

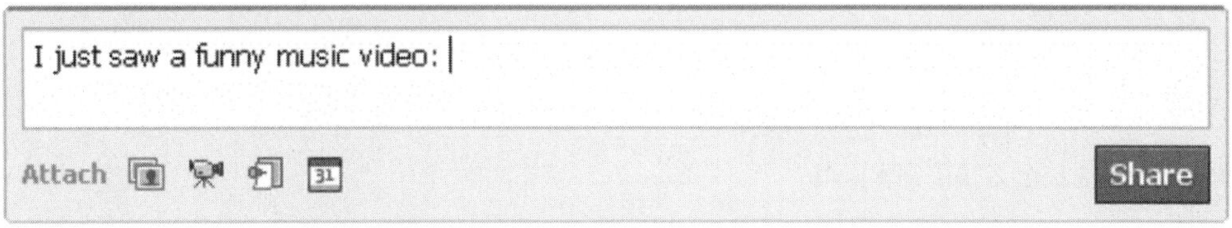
I just saw a funny music video:
Attach
Share

Figure 3-66. Area to type in, beneath the Wall tab

Paste in a link. As soon as you do, Facebook may automatically add it (see Figure 3-67).

I just saw a funny music video: http://www.youtube.com
/watch?v=9aIyZH1fKVo
Link
She's My Gerbil
http://www.youtube.com/watch?v=9aIy...
This is the She's My Gerbil video, featuring Binky, Boojy, Sparky and Nergil.
Share

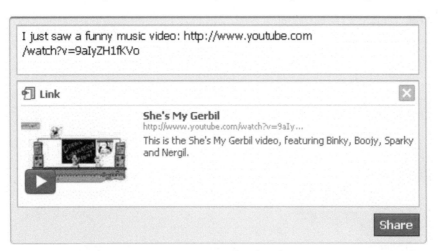

Figure 3-67. Facebook can sometimes automatically add a link as soon as you type or paste it in.

You can also type in a message and click the Link icon (see Figure 3-68).

Figure 3-68. *The Link icon is the sure-fire way to get a link in a post.*

Then, paste a link in, and click Attach (see Figure 3-69).

Figure 3-69. *Attaching a link to a post*

Then click the Share button, and voila! Linkerific: the link appears on your Wall (see Figure 3-70).

Figure 3-70. *When you share a link on your page, it appears on your Wall.*

The link also appears on the Home page of anyone you're friends with, because the Facebook News Feed carries it there. In Figure 3-71, you see how the link that Jonathan Doe posted as shown in the previous figures also appears on Todd Kelsey's Home page, thanks to the magic of the Facebook stream. The best way to understand this is to log on to Facebook and click the Home tab. You'll see things other people have posted. Then, you can click their name to see their profile—and you'll see that what they just posted shows on their profile, too.

Figure 3-71. The link and the preview of the page appear.

Hide and Seek with the Hide Function: One of the Most Important Things to Learn on Facebook

As you add friends on Facebook, some post more than others, and you may not want to have to read all those posts. You may still want to remain friends with someone, but you may not want to have their posts show up in your News Feed.

Remember, you can always roll your mouse over one of their posts and click the Hide button (see Figure 3-72).

Figure 3-72. Roll over a post, and click Hide.

If you want to add someone back, click Home and then News Feed. Then, look for the Edit Options link shown in Figure 3-73, and click it; scroll all the way to the bottom of the News Feed if you need to.

Figure 3-73. Home ➤ News Feed ➤ Edit Options

Find the friend you hid, and click the Add To News Feed button to unhide them so you start seeing their posts again in your News Feed (see Figure 3-74).

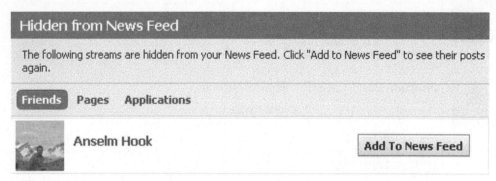

Figure 3-74. Restoring a poster to their former place of honor

Click the Close button when you're done. That's it! Definitely a useful feature.

■ **Note** You may see a different screen than the one in Figure 3-74. Sometimes, some Facebook features aren't consistently available to all users, especially when the site is in the midst of a redesign. According to *Economist* magazine, as of February 2010, Facebook has 400 million users, and when they're rolling things out it may take some time.

Changing Your Profile Picture

Changing your profile picture can be fun and a way to add some variety, to express yourself, to make your cat famous, or whatever you can think of.

■ **Note** The first Twitter chapter contains a section on a helpful tool called Pic Resizer, which makes it easy to crop pictures.

To change your profile picture, go to your profile, roll the mouse over your picture, and click Change Picture (see Figure 3-75).

Figure 3-75. Roll over the picture, and click Change Picture.

Choose the Upload a Picture option, as shown in Figure 3-76.

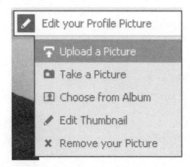

Figure 3-76. Upload a Picture link

■ **Tip** The menu shown in Figure 3-76 also allows you to perform other actions. The Edit Thumbnail option lets you change the position of the thumbnail image that Facebook uses. Facebook makes a small version of your larger image compared to the big version; sometimes you may wish to adjust what portion of a picture Facebook chooses for the thumbnail.

Click the Choose File button (see Figure 3-77).

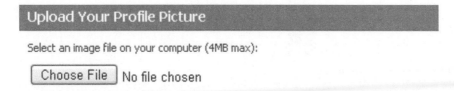

Figure 3-77. After clicking the Choose File button, you can locate and select a file.

The new profile picture appears, as shown in Figure 3-78.

Figure 3-78. *New profile pic*

When you've uploaded several profile pictures, you can switch back and forth between profile pictures. To try it, click Change Picture (see Figure 3-79).

Figure 3-79. *Change Picture link*

Click Choose from Album (see Figure 3-80).

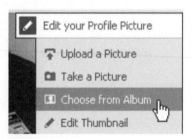

Figure 3-80. *Choose from Album link*

The screen shows a list of available profile pictures. Click the one you want (see Figure 3-81).

Your Photos - Profile Pictures
Back to Profile
2 photos | Edit Photos | Change Profile Picture

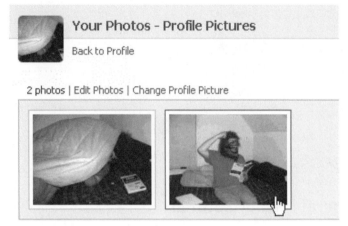

Figure 3-81. Pictures to choose from

You'll get a close-up of the profile picture (see Figure 3-82).

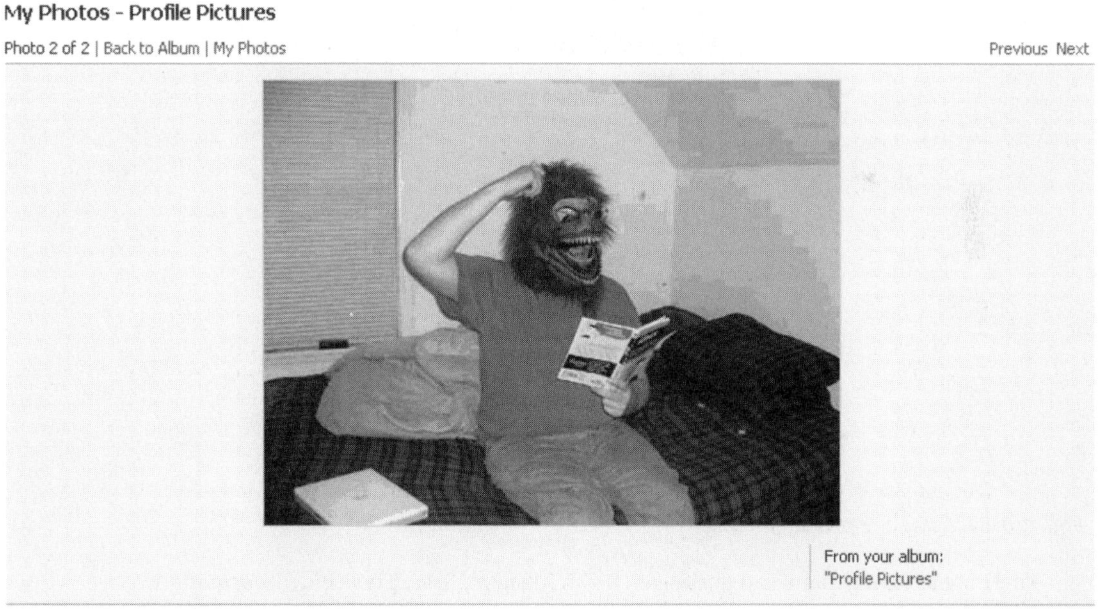

My Photos - Profile Pictures
Photo 2 of 2 | Back to Album | My Photos
Previous Next
From your album:
"Profile Pictures"

Figure 3-82. The big version of the picture

When you're looking at the picture, there's one more step to complete. You have to scroll down and click Make Profile Picture (see Figure 3-83).

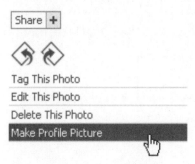

Figure 3-83. *Make Profile Picture link*

Adjusting General Privacy Settings

Adjusting privacy is a good thing to be familiar with. It may save you embarrassment or make you feel more comfy. Refer back to the "Posts and Privacy" section earlier in this chapter for more details.

To access privacy settings, click Account ➤ Privacy Settings in the upper-right corner of Facebook (see Figure 3-84).

Figure 3-84. *Accessing privacy settings*

There are several general categories, as shown in Figure 3-85. Try Profile Information.

Privacy Settings

Profile Information
Control who can see your profile and who can post to your Wall

Contact Information
Control who can contact you on Facebook and see your contact information and email

Applications and Websites
Control what information is available to Facebook-enhanced applications and websites

Search
Control who can see your search result on Facebook and in search engines

Block List
Control who can interact with you on Facebook

Figure 3-85. Privacy Settings page

Click to change your privacy settings as desired (see Figure 3-86). For example, you can click the button in the Personal Info row and switch from Only Friends to Everyone so that anyone who visits your profile can see your personal information.

Privacy Settings ▸ Profile Information

◀ Back to Privacy	Preview My Profile...
About me About Me refers to the About Me description in your profile	🔒 Everyone ▾
Personal Info Interests, Activities, Favorites	🔒 Only Friends ▾
Birthday Birth date and Year	🔒 Friends of Friends ▾
Religious and Political Views	🔒 Friends of Friends ▾
Family and Relationship Family Members, Relationship Status, Interested In, and Looking For	🔒 Everyone ▾
Education and Work Schools, Colleges and Workplaces	🔒 Everyone ▾
Photos and Videos of Me Photos and Videos you've been tagged in	🔒 Friends of Friends ▾

Figure 3-86. Privacy Settings ➤ Profile information

Facebook Messages and Notifications

One common thing you'll probably end up getting involved in is sending and receiving Facebook messages. Typically, it starts when you join Facebook, and people begin sending you messages. Most likely you'll get an e-mail like the one shown in Figure 3-87.

☐ ☆ Facebook (2)   E. John Walford sent you a message on Facebook...

Figure 3-87. An e-mail that lets you know you have a message on Facebook

When you click the link in the e-mail, you're taken directly to the message.

You can control whether Facebook notifies you about such things by going to the top of the Facebook screen and selecting Account ➤ Account Settings, clicking the Notifications tab, and checking (or unchecking) the appropriate option to tell Facebook whether you want to get an e-mail. In fact, when you start a Facebook account, I definitely recommend visiting this area and looking at the settings to see if they suit you (see Figure 3-88).

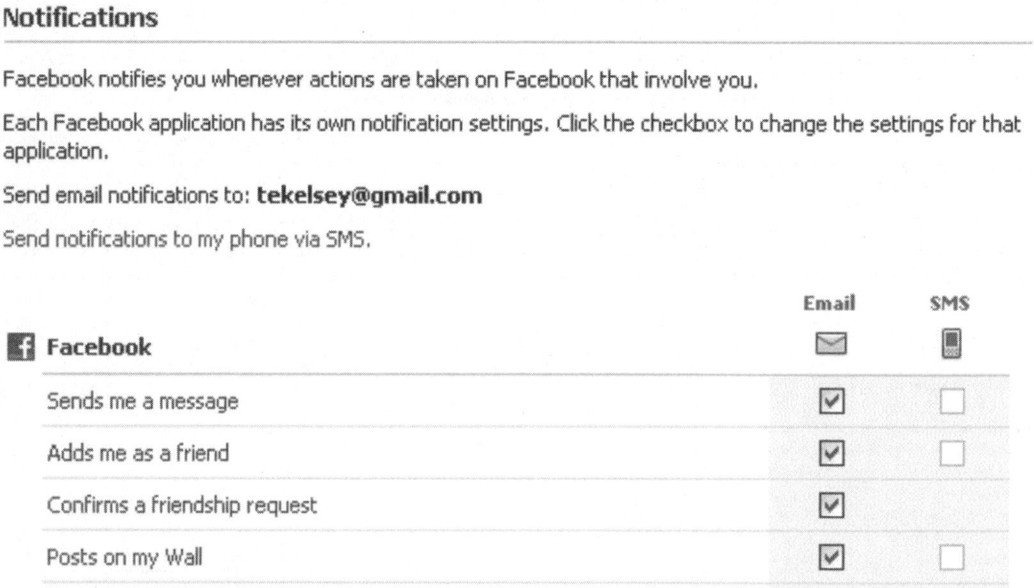

Notifications

Facebook notifies you whenever actions are taken on Facebook that involve you.

Each Facebook application has its own notification settings. Click the checkbox to change the settings for that application.

Send email notifications to: **tekelsey@gmail.com**

Send notifications to my phone via SMS.

	Email ✉	SMS 📱
📘 **Facebook**		
Sends me a message	☑	☐
Adds me as a friend	☑	☐
Confirms a friendship request	☑	
Posts on my Wall	☑	☐

Figure 3-88. Notifications are worth exploring.

Be sure to click the Save Changes button when you're finished.

As for me, I like to be notified. Once in a while it can get annoying; but remember, you can come back here and change things. If you turn off notifications, remember that a lot of people treat Facebook as if it were e-mail (reportedly, some younger people don't even use e-mail anymore); so at the very least, it's a good idea to log in at least once a week and check your inbox if you've turned off notifications. (To check your Inbox, log in and click the Messages icon at the top of the screen.)

One other thing is worth mentioning about Facebook messages. In the current version, if you write a message to multiple people or receive a message that has been sent to multiple people, it's easy to click the wrong button and reply to everyone, when you only mean to send the message to an individual person. The simple thing to remember is this: only click Reply All if you really mean to.

For example, when you're in your Inbox and click Compose Message, you can start typing your friends' names in the To field, and Facebook will suggest a list of friends. You can select the friend you want to send a message to (see Figure 3-89).

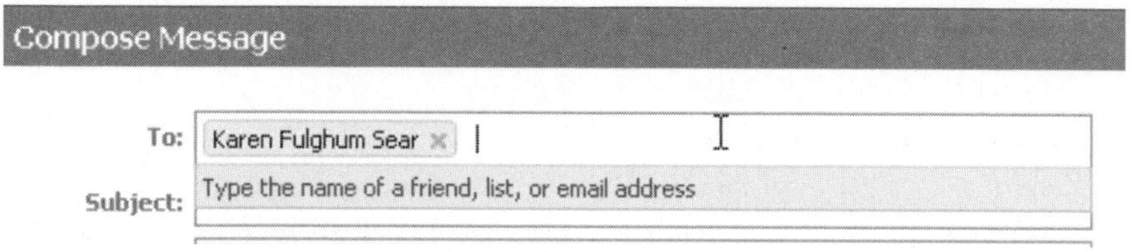

Figure 3-89. Choosing a recipient

You can send the message to more than one person by typing someone else's name and selecting that person, as shown in Figure 3-90.

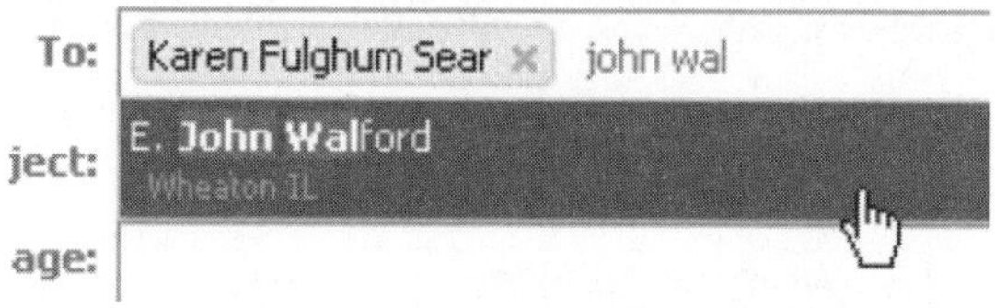

Figure 3-90. When you start typing in letters, Facebook suggests options.

Then, type a subject and a message, and click the Send button (see Figure 3-91).

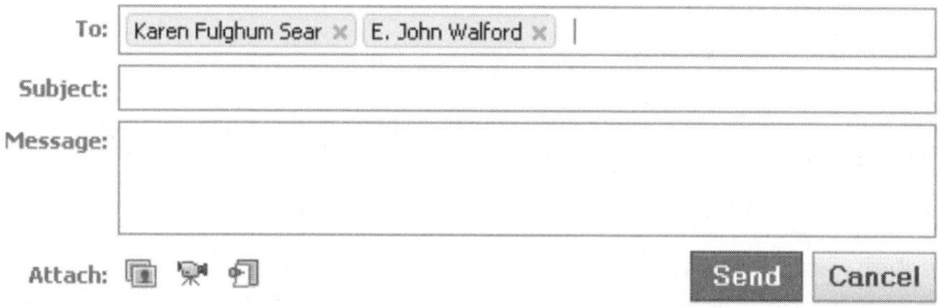

Figure 3-91. Adding multiple recipients

When people begin replying, you may be tempted to click the Reply All button, as you see me about to do in Figure 3-92—but unless you want your message to go to everyone, you need to click the Reply link instead.

Figure 3-92. *A very important thing to remember, lest you send a private reply to everyone who received the original message. Be conscious in Facebook messages of whether you are "replying" or "replying to all."*

Facebook opens a Compose Message window (see Figure 3-93). Type your message, and then click Reply.

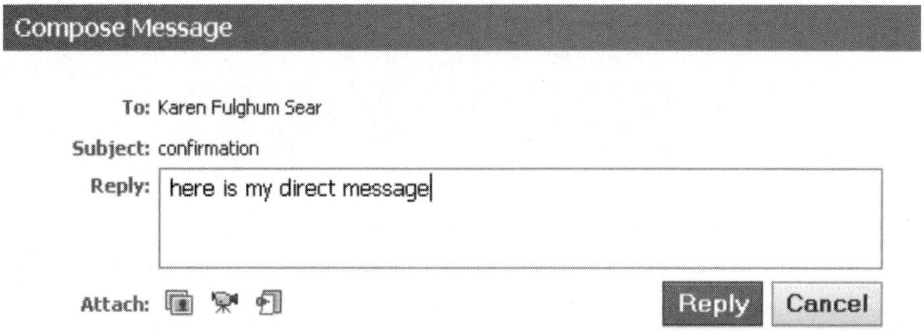

Compose Message

To: Karen Fulghum Sear

Subject: confirmation

Reply: here is my direct message|

Attach:

Reply   Cancel

Figure 3-93. *Compose Message window*

In this way, you can open a thread between you and that person. Notice how Figure 3-94 says *Between Karen Fulghum Sear and You*; this means it's a direct conversation.

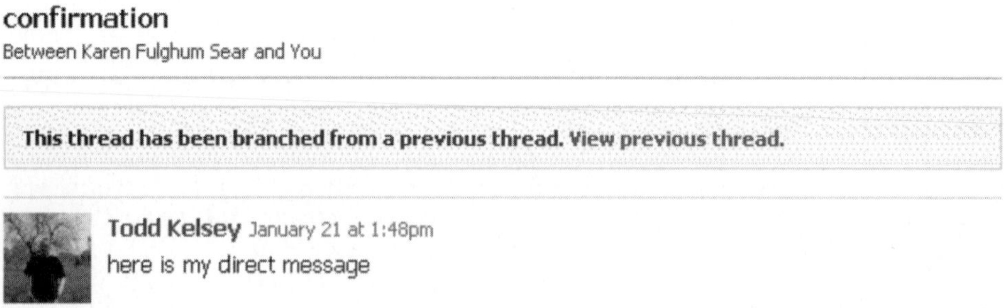

confirmation

Between Karen Fulghum Sear and You

This thread has been branched from a previous thread. View previous thread.

Todd Kelsey January 21 at 1:48pm
here is my direct message

Figure 3-94. *A message between two people*

Help!

Sometimes, in spite of well a book is written or how much you've explored, you may need a little help. So remember, Facebook has a Help Center link, way down in the lower-right corner of the screen (see Figure 3-95).

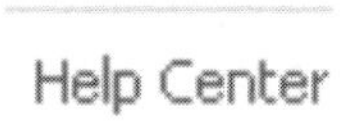

Help Center

Figure 3-95. Help Center link

The Help material for Facebook is well written and well organized (see Figure 3-96). Click away!

Figure 3-96. Lots of goodies to click. I recommending getting something from Starbucks (or Caribou), and clicking away!

Trying Applications

You can add gazillions of applications on Facebook: games, utilities, tools for sharing, applications that allow you to give gifts, and so on. As with other aspects of Facebook, I learned about most applications by seeing them mentioned in posts from other people.

Browsing Applications

Browsing applications is a nice way to get acquainted with what's out there. To browse applications, click the Home link at the top of Facebook and then the Applications link on the left (see Figure 3-97).

Todd Kelsey
View My Profile

News Feed

Messages (107)

Events (5)

Photos

Friends

Applications

Games

Figure 3-97. Applications link

Microsoft, and perhaps even Google, may wonder just how many free applications will be created and used on Facebook. Who knows? But there are some really interesting ones, as you can see in Figure 3-98.

Business	Education	Entertainment
Marketplace	Causes	Mobile
NetworkedBlogs	God wants You to Know	Music
Promotions	Quiz Monster	Photo of the Day
Social RSS	(Lil) Green Patch	Daily Horoscope
Your Birthday	My Personality	Movies
Sweepstakes	What's your Actual…	Zoosk
Contests	Quizzes	Bumper Sticker
Payvment E-Commerc…	Dr. Phil's Persona…	Slide FunSpace
Memorable Web Addr…	Interview	RockYou Live
Fan Appz	Quiz Creator	Sketch Me
Business ▸	**Education ▸**	**Entertainment ▸**

Friends & Family	Just For Fun	Lifestyle
FamilyLink.com	Friends Exposed	Astrology
Top Friends	Social Interview	Cities I've Visited
Entrevista tus Amigos	Friend Facts™	Friend Hug
Birthday Album	Quiz Planet!	Are YOU Interested?
Yearbook	Graffiti	Likeness
My Top Fans	Pieces of Flair	The Fortune Teller
My BFFs	LivingSocial	Where I've Been
Photos I Love!	Status Shuffle	Online People
Honesty Box	Funny Photo Widget	Ma Fiche
Circle of Moms	Tarjetitas	Life Box
Friends & Family ▸	**Just For Fun ▸**	**Lifestyle ▸**

Figure 3-98. When you're browsing for applications, you can click anything you like.

Each category area has a list of featured applications that you can click and explore; you can also click the link at the bottom of the list (for example, Friends & Family) to see an entire list of applications in that category(see Figure 3-99).

Friends & Family

FamilyLink.com
Top Friends
Entrevista tus Amigos
Birthday Album
Yearbook
My Top Fans
My BFFs
Photos I Love!
Honesty Box
Circle of Moms

Friends & Family ▶

Figure 3-99. Friends & Family category

Trying an Application: Scrabble

Speaking of friends and family… Scrabble? On Facebook? Are you serious? Why would I want to do that? There's a very good reason why, so please read on. (And don't tease me about liking Scrabble. It will expand your vocabulary, provide you with a convenient tool for intergenerational gaming, and make all your dreams come true.)

Scrabble happens to be an excellent example of a cooperative-play game, which is why it's so wonderful—you can play it with several other people, live, and they can be anywhere.

To search for games, and in particular, Scrabble, enter the name in the search box at the top of Facebook, as shown in Figure 3-100, and press Enter.

Figure 3-100. Search box.

Scrabble comes up in the search results (see Figure 3-101).

Figure 3-101. Scrabble Facebook application

To go further, click the title (see Figure 3-102).

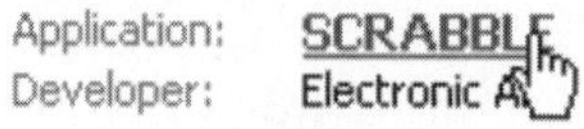

Figure 3-102. *Clicking the title*

Then, click Go to Application (see Figure 3-103).

Figure 3-103. *Go to Application button on the Scrabble page*

When you add an application, you see a screen like the one shown in Figure 3-104. Don't be afraid; the application isn't going to sell your private information, it's just going to use it so you can play Scrabble with your friends.

Figure 3-104. *Allow button*

■ **Caution** Not all applications are created by large, reputable companies. Some applications are created by individuals, and not all individuals are equally reliable. Some applications don't work well, and some haven't been created by Facebook. Some are verified by Facebook, and others aren't. When you first look at an application in your search results, look at who developed it and how many people are using it. The more people are using it, probably the better it is and the more reliable it is.

After you add the application, it takes a minute or two to load. Then, you see a screen like the one in Figure 3-105.

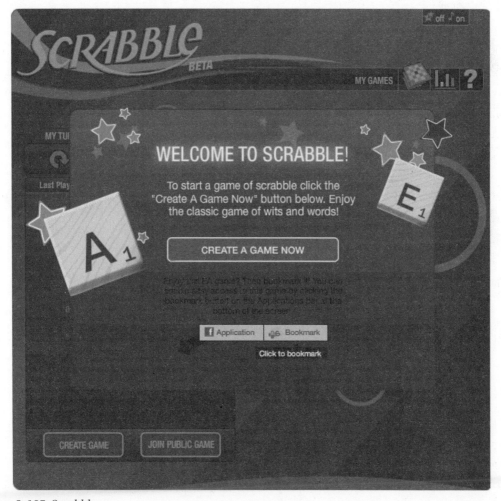

Figure 3-105. Scrabble

After you've added it, to access Scrabble, click the Home link at the top of Facebook, and then click the Games link on the left. Scrabble shows up in your list of games (see Figure 3-106).

Figure 3-106. Scrabble appears in your Games list.

To join the fun, start Scrabble (Home ➤ Games ➤ Scrabble), and click Create a Game Now (see Figure 3-107).

Figure 3-107. Create a Game Now

Name the game, if you wish; begin typing the name of a friend; and click the friend's name, as shown in Figure 3-108. (They need to be someone you've already added as a friend in Facebook.)

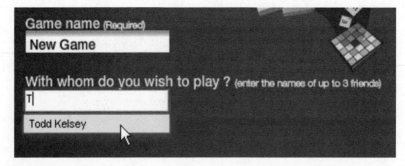

Figure 3-108. Inviting a player

After you type the name, it shows up on the right (see Figure 3-109). You can play with more than one person.

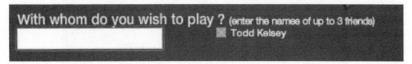

Figure 3-109. *The name appears on the right.*

Then, click Start (see Figure 3-110).

Figure 3-110. *Start button*

You see your name on the screen (see Figure 3-111). Generally, you'll want to make arrangements with your friend to be online at the same time.

Figure 3-111. *List of players*

If you don't see a board come up on the screen, click the "click here" link to see your active games (see Figure 3-112). This is also how your friend can see the game when they get the application.

Figure 3-112. *Active games*

You and your friend see a list of active games, as shown in Figure 3-113.

Figure 3-113. List of games to choose from

Click the Play This Game button, shown in Figure 3-114.

Figure 3-114. Play This Game button

In some cases, if things are slow or you're not sure what's going on, you may need to click the Refresh button in the browser (see Figure 3-115). Then, go to your active games, and click Play This Game.

Figure 3-115. You may need to click the Refresh button in your browser.

You see a Scrabble board, as shown in Figure 3-116. Wonderful! Drag letters into place, as shown in Figure 3-117, and click the green arrow to play your turn. Depending on how far away your friend is and how many people are playing Scrabble at the same time, the delay between moves can last a few moments.

Figure 3-116. The blank Scrabble game board, ready to go

Figure 3-117. Drag letters from the bottom up to the middle of the board (one has to be in the center). Then, click the green triangle button at the bottom of the game board (see Figure 3-116).

After you play your turn, the other person's name is highlighted, their green arrow is highlighted, and they can drag letters into place, as shown in Figure 3-118.

Figure 3-118. On the next turn, just like in real scrabble, letters are dragged into place.

Scrabble keeps tracks of the players' words and points, as shown in Figure 3-119.

PLAYER	WORD	PTS	TOTAL
Jonathan	FINE	14	14
Todd	WIG	7	7

Figure 3-119. Scores are automatically calculated.

Scrabble is an example of a really nice cooperative-play game. In the future, may there be many more like it! How cool that you can get family and friends together and play a game like that.

■ **Tip** For extra fun, have everyone install Skype on their computers, and learn how to do a conference call. Or if these sites are still around, try www.freeconferencecall.com or www.freeconference.com—and have everyone dial in while you're playing Scrabble!

Q/A

Q: Is there any reason to have multiple Facebook accounts?
A: Some people like to have both a personal and a professional Facebook account. That way, they can connect with business friends through one but not have to worry about whether to make personal comments. Technically, as you learn in these chapters, you can control who you post messages to, even if all your friends are connected to a single Facebook account. But you may find it easier to maintain separate Facebook accounts. You can accomplish this by creating a separate Gmail address (www.google.com/gmail), starting a professional Facebook account, and adding –*Professional* after your name, such as Todd Kelsey-Professional. This way, people can distinguish between your personal and professional accounts when they search for you on Facebook. Or if you don't want a suffix on your last name, you can wear a professional-looking, corporate-type outfit for your professional account.

Q: I like this book, but there are only four chapters about Facebook. Where can I read more?
A: If you like this book and this chapter or section, keep your eyes open for an entire book about Facebook from CFTW Press. If you want to keep up to date about the book's progress, go on Facebook and search for (and join) the Social Networking Spaces group, or search for (and become a fan of) the Social Networking Spaces Facebook page. I'll post messages once in awhile to both. Just as with this book, all author proceeds will be donated to CFTW. (See the Introduction to this book.)

Q: Who exactly are the gerbil and the other 3D characters in this book?
A: See http://tinyurl.com/aboutrgb. Originally, Mr. Green was an idea for a character to be in a kind of open source *Finding Nemo* 3D adventure film, to help kids learn about the environment. If you like the characters, let me know, and that will give some extra encouragement to Alexandra, who made the characters.
Maybe, if enough people like them, that will convince us to do a children's book, as we've considered doing. And then maybe that will turn into enough interest and computing power that we'll try to make a video. The original idea was to make something for the kids of One Laptop Per Child (http://laptop.org/en/), something they could watch on their laptops (in far-flung places of the world, like Peru and Afghanistan). But it takes effort and resources. If this sounds interesting to you, in the spirit of social networking, check out this book's web site at www.snspaces.com, and check out Appendix A—

Kahonua. Also, feel free to friend me and look at the Kahonua Facebook photo album, or visit `http://tinyurl.com/kahonua1`—it explains more about the imaginary chain of islands.

> Q: Wait! I have another question! Where can I ask it?
> A: On `www.snspaces.com`.

Conclusion

Dear Reader,

In this chapter, you took a whirlwind tour of Facebook and learned a few of the things you can do. Remember to have fun and explore, and don't hesitate to try the Help link in the lower-right corner of the screen to learn more about how things work (and to learn new things you didn't know).

In the next chapter, you look at a themed use of Facebook, one of the most meaningful and perhaps the most fun ways to use Facebook—to capture, preserve, and share your life story. You learn to upload pictures and videos, make notes, connect blogs, and tell your friends and family about what you've shared.

And if you're wondering why anyone would be interested in your life story, then ask yourself this: wouldn't it be cool if your grandparents or great-grandparents had Facebook pages, or pictures or notes (or film, or video) about bits of their life?

Wouldn't it be really interesting (and meaningful) to be able to experience those pages?

Don't make the mistake of thinking that supposedly mundane bits of your life aren't interesting. If you ever have descendants, I can guarantee they'll be glad you made the effort to capture some of your life story. Even if you never plan to have descendants, you may change your mind. And you may be surprised how many people who are alive right now would be interested in your life. It really is worth doing.

If you stubbornly refuse to believe anyone would be interested in your life or share your interests, I'll bet you 100 sunflower seeds that you're wrong. (Sunflower seeds are destined to become a new form of currency.)

To prove it, try entering your interest in the search box in Facebook. I dare you.

Regards,

–Todd

P.S. If you've read Chapter 1, you may already know that the Life Story Suitcase is an experimental tool for gathering all your life media from Facebook, Blogger, and so on. If you like, when you've had a chance to start a Facebook account, you're welcome to come by `www.lifestorysuitcase.com` and tell us how good or bad the experiment is.

snspaces.com

Come and visit the Social Networking Spaces companion web site at www.snspaces.com, where you can find more tips and updates and have an opportunity to share your thoughts or ask questions.

In Living Color: You can visit www.snspaces.com/pics to see full-color versions of all the pictures from this chapter.

CHAPTER 4

Capturing Your Story on Facebook

In This Chapter:

- Uploading photos and videos
- Capturing your thoughts with notes
- Sharing what you've created and uploaded on Facebook
- Privacy: deciding who can see what you share

snspaces.com

Come and visit the Social Networking Spaces companion web site at www.snspaces.com, where you can find more tips and updates and have an opportunity to share your thoughts or ask questions.

In Living Color: You can visit www.snspaces.com/pics to see full-color versions of all the pictures from this chapter.

Introduction

In this chapter, you look at what can be an enjoyable and meaningful way to use Facebook: capturing, preserving, and sharing stories from your life. You look at uploading pictures and videos, making notes, and telling your friends and family what you've shared (as well as how to change the privacy settings to share with only the people with whom you want).

My personal perspective: when I encourage people to consider capturing their life somehow to share with future generations, family, or friends, sometimes people feel like their life isn't interesting, or think that no one would want to know the supposedly mundane details of their life. I usually ask them to consider the following question: "Wouldn't it be cool if your grandparents or great grandparents had left a diary, or pictures or notes (or film, or video) about bits of their life? And if they did, even if it was everyday bits, wouldn't it be really interesting (and meaningful) to be able to access them?" You may not have children, or not plan to have children; but if you do, I can guarantee your descendants will be glad you made the effort to capture some of your life story. There are also relatives to consider.

Facebook is a nice way to get started, in part because, as you add friends, it's a good environment for "show and tell." When you capture some element of your life, be it a picture, a note, or a video, there's usually someone who will see and enjoy it (even if they don't comment on it). And remember, you can make new friends on Facebook by joining groups. You can meet people who have similar interests, who will be interested in your life story.

If you stubbornly refuse to believe there's anyone out there who would be interested in your life story or share your interests, I'll bet you 100 sunflower seeds you're wrong. (Sunflower seeds are destined to become a new form of currency.)

To prove it, try entering your interest in the search box in Facebook. I dare you.

Photos

The Photos application is one of the built-in applications in Facebook. If you like, you can access it by going to the Applications menu at the lower-left corner of the screen. The Photos tab on your Profile is a handy way of accessing it, too.

Creating a Photo Album

You can create as many photo albums as you like, and you can always come back later to add more photos, to reorganize them, or to delete them. As you see, the photo albums automatically appear on the home pages of your Facebook friends, but you can change the privacy settings. And you can also share photos with people who aren't on Facebook.

To get started, first click your Profile, then the Photos tab (see Figure 4-1). If you don't have a Photos tab, you can click the + tab and choose Photos.

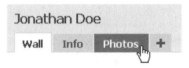

Figure 4-1. *The Photos tab*

The Photos tab displays any photo albums you have, including an album that contains any profile pictures you've uploaded (see Figure 4-2). To create a new album, click the Create Album button.

Figure 4-2. Photo albums, including your Profile Pictures album, can be viewed by clicking the Photos tab.

Enter a name for your album (and a location and description, if you like), and click the Create Album button (see Figure 4-3).

Figure 4-3. The Create Album button

You can adjust the privacy settings before creating an album (see Figure 4-4), or you can come back and do this after you create an album.

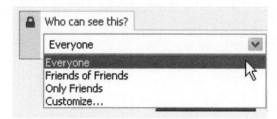

Figure 4-4. Privacy settings let you control who can see your album.

The Everyone setting allows anyone on Facebook to see the album. Friends of Friends means, say, if you have a friend named Joe, he can see the album, and anyone who is his Facebook friend can see it, too. Only Friends means only your Facebook friends can see the album. Custom allows you a greater degree of control, allowing you to specific who can see and who can't. See Figure 4-5.

Figure 4-5. Customizing who can access your album

If you click Some Friends, you can select the specific friends to whom you want to grant access to your album. See Figure 4-6.

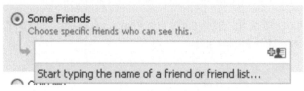

Figure 4-6. Selecting the friends you want to have access to your album

You don't have to type the name of each friend. Begin typing a name, and Facebook guesses which friend you mean. When the correct name is suggested, click it. See Figure 4-7.

Figure 4-7. Click a name to add it to the Some Friends list.

After you click the name, it appears in the list. A box appears where you can add more names. When you're done, click OK at the bottom of the screen.

Figure 4-8. Adding more names to your Some Friends list

Uploading Photos

There are two ways to upload photos. When you create a photo album, click Upload Photos. Note that the Uploader requires Java, so you may be asked to install/authorize Java. If the Upload Photos button doesn't appear or doesn't work, you can always use the Simple Uploader. This appears as a link at the bottom of the uploading area. See Figure 4-9.

Trouble uploading photos? Try the Simple Uploader.
Got a camera phone? Upload photos straight from your phone.

Figure 4-9. Choose the Simple Uploader if the Upload Photos option doesn't work or appear.

■ **Note** You can always return to a photo album under your Photos tab to add more photos. Just select the desired photo album, and click the Add More Photos button.

The Uploader

Assuming the Uploader does appear and work correctly, it's the easiest option. First, select the photos you want to include in your album from wherever they're stored on your computer (see Figure 4-10).

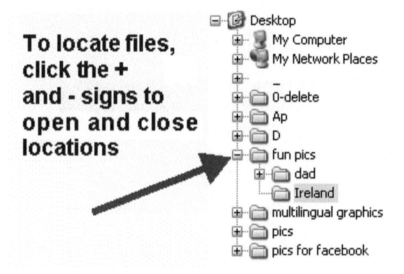

Figure 4-10. Locate photo files on the left side of the Uploader screen.

Then, select the photos using the little check boxes (or the Select All button), and click the Upload button (see Figure 4-11).

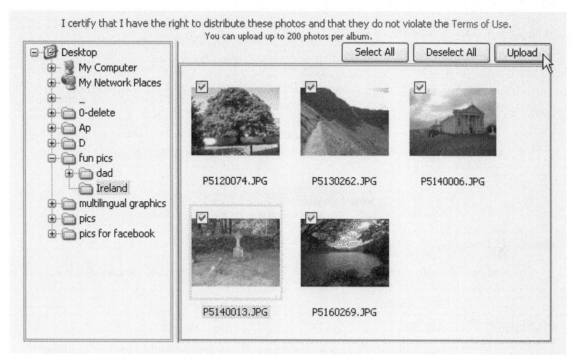

Figure 4-11. *On the right, select the photos you wish to include in your album.*

Notice that, while you're selecting images, little Rotate icons appear when you roll your cursor over each thumbnail. See Figure 4-12. If you've taken a picture and it's at a right angle, you can use these icons to rotate the picture before uploading it.

Figure 4-12. *Rotating images*

The Simple Uploader

As mentioned previously, if you can't get the Uploader to appear or work properly, you can use the Simple Uploader, shown in Figure 4-13.

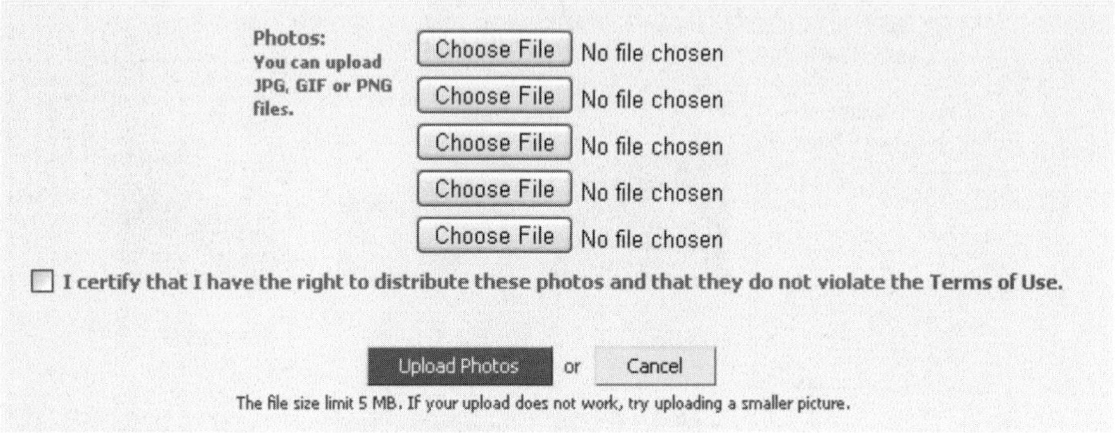

Figure 4-13. Using the Simple Uploader

To upload photos with the Simple Uploader, click the Choose File buttons, locate the desired photos, and then click the Upload Photos button.

Publishing Your Album

After you've uploaded your photos, Facebook may ask you if you want to publish your album straight away (see Figure 4-14). I tend to wait to publish until after I've added captions to pictures. You can click Publish Now or Skip.

Figure 4-14. Skip publishing, for now.

You then see the Edit Photos tab, shown in Figure 4-15.

🖼 Edit Album - New Pictures

| Edit Photos | Add More | Organize | Edit Info | Delete | Back to Album |

Figure 4-15. Edit Photos tab

Click the Edit Photos tab to add captions, or you can do so at a later time. See Figure 4-16.

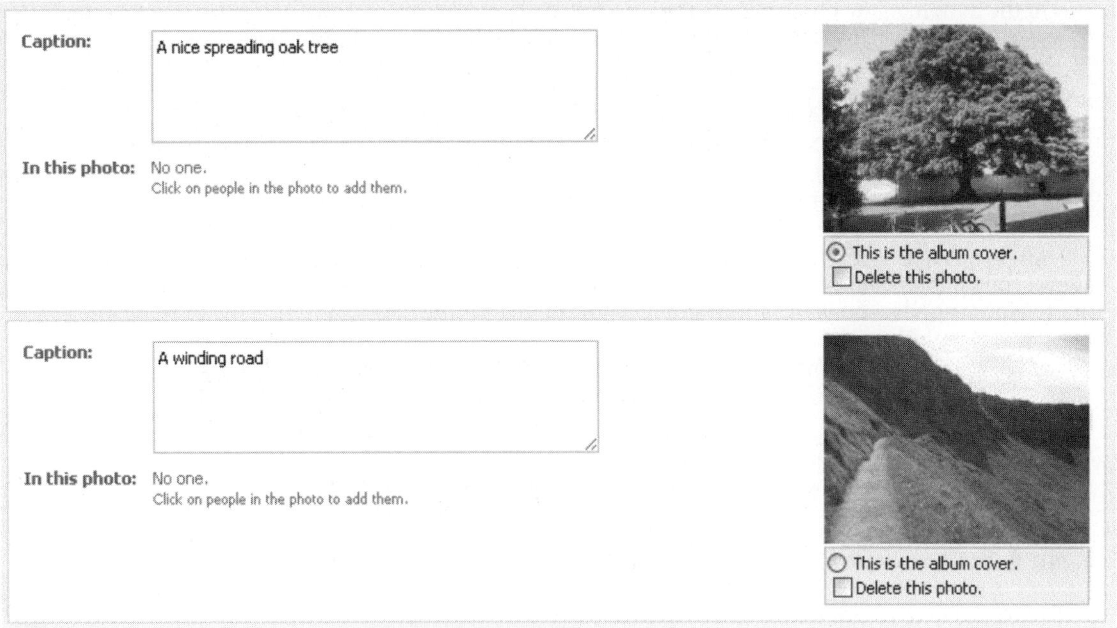

Caption: A nice spreading oak tree

In this photo: No one.
Click on people in the photo to add them.

⊙ This is the album cover.
☐ Delete this photo.

Caption: A winding road

In this photo: No one.
Click on people in the photo to add them.

○ This is the album cover.
☐ Delete this photo.

Figure 4-16. Adding captions

In the Edit Photos tab there is also an option to add an album cover, as in Figure 4-17.

○ This is the album cover.
☐ Delete this photo.

Figure 4-17. Adding an album cover

When you have completed all your photo edits, click Save Changes, as in Figure 4-18.

Save Changes   Cancel

Figure 4-18. Saving changes to photo album

At the bottom of the photo album, there's a link that you can select, copy, and paste into an e-mail or message to share the album with anyone, regardless of whether they're on Facebook. See Figure 4-19.

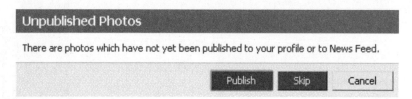

Share this album with anyone by sending them this public link:
http://www.facebook.com/album.php?aid=4953&id=1000001094866468&l=6745593e40

Figure 4-19. Sharing your album

After you click Save Changes, Facebook may ask you if you want to publish (see Figure 4-20). This allows you to publish to your News Feed. *Publishing* simply means that a promotional blurb for the photo album appears on your profile and on your friends' Home pages the next time they log in.

Figure 4-20. Choosing to publish edited photos

Click Home to see your blurb (see Figure 4-21).

Figure 4-21. To see the promo blurb for your new album, you can click the Home or Profile link at the top of the screen.

When you create a new album or add photos, Facebook selects some of the photos and adds a blurb on your Wall (the same thing as the Home link) and on your profile. See Figure 4-22.

Figure 4-22. Facebook announces your new photos or album.

To access the album, click your Photos tab, and select the album. See Figure 4-23.

Figure 4-23. Selecting from your list of albums

When you've selected an album, you can use a variety of functions to update or share it. These are discussed in the following sections.

Sharing an Album (or Individual Pictures)

To share an album, you can select it and then select the Share This Album link shown in Figure 4-24.

Figure 4-24. *Sharing an album*

When sharing the album, the Post to Profile feature allows you to do the same thing as when you're asked if you want to publish. If you don't choose to publish the album so that it appears on your profile and on your friends' pages through the News Feed, this function allows you to come back and place a blurb on your profile. See Figure 4-25.

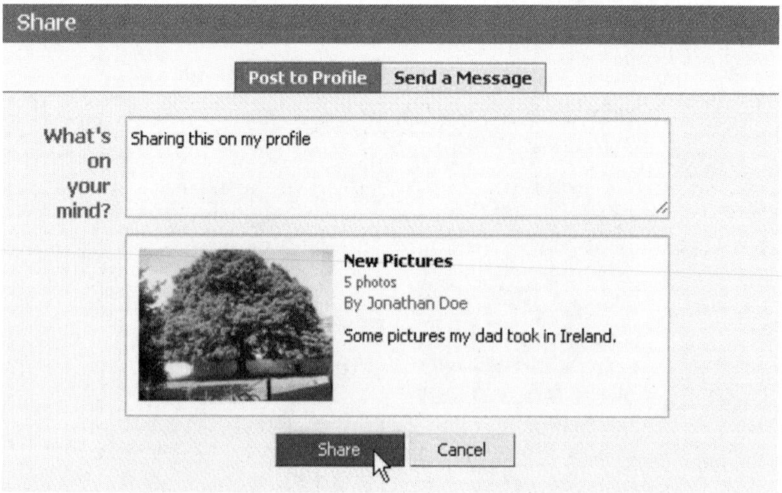

Figure 4-25. *Announcing your album with a post*

The Share function also has a Send a Message tab, which you can click (see Figure 4-26); this is how you can send a message to people on Facebook or via e-mail to directly announce the album and invite them to check it out.

Figure 4-26. The Send a Message tab

After you click the Send a Message tab, you can type the name of a Facebook friend, the name a friend list (which you can create in the Friends area), or an e-mail address to indicate to whom you'd like to send a message. See Figure 4-27.

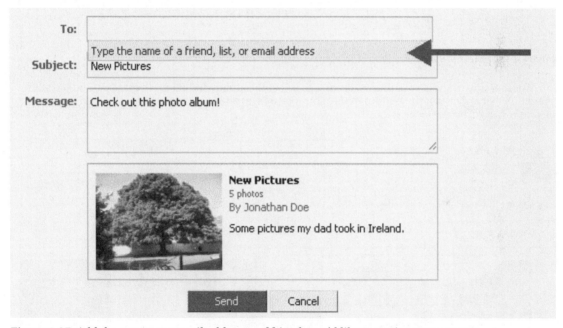

Figure 4-27. Add the names or e-mail addresses of friends you'd like to receive your message.

If you e-mail someone about your photo album, they get a message something like what is shown in Figure 4-28.

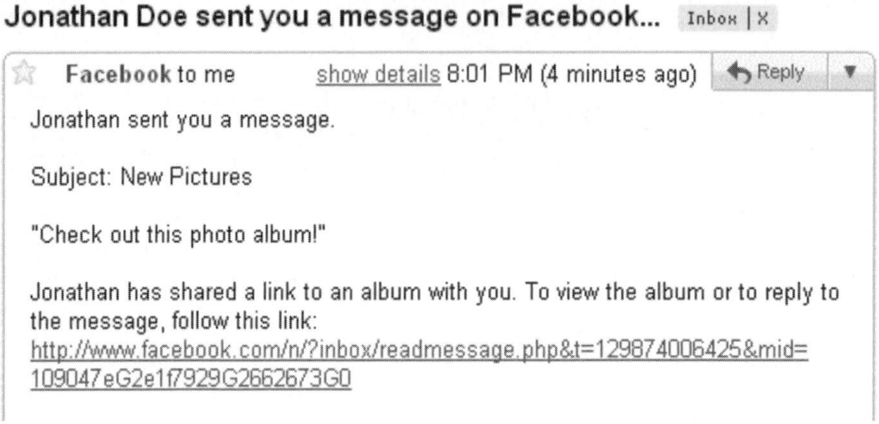

Jonathan Doe sent you a message on Facebook... Inbox | X

☆ **Facebook** to me   show details 8:01 PM (4 minutes ago)   ↩ Reply   ▼

Jonathan sent you a message.

Subject: New Pictures

"Check out this photo album!"

Jonathan has shared a link to an album with you. To view the album or to reply to the message, follow this link:
http://www.facebook.com/n/?inbox/readmessage.php&t=129874006425&mid=109047eG2e1f7929G2662673G0

Figure 4-28. An e-mail message announcing your new album

Another way to share your photo album is to select the album and then select, copy, and paste the share link that appears at the bottom of the album (see Figure 4-29). You can paste this into an e-mail or instant message, or whatever.

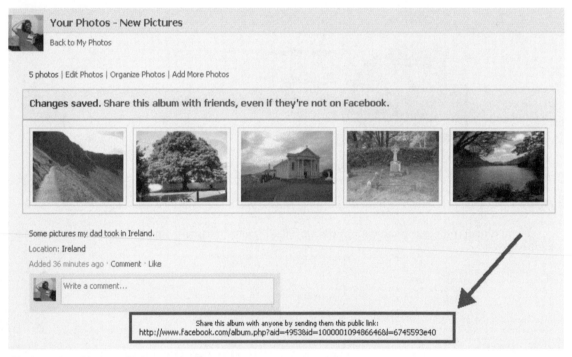

Your Photos - New Pictures
Back to My Photos

5 photos | Edit Photos | Organize Photos | Add More Photos

Changes saved. Share this album with friends, even if they're not on Facebook.

Some pictures my dad took in Ireland.
Location: Ireland
Added 36 minutes ago · Comment · Like

Write a comment...

Share this album with anyone by sending them this public link:
http://www.facebook.com/album.php?aid=4953&id=1000001094866468l=6745593e40

Figure 4-29. Sharing a link to your album

If you send the public link to someone and they aren't on Facebook, they can still see your album; it appears something like what is shown in Figure 4-30 (and this may prompt them to create their own Facebook account).

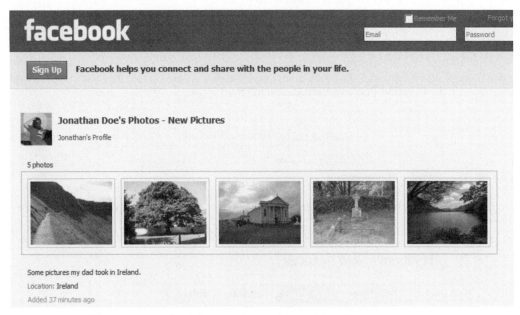

Figure 4-30. Your album appears like this to someone without a Facebook account.

You can also share an individual photo, using the share link, which works like the share link for an album. Or, when you've select a photo in a photo album, a link at the bottom leads just to that photo. See Figure 4-31.

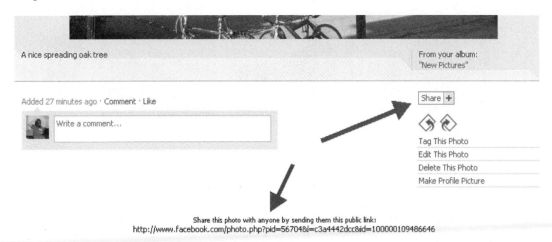

Figure 4-31. Sharing a link to an individual photo

125

■ **Note** If you send someone the public link for an individual photo, it shows that individual picture, but there won't be a next or back link to go through the other photos in the album.

Organizing Photos

After you upload photos, you can rearrange them into whatever order you like. To do so, select the photo album, and click the Organize Photo option, shown in Figure 4-32.

Figure 4-32. The Organize Photos option

To rearrange photos, roll the mouse pointer over the desired photo; an arrow icon appears. See Figure 4-33.

Figure 4-33. Selecting a photo to rearrange

You can click and drag the photo into a different position, as shown in Figure 4-34.

Figure 4-34. Dragging a photo to a new position

When you're satisfied with your arrangement, click Save Changes (see Figure 4-35).

Figure 4-35. Save your changes.

Sharing Photos with a Facebook Group

One of the nice things you can do when you have photos in an album is to share them with the members of a Facebook group that you've chosen to join. (See the previous chapter for info on how to join a group.) Click the Groups icon to access the Groups application. See Figure 4-36.

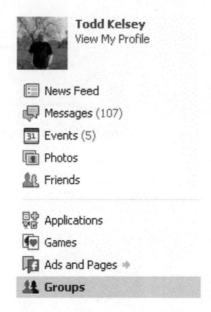

Figure 4-36. The Groups link

Find and select the group with which you'd like to share photos (click the title of the group), as shown in Figure 4-37.

Figure 4-37. Selecting a group

Then, select the Photos tab, and click Add Group Photos (see Figure 4-38).

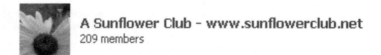

Figure 4-38. Add Group Photos

You're taken to a list of albums that appear beneath the Add from My Photos tab. See Figure 4-39.

Figure 4-39. The Add from My Photos tab

When you're visiting a Facebook group and using the Add From my Photos feature, Facebook brings you back to a list of your photo albums and allows you to select an album from which to select photos. See Figure 4-40.

Figure 4-40. Selecting an album

Click the check boxes on the photos you'd like to add, and then click the Add Selected Photos button (see Figure 4-41).

Figure 4-41. Selecting photos to share with the group

More Ways to Upload

You can visit www.facebook.com/mobile to explore more ways to upload photos. One method is through the Upload Photos via E-mail function. Facebook gives you a custom e-mail address to which you can upload photos; see Figure 4-42.

Upload Photos via Email

Use a personalized upload email to send photos and videos straight to your profile. Your personal upload email is:

folio215gaunt@m.facebook.com

Send my upload email to me now

Find out more

Figure 4-42. Uploading via e-mail

Facebook for Your Phone

Facebook for your phone is a wonderful function for camera phones. You need to have a phone with a camera and an Internet plan. See Figure 4-43.

Facebook for your phone

Download rich, interactive applications built for your phone. Available for:

iPhone	Blackberry
Palm	Windows Mobile
Sony Ericsson	Widsets
INQ	

Figure 4-43. Facebook for your phone

Personally, I think Facebook for your phone is one of the coolest things to come around in a long time. It's similar to the mobile application you can get for Flickr, and they both basically allow you to take pictures on the spot and upload them directly.

Part of the reason I like Facebook Mobile so much is it allows me to be more spontaneous. I think that anything that makes it easier to capture and share aspects of your life is wonderful.

I've been known to take pictures with my traditional digital camera and for them to sit for weeks on the camera because of the effort required to load them onto the computer, upload them, and so on. But I think Facebook Mobile is worth exploring, even if you have to stretch a little in order to get a camera phone or a wireless plan with Internet access—because if you're anything like me, it will result in you being more likely to capture parts of your life online. And I'm convinced that in most if not all cases, you'll be glad you did.

Video

This section explains the process for adding video to Facebook, which is similar to uploading pictures. The first step is to add the Video tab to your Profile, if it isn't already there.

Adding the Video Tab to Your Profile

Adding a Video tab to your Facebook profile gives you an easy way to upload video, as well as an easy way for people who are visiting your profile to look at what you've uploaded. To add a Video tab, click the + tab on your profile. See Figure 4-44.

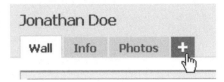

Figure 4-44. The "Add a new tab" button

From the "Add a new tab" menu that appears, select Video, as shown in Figure 4-45.

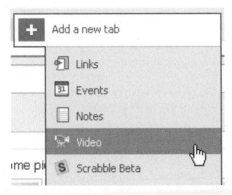

Figure 4-45. Adding a Video tab

131

After you have a Video tab, you can roll over it to get the pencil icon if you ever want to delete it. See Figure 4-46.

Figure 4-46. The pencil icon appears when you scroll over the tab.

When you see the pencil and the accompanying Tab Options, you can choose to delete your Video tab (or any tab). See Figure 4-47.

Figure 4-47. Choosing to delete a tab

Uploading Videos

To upload a video, click the Video tab on your profile after adding it, and click the Upload button, as shown in Figure 4-48.

Figure 4-48. The Upload button

If you'd like a sample video file to work with visit: `http://tinyurl.com/snfiles` or `https://sites.google.com/site/snsamplefiles`. You're welcome to download it to your computer and try uploading it to Facebook.

Facebook supports most popular formats of video. Generally speaking, the smaller the file size, the better; and most modern digital cameras with video capability use formats that have pretty good quality with relatively small file size. (If you don't have a camera but want to try it, check out the FlipVideo on Google.) Specific file formats that Facebook supports are shown here:

- 3g2 (Mobile Video)
- 3gp (Mobile Video)
- 3gpp (Mobile Video)
- asf (Windows Media Video)
- avi (AVI Video)
- dat (MPEG Video)
- flv (Flash Video)
- m4v (MPEG-4 Video)

- mkv (Matroska Format)
- mod (MOD Video)
- mov (QuickTime Movie)
- mp4 (MPEG-4 Video)
- mpe (MPEG Video)
- mpeg (MPEG Video)
- mpeg4 (MPEG-4 Video)
- mpg (MPEG Video)

- nsv (Nullsoft Video)
- ogm (Ogg Media Format)
- ogv (Ogg Video Format)
- qt (QuickTime Movie)
- tod (TOD Video)
- vob (DVD Video)
- wmv (Windows Media Video)

The video upload feature is similar to the photo upload feature. To upload a video, click the Choose File button. See Figure 4-49.

File Upload
Mobile Video
Record Video
Back to My Videos
Select a video file on your computer.
Want a bigger limit? Verify your account.
Choose File
No file chosen
Please upload a file only if:
The video is under 100 MB and under 2 minutes.
The video was made by you or your friends.
You or one of your friends appears in the video.

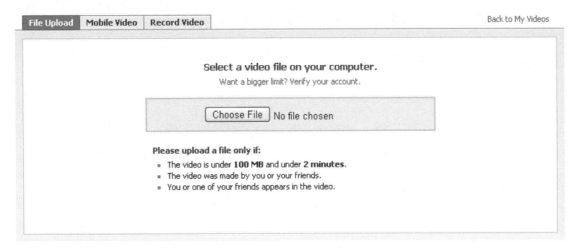

***Figure 4-49.** The Choose File button*

The first time you try to upload, if you haven't verified your Facebook account, the limit on the file size is 100 megabytes and the length is limited to 2 minutes. After verifying, shown in Figure 4-50, you can upload up to a gigabyte (1024 megabytes) and have a longer video, up to 20 minutes.

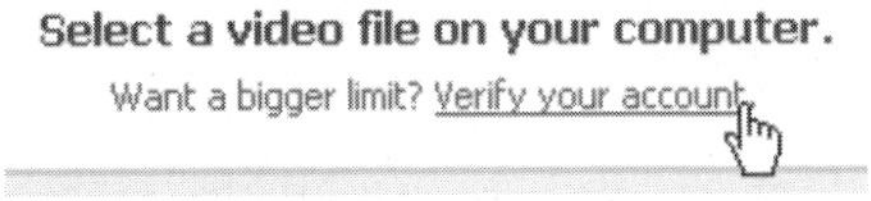

Select a video file on your computer.
Want a bigger limit? Verify your account.

***Figure 4-50.** Verifying your account*

When you verify your account, Facebook may ask you to confirm your phone (see Figure 4-51). You can enter a mobile phone number, and Facebook sends you a text code.

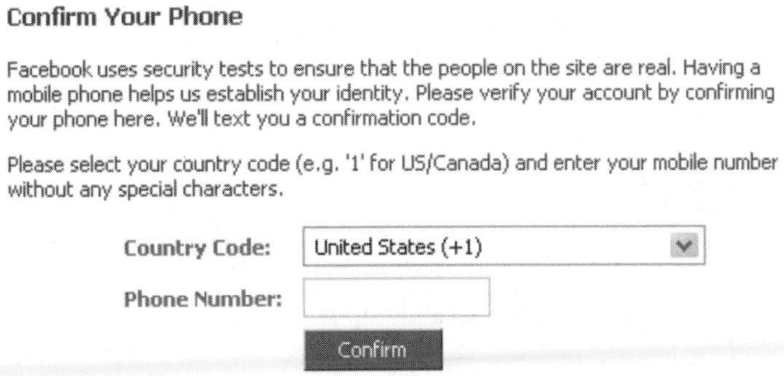

Confirm Your Phone
Facebook uses security tests to ensure that the people on the site are real. Having a mobile phone helps us establish your identity. Please verify your account by confirming your phone here. We'll text you a confirmation code.
Please select your country code (e.g. '1' for US/Canada) and enter your mobile number without any special characters.
Country Code:
United States (+1)
Phone Number:
Confirm

***Figure 4-51.** Verifying your phone*

Then, your uploading begins. While this is happening, Facebook displays a progress indicator, as shown in Figure 4-52. Depending on the speed of your Internet connection and the length of the video, the upload can take seconds or minutes.

Please wait while your video is uploading.

| | Cancel |

1.02 MB of 2.98 MB (148.64 KB/sec) -- 14 seconds remaining

Figure 4-52. Upload status indicator

If all goes well, you get an Upload Successful message. See Figure 4-53.

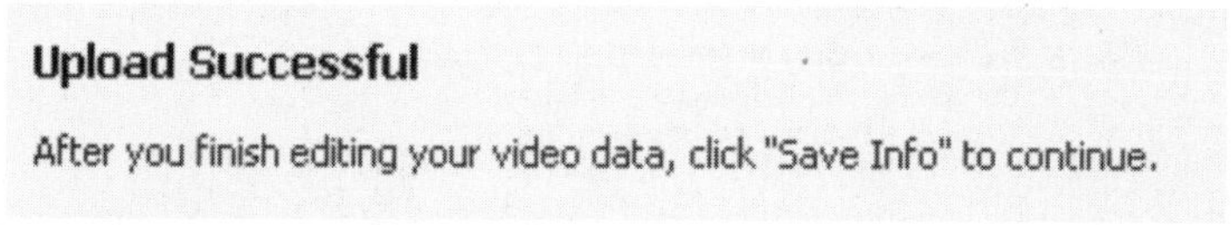

Upload Successful

After you finish editing your video data, click "Save Info" to continue.

Figure 4-53. Upload confirmed!

You can enter the Title and Description and set Privacy while uploading, or you can do after the video has uploaded. When you're finished, click Save Info. See Figure 4-54.

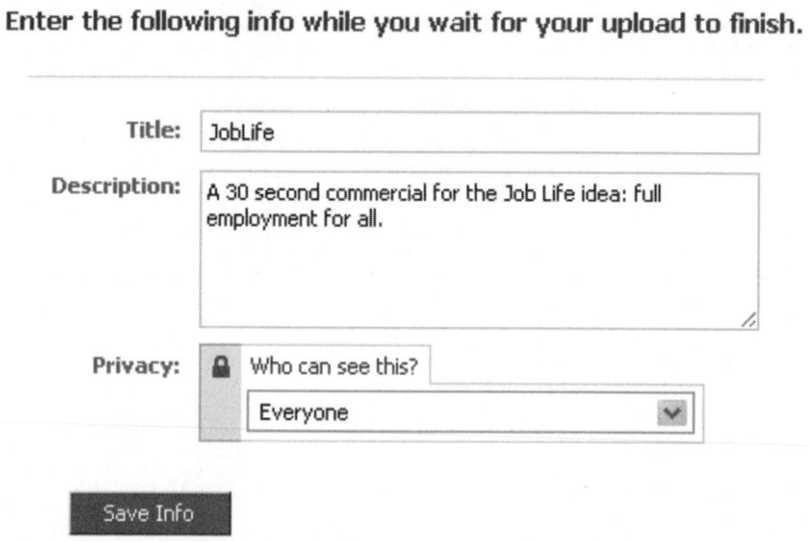

Enter the following info while you wait for your upload to finish.

Title: JobLife

Description: A 30 second commercial for the Job Life idea: full employment for all.

Privacy: 🔒 Who can see this?

Everyone

Save Info

Figure 4-54. Add and save a description.

Next, determine the privacy settings, just as with photos. See Figure 4-55.

134

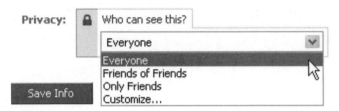

Figure 4-55. Setting privacy preferences

When the video is finished, it appears as a preview. See Figure 4-56.

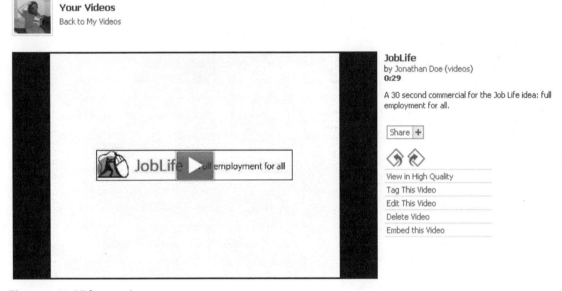

Figure 4-56. Video preview

After it's uploaded, your video appears on your Wall, as shown in Figure 4-57.

Figure 4-57. Your video on your Wall

The video also appears under the Video tab you added to your profile, as shown in Figure 4-58.

Figure 4-58. Your video in the Video tab

■ **Tip** Visit the section on www.snspaces.com that corresponds to this chapter for a tutorial on how to change the thumbnail image that displays for video. You can also ask questions about other things you're trying to figure out. (You may also want to try searching in Facebook Help.)

Sharing Videos

It's easy to share videos. Just go to the Video tab that you added to your profile, select a video, and then click the Share link, shown in Figure 4-59.

Figure 4-59. *The Share link*

Just as with photos, you can select the Post to Profile tab or the Send a Message tab. The Send a Message tab allows you to type the name of a Facebook friend, an e-mail address, or a list in the To field. When you're ready to share, click Send, as shown in Figure 4-60.

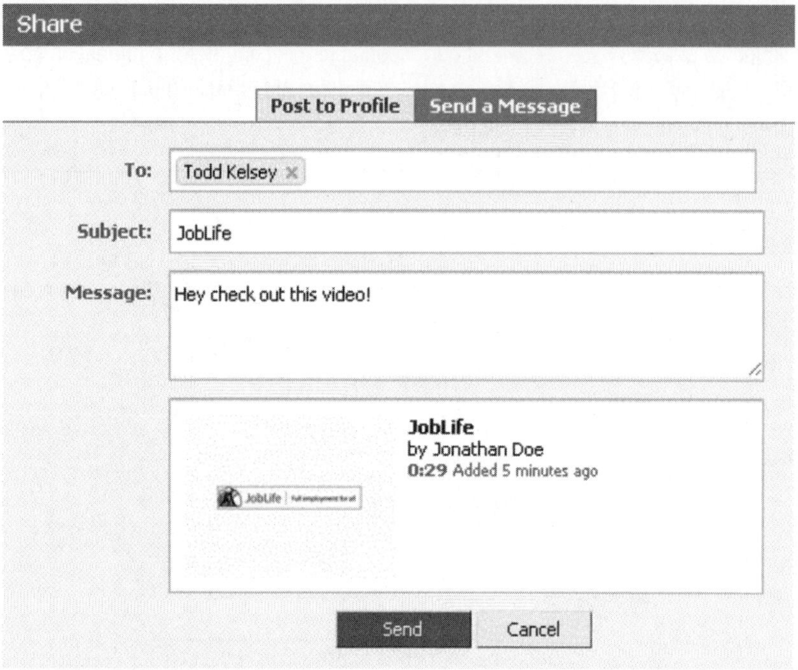

Figure 4-60. Sharing videos

■ **Note** At the time of writing, Facebook doesn't offer a link for videos that can be shared with "anyone." With photos and photo albums, you get a public link that lets you share them with anyone, on or off Facebook. But in order to see a video that you post on Facebook, other people must register with Facebook and sign in.

Notes

Notes are another nice way to share parts of your life in written form; you can also include pictures.

Mostly, when sharing stories on Facebook, I upload pictures and add comments in the captions, which can contain multiple paragraphs. But if I want to write something with more text, more like a blog post, I use a note.

Adding the Notes Tab to Your Profile

The first thing you have to do is add the Notes tab to your profile. To do so, click the + icon on your profile. See Figure 4-61.

Figure 4-61. Select the + icon to add a tab.

Then, select Notes, as shown in Figure 4-62.

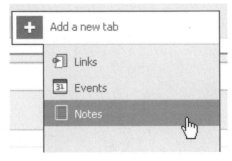

Figure 4-62. Select the Notes option.

Making a Note

Creating a note is as easy as clicking the Notes tab and clicking the Write a New Note button, as shown in Figure 4-63.

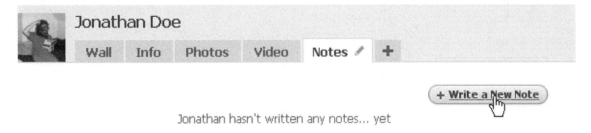

Figure 4-63. The Write a New Note button

Enter a title and add text. If you want to actively invite people in the note, especially if they're mentioned in it, you can use the "Tag people in this note field" to tag Facebook friends. Facebook sends them a message saying they've been tagged. See Figure 4-64.

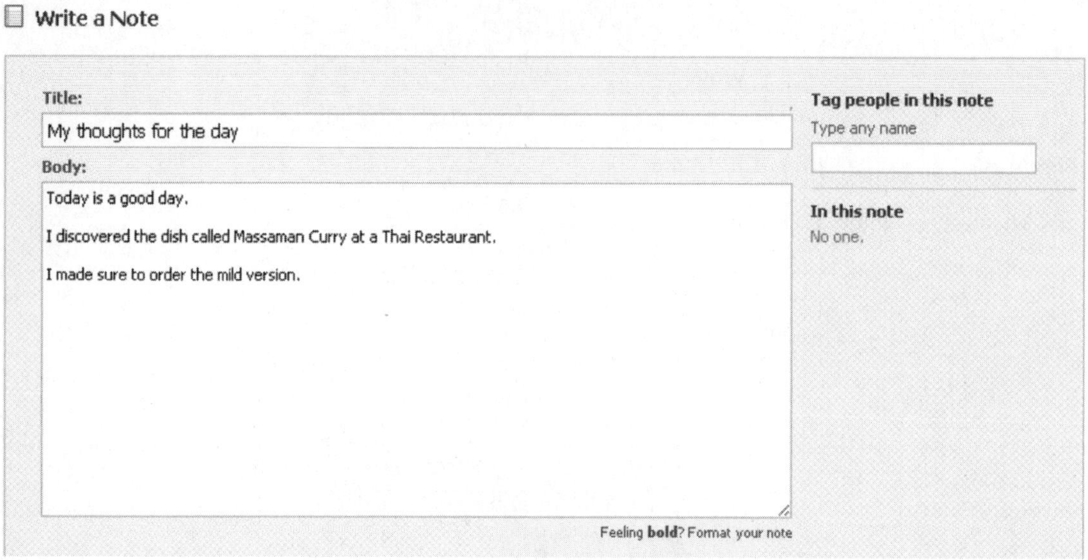

Figure 4-64. Adding a note

The lower section of the note allows you to upload a photo, or to import one from a photo album, and to set privacy. When you're done, click Publish.

A note may be a nice way to experiment with capturing a family recollection or life story, and to practice setting privacy to only your family members and relatives. It may also give you an occasion to invite some family to be your friends (see Figure 4-65).

Figure 4-65. Practice sharing memories with your friends and family.

You might like to try thinking of life events and capturing your thoughts about them. These may include the following:

- High school graduation

- A teacher you remember from school or college

- A trip you went on with friends in school or college

- A family trip you went on

- What is was like when you became a parent

- A music concert

- A time you did something with your grandpa or grandma

- A time you did something with your dad, or mom, or sister, or brother

- A major event that you lived through

- A significant turning point in your life, when you decided to (…)

- Something you really enjoy doing, just for the fun of it

All of these things may lead to notes—and are worth of remembering! You can start with text, and add pictures. Or you may want to start with pictures and see what you can remember about them.

I'd suggest taking a few pictures, like the top three to five pictures from an event, making a photo album on Facebook, and adding thoughts in the captions, based on the memories or stories they inspire. Then, I'd suggest taking the same pictures, adding them to a note, and writing about them there, giving yourself more space. Think of it as though you're sitting at a table at dinner, and a friend or family member asks you to tell them a story about … (see the list, or think of your own).

If you're interested in an example of how to do something I've described here, please feel free to visit www.snspaces.com; if I haven't written a tutorial yet, ask me nicely, and I'm happy to write one.

■ **Tip** Remember that you can *scan* pictures and share them on Facebook, with your family, relatives, or Facebook friends. (If you're not sure how, come and visit www.snspaces.com.)

When you've typed out your thoughts, Facebook asks you if you want to share them. See Figure 4-66.

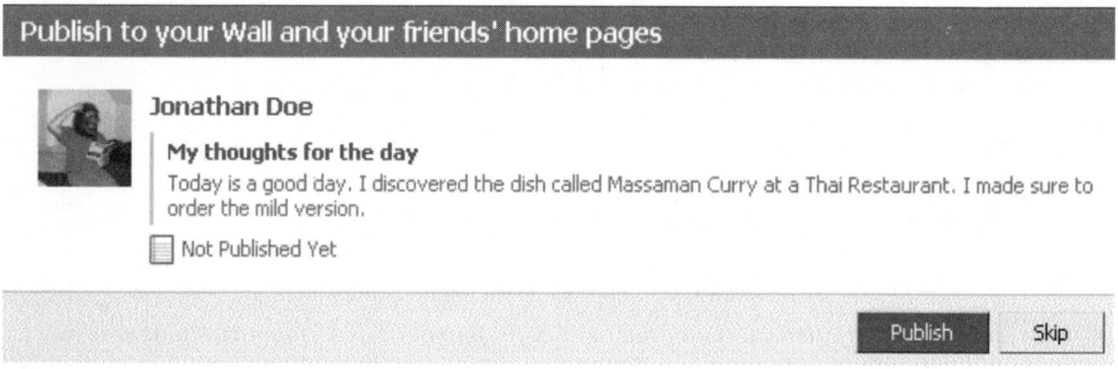

Publish to your Wall and your friends' home pages

Jonathan Doe

My thoughts for the day
Today is a good day. I discovered the dish called Massaman Curry at a Thai Restaurant. I made sure to order the mild version.

▢ Not Published Yet

Publish · Skip

Figure 4-66. Facebook asks if you want to publish.

When you're done, you can always go back to the Notes tab you added, to see your notes. See Figure 4-67.

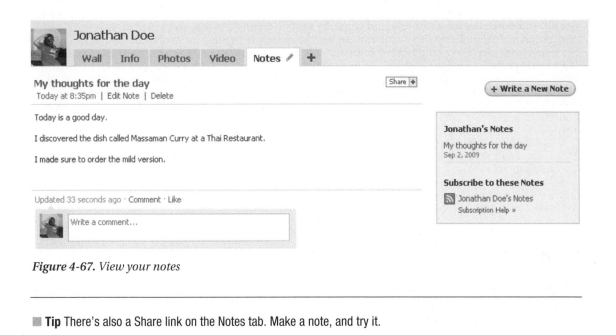

Figure 4-67. *View your notes*

■ **Tip** There's also a Share link on the Notes tab. Make a note, and try it.

Q/A

Q: How do I share a video from YouTube on Facebook?
A: Get the link from YouTube, go to Facebook, and paste the link into the What's On Your Mind? field on your Profile/Wall/Home page.

Q: How do I get into using video on Facebook?
A: I suggest learning about megabytes and gigabytes, and getting in the habit of making videos that are shorter, so that they take less time to upload. I personally recommend the popular a FlipVideo, or an inexpensive digital camera such as a Kodak V1253, which can take pictures but can also shoot good-quality video with audio (and get an extra chip with space). Then, you can always edit the video using a program like Windows Movie Maker (Windows) or iMovie (Mac), or you can upload the clips as-is.

Q: What about longer video?
A: For longer video, you may wish to break it up into segments before uploading into Facebook, depending on the file size. One of the reasons it's nice to work with video from a hand-held digital camera, or something like a FlipVideo (see www.flipvideo.com) is that it *compresses* the video, so you get a longer video with a smaller file size (which makes it easier to upload).

Q: Should I use YouTube or Facebook?
A: Facebook is convenient for posting and sharing video with your Facebook friends, and through a Facebook page if you're promoting something. (See the next chapter for more info about Facebook pages.) YouTube is a good place if you want to try to get as much exposure as possible. If you want to promote or otherwise share video with as many people as possible, do both.

Q: I like this book, but there are only four chapters about Facebook. Where can I read more?
A: If you liked this book and this chapter or section, keep your eyes open for an entire book from CFTW Press on Facebook. If you want to keep posted about the book's progress, go on Facebook and search for (and join) the Social Networking Spaces Group, or search for (and become a fan of) the Social Networking Spaces Facebook page. I'll post messages once in a while to both. Just as with this book, all author proceeds will be donated to CFTW. (See the Introduction to this book.) And don't worry if you don't know how to join a group or become a fan. You can learn by reading the Facebook chapters in this book!

Q: What the heck is JobLife?
A: See `www.JobLife.org`. It's an idea for developing free learning materials to help the 1 in 10 people who are unemployed.

Q: Wait! I have another question! Where can I ask it?
A: On `www.snspaces.com`.

Conclusion

Dear Reader,

In this chapter, you've taken a closer look at Facebook and how to get started sharing your memories and thoughts. I hope it's inspired your somewhat. Don't be afraid to start clicking everything and experimenting with Facebook!

As the book was being written, Facebook made some changes to Facebook itself, as well as to privacy options. The chapter was updated, but things could always change, so one of the things you should probably do is to get comfy with how privacy works.

The easiest way to do this is to visit the Help link at the bottom of the Facebook screen and look for updated information on privacy. The other thing you can do is click Account at the top of the Facebook screen and then click Privacy Settings, and explore privacy there—just wander through it.

As for me, in general I make everything public to just about everyone. But there may come a time when there's a photo album I'd like to make private, for family or friends only, so I think that's worth doing. It's also been helpful for me to realize that, when you comment on someone else's Wall or on their pictures, and so on, Facebook may publish these activities on your News Feed.

Someone could write a whole book on Facebook privacy, but you can learn enough to get up and running by reading through Facebook's help material and also checking `www.snspaces.com`. If you don't find the information you need, ask the question on `www.snspaces.com`, and either I or a kind volunteer will answer.

In general, I'd suggest that you not worry about privacy settings too much, but focus on having fun and exploring. Then, once in awhile, spend some time learning how to adjust privacy settings.

Regards,

–Todd

P.S. If you've read Chapter 1, you may already know the Life Story Suitcase is an experimental tool for backing up your pictures and posts from Facebook, Blogger, Twitter, and so on. The tool helps you to weave the pictures and posts together, to capture and preserve stories from your life. The idea is to share the stories with your family and friends. If you like, when you've had a chance to try Facebook, you're welcome to come by www.lifestorysuitcase.com and tell us what you think of the experiment.

Come and visit the Social Networking Spaces companion web site at www.snspaces.com, where you can find more tips and updates and have an opportunity to share your thoughts or ask questions.

In Living Color: You can visit www.snspaces.com/pics to see full-color versions of all the pictures from this chapter.

■ ■ ■

CHAPTER 5

Branching Out: Facebook Pages and Facebook Advertising

In This Chapter:

- Introduction: Gives some general background on Facebook promotion

- Facebook pages: An introduction to Facebook's pages, including how to create a page and inviting people to become fans

- Facebook advertising: An introduction to Facebook advertising, an easy-to-use paid service that reaches out to specific groups of people on Facebook

snspaces.com

Come and visit the Social Networking Spaces companion web site at www.snspaces.com, where you can find more tips and updates and have an opportunity to share your thoughts or ask questions.

In Living Color: You can visit www.snspaces.com/pics to see full-color versions of all the pictures from this chapter.

Introduction

Facebook can be used to promote any organization such as a band, a cause, a business, or anything else. Facebook provides an ideal platform for spreading the word about anything from a garage sale to an international movie release, because of the social context.

Facebook, like most social networking sites, is always changing, and the options and opportunities are always being improved. This chapter is an introduction to the basics, but I encourage you to click around and explore things that either I don't have space to talk about in this chapter or have been updated or changed by Facebook. Mainly, I'm hoping to help guide you in the following pages in the spirit of exploration, so click anything that looks even remotely interesting or helpful.

In the end, you can never force anyone to like something; but if you have something that you think people may like hearing about, chances are that some of those people would be willing to pass the word on to other people—especially if you ask them to, and especially if they know you. This is the power of social networks: word-of-mouth referral. The idea in Facebook promotion is to put something out there and then use the tools that Facebook provides to tell people about it.

If you're interested in digging deeper, a variety of tools, methods, and approaches for Facebook promotion are available—enough for a book, or several books, which is why a number of books have already been written. You may enjoy looking at Amazon.com and checking out *The Facebook Era: Tapping Online Social Networks to Build Better Products, Reach New Audiences, and Sell More Stuff* by Clara Shih (Prentice Hall, 2009) or *Facebook Marketing: Designing Your Next Marketing Campaign* by Steven Holzer (Que, 2010), which are also listed in the "For Further Reading" section of this chapter. Alternatively, you can type in the phrase "social media marketing" on Amazon and see what happens.

If you'd like to start out simple, there are a couple of things you can try, such as Facebook pages and Facebook ads.

Understanding Facebook Pages

A Facebook page is a page on Facebook that you can create, and it can be about anything you want to promote. It doesn't have to be about a famous person or a band, although it can be. On the page, you publish news; the idea is to make announcements and updates or upload pictures, just like you would with a regular account. However, instead of being friends with people, you can invite people to be *fans* of a page.

■ **Tip** There's a nice overview of Facebook pages at `www.facebook.com/advertising/?pages`.

Figure 5-1 shows the top portion of a Facebook page, which is very similar to a Facebook profile.

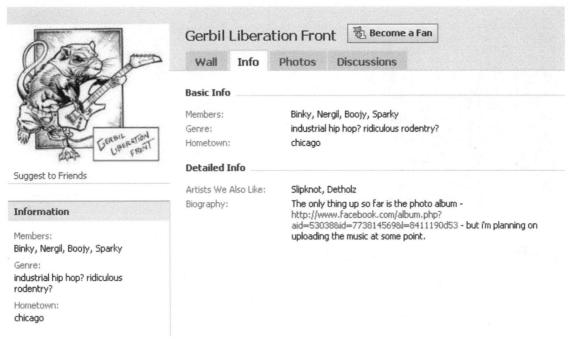

Figure 5-1. Top of a Facebook page

People may search for your page, and there's a function to become a fan right in the search results, as shown in Figure 5-2.

Figure 5-2. When you find a Facebook page you like, you can click Become a Fan without even looking at the page.

When you visit a page, you can click to become a fan, and you can suggest that your friends become fans (see Figure 5-3).

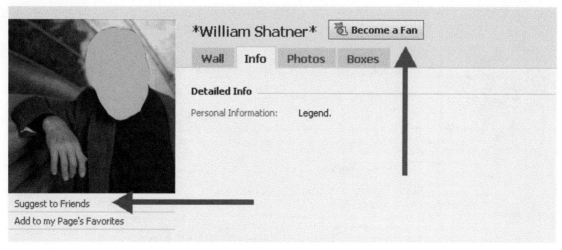

Figure 5-3. Who wouldn't want to become a fan of William Shatner?

This represents the power of word-of-mouth referrals on a social network—from fans of a movie star to fans of a local cake decorating business to a humanitarian cause.

When someone becomes a fan of something, it shows up in their profile, so other people may see the announcement (see Figure 5-4).

Figure 5-4. An announcement shows up whenever you do something on Facebook. People know if you become a fan of something, and they may investigate it, too. Who in the heck is Ardi? Exactly. Curiosity killed the cat. Search for Ardi on Facebook, or friend me and look at my pages.

When you're a fan of a Facebook page, it also shows up in the Pages section of your profile under the Info tab. If someone is exploring your profile, they can see who or what you're a fan of, as shown in Figure 5-5.

Pages _____ See All (9)

         One Laptop Per Child
         Non-Profit

         Ardi
         Other Public Figure

Figure 5-5. There's Ardi. People who visit my profile can see a few of the pages I'm a fan of and click the page titles to explore them. They can click the See All link to see the other pages I'm a fan of as well.

The "Creating Facebook Pages" section later in this chapter provides an introduction to how to create a Facebook page as well as some options for promoting the page.

Understanding Facebook Ads

When you see ads on Facebook, they're usually pretty simple. They most often advertise a product or web site, but they may also advertise a Facebook page or group (see Figure 5-6).

A Sunflower Club

Open club where kids of all ages grow monster sunflowers, share seeds and add to a family tree of sunflowers. No green thumb required.

Figure 5-6. A Facebook ad

Facebook ads are paid ads, and there are two ways to keep track of them:

- You can pay a certain amount per thousand impressions (also known as CPM), which means the number of people who see the ad. Facebook keeps track of how many people click it. You can also pay for each time a person actually clicks an ad. This is known as cost per click (CPC).

- You can keep everything very simple by seeing if you can get some extra traffic, fans, or sales, or you can get sophisticated and carefully monitor the traffic to see if you can calculate your return on investment (ROI). You can spend as little or as much as you want. Generally, the strategy is to try running an ad over a certain period of time such as a week or a month and see how many people view it.

If you're advertising a Facebook page, you can see how many people become fans based on a certain number of dollars spent, if you're selling a product. Ideally, you see how many sales of the product result.

■ **Tip** If you're selling a product, the simplest way to keep track of your ROI is to have the ad lead to a *landing page*: a simple web page that welcomes the person who clicked the ad and offers them some kind of discount coupon code, which they can enter in the shopping cart. This way, you know exactly how many sales are the result of the money you spent on a particular ad. This puts you in the position of knowing how much revenue you generate with the amount spent on ads.

Later in the chapter, in the "Facebook Advertising" section, I introduce you to the process of creating a Facebook ad.

The Facebook advertising platform is easy to use and is also fun. Online advertising professionals will find familiar capabilities, but you don't necessarily need to be a professional to use it. You may enjoy trying it and having some fun, and then discover that you're interested in learning more about online advertising as a career.

Here's an invitation to stay-at-home moms/dads looking for extra income and job seekers: My personal impression is that of all the online advertising going on, the Facebook Ads platform represents the easiest (and most enjoyable) way to get your feet wet, if you're looking for a new career or way to make money on the side. If you have some graphic design skills, great; if not, you can learn the basics or work with freelancers. You may start small by creating a Facebook group, running an ad, and then learning about Facebook pages.

If you find you enjoy it, you can approach local businesses, help them try an ad campaign, and see if you can also help them find a way to track the dollars they spend and how much sales they generate (so that they can confidently spend more). If this seems like an interesting path, then you can always explore more education, or go through the free Google Analytics and/or Google AdWords certification training material. Finally, if you really get into it, look at the `www.snspaces.com` site to see if there are any links or tutorials about this area. If not, feel free to send some in or to bug me (snspaces "at" gmail "dot" com). I'll be happy to post some tutorials and tips.

The best way to start is by having some fun and trying out Facebook pages and Facebook ads throughout the rest of this chapter.

Creating Facebook Pages

To begin the process of creating a Facebook page, visit the following link:
`www.facebook.com/pages/create.php` or `http://tinyurl.com/fbcreate`. You can also visit `www.facebook.com/pages` and click the Create a Page button. At both, you're asked to choose a category for your page. You may wish to make a practice page and invite a few friends to become fans, to see how the process works. You can always delete it later if you like.

To choose a category, click the radio button on the left (such as next to Local, Brand/Product/Organization, or Artist/Band/Public Figure), and choose a drop-down menu option, as shown in Figure 5-7. The Local category has a number of types. Other Business is a generic menu option that covers just about anything.

Figure 5-7. In order to create a page, you have to choose a type. If you're making a page for a business, I recommend reading as much as possible in the Facebook Help section about Facebook pages. Then, through some trial and error, explore what Facebook allows you to do with pages.

I recommend fully exploring every option in the drop-down menu. After you create a Facebook page, at the time of writing, you *can't* change the category (although this could change). Therefore, you should make sure you have your desired category before you put too much work into a page or before you invite too many people, because the category appears in search results. For example, when I created the Facebook page for this book, at the time of writing there isn't a category for "book," so I tried Other Business. Then, I decided this category didn't make a lot of sense, so I'm going to create a new Facebook page in the Education category. You can always delete a Facebook page after you've created it and make another one. I recommend playing around a bit before you get serious and do too much work, including searching for your page, becoming a fan, and so on, to see how things work.

Next, type in the name of your page (for example, the name of your business or band), and click the Create Page button (see Figure 5-8).

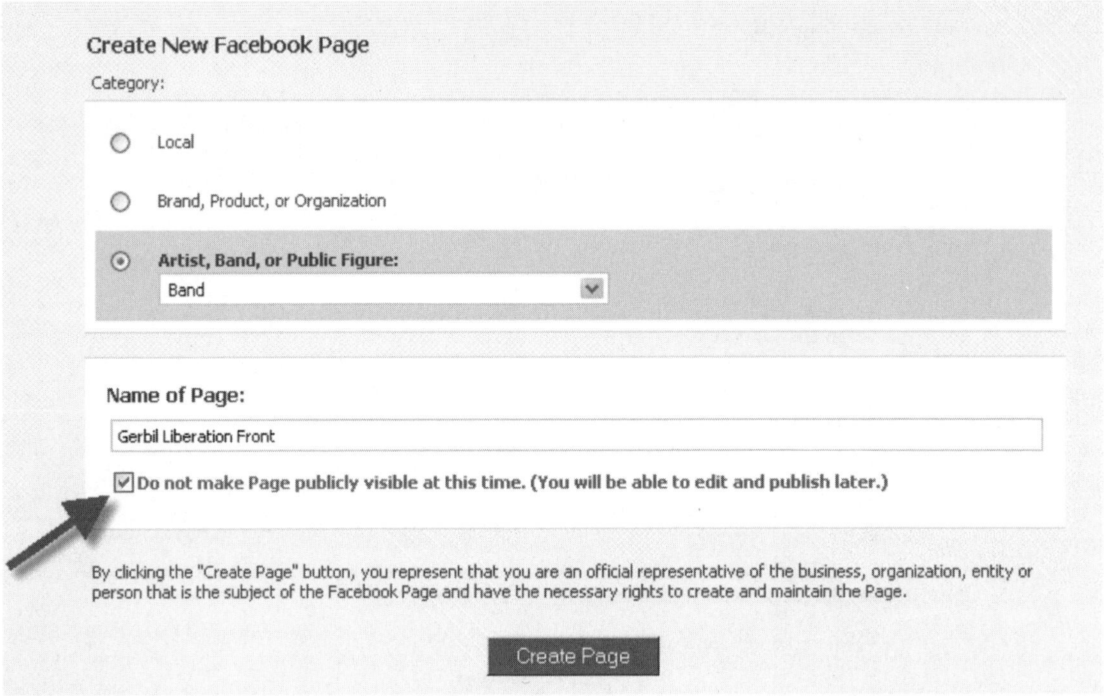

Figure 5-8. The Create New Facebook Page screen

■ **Note** You may also want to click the "Do not make Page publicly visible" option, if you want to work on it before you go live. The examples in this chapter assume that you're working privately at first and will publish the page later. If you don't check the box, the page is automatically published, and you won't see some of the options discussed in the following, such as Publish this Page.

After your page displays, it may have some promotional messages at the top, such as Link Your Page to Your Twitter Account.

At this point, you may wish to bookmark the Facebook page in your browser. Sometimes it's nice to have the direct link to your Facebook page so you can put it in Twitter or send it to someone by e-mail. However, people don't necessarily have to be on Facebook to see the page. The link looks something like the following:

```
http://www.facebook.com/pages/Blahbie-Doobie/206360751414
```

If you see anything at the end beyond the numbers, like ?Create, keep in mind you don't need that information. Later, you'll also see how you can access the page through Facebook.

One of the easiest ways to get the link is to become a fan of a page: go to your Info page (see Figure 5-9), roll your mouse over the link to your page, right-click (Windows) or hold Ctrl down, click (Mac), and copy the link.

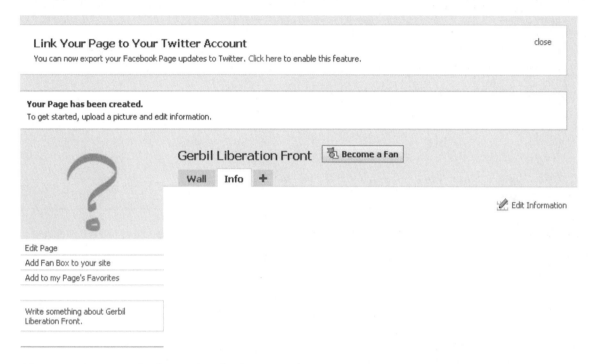

Figure 5-9. *A new Facebook page. Woohoo!*

To add a page profile picture, roll your mouse over the question mark on the Facebook page, and choose the Change Picture link (see Figure 5-10). Exactly like Facebook profiles, you can upload and change the picture as often as desired.

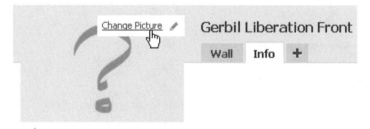

Figure 5-10. *The first thing you may want to do after you create a Facebook page is to change the profile picture.*

The profile picture appears in the News Feed when you post something and shows up in your fans' pages. It also appears in their Pages section when they become a fan (see Figure 5-5 earlier in this chapter).

To add basic information, click the Info tab on the page, and click the Edit Information link (see Figure 5-11).

Figure 5-11. The Edit Information link under the Info tab

■ **Tip** This section is meant as a simple introduction to Facebook pages, but there are a lot of options for adding material. Exactly like a Facebook profile, you can click the + tab to add new sections such as photos and videos.

A Facebook page has a Wall, like a regular Facebook profile. As Figure 5-12 shows, when people visit your page, they can click the Become a Fan button.

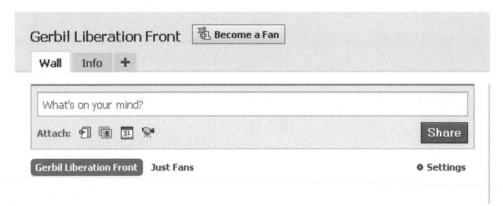

Figure 5-12. The Become a Fan button. May your Facebook page gain many fans!

When you're on the page, one of the ways you can share information with fans is to keep a regular stream of updates, pictures, video, and links going. Update regularly, but not annoyingly so. How much is too much? Ask people.

Publishing the Page

Remember to publish the Facebook page after it's created, when you're ready for it to go live. If all goes well, there is a Publish box at the top of the page, and you can click the red "publish this Page" link (see Figure 5-13).

 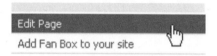
This Page has not been published. To make this Page public, publish this Page.

Figure 5-13. Facebook provides a reminder to publish your page.

You can also publish the Page by clicking the Edit Page link on the side (see Figure 5-14).

Edit Page
Add Fan Box to your site

Figure 5-14. On your Facebook page, there is an Edit page link.

After you click the link, if the page hasn't yet been published, the box shown in Figure 5-15 appears on the right side of the page. You can then click the red "publish this Page" link.

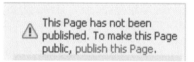
This Page has not been published. To make this Page public, publish this Page.

Figure 5-15. The "publish this Page" link appears in red and is clickable.

■ **Note** You don't have to publish the page every time you add something. It's a one-time thing that you do when you first want to release the page. After you publish the page for the first time, it's automatically updated whenever you add something.

Getting Help!

Facebook has some good tutorials that discuss how to create, edit, and promote your Facebook pages. For example, there's a good overview of creating a Facebook page at the following address: www.facebook.com/help.php?page=904 or http://tinyurl.com/pagesfb. To get to it, go all the way to the lower-right corner of Facebook, and click the Help link (see Figure 5-16).

Figure 5-16. The Help link contains an entire world of useful information.

Then, in the Ads and Business Solutions section, click the Facebook Pages link, as shown in Figure 5-17.

Figure 5-17. There's a variety of helpful info for business types.

■ **Tip** If you're interested in Facebook promotion, you may want to bookmark this section of Facebook Help so you can come back and wander through it later.

The Facebook Pages section of help has several articles (see Figure 5-18).

Figure 5-18. Bingo! Creating, Administering, and Editing your Page.

■ **Note** There's a nice overview of Facebook Pages at www.facebook.com/advertising/?pages.

Additional Fun

As I mentioned, Facebook has a lot of good information to explore. For example, you want like to explore the following:

- *Page badges*: A page badge allows you to advertise your Facebook page on your blog. If you're on Blogger or Wordpress, it will automatically help you to place the badge on the blog. There's also a piece of code you can paste into any web page: www.facebook.com/facebook-widgets/pagebadges.php or http://tinyurl.com/pagebadges. (For more information on blogging, see Chapter 8.)

- *Widgets*: A page badge is one of the many widgets available that you can use to help promote your Facebook page (www.facebook.com/facebook-widgets/ or http://tinyurl.com/widgetsfb).

Linking to Twitter

One nice thing about Facebook and Twitter is that they're always thinking of new ways to connect the two. In the case of Facebook pages, you can consider also making a Twitter account. Just as with Facebook, people are spending increasing amounts of time on Twitter and using it as a platform to communicate with each other. To promote your entity, you can go to www.twitter.com, create an account, and then post tweets. You can also link things so that your Twitter page automatically gets whatever you post on your Facebook page.

■ **Tip** If you're just starting out, you may want to read the chapters on Twitter in Part 3 before trying this section.

To try this, visit www.facebook.com/twitter, and click Link a Page to Twitter, as shown in Figure 5-19.

Figure 5-19. There are a variety of ways to connect Facebook and Twitter. This is one of them.

Figure 5-20 shows the set of graphics that help get the concept across. Basically, you can send everything that happens on the Facebook page to Twitter, or just some of the information.

Share status updates, links, photos, notes, and events with your followers on Twitter, directly from your Facebook Page.

Choose the kinds of things you want to share both on Twitter and Facebook.

Figure 5-20. Thanks, Facebook, for such helpful visuals.

Facebook allows you to choose which pages you're working on that you want to link to your Twitter account (see Figure 5-21).

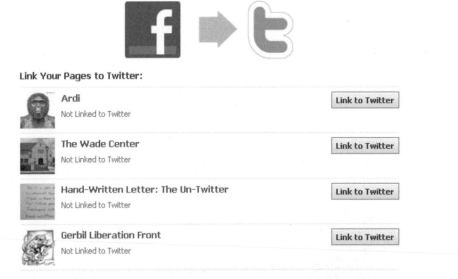

Figure 5-21. Ardi is a hominid, but she likes to keep up with current technology. Maybe she should have her own Twitter account. If she did, you could make it easy for her to log on to Facebook, make a post on the Facebook page, and link accounts so her Facebook posts would appear on Twitter.

If you have more than one Twitter account, and you have your Internet browser set up to remember the password and login information, Twitter can set up the link to the last Twitter account you were logged in to on your computer. As you can see in Figure 5-22, there is a "Sign out" link so you can sign out of one Twitter account and sign in to another account. In this case, Twitter may remember what's going on, or you may need to start the process over again in Facebook after you're signed into the right account in Twitter.

Figure 5-22. Not only do people connect with each other, but social networks also now connect with each other.

Click the Allow button when you're ready. Then, in Facebook, on the www.facebook.com/twitter page, you can always unlink from Twitter or use the check boxes next to a particular page. Finally, click the Save Changes button (see Figure 5-23).

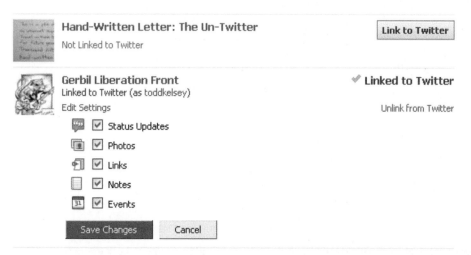

Figure 5-23. Should you send everything from Facebook into Twitter? What happens when you make these various kinds of posts? What will they look like on Twitter? It sure would be interesting to find out. Maybe it would be fun to try…

In Figure 5-24, you see a post on the Facebook page, where I entered something on the Wall and clicked the Share button. When you post only text, like on your regular Facebook profile, it ends up on your Wall and as the status. However, if you post a link or video/photo, it's more than a text message, so it shows up on your Wall but doesn't change the status.

Figure 5-24. A Wall post made on a Facebook page

When I linked the Gerbil Liberation Front page to the www.twitter.com/toddkelsey account, the post automatically appeared on Twitter, as shown in Figure 5-25.

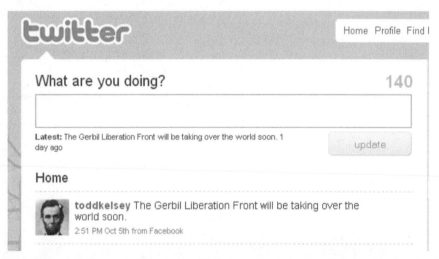

Figure 5-25. Some may say that it would have made better sense to make a Twitter account for the Gerbil Liberation Front. But you can link a Facebook page to whatever you want. Therefore, I thought it would be funny if Abe Lincoln made announcements for the Gerbil Liberation Front (he is my profile icon on Twitter). The possibilities are endless, whether they're serious or silly, or both.

Accessing, Editing, and Expanding Your Facebook Page

After you've created your Facebook page, you can do a lot with it. To access your page, if you ever lose your way, you can always visit www.facebook.com/pages and click the Pages I Admin link.

Facebook automatically adds a new Ads and Pages link on your Home page after you've created a Facebook page. This is the easiest way to access the Facebook page management area, as shown in Figure 5-26.

Figure 5-26. Click the Home link at the top of Facebook, and you see these links on the left side of your Home page. After you've created a Facebook page, the Ads and Pages link appears here.

■ **Note** If you've created only one page, the Ads and Pages link takes you directly to that page.

When you've created more than one page, the Ads and Pages link shows you a list of your pages. You can look and see how many fans each page has. You can click the title of the page to access it directly or use the various links to Edit, Advertise, View Insights, or Delete the page (see Figure 5-27).

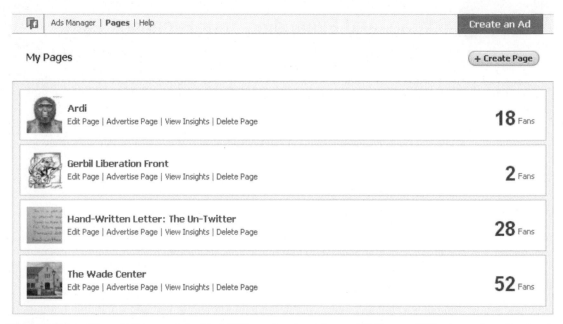

Figure 5-27. Ardi has 18 fans, and the Gerbil Liberation front has only 2! I guess I'd better make a Facebook ad to promote the Gerbil Liberation Front page. Or, maybe I should post things more often on the GLF Facebook page, so the posts show up in fans' News Feeds and the word gets out, and so on.

To access the page so as to view it as the public sees it, use the regular features such as posting something to the wall, but click the title (see Figure 5-28).

Figure 5-28. In Facebook, it's a good idea to click just about anything that looks clickable.

When you're on the page directly, as in Figure 5-29, you can view or add material to the page just as you can on your own personal account (for example, enter an update, and then click the Share button).

Figure 5-29. When you're on the Facebook page, you can make a post.

When people visit your page and click the Become a Fan button, not only do your posts appear on your Facebook page, but the posts also appear on your fans' Facebook Home pages, courtesy of the News Feed.

Think of your Facebook page like a newspaper. When people become fans, they're subscribing to your Facebook page.

In Figure 5-30, you see this in action. You're looking at my News Feed. I visited the Gerbil Liberation Front Facebook page and became a fan. So, I received the update that was posted to that Facebook page (which was done in Figure 5-29).

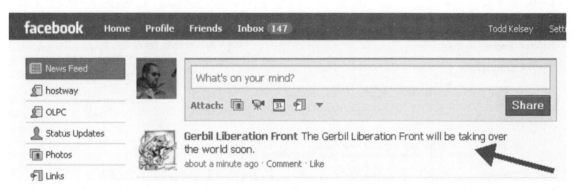

Figure 5-30. The post that was entered on the GLF Facebook page appears in the News Feeds of fans.

Editing a Page

To edit a page, choose the Edit Page link from the list of pages, as shown in Figure 5-31.

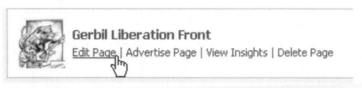

Figure 5-31. Edit Page link

Editing the page is the headquarters of working on a Facebook page. I highly recommend exploring all the areas on the page, however. To adjust settings, Wall settings, or explore Facebook Mobile, click the pencil icons in the upper-right corner of those rectangular areas. Otherwise, click around on the other links to explore. For example, in the Applications area, you can find a number of applications that are designed to help you put up content, as shown in Figure 5-32. (Note: The types of applications that appear on the Edit page are determined by what type of page you have.)

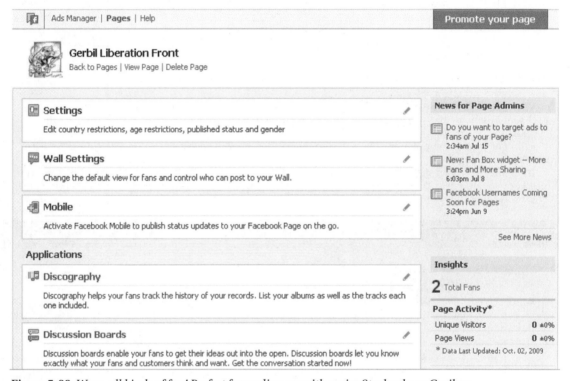

Figure 5-32. *Wow, all kinds of fun! Perfect for curling up with a nice Starbucks or Caribou.*

■ **Note** As an alternative to twittering into Facebook, you can use the Facebook Mobile application to update your status and do other wonderful things like uploading pictures directly from your mobile device into Facebook. See www.facebook.com/mobile/.

It's not clear whether Facebook Mobile allows you to differentiate between sending a status update to your personal profile or a specific Facebook page. It may go to both, or you may have to choose one or the other.

Facebook Page Promotion

There's a nice overview of Facebook pages, including information about promotion, at `http://tinyurl.com/fbadpages` or `www.facebook.com/advertising/?pages`. Don't forget the ? in the web address, because you need to type it in.

You can also go to the Help section as described in the "Getting Help!" section earlier in this chapter. In the lower-right corner of Facebook, choose the Help link ➤ Facebook Ads and Pages section ➤ Facebook Pages; but this time, you can explore "Promoting your Page and Page Insights," as you can see in Figure 5-33.

Figure 5-33. Explore!

Remember, the best thing to do in general is to get in the habit of exploring, whether it's exploring the features when editing your page or exploring an article in the Help section, as shown in Figure 5-34.

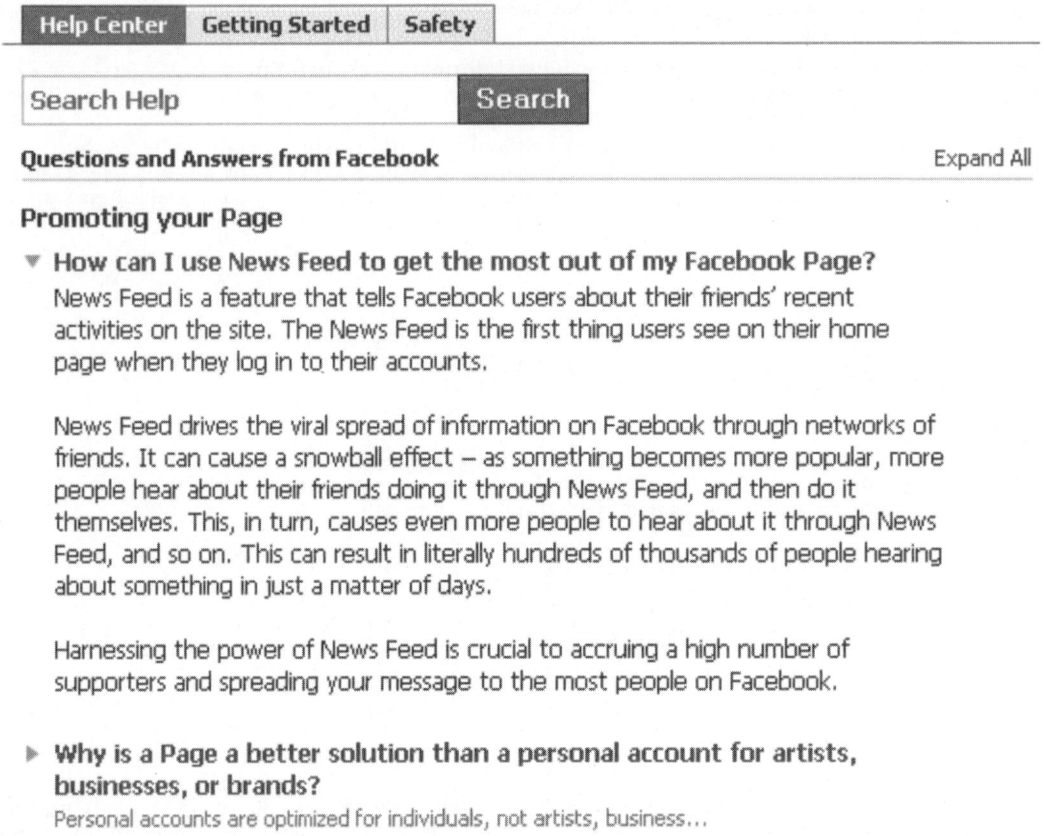

Figure 5-34. *You may actually wish to read the entire text contained in this image. Then, maybe find the* "Why is a Page…" *article. News Feed + Facebook page = getting the word out. Just remember: 400,000,000 people and counting.*

Facebook Advertising

This is a little high-level tour of Facebook advertising. No frills, no chills, and no spills. For specific information, visit and explore www.facebook.com/advertising. For general information about promotion and marketing on Facebook, visit Amazon.com and see the book *Facebook Marketing: Leverage Social Media to Grow Your Business* by Steve Holzner (Que, 2010); or, to get serious in a business way, see *The Facebook Era: Tapping Online Social Networks to Build Better Products, Reach New Audiences, and Sell More Stuff* by Clara Shih (Prentice Hall, 2010). You can also view a free tutorial about Facebook advertising at www.snspaces.com.

Let's do a bit of exploring based on a sample ad, so you can get your feet wet. My first time, I was a little intimidated at the prospect, but I was very impressed with the ease of use of the platform. If you want to jump right in, go to www.facebook.com/advertising and click the Create an Ad button.

There are also other ways to get to the Ad platform. Links are scattered throughout Facebook, such as "Advertise your group" when you've created a group, Promote your Page, or Advertise your Page, because the folks at Facebook would be happy for you to spend a few dollars (or many dollars) on ads.

The Ad

The purpose of the ad in Figure 5-35 was to invite people to join the Sunflower Club. As you can see, I geared the language to invite anyone who might be interested.

A Sunflower Club

Open club where kids of all ages grow monster sunflowers, share seeds and add to a family tree of sunflowers. No green thumb required.

Figure 5-35. It was a great deal of fun to make this ad. Even if you're slightly frightened by the idea of making an ad, I recommend trying it. You may be surprised; it can be empowering.

Ad Design

The user experience for ad creation is simple, straightforward, and friendly. If you've always wanted to try making an online advertisement, here's your chance!

Scenario: Advertising a Facebook Group

When creating an ad, you enter a title and some body text for the ad, and then you can upload an image. In this case, I clicked the "Advertise your group on Facebook" link within the Sunflower Club Facebook group. As you can see in Figure 5-36, in the Facebook Content section, the drop-down menu was set automatically.

Figure 5-36. The Design screen gives a nice preview of your ad, and it updates as you make changes.

■ **Tip** I accessed the ad-creation function by visiting the Facebook group I'd created and choosing the "Advertise your group" function. When you choose this link, the Ad Manager automatically links to your Facebook group or page.

Scenario: Advertising an External Site

If you want to advertise an external web site on Facebook, you can go directly to
www.facebook.com/advertising. When you create an advertisement, the box shown in Figure 5-35 looks a little different.

Next, you're given the opportunity to enter in a link to your web site that you wish to promote (see Figure 5-37).

Figure 5-37. The Destination URL area. Don't use https:// unless you know you need a secure connection. Generally speaking, use http://.

Advertising a Facebook Page

After you've created a Facebook page to represent your idea, project, company, or organization, a Facebook ad is a good way to bring some attention to it.

When looking at a Facebook page you've created, you can click the Advertise Page link, as shown in Figure 5-38. (For more information on pages, see the "Facebook Pages" section in this chapter.)

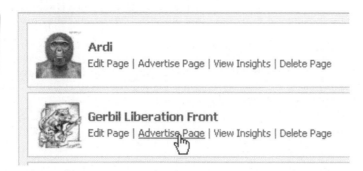

Figure 5-38. *Advertise Page link*

The system then automatically connects your ad to the Facebook page in the Facebook Content drop-down menu. In this case, Facebook may put in sample body text that it grabs from your Facebook page, but you can replace it with anything you like (see Figure 5-39).

Figure 5-39. *The Design Your Ad screen is based on advertising a Facebook page.*

■ **Tip** Facebook has the "I want to advertise a web page" link right beneath the Facebook Content drop-down menu. Basically, Facebook is trying to make it easy for you to advertise Facebook pages and groups, and it makes the ones you manage available in the drop-down menu. However, if you have a link to an external web site, you can use that too.

In the Body Text area, you don't need to put a link. Generally, the idea is simply to put some text that will result in people clicking the ad. Try to think of a title, picture, and body text that might cause you to click.

Remember, if you aren't choosing the Advertising Manager from within a Facebook group or Facebook page, but are accessing it directly via `www.facebook.com/advertising`, Facebook expects that you want to put an ad on Facebook leading to an external web site. Notice in Figure 5-40 that there is a link called "I want to advertise something I have on Facebook," which you can use to indicate a Facebook page or group that you manage.

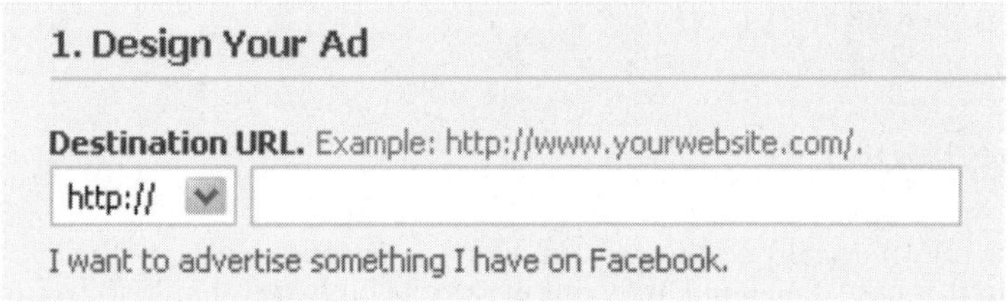

Figure 5-40. Pointing an ad to a web address

In short, there's always a way to point your ad in the right direction—whether the ad will lead to a Facebook group, a Facebook page, or an external web site. The destination will be wherever you want people to land when they click your ad.

Targeting Choices

In the Facebook ad-creation process, after you fill in the basic information and click the Continue button, the targeting choices are added at the bottom of the Design section. This can be a fun process.

The idea is to choose a location, age range, keywords (for example, *sunflowers*), and other options, as shown in Figure 5-41. For example, a person may have certain words/interests listed in their profile.

2. Targeting

Location:
United States ✕

- ⦿ Everywhere
- ○ By State/Province
- ○ By City

Age: 18 ▾ - Any ▾

Birthday: ☐ Target people on their birthdays

Sex: ☐ Male ☐ Female

Keywords: Sunflowers ✕

Education:
- ⦿ All
- ○ College Grad
- ○ In College
- ○ In High School

Workplaces: Enter a company, organization or other workplace

Relationship: ☐ Single ☐ In a Relationship ☐ Engaged ☐ Married

Interested In: ☐ Men ☐ Women

Languages: Enter language

Connections: Target users who are connected to:
Enter your Page, Event, Group or Application

Target users who are not already connected to:
A Sunflower Club - www.sunflowerclub.net ✕

Estimate: **13,780** people
- who live in the **United States**
- over the age of **18**
- who like **sunflowers**
- who are not already connected to **A Sunflower Club - www.sunflowerclub.net**

Targeting
By default, Facebook targets all users 18 and older in the default location. You can change any targeting specifications you wish.

Location
Facebook Ads uses IP address and a user's profile information to determine a user's location.

Keywords
Keywords are based on information users list in their Facebook profiles, such as Activities, Favorite Books, TV Shows, Movies, etc.

Connections
Connections are users who have become a fan of your Facebook Page, a member of your Group, RSVP'd to your Event or authorized your Application.

More Help
Ad Targeting FAQ

Continue

Figure 5-41. Enter your ad criteria. When you're ready to move on, you can click Continue.

Facebook keeps a running count that estimates how many people the ad can be displayed to, based on what choices you make. This is a good screen to play around on. (Plus it's a lot of fun!) When a campaign is running, using the Ad Manager, you can always go back and adjust criteria and create and test a new campaign. When you're ready to move on, you can click Continue.

■ **Tip** Teachers, professors, and others may wish to use the ad-creation process and the targeting feature specifically as a class exercise. It can be an interesting tool to identify various demographic segments, like how many people on Facebook in a certain area fit a certain profile. For a class or an individual exercise, the students can make an ad and then run it. If you really want to have fun, have the students make a survey using a tool like Limesurvey or Surveymonkey, and try to collect responses from the people who respond to the ad.

Campaigns, Pricing, and Bidding

In this section, you can choose a currency for payment, make a name for the ad campaign, and set a daily budget. I suggest starting with a low budget to experiment, and work on a strategy of identifying what a return on investment would be, such as a certain number of visitors, new fans, group members, or sales on your site. If you're selling anything, you may wish to explore learning about online advertising techniques and experimenting with creating a landing page that you can direct people to. For example, perhaps you can advertise with a coupon code that people can use to enter into a shopping cart to receive a discount. Then, you can exactly track how many purchases result from your ad campaign (see Figure 5-42).

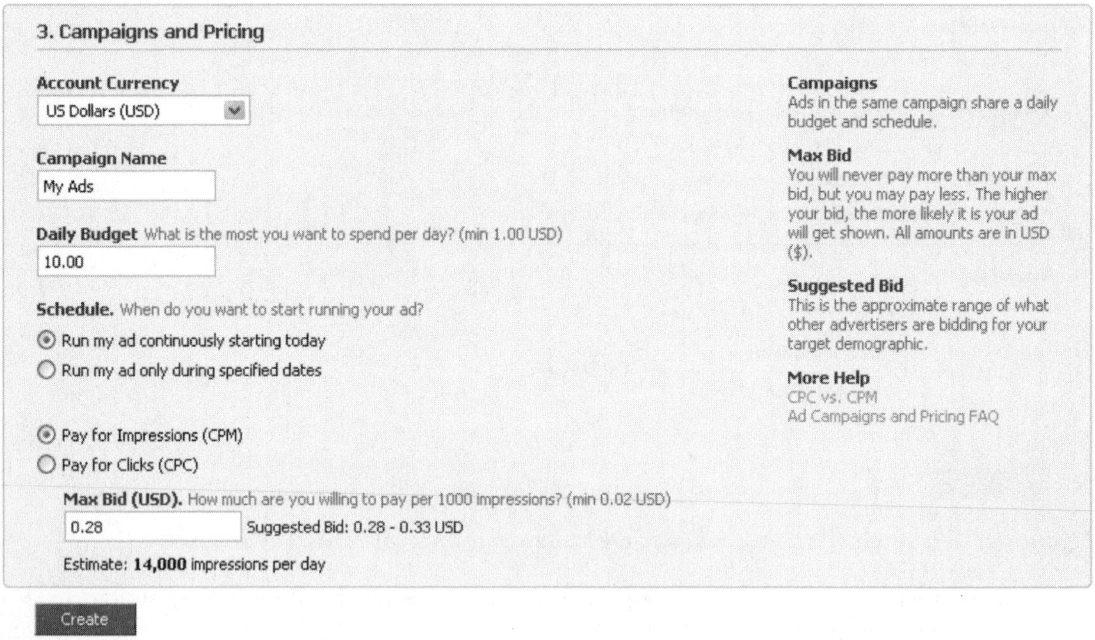

Figure 5-42. A sort of distant cousin to eBay. Click the Create button to start the campaign.

At the bottom, you can choose CPM or CPC. I'd suggest starting out with CPM and looking at the More Help section on the right, like CPC vs. CPM and Ad Campaigns and Pricing FAQ. You can also search on Google and Wikipedia for things like "CPM advertising" or "CPM advertising tutorial." Finally, click the Create button to start the campaign.

Review and Payment

As you can see in Figure 5-43, you're given an opportunity to review everything and to go back and change things as needed or desired.

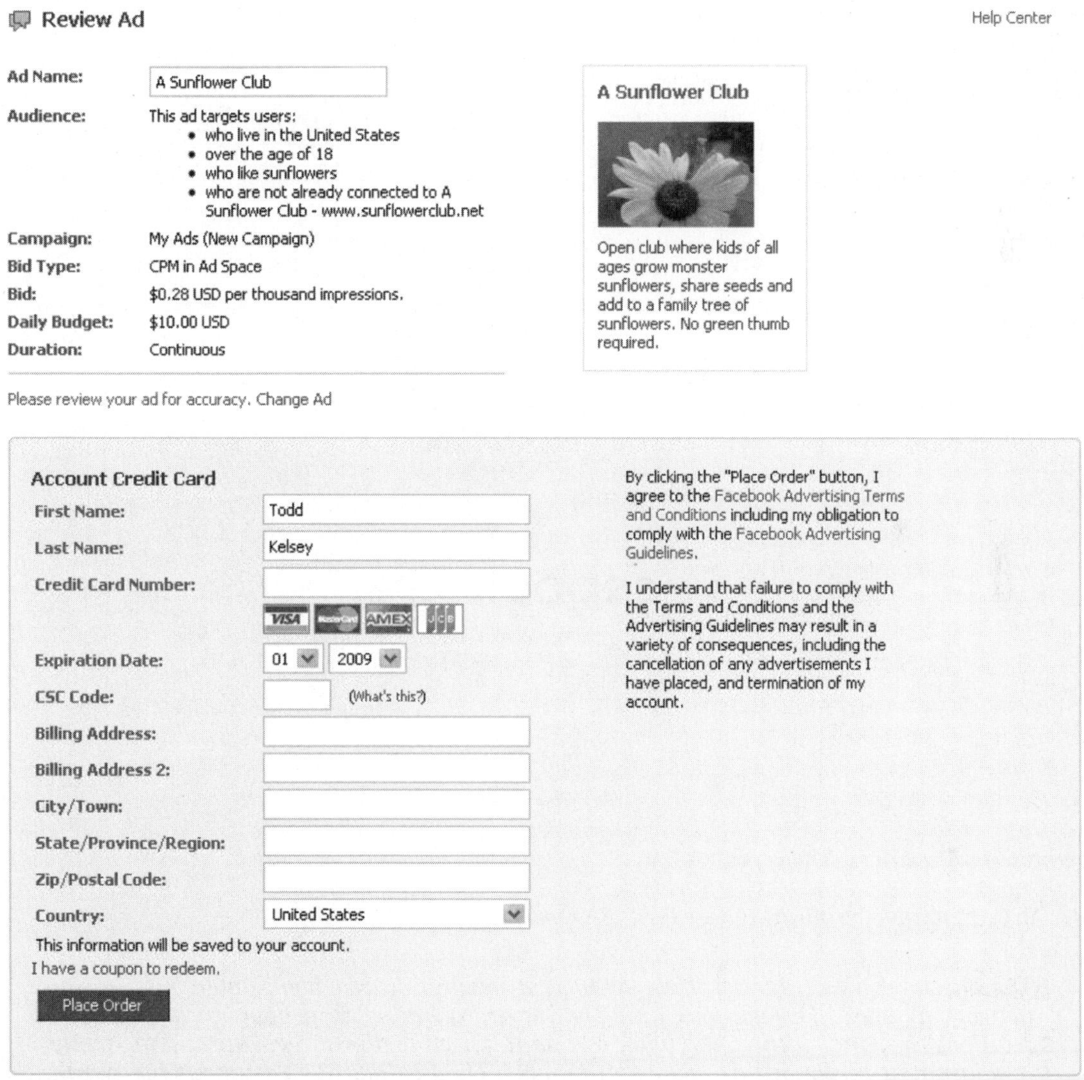

Figure 5-43. *Review, enter your credit card information, and click Place Order.*

Finally, enter your credit card information, and click Place Order.

Ad Launch

After you create the ad, it shows up in the Ad Manager (www.facebook.com/ads/manage). Initially, it says Pending Review. You can come back to the Ad Manager and monitor the performance of your ad, such as viewing how many people have clicked it.

For Further Reading

If you're interested in the emerging world of using Facebook as a tool for marketing and advertising, you may be interested to read *The Facebook Era: Tapping Online Social Networks to Build Better Products, Reach New Audiences, and Sell More Stuff*, by Clara Shih (Prentice Hall, 2009), shown in Figure 5-44, or *Facebook Marketing: Designing Your Next Marketing Campaign*, by Steven Holzer (Que, 2010).

Figure 5-44. The cover of The Facebook Era

An excerpt from the official release for *The Facebook Era* follows:

The Facebook Era (Prentice Hall 2009) is a newly released book about how social networking sites like Facebook and Twitter are ushering in a new era of business, relationships, and culture, and what companies need to do strategically and tactically to adapt and thrive in this new environment. The last decade was about the World Wide Web of information and the power of linking content pages. Today, it's about the World Wide Web of people and the power of the social graph. You're undergoing a radical transformation as traditional one-sided CRM gives way to bidirectional visibility and access, and an unprecedented degree of trusted online identity and access to people are forever changing human relationships and business transactions. Facebook, Twitter, and LinkedIn are changing everything you thought you knew about sales, marketing, and product development—and empowering companies with new tools, insights, and ability to transform customers into true partners and your most effective sales force.

Q/A

Q: I've heard of Google Adwords. Should I use Facebook ads instead of Google advertising?

A: It depends. Google Adwords reaches people that Facebook doesn't and vice versa. The very interesting thing about Facebook ads is the social context; Facebook's tools aren't as sophisticated as Google's (yet), and there are differences, but they're both worth exploring. Ultimately, the best thing to do is to explore something like Google Analytics (try searching for it on Google) and use it as a tool to see where your visitors are coming from. When you set it up right, you can see how effective your Google Adwords campaign and Facebook advertising campaign are. If you haven't heard of Google AdWords, try searching for it on Google or Wikipedia.

Q: I have a nonprofit organization that is a 501(c)3 registered charity. Our resources are limited, but I want to explore online advertising. What do we do?

A: You can apply for a Google Grant, which is a great program that in some cases can result in free advertising on Google. If you need free help applying for a grant, e-mail me at tekelsey@gmail.com. If you feel like it, let's get together and make a petition for Facebook to start a similar program.

Q: For promoting my web site, if I had to decide between a Facebook group and a Facebook page, which should I use? There are so many options out there. I don't know where to start. Do I use Twitter? I feel overwhelmed.

A: Never fear. Try starting simple, experimenting with a Facebook page. Once in a while, post something about what you're doing. Tell your organization or company's story. Think of it as a little press release. Then, branch out and try posting pictures of people, or events, or products. These will all end up on your fans' News Feeds. Then, get your feet wet with video. Try buying a FlipVideo and making some videos. Post them on your Facebook page. At some point, explore Twitter. When you're comfortable with posting to Facebook, you'll be more comfortable posting to Twitter. Telling the story of your company or organization will go a long way.

Q: I'd like to make an image for a Facebook ad, but I don't have graphic skills. What do I do?

A: One possibility is to check with your local high school, community college, or university to see if any budding graphic designers can help you. There may be ad agencies in town, and you're also welcome to drop me a line. Alexandra Constantin (who made the 3D images of some of the animals that appear at the beginning and end of chapters) is looking for freelance work. Visit www.cgadvertising.com/, and tell Alexandra I sent you.

Q: I need to run online ads, but I'm intimidated by all the information on the Facebook ad page, and I'm scared of Google AdWords. What do I do?

A: Come on www.snspaces.com and see if any ad agencies that have posted and can help you out. A couple of editor/writers have reviewed this book, and they can help with copywriting the text of your ad, Facebook page, and so on. There's bound to be someone, possibly even myself, who can help you. (And if you have some kind of service to offer, feel free to post your offer on www.snspaces.com.) There's also a book I've been reading that I've found to be helpful in online advertising, which you may want to check out: *Winning Results with Google Adwords*, by Andrew Goodman. It provides some good perspectives on online advertising in general. Check out that book, and maybe *Facebook Marketing*, and then bug me; I'll either put up some tutorials (or maybe someone else will) at `www.snspaces.com` or perhaps, if there's enough interest, write a whole book on Facebook advertising.

Q: Wait, don't go, I have more questions!

A: If you're interested in leveraging social media for promotion, you may wish to search for a LinkedIn group (see Part 6 of this book, on LinkedIn). You'll wind up with a community of people who share your interests. There may also be a good Facebook group you can find. Try searching on Facebook's help pages. And by all means, feel free to come on `www.snspaces.com`, see if someone has already asked or answered your question; if not, ask me directly, and I'll post an answer. I hope a few folks will join me on `www.snspaces.com` in answering questions or posting links, so that I can get enough sleep!

Q: I like this book, but there are only four chapters on Facebook. Where can I read more?

A: One of the challenges in writing this book was that it felt like each chapter could become an entire book. Still, I had the desire to give an overview of a number of different social networks in a single book. If you liked this book and this chapter or section, keep your eyes open for an entire book from CFTW Press on Facebook or Facebook advertising. If you want to keep posted about the book's progress, go on Facebook and search for (and join) the Social Networking Spaces Group, or search for (and become a fan of) the Social Networking Spaces Facebook page. I'll post messages once in a while to both. Just as with this book, all author proceeds will be donated to CFTW (see the Introduction to this book). Don't worry if you don't know how to join a group or become a fan. You can learn by reading the Facebook chapters in this book!

Q: Who the heck is Ardi?

A: Well, go on Wikipedia.org and find out. Or, search for "Ardi" on Facebook, and look for the Facebook page. Finally, you can add me as a friend and find her on my list of pages on my profile (if she's not there, you may need to click the See All link to see all the pages I'm a fan of). Basically, Ardi is a four-million-year-old woman, and I'm a fan of hers. I figure if she can wind up on Facebook millions of years later, I have a chance to live to be at least 100 and that there will be a Facebook page about me. Part of the point is, there's a page on Facebook for just about anything, and it can be fun (and easy) to make a Facebook page.

Conclusion

Dear Reader,

This chapter provided an introduction to the possibilities of using Facebook pages and the Facebook Advertising platform in order to promote something on Facebook or an external web site. The possibilities are endless, and the best thing to do is to explore.

Regards,

–Todd

P.S. If you've read Chapter 1, you may already know the Life Story Suitcase is an experimental tool for backing up your pictures and posts from Facebook, Blogger, Twitter, and so on. The tool helps you to weave the pictures and posts together, to capture and preserve stories from your life. The idea is to share the stories with your family and friends. If you like, when you've had a chance to try Facebook, you're welcome to come by `www.lifestorysuitcase.com` and tell us what you think of the experiment.

snspaces.com

Come and visit the Social Networking Spaces companion web site at www.snspaces.com, where you can find more tips and updates and have an opportunity to share your thoughts or ask questions.

In Living Color: You can visit www.snspaces.com/pics to see full-color versions of all the pictures from this chapter.

CHAPTER 6

■ ■ ■

What the Heck Is Twitter?

In This Chapter:

- Introduction: some general background about what Twitter is and a few things it does

- Signing up and getting started: step-by-step instructions for signing up for Twitter and adding a profile icon

- Making your first tweet, "following" someone, and seeing who your followers are

---

snspaces.com

Come and visit the Social Networking Spaces companion web site at `www.snspaces.com`, where you can find more tips and updates and have an opportunity to share your thoughts or ask questions.

In Living Color: You can visit `www.snspaces.com/pics` to see full-color versions of all the pictures from this chapter.

Twitter Users: To follow Social Networking Spaces on Twitter, visit `www.twitter.com/snspaces`, and click Follow.

Introduction

You've probably heard about Twitter by now. You may be wondering, what the heck is a *tweet*? And when a company says on television, "Follow us on Twitter," or you come across that phrase on a web site, what does it mean?

Twitter is basically a microblogging web site. A "micro" blog is a blog with really short entries—and blogs are like online journals or diaries (see Chapter 8).

According to Wikipedia, "Twitter is a free social networking and micro-blogging service that enables its users to send and read messages known as tweets. Tweets are text-based posts of up to 140 characters displayed on the author's profile page and delivered to the author's subscribers who are known as followers" (see `http://en.wikipedia.org/wiki/Twitter`).

The heart of Twitter, like Facebook, is a *stream*—but in this case, it's entirely made up of 140-character messages, which are the *tweets*. If you like, you can use Twitter to read other peoples' posts, or tweets, and you never have to make a tweet of your own—but it might be fun to try.

Figure 6-1 shows a very simple collection of three tweets that I saw just now when I logged onto Twitter for the Social Net Spaces account.

snspaces I am writing the book Social Networking Spaces From Facebook to Twitter and Everything in Between.
21 minutes ago from web

WilliamShatner RT @SOCMusicWe are very excited to have a Christmas song from @WilliamShatner on one of our label's first releases!--> http://bit.ly/3fAHuf
about 4 hours ago from web

toddkelsey 15 min. on elliptical.
11:02 AM Aug 4th from txt

Figure 6-1. *The Social Networking Spaces Twitter account, showing the latest tweets from three different sources: snspaces, William Shatner, and Todd Kelsey.*

The snspaces account *follows* Todd Kelsey and William Shatner, so any tweets show up on this account. Generally people on Twitter log on, look at the tweets of people they're following, and make tweets of their own.

You can also tweet directly from your mobile device, as shown in Figure 6-2. When you set up your Twitter account to speak with your mobile device, you're given a *short code* to send your messages to. It only works after you set up the phone by logging on to Twitter and adjusting your settings. Then, you use the standard text-messaging feature on your phone to send the message, and it appears on the Twitter site (and is sent to anyone who is following your Twitter account).

Figure 6-2. *With Twitter, you can use your mobile phone to send a message that will appear on your Twitter home page, and the pages of anyone who is following you. Just like if you were a news correspondent and sending everyone the latest news instantly, from wherever you are.*

Some Twitter users rarely visit the web site. If you like, you can have messages from anyone you're following sent directly to your phone as text messages. (I don't particularly recommend this unless you're *sure* you want to do it—the more people you follow, the more you'll get interrupted all the time by your mobile phone.)

Decoding a Tweet

Let's take a closer look at William Shatner's tweet, shown in Figure 6-3. What the heck is all that stuff he's babbling about?

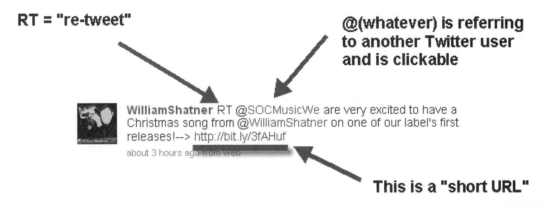

Figure 6-3. *Decoding a tweet*

Over time, an entire vocabulary of code words and techniques has evolved because of the 140-character limit of Twitter messages. William Shatner's tweet uses the following:

- *RT (re-tweet):* Originally, when people liked someone else's tweet, they copied and pasted it onto their own Twitter page and indicated who they were re-tweeting by putting *RT*, an @ sign, and the Twitter account name. You probably won't see this as much now, because you can use the built-in re-tweet function (see Chapter 7).

- *@username:* When you put this in a message on Twitter, you're referring to another Twitter account. People on the Web can click that name in Twitter to go to their account. You might do this for a variety of reasons, but the most common may be a reply. People began putting @(*twitteraccount*) on their tweets to indicate that they were replying to someone, and now the reply feature is built into Twitter. In general, Twitter messages were and are public, but it's possible to send a direct, private message via Twitter. (See Chapter 7.)

- `http://bit.ly/(whatever)`: This is an example of a *URL shortener*. Because you can use only 140 characters, instead of including a long link (links are getting increasingly longer these days, especially to news articles), you can make an encoded URL. You'll learn more about *short URLs* in Chapter 7. Basically, services like `http://tinyurl.com` and `http://bit.ly` allow you to enter a long web address, and they provide a short link. When someone clicks it, they go to the same web site—the short URL forwards them to the long URL. (URL = web address—or, technically speaking, Uniform Resource Locator.)

Messages have a 140-character limit because this is the length limit for text messages sent between mobile phones. By limiting a tweet to 140 characters, Twitter ensures that someone who is reading tweets on their mobile phone gets the entire message. (Technically, Twitter—on the web site, at least—accepts messages longer than 140 characters, but the only way to view them is on the web site. It's best to stick to 140 characters. Also, some mobile devices can send messages up to 160 characters, but standards vary from country to country and device to device, and 140 is the magic number.)

■ **Tip** For more information about Twitter jargon, see `http://weblogs.about.com/od/microblogging/tp/TwitterTerminology.htm`.

Signing Up and Getting Started

The best way to explore Twitter is to sign up and get started! To begin, visit `www.twitter.com` (see Figure 6-4), and click the Sign Up Now button. In the window that opens, shown in Figure 6-5, choose a username.

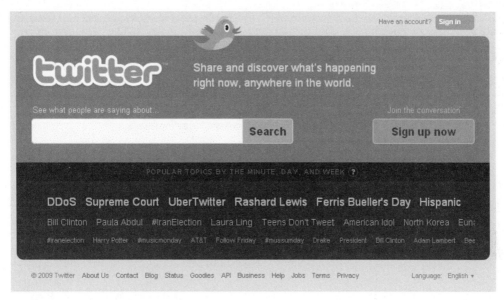

Figure 6-4. The screen you see when you visit Twitter.com

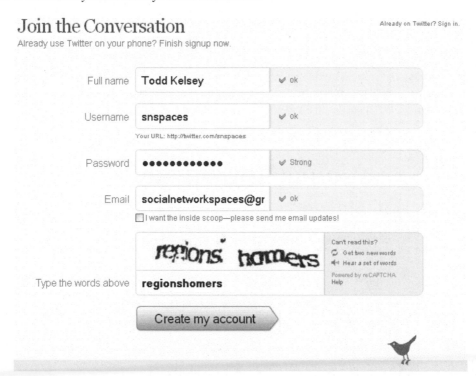

Figure 6-5. Choose a username.

Twitter can check your web mail account (such as Gmail), analyze your contacts, and see if any of them are on Twitter (see Figure 6-6). Twitter contacts Gmail (or Yahoo or AOL) and loads your contact information (see Figure 6-7). If Twitter finds a contact, you can select it and follow that person, as shown in Figure 6-8; this means you're subscribing to their tweets.

Find people. Follow them.

Find on Twitter	Find on other networks	Suggested Users

M Gmail

Y! Yahoo

AOL

Your Email **socialnetworkingspaces@**

Email Password ●●●●●●●●●●●

🔒 **Email Security**
We don't store your login, your password is submitted securely, and we don't email without your permission.

Continue

Figure 6-6. Entering your webmail information so Twitter can check and see if anyone you contact via e-mail is also on Twitter. Pretty cool.

Contacting Gmail...

We're loading your contacts.
(This can take a while if you've got a large address book.)

Figure 6-7. It may take a few minutes to load and process your contacts.

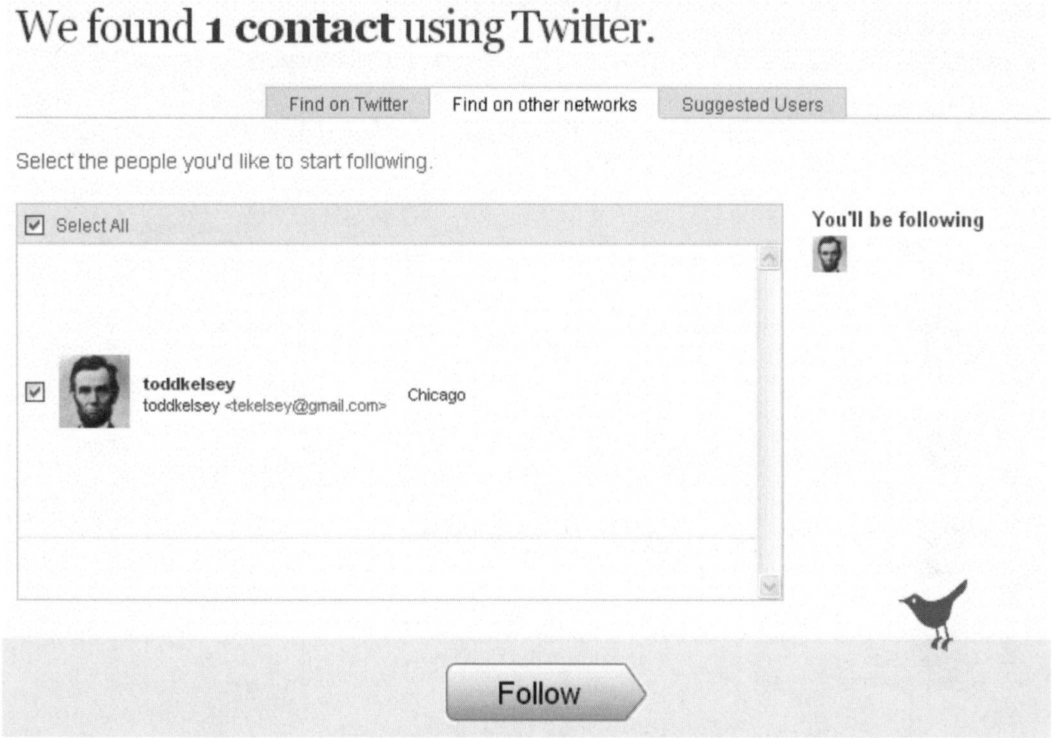

We found **1 contact** using Twitter.

Find on Twitter   Find on other networks   Suggested Users

Select the people you'd like to start following.

☑ Select All

You'll be following

☑ **toddkelsey**
toddkelsey <tekelsey@gmail.com>   Chicago

Follow

Figure 6-8. After Twitter finds your contacts, you can click the check box next to the people you want to follow and then click the Follow button. Following someone is also a way of letting people know you're on Twitter—when you follow them, they may also end up following you.

After you sign up (if you've chosen one or more followers during the sign-up process), your Twitter home page appears, with tweets from anyone you're following, as shown in Figure 6-9.

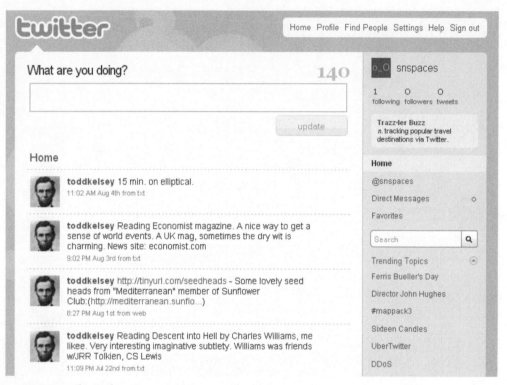

Figure 6-9. Done! This is the snspaces Twitter account. Because it's set to follow toddkelsey (my personal Twitter account), posts from the toddkelsey Twitter account now show up on the snspaces page. If you're confused, think of it like a magazine subscription—when you follow someone, it's like you're subscribing to anything they publish (on Twitter), and your subscription appears on your Twitter page.

Figure 6-10 shows a close-up of a new Twitter home page. This account is following one person and has zero followers (because it's new), and zero tweets have been made.

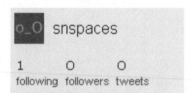

Figure 6-10. Just starting out—the basic info where you can see your main stats

Following Someone

The next order of business, now that you have your Twitter account, is to try following someone (and sometimes, when you follow someone, they'll follow you in turn). Adding followers to your Twitter account is easy.

To search for someone on Twitter, click the Find People link, as shown in Figure 6-11. Then, type in a name (see Figure 6-12). If you don't want to follow William Shatner, you can type another name or "Social Net Spaces."

Figure 6-11. The Find People link that appears at the top of your Twitter page when you're logged in

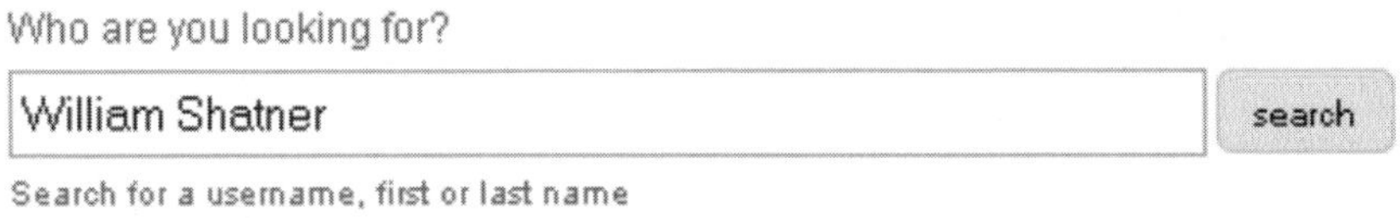

Who are you looking for?

| William Shatner | search |

Search for a username, first or last name

Figure 6-12. You can type in a person's username if you know it, or their first and/or last name.

When the search results appear, as shown in Figure 6-13, you can follow the Twitter account by clicking the little gear-looking icon on the right and choosing the Follow option.

Figure 6-13. Search results

When you've chosen someone to follow, click the Home link (see Figure 6-14). The person's tweets appear on your home page (see Figure 6-15)

Figure 6-14. Home link

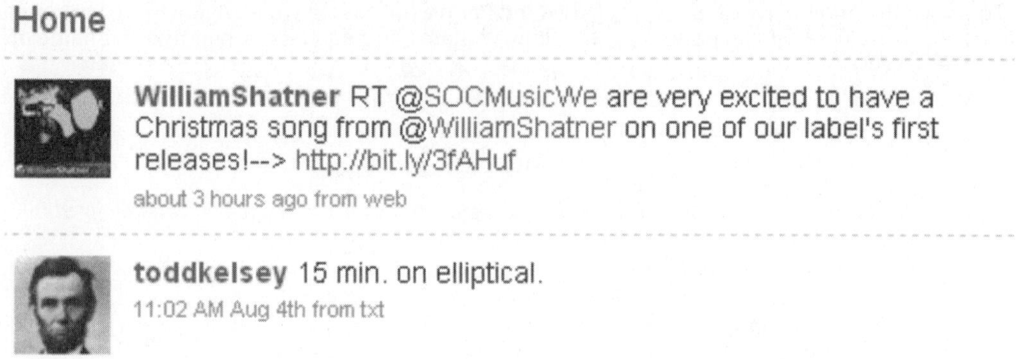

Home
WilliamShatner RT @SOCMusicWe are very excited to have a Christmas song from @WilliamShatner on one of our label's first releases!--> http://bit.ly/3fAHuf
about 3 hours ago from web
toddkelsey 15 min. on elliptical.
11:02 AM Aug 4th from txt

Figure 6-15. *After you've started following someone, their tweets appear on your home page.*

Another Way to Follow Someone

You just learned how to follow someone by searching for them on Twitter. Another way to follow someone uses the links you increasingly find on the Web, such as a Follow Me link on a news web site. You may also see the Twitter icon posted on a site.

These things, called *Twitter badges*, lead you to a Twitter user's profile page. When you get there, you can sign in and click Follow, as shown in Figure 6-16.

http://twitter.com/snspaces
twitter
Home
snspaces
Follow
I am writing the book
Social Networking Spaces - From
Facebook to Twitter and Everything
in Between.
3 minutes ago from web

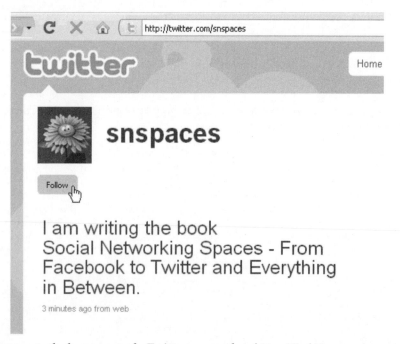

Figure 6-16. *If you go to the home page of a Twitter user, such as* `http://twitter.com/snspaces`*, you can click the Follow button.*

Adding a Profile Icon

You may notice when you sign up that Twitter assigns a generic default icon (see Figure 6-17). This profile icon appears with all your tweets unless you change it. You don't have to change it, but it certainly can be a fun thing to do.

Figure 6-17. *The generic default profile icon (appearing to the left of your username)*

If you'd like a practice icon to use, you can go to `www.cftw.com/snspaces` and use the icon I've uploaded.

■ **Note** If you'd like to use an image that's on the Web (and that isn't copyrighted), you can download it by right-clicking (Windows) and choosing Save Image As (Firefox) or Save Picture As (Internet Explorer). On a Mac, hold down the Ctrl key, click the image, and choose Download to Disk.

The best image for a profile icon is a cropped image, such as a picture of yourself, your dog, or something like that—the idea is to focus on something you can recognize even at the smaller size. If you're not sure how to prepare an image, see the next section, which explains how to use a simple web-based tool called Pic Resize.

When you have an image ready, click the default profile icon, as shown in Figure 6-18. Doing so takes you to your profile (see Figure 6-19). Your Twitter address is `http://twitter.com/`*username* (with or without the www). To add a photo for a new profile icon, click the Add a Photo box. (When you're following someone, their profile icon appears on your profile.) Then, in the window shown in Figure 6-20, click the Browse button to locate your picture, and click Save.

Figure 6-18. *Step 1: Click the default icon next to your username.*

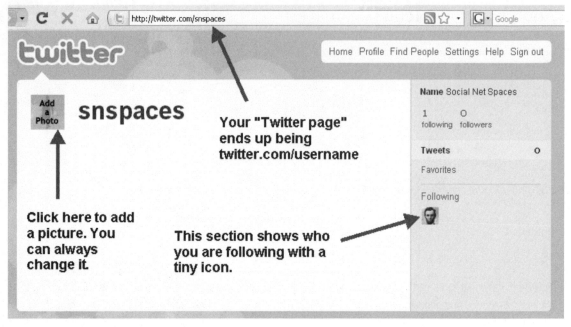

Figure 6-19. Step 2: Click the Add a Photo box on your Twitter home page.

Figure 6-20. Now, you can click the Browse button and locate a picture, and then click Save when you're done.

Figure 6-21 shows what Twitter has to say about profile pictures.

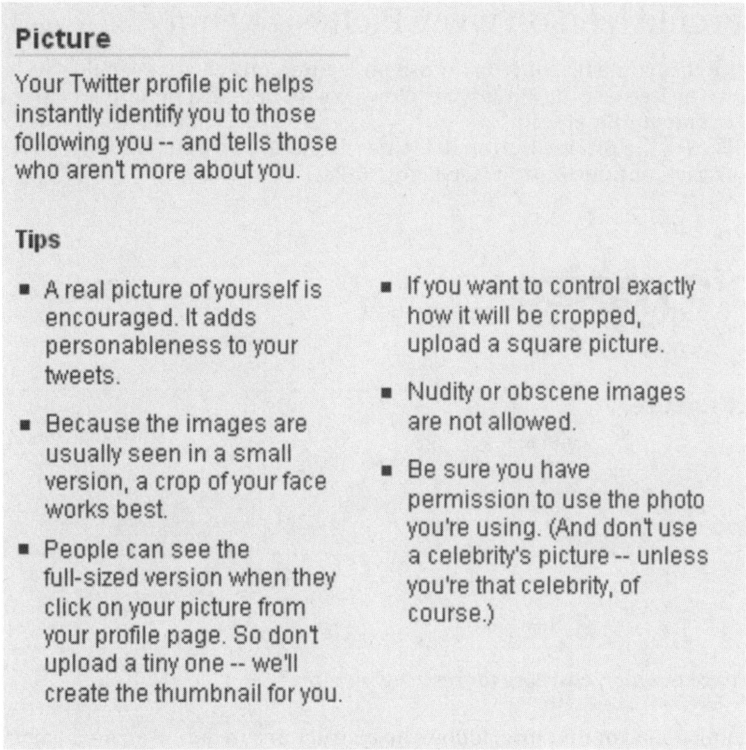

Picture
Your Twitter profile pic helps instantly identify you to those following you -- and tells those who aren't more about you.
Tips
A real picture of yourself is encouraged. It adds personableness to your tweets.
Because the images are usually seen in a small version, a crop of your face works best.
People can see the full-sized version when they click on your picture from your profile page. So don't upload a tiny one -- we'll create the thumbnail for you.
If you want to control exactly how it will be cropped, upload a square picture.
Nudity or obscene images are not allowed.
Be sure you have permission to use the photo you're using. (And don't use a celebrity's picture -- unless you're that celebrity, of course.)

Figure 6-21. *Some tips from Twitter about profile pics*

When you're finished, click the Home link (see Figure 6-22). The new profile picture replaces the default profile picture and appears next to all your tweets for people who follow you (see Figure 6-23).

Home
Profile

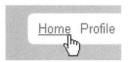

Figure 6-22. *The Home link gets you back home.*

snspaces
1 following
0 followers
0 tweets

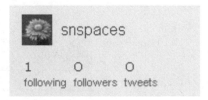

Figure 6-23. *The new profile pic shows up next to your username.*

Congratulations! You just changed your profile icon.

Creating a Profile Icon on www.PicResize.com

If you have a picture that you'd like to crop for use on Twitter, one easy way to do this is to visit
www.picresize.com. The free web-based service allows you to upload a picture, make changes, and then
save a new copy to your computer.

At the web site, click the Browse button to locate the picture on your computer that you'd like to
crop, and then click the Continue button (see Figure 6-24).

Figure 6-24. Pic Resize is a nice, easy tool for resizing pictures.

When you've uploaded your picture, follow the instructions to define an area (such as your face) to
which you'd like to crop the picture (see Figure 6-24). You basically click once, let go of the mouse
button, move your mouse down and to the right, then click again.

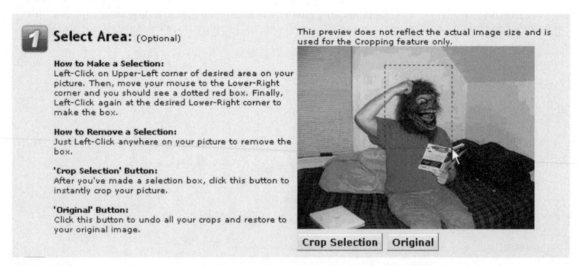

Figure 6-25. You can select an area of a larger picture to get a head shot, if you like.

After you've defined the area, click the Crop Selection button, shown in Figure 6-26.

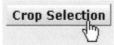

Figure 6-26. Crop Selection. Cropping is the process of defining a smaller area within a picture and cutting away everything else.

The cropped image is displayed, as shown in Figure 6-27. Don't worry about resizing the image; you can save it as the cropped version. If you're working with digital pictures from a powerful camera (several megapixels), you should probably learn how to resize images so the pictures and file sizes are smaller.

Figure 6-27. The cropped image

When you're happy with the cropped image, scroll down to the bottom of the screen, and click the Resize Pic button (see Figure 6-27).

Figure 6-28. The Resize Pic button finalizes the process.

On the next screen, click Save to Disk (see Figure 6-29)—and voila! You have a cropped profile icon, suitable for Twitter. Free, and no muss, no fuss.

Figure 6-29. Use this link/button to save a copy of the image to your computer in a place where you can find it. (If you're not sure how to work with folders, you might try saving to your desktop.)

Making Your First Tweet

The heart of Twitter is tweeting, so get ready to make your first tweet. Sign in to Twitter, and prepare to type!

If you need to, click the Home link shown in Figure 6-30 to make sure you're in the right place.

Figure 6-30. Home link

Now, click in the blank Twitter box, shown in Figure 6-31, and start typing. Be aware that you only have 140 characters to work with. When you're finished, click the Update button (see Figure 6-32). You've made a tweet!

What are you doing?   140

                                                                    update

Figure 6-31. Click in the white area beneath the question "What are you doing?" and begin typing.

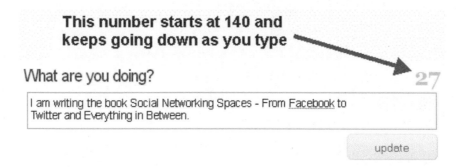

This number starts at 140 and keeps going down as you type

What are you doing?

I am writing the book Social Networking Spaces - From Facebook to Twitter and Everything in Between.

update

Figure 6-32. When you type, the number begins counting down to tell you how many characters you have left.

The tweet appears on your home page, along with tweets from anyone you're following (see Figure 6-33). Anyone who is following you also gets your tweet, either on the Web or on their mobile device.

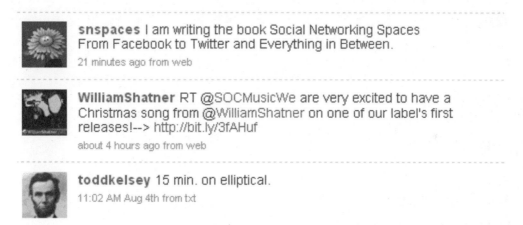

snspaces I am writing the book Social Networking Spaces From Facebook to Twitter and Everything in Between.
21 minutes ago from web

WilliamShatner RT @SOCMusicWe are very excited to have a Christmas song from @WilliamShatner on one of our label's first releases!--> http://bit.ly/3fAHuf
about 4 hours ago from web

toddkelsey 15 min. on elliptical.
11:02 AM Aug 4th from txt

Figure 6-33. After you click the Update button, the tweet appears.

Checking on Your Followers

You can invite people directly to be your followers by e-mail, by posting your new Twitter page on Facebook, or by putting a Twitter badge on your blog or web page. (See Chapter 7.) Also, when you follow others, sometimes they'll follow you in turn.

To check on your followers, sign in to Twitter, and click the Followers link (see Figure 6-34). Twitter displays a list of followers, as shown in Figure 6-35. Don't feel bad if you don't have any followers when you create your account. It's time to read the next chapter and get busy tweeting!

197

Figure 6-34. You can see who is following you by clicking the "followers" link.

Figure 6-35. Woohoo! There's a follower!

Q/A

Q: Is Twitter worth exploring?
A: Absolutely, and you may even have fun!

Q: Should everyone be on Twitter?
A: In my opinion, it doesn't really matter. Each to their own; carpe diem.

Q: What if I'm a business?
A: You should definitely learn about the emerging trends in Twitter, such as brand monitoring and instant customer service.

Q: Oooh! Can I put my Twitter address on my business card?
A: Yes, you can. The address is http://twitter.com/*username* (for example, http://twitter.com/toddkelsey or http://twitter.com/snspaces). You can also say something like "Follow (*username*) on Twitter."

Q: How can I find out more?
A: Try http://mashable.com, or drop by www.snspaces.com to explore the links (and feel free to contribute your own).

Q: Is there a downside to Twitter?

A: I guess the downside may be inanity. People will tweet about just about anything; and if you end up feeling like Twitter is one more thing you have to monitor or participate in, you may get burned out. On the other hand, there's no reason you have to read Twitter—you can just share your thoughts. If someone wants to follow you, cool. If not, no biggie. But like many tens of millions of people, it may become a conversational medium for you.

Q: I like this book, but there are only two chapters about Twitter. Where can I read more?
A: If you liked this book and this chapter or section, keep your eyes open for an entire book from CFTW Press about Twitter. If you want to be posted about the book's progress, go on Facebook and search for (and join) the Social Networking Spaces group, or search for (and become a fan of) the Social Networking Spaces Facebook page. I'll post messages once in a while to both, and maybe to the `http://twitter.com/snspaces` account too, if you'd like to follow it. Just as with this book, all author proceeds will be donated to CFTW. (See the book's Introduction). And don't worry if you don't know how to join a group or become a fan. You can learn by reading the Facebook chapters in this book!

Q: Which is better, Twitter or Google Buzz?
A: I think both are worth trying. If you haven't heard of Google Buzz, go to `www.google.com` and type in "google buzz". It gives you a Twitter-like ability to post messages, but it's within the framework of Gmail. Personally, I think Gmail is great. My opinion on Buzz is that it's nice, because it's right within Gmail.

I'm keeping an eye on it to see if it gets too cumbersome. With Twitter, I post to it, but I don't have Twitter set to send me e-mails of the tweets of people I follow, and I don't have my phone set to receive tweets. I like it that way—if/when I want to see what's up, I can go on Twitter and see the posts of people I follow. With Google Buzz, the messages show up as though you have e-mail, so there's a bit more compulsion. So far, I've felt like unfollowing a lot of people on Google Buzz, so I keep a very short list of people I follow. It's more focused.

I like keeping tabs on people by going to Facebook and seeing what people have posted there, but for my closest friends, it's nice to have Google Buzz. I also think it's interesting how you can connect Google Buzz to other things, like Twitter.

Q: Why the heck is William Shatner's face all grayed out in the screenshots in this chapter?
A: Because I was waiting to hear back about an inquiry for permission to use his likeness. If you really want to see his face, search for him on Twitter. And if you know him, ask him if we can use his picture—and maybe if this book sells enough copies, we can fix it in the reprint!

Q: Wait! I have another question! Where can I ask it?
A: On `www.snspaces.com`.

Conclusion

Dear Reader,

In this chapter, you've taken a tour of Twitter and set out on your way toward tweeting. One of the interesting things about Twitter is that when you begin tweeting, people will begin following you. Tens of millions of people use Twitter, and whether you're using it for personal fun or for business, a lot of people are out there searching for tweets. People may end up finding you when they search for certain words on Twitter—and because there are so many users, chances are someone will find you.

Twitter, like Facebook, is just a tool. It can be fun, and it probably makes sense to try it and become familiar with it. There's no need to receive tweets on your phone; but like Facebook, Twitter is a nice way to share what's going on with you. And if you have a show-and-tell streak, you may find that you like sharing information.

For businesses, the case is easier: you should definitely be thinking about Twitter. So many people are on it that businesses are starting to use it for anything from marketing to customer service (searching for mention of your company's name, positive and negative).

As time has gone by, I've seen Twitter grow, and it seems to be here to stay; I tried it more often and found it to be fun for updating people who follow me. I like sharing links, so I use it for that purpose. I enjoyed hooking up my mobile phone so I could share thoughts, or tweet when I've gone to the gym—I even added the Twitter for Facebook application (see the "Connecting Twitter to Facebook" section in Chapter 7). When you activate this application, your tweets automatically change your Facebook status—with one text, you can send a tweet to Twitter followers, and your Facebook friends also see what you're up to. This is a good thing for me to do, because it gives me some accountability for going to the gym, and friends and family can root me on as I work toward getting to my healthy weight. Sometimes I emerge from the gym, get in the car, and tweet how many minutes I've spent on the elliptical machine. Not earth-shattering, but helpful.

I've grown to enjoy Twitter, and I think it's important. I think it represents the power of simplicity and focus. Over the last year or two, I've learned more about mobile usage, especially in the developed world, and particularly in places like Africa, China, and Japan, where many people are more likely to access the Internet using mobile devices. In some parts of Africa, a mobile phone may be the only way a person can communicate electronically; and even if they don't have Internet access on their phone, they're likely to have texting access.

So Twitter, to me, highlights what I call the common denominator of communication: hundreds of millions of people around the world have in common this ability to text. It's been interesting to see Twitter evolve, capture the public imagination, and become a political issue—for example, when Twitter is blocked by particular governments during times of unrest.

My recommendation is that you explore; and if you choose to try Twitter, make it sustainable. Share things that are meaningful to you and your friends, family, and followers. I suggest making it part of capturing your life story, by occasionally jotting down thoughts, reflections, or reactions, which might otherwise be lost.

I also encourage you to consider adding the Twitter for Facebook application (see Chapter 7), so you can easily share your thoughts with your followers on Twitter as well as your friends and family on Facebook. Once in a while, someone may comment, and it may turn into a conversation—and who knows, it may lead to something you never expected.

Chapter 7 takes a closer look at Twitter and how to get the most out of your tweets, including setting up your mobile phone; connecting to Facebook, and trying a URL shortener (so you can shorten a lengthy web address so it will fit into a 140-character tweet). You look at a few ways to promote your Twitter page, including the ever-more-ubiquitous Twitter badges.

Have fun, and best wishes with your tweets!

Regards,

–Todd

P.S. If you've read Chapter 1, you may already know the Life Story Suitcase is an experimental tool for backing up your pictures and posts from Facebook, Blogger, Twitter, and so on. The tool helps you to weave the pictures and posts together, to capture and preserve stories from your life. The idea is to share the stories with your family and friends. If you like, when you've had a chance to try Twitter, you're welcome to come by www.lifestorysuitcase.com and tell us what you think of the experiment.

snspaces.com

Come and visit the Social Networking Spaces companion web site at www.snspaces.com, where you can find more tips and updates and have an opportunity to share your thoughts or ask questions.

In Living Color: You can visit www.snspaces.com/pics to see full-color versions of all the pictures from this chapter.

Twitter Users: To follow Social Networking Spaces on Twitter, visit www.twitter.com/snspaces, and click Follow.

■ ■ ■

Making the Most of Your Tweets

In This Chapter:

- How using shortened links can save space for your Twitter messages (called *tweets*)
- Setting up your phone/mobile device to send tweets
- How to use the new *re-tweet* feature to pass along something you like
- Some amazing Twitter goodies you can use to include Twitter on your blog or Web page

snspaces.com

Come and visit the Social Networking Spaces companion web site at www.snspaces.com, where you can find more tips and updates and have an opportunity to share your thoughts or ask questions.

In Living Color: You can visit www.snspaces.com/pics to see full-color versions of all the pictures from this chapter.

Twitter Users: To follow Social Networking Spaces on Twitter, visit www.twitter.com/snspaces and click Follow.

Introduction

On the surface, using Twitter is pretty simple. You just type in a message of fewer than 140 characters and read the short messages shared by other Twitter users. But because of the growth and evolution of the Twitter community, Twitter's uses have expanded, and a lot of interesting phenomena have happened. There are Twitter applications that allow you to use Twitter in new ways, and uses that have evolved because of people's creativity and innovation: things that Twitter's founders probably never imagined.

So much is out there, an entire book wouldn't be enough to hold it; so for some of the things you may enjoy looking at, I'll take all the links I've gathered during the course of looking into Twitter, and I'll put them on www.snspaces.com. (You're welcome to go on www.snspaces.com and suggest links of your own, including if you have a Twitter-related article, site, or program you like or want to promote, or if you want to promote your Twitter page.)

This chapter looks at some of the things you can do to get more out of Twitter, in terms of having fun and trying new things, based on my own experiences. I'll keep it simple but try to make it fun; then, if you want more, check out the links on www.snspaces.com.

Tweeting Within Budget

One of the things about Twitter is, as I mentioned, you only have 140 characters to work with; so, if you're typing a message and then want to share a link, you may have some issues. In Figure 7-1, you see a message, and there's not enough room to paste a link. The 6 at upper right means there are only six characters left.

What are you doing?   6

> This is a test tweet to see what happens when you type a message but are running out of characters, and you need to post a long link.

Figure 7-1. Only six characters left to go!

If you do paste a link, even a relatively short one like that shown in Figure 7-2, you may *go negative*; then, in the current version of Twitter, you can't post the message. The -31 means you've gone 31 characters over. Think of 140 characters like a budget. With Twitter, there's no overspending.

What are you doing?   -31

> This is a test tweet to see what happens when you type a message but are running out of characters, and you need to post a long link. http://www.upstartgirl2.blogspot.com/

Figure 7-2. You have overspent by 31 characters.

What has evolved is, probably in large part because of Twitter, a collection of web sites that can take a long link and make it shorter. Let's say you want to share a CNN news article on Twitter. The article's web address may have quite a number of characters in it. (See Figure 7-3.)

http://www.cnn.com/2009/TECH/11/12/cnet.xbox.live.ban/index.html

Figure 7-3. A long URL

If you post a CNN-length link after your original Twitter message, you go ever further into the negative as far as character budget (see Figure 7-4).

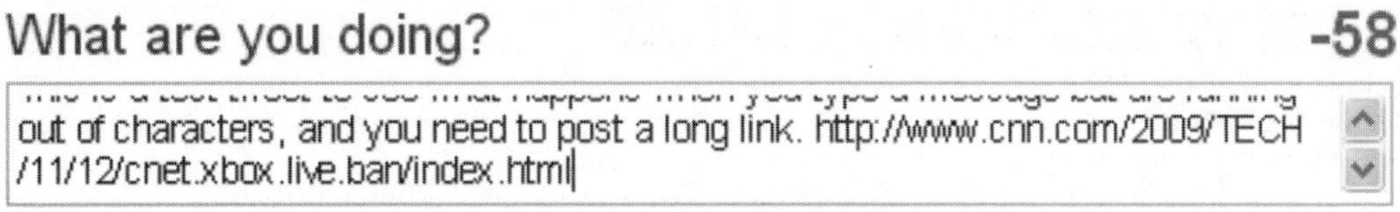

What are you doing?   -58

```
out of characters, and you need to post a long link. http://www.cnn.com/2009/TECH
/11/12/cnet.xbox.live.ban/index.html
```

Figure 7-4. Long URLs can throw you way off your character budget.

One way you can get away with posting a link in a Twitter message is to shorten your original message, but why give up all those characters if you can shorten your link?

Basically, people figured out that you can have a free service where you paste in a link, and the service gives you back a shorter link to the same site. All the short link does is send you to the long link. It's kind of like call-forwarding on the Internet, but for links.

TinyURL.com

TinyURL.com is one of the popular services. It gives you a typical short link: it's coded, such as `http://tinyurl.com/ks3ds`, and it leads to your site.

One of the other nice things I've enjoyed about TinyURL is that you can enter your own ending for the link. The result is still a short link, but it allows you to give the link some context. Let's take a look so you have some idea of what the heck I'm talking about.

(By the way, a URL is just a fancy name for a link; it stands for Uniform Resource Locator. Go to `http://en.wikipedia.org/wiki/Url` to learn more.

You can take the lengthy link from CNN, visit TinyURL.com, and paste it into the field titled "Enter a long URL to make tiny." See Figure 7-5.

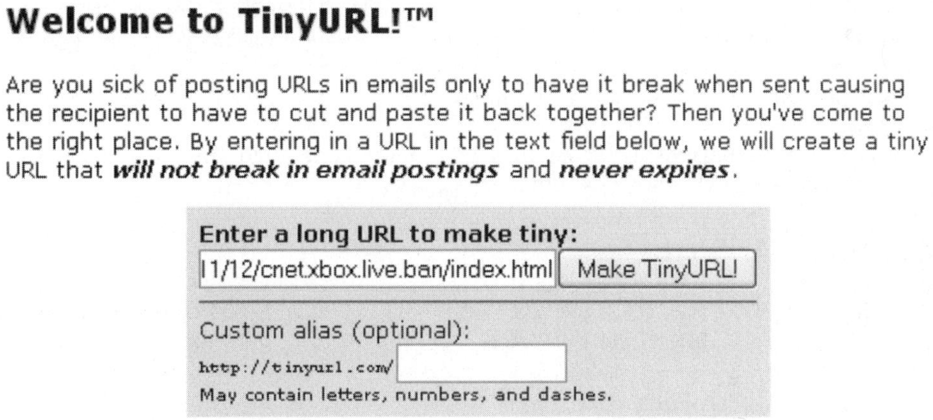

Welcome to TinyURL!™

Are you sick of posting URLs in emails only to have it break when sent causing the recipient to have to cut and paste it back together? Then you've come to the right place. By entering in a URL in the text field below, we will create a tiny URL that **will not break in email postings** and **never expires**.

Enter a long URL to make tiny:

| 1/12/cnet.xbox.live.ban/index.html | Make TinyURL! |

Custom alias (optional):
`http://tinyurl.com/` [   ]
May contain letters, numbers, and dashes.

Figure 7-5. Shrink a link with TinyURL.

After you paste in a link, you click the Make TinyURL! button, and you get a confirmation, such as what is shown in Figure 7-6.

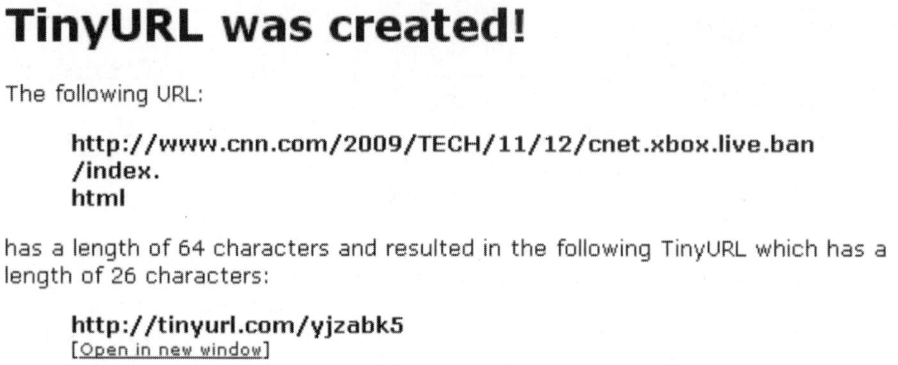

TinyURL was created!

The following URL:

> http://www.cnn.com/2009/TECH/11/12/cnet.xbox.live.ban
> /index.
> html

has a length of 64 characters and resulted in the following TinyURL which has a length of 26 characters:

> http://tinyurl.com/yjzabk5
> [Open in new window]

Figure 7-6. Voila, a shorter link results.

The long URL was changed into a short URL or short link.

In this example, the link ending in yjzabk5 leads to the same online location as the original link. This is perfect for copying and pasting into a Twitter message. Notice how the original link was 64 characters, whereas the shorter link is only 26 characters. That leaves more room for a Twitter message.

You can see that when you past a shortened URL back into the original message, it only goes negative by 20 characters (see Figure 7-7). This happens to me sometimes; I'll type something in, put a link, and then go back and shorten the message.

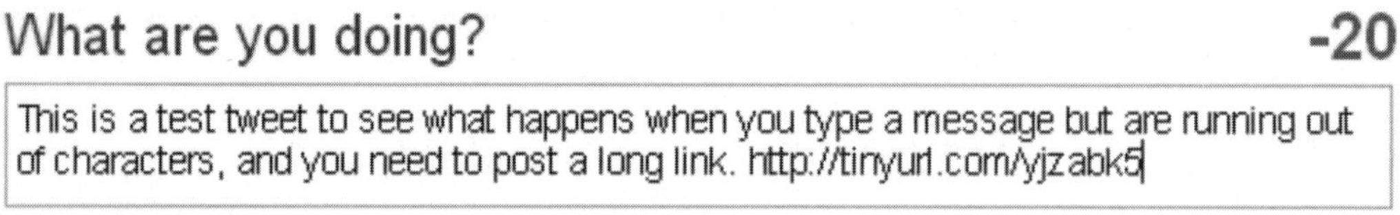

What are you doing?   -20

> This is a test tweet to see what happens when you type a message but are running out
> of characters, and you need to post a long link. http://tinyurl.com/yjzabk5

Figure 7-7. Still over budget with a shorter link, but less so

And this is what an actual message might look like: a reasonable-sized sentence, which has more room to breathe, because I'm using a short URL. See Figure 7-8.

What are you doing?   8

> I saw this article about how Microsoft banned a million people from XBox live for using
> pirated software: http://tinyurl.com/yjzabk5

Figure 7-8. An acceptable length tweet, with link

Making a Short URL with a Custom Alias

This sounds really sophisticated and difficult, but it's actually very simple. *Custom alias* means that, instead of getting a random code in your link, you can use words to give context. For example, in the previous sections you made a short URL, and the link ended up being http://tinyurl.com/yjzabk5. There's nothing wrong with that, but sometimes it's nice to include some meaning, some context, within the link. You can go to TinyURL.com and, if someone hasn't already used the same custom alias, TinyURL makes it for you.

In Figure 7-9, I entered "xboxbanned" in the custom alias field, after pasting in the CNN link.

Enter a long URL to make tiny:
http://www.cnn.com/2009/TECH/11
Make TinyURL!
Custom alias (optional):
http://tinyurl.com/
xboxbanned
May contain letters, numbers, and dashes.

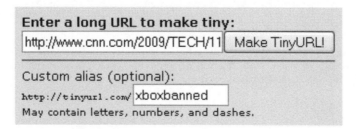

Figure 7-9. Going the custom alias route

TinyURL created the link shown in Figure 7-10.

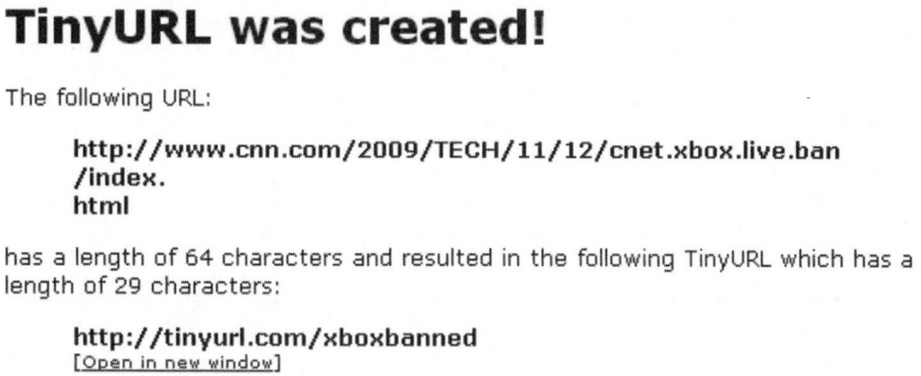
TinyURL was created!
The following URL:
http://www.cnn.com/2009/TECH/11/12/cnet.xbox.live.ban/index.html
has a length of 64 characters and resulted in the following TinyURL which has a length of 29 characters:
http://tinyurl.com/xboxbanned
[Open in new window]

Figure 7-10. Custom alias created

I personally like using a custom alias when I can, because it makes a link easier to share and is a little more elegant, as you see in Figure 7-11.

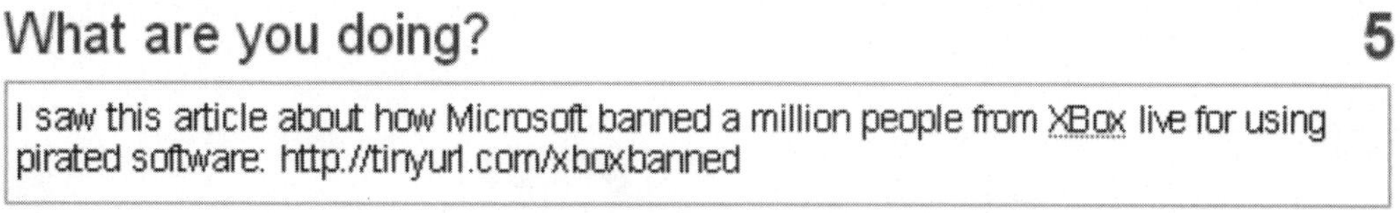
What are you doing?
5
I saw this article about how Microsoft banned a million people from XBox live for using pirated software: http://tinyurl.com/xboxbanned

Figure 7-11. A custom alias provides context and elegance.

You can see how the final tweet looks in Figure 7-12.

snspaces I saw this article about how Microsoft banned a million people from XBox live for using pirated software: http://tinyurl.com /xboxbanned

less than 5 seconds ago from web

Figure 7-12. *Final tweet, ready to share*

If you have Twitter connected to Facebook, whenever you tweet something, it also gets automatically shared with your Facebook friends. So when you post it, your tweet (along with a short URL), is carried into Facebook, as shown in Figure 7-13.

Figure 7-13. *Connecting Twitter and Facebook*

I cover how to connect Facebook and Twitter later in this chapter, in the "Goodies" section.

Other URL Shorteners

There are a number of URL shorteners out there. Twitter has an official relationship with one called bit.ly, so it's worth investigating. See Figure 7-14.

Figure 7-14. *The bit.ly URL shortener*

Bit.ly has some nice features, including giving you a complete history of all the links you've created using it.

Is.gd is another URL shortener with a nice, very short address. The link Tinyurl.com is taking up, oh my gosh, 10 characters! That's a few characters I could be using in my tweet! Because of Twitter mania, very short web site names, such as is.gd, offer the very shortest in short URLs.

Luke Skywalker, I Am Your Father: The Dark Side of URL Shorteners

One issue with URL shorteners is that when you make a link, if you expect people to come across the link and use it in the future, it would be nice to know that the URL was going to work forever. It can be a challenge to make a URL shortener service sustainable, because it's free; but a lot of people use it, so it can use up a lot of computer power. For the creator, this can be tricky. And this is one reason why there are people who are against URL shorteners: they think short URLs are too risky and clutter up the Internet. Basically, they're concerned about what happens if a URL shortener business goes belly up and all your links are broken.

Some people are also concerned that a URL shortener service technically would have the capability to suddenly redirect all traffic from all the links people have created to whatever they want, such as a porn site. So the short URL leading to a CNN article about the latest Disney movie that you sent to your mother in law could suddenly be pointing at some unmentionable site offering to enlarge something for a price.

My personal perspective on the "dark side" is that there's a strong demand for URL shorteners, they aren't going away, and the best thing to do is to stick with established, more reliable ones. Yes, some larger URL shortener services have gone down, but bit.ly is pretty safe because it's now connected to Twitter, and both tinyurl.com and is.gd seem to be doing well.

Texting Refresher

If you have used your cell phone for texting, you may know this, but some people reading don't, so I'll go ahead and review. When you're shortening text messages, there are a few different techniques you can use.

For example, if you want to be shortening messages, you can change the words.

I can take the previous sentence and compress it using abbreviations, as shown below:

4 example, if u want 2b shortening msgs, u can change words.

See how it becomes shorter? This kind of abbreviation can help on Twitter, when you're texting with a mobile phone, or when you're chatting. (It's also useful for driving teachers, professors, or editors crazy when you e-mail them or turn in a paper.) There's a very informative article about many such abbreviations at http://en.wikipedia.org/wiki/SMS_language.

But the quickest way to learn the ins and outs of texting is probably to ask the nearest teen. If you'd like to tweak them a bit, you can always ask them if they heard about how Morse code beat texting in a speed competition. (See the article "*Morse code trumps SMS in head-to-head speed texting combat*" at http://tinyurl.com/morsetexting.) And if you happen to be an engineer, let's make a keychain that allows you to send and receive SMS messages via Morse code! Maybe it would be fun to make Morse code fashionable again. Or at least my Abraham Lincoln profile icon would think so.

While I'm on the subject of Abraham Lincoln, let me mention how much fun it was to come across this little gem at the Chicago Tribune building, showing a letter where Abe was renewing his subscription to the newspaper. 150 years later, I guess it would be an e-mail or a tweet.

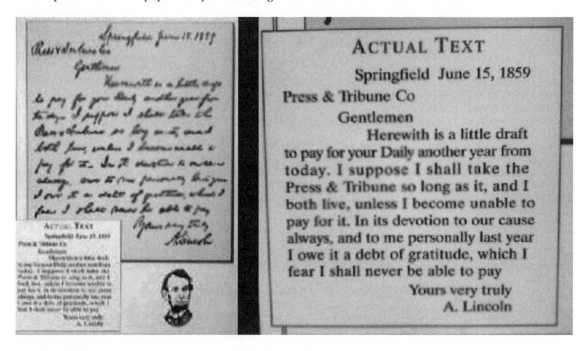

■ **Tip** If you can't see these pictures clearly enough, take a look at the Facebook photo album mentioned next– sometimes digital pictures come out better online than in print; plus they're in color!

And yes, this section is related to the book. In order to share the pictures on Twitter, which were originally placed in a Facebook photo album, I look the long URL
`http://www.facebook.com/album.php?aid=90362&id=773814569&l=1632c1c140`
and made it into a short URL:
Then, I tried making a short Twitter message and used a bit of textese (for example, *2* instead of *two*, *w/a* instead of *with a*, and so on, as shown in Figure 7-15.

toddkelsey FB album: includes visit 2 Chicago Tribune bldg, w/a letter Abraham Lincoln wrote 2 renew his subscription http://tinyurl.com/tkvisits

less than 5 seconds ago from web

Figure 7-15. A shortened tweet, featuring Abe Lincoln

OK, I'm having 2 much fun here trying 2 inspire u so I'd better get moving w/the chapter!

Using Twitter on Your Cell Phone or Mobile Device

I do have to say that I was just thinking about how misleading a term *mobile device* is. Because I have a mechanical typewriter sitting not too far off, and it's mobile. It has a carrying case and everything. But you can't use Twitter on it.

Or can you?

The following message is under 140 characters:

My mom used this mobile device to type her papers in college. Go mom!

I guess you'll have to leave the question of whether you can tweet on a typewriter to the philosophers. Alas, even though you can quickly type a <140 character message on it, there's not currently a method to connect this mobile device to Twitter.

But for just about everyone else, luckily, there is a way to connect Twitter to your mobile device or cell phone.

Why bother? Well, it's actually fun. If you're the kind of person who has fun on Twitter, then you're likely to have fun knowing that wherever you are, if you have a thought or notice something interesting, you can tweet about it. That's part of the immediacy, the little thrill of Twitter: immediate self-publishing to a following, a good example of show and tell.

As for me, I do enjoy tweeting from my phone sometimes. I actually end up using Twitter as a way to keep myself accountable on health goals. I go to the gym and then tweet how many minutes I spent on the elliptical machine. (See http://twitter.com/toddkelsey, and feel free to kick my butt if you don't see evidence that I'm exercising!)

The first thing you do to get started is to log in to Twitter.com and click Settings, as shown in Figure 7-16.

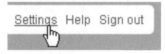

Figure 7-16. Setting up to tweet on your mobile device

Then, click the Mobile tab, shown in Figure 7-17.

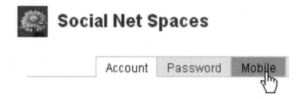

Figure 7-17. Click Mobile.

Twitter provides some simple instructions for getting started. Basically, you need to send a text message to a *shortcode*, which is like a shortened phone number (see Figure 7-18).

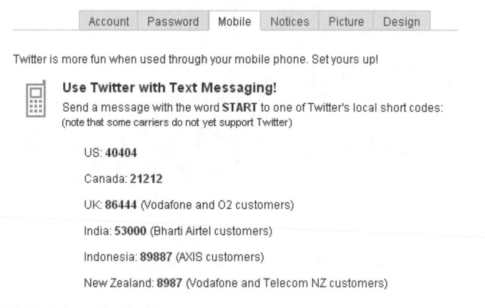

Figure 7-18. Use Twitter with your phone.

The way mobile devices work with text messaging varies widely, but generally you enter someone's phone number, type a message, and use a *send* function. In this case, Twitter needs to verify that a

Twitter user is really the owner of the phone, so you need to send some messages back and forth. This example uses my faithful yet rapidly degenerating Treo. Maybe the president of Sprint will have pity on me and give me a new device, or maybe Steve Jobs will read this book and give me an iPhone.

Whatever mobile device you use, the first thing you do is to consult the Mobile tab on your account page in Twitter and, depending on where you live, type in the shortcode provided, and send a message. You can put the word *start* if you want, or something else. See Figure 7-19.

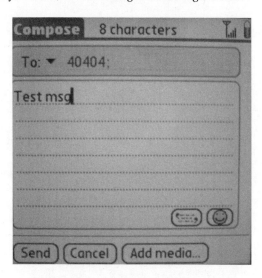

Figure 7-19. A test message

Twitter responds, asking you to type in your username. Type in your username, and send another message, as shown in Figure 7-20.

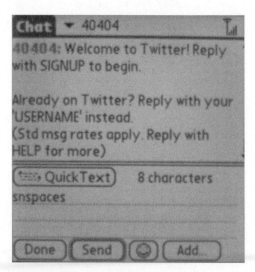

Figure 7-20. Include your username, and send another message.

Next, you need to type in your password. You need to really pay attention to your mobile device when you do this, because passwords on Twitter are case-sensitive, and some phones auto correct when you type in letters. For example, if your password is

hongkongphooey

then when you typed this, your phone may make the first letter uppercase, so it's now

Hongkongphooey

Just make sure you're paying attention to what your phone does (if it makes the first letter capital, type the rest of the password in, and then go back and replace the wacky letter.) See Figure 7-21.

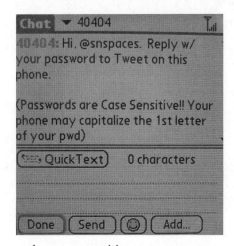

Figure 7-21. Be aware that passwords are case sensitive.

After you type in your password (I removed mine from Figure 7-22), you get a confirmation screen. You need to respond with a message that says OK for final confirmation.

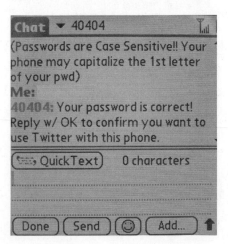

Figure 7-22. Password confirmed.

Then, you get a final confirmation message, and you're ready to tweet! See Figure 7-23.

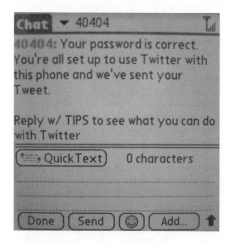

Figure 7-23. Ready to tweet!

Thereafter, you can send a message to your code (in the U.S., the code is 40404), and the message goes to your Twitter account. See Figure 7-24.

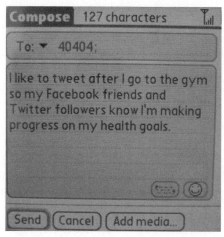

Figure 7-24. You tweet on your phone …

Your mobile tweet now appears on Twitter, as shown in Figure 7-25.

Home

 snspaces I like to tweet after I go to the gym so my Facebook friends and Twitter followers know I'm making progress on my health goals.

4 minutes ago from txt

Figure 7-25. *Your tweet appears on Twitter.*

Your tweet also appears on your Facebook account, as shown in Figure 7-26, if Twitter is connected to Facebook (see the "Goodies" section in this chapter).

Figure 7-26. *Your tweet can also appear on Facebook.*

■ **Note** Some phones allow you to type in a text message longer than 140 characters. When you're on the Twitter web site, it shows a negative number when you go beyond 140 characters. But on your phone, even if you can type up to 160 characters and can tweet the message, it won't be a standard Twitter message (people can click a link to see more on the site, but anyone who is following you and receiving updates on their mobile device won't get the full message).

Here's another important thing: unless you want to receive text message updates on your mobile device of anyone you're following on Twitter, you should go back to the Mobile tab (Twitter.com ➤ Settings ➤ Mobile), click the "Device updates" drop-down menu as shown in Figure 7-27, and switch it to Off. Then, click the Save button.

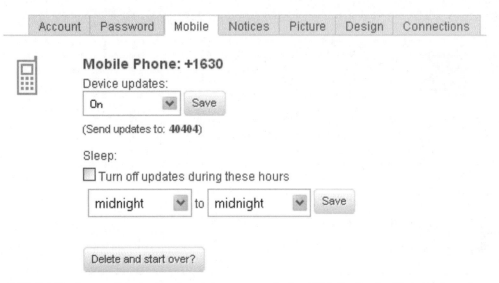

Figure 7-27. *Setting it up so you don't get updates on your device. Click the Device Updates drop-down menu, switch it to Off, click Save.*

You'll notice there's also a helpful feature for those people who would like to receive tweets on their phone but want to turn it off while they're asleep, or reading this book, or pruning bonsai, or sowing sunflower seeds, or something.

If you no longer want to have Twitter connected to your phone, you can go to the Mobile tab and click the "Delete and start over?" button. It clears the connection between your phone and Twitter; then, you can connect the Twitter account to another device, or not use the mobile feature at all. (Note: you can only tweet to one device at a time with the built-in Twitter mobile feature.)

Re-tweeting

In this section, I'll expand a bit on re-tweeting. *Re-tweeting* is a feature of Twitter that lets you pass on a tweet you like by sending it to your own followers. (People started using the code *RT* before a message to indicate they were re-tweeting, and it was customary to indicate whose message you were re-tweeting, as a courtesy to the original tweeter. Twitter decided to make this feature [duh] an official part of Twitter.)

For example, in my toddkelsey Twitter account, I'm a follower of the snspaces Twitter account. So when snspaces posts messages, they show up on my page. All you need to do in order to re-tweet is roll over the right side of a message and click the Retweet link, shown in Figure 7-28.

Figure 7-28. *Re-tweeting*

The Reply link enables you to post a tweet that will appear on your page and also show up on the Replies tab of the Twitter account you're following.

Twitter asks you to confirm if you want to pass the message along to your followers, as in Figure 7-29.

Figure 7-29. *Confirming your wish to re-tweet*

After you use this function, the re-tweeted message is sent on to all your Twitter followers, and a little "Retweeted by" label appears underneath, as in Figure 7-30.

Figure 7-30. *The Re-tweeted label "Retweeted by you" appears underneath the snspaces tweet.*

Twitter Goodies

There are some treasures buried in a section on Twitter called Goodies, which allow you to use Twitter in different ways. A series of widgets (widgets = tools) allow you to do interesting things, and a Facebook application lets you connect Twitter to Facebook so you can make a tweet and have it show up in your status on Facebook.

To explore, click the Goodies link at the bottom of the screen, shown in Figure 7-31.

Twitter About Us Contact Blog Status Goodies API Business Help Jobs Terms Privacy

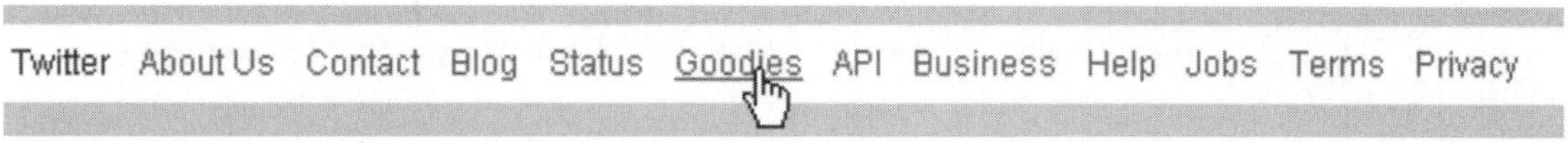

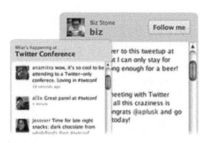

Figure 7-31. *The Goodies link*

Then, click the Widgets link/title, shown in Figure 7-32.

Twitter Goodies
biz
Follow me
Twitter Conference
Widgets
Put your updates anywhere or create a live stream for an event.
Compatible with Facebook, MySpace, Blogger etc.

Figure 7-32. *Click Widgets.*

You're given a chance to select a widget. Each widget performs different functions, but basically they offer ways of connecting to other social networking sites. See Figure 7-33.

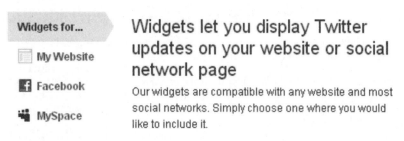

Select Your Widget
Widgets for...
My Website
Facebook
MySpace
Widgets let you display Twitter updates on your website or social network page
Our widgets are compatible with any website and most social networks. Simply choose one where you would like to include it.

Figure 7-33. *Selecting widgets*

For example, in the My Website section is a series of widgets that produce code you can paste into your web site, which adds new functions. As you'll see, in certain cases, there's an easy way to add the

My Website code to a blog. Normally, with something like this, you need to be comfortable with copying and selecting code and then pasting it into the code in your web site; but if you have a Blogger blog (wink wink, nudge nudge, hint: read Chapter 8 and Chapter 9), a button makes the process easy. Let's look at the Search Widget: click the My Website option on the left and then the Search Widget link/title, as shown in Figure 7-34.

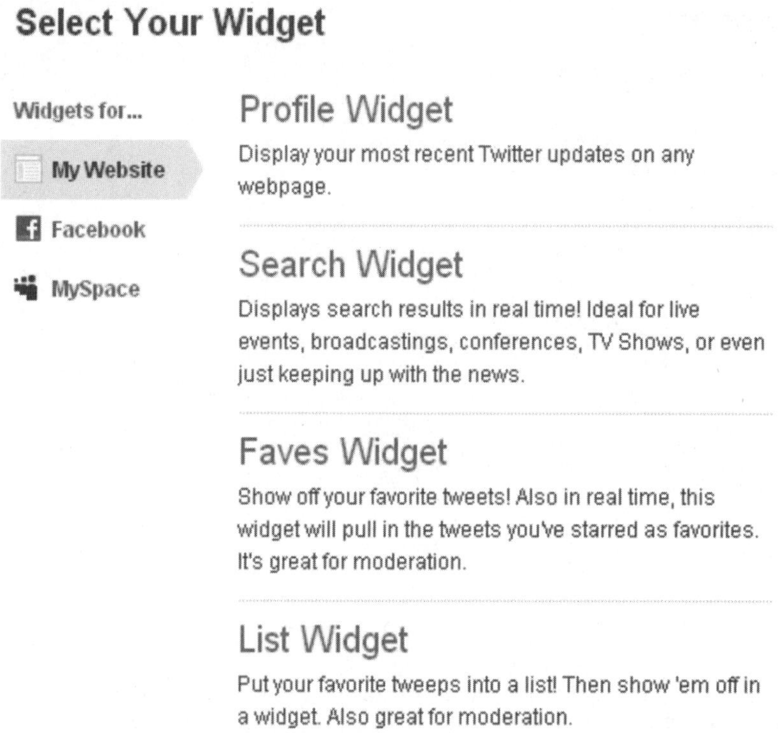

Select Your Widget

Widgets for...

📋 **My Website**

f **Facebook**

👥 **MySpace**

Profile Widget

Display your most recent Twitter updates on any webpage.

Search Widget

Displays search results in real time! Ideal for live events, broadcastings, conferences, TV Shows, or even just keeping up with the news.

Faves Widget

Show off your favorite tweets! Also in real time, this widget will pull in the tweets you've starred as favorites. It's great for moderation.

List Widget

Put your favorite tweeps into a list! Then show 'em off in a widget. Also great for moderation.

Figure 7-34. Selecting My Website

Adding a Twitter Search Widget to a Blogger/Blogspot Blog

A search widget adds a fascinating real-time stream of tweets on a certain topic. This can be a really interesting way to gather information on something that relates to your web site. Serious business types use Twitter searching to do *brand monitoring,* to look for any mention of their product on Twitter (this is an entire world unto itself: try looking at the Twitter links on www.snspaces.com for more information about Twitter applications and techniques). This is a simple bit of fun but pretty fascinating.

If you like the idea, I recommend reading Chapters 8 and 9 on making blogs and then coming back and trying adding a Twitter search widget.

After you click the Search Widget link, it brings you to a sample page – on the right, you see a real-time stream of tweets, and it may have something like "omg" on the left (which stands for "oh my gosh" or "oh my god"). Basically, you can play around with different search queries by typing words or phrases in the Search Query box and pressing the Enter key to trigger things to see what appears on the right.

The purpose of this widget is to allow you to enter custom settings: the search query represents the kind of tweets you'd like to appear in the widget when you place it on your blog or web site. You can also type in a Title and Caption, which change the appearance of the preview on the right. See Figure 7-35.

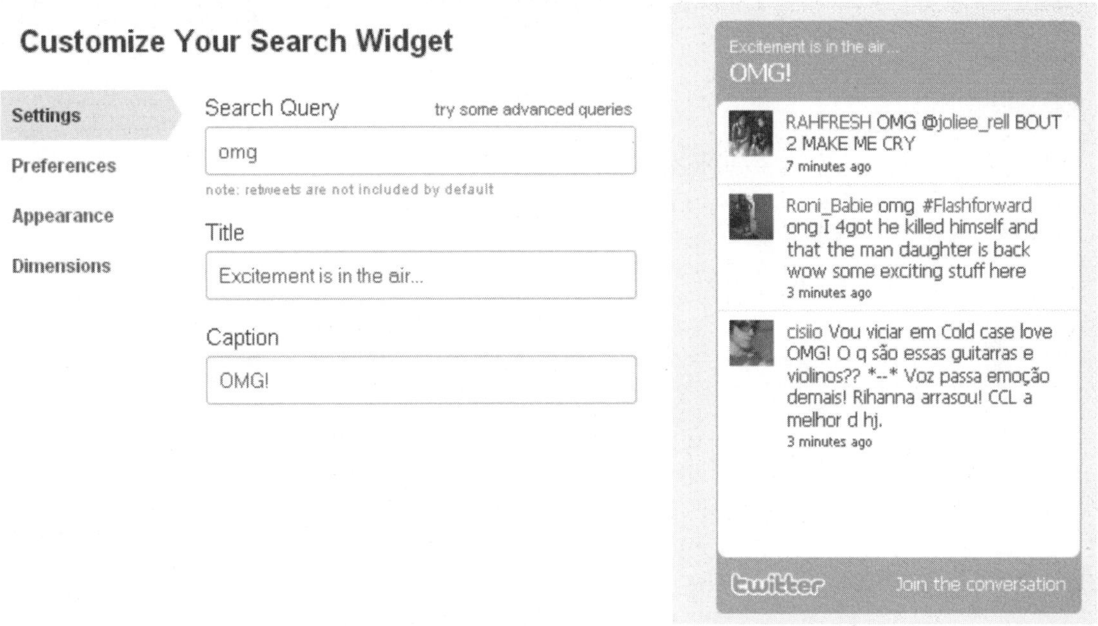

Customize Your Search Widget

Settings	**Search Query** try some advanced queries
Preferences	omg
	note: retweets are not included by default
Appearance	**Title**
Dimensions	Excitement is in the air...
	Caption
	OMG!

Preview:
Excitement is in the air...
OMG!

RAHFRESH OMG @joliee_rell BOUT 2 MAKE ME CRY
7 minutes ago

Roni_Babie omg #Flashforward ong I 4got he killed himself and that the man daughter is back wow some exciting stuff here
3 minutes ago

cisiio Vou viciar em Cold case love OMG! O q são essas guitarras e violinos?? *--* Voz passa emoção demais! Rihanna arrasou! CCL a melhor d hj.
3 minutes ago

twitter   Join the conversation

Figure 7-35. Customizing your search widget

Here, I'm trying the phrase "google wave": it's a hot topic, so a stream of tweets is coming in (see Figure 7-36). Remember, after you type in a search query, you need to press the Enter key on your keyboard to trigger the preview. If you just type a word or phrase and then click another field, you won't see anything on the right. Also, if you type in a word that no one happens to be tweeting about, nothing will appear, so try a different word or phrase. And, try multiple words or phrases separated by commas.

Customize Your Search Widget

Settings

Preferences

Appearance

Dimensions

Search Query   try some advanced queries

google wave

note: retweets are not included by default

Title

Social Networking Spaces

Caption

Real-time tweets about Google Wave

Social Networking Spaces
Real-time tweets about Google Wave

ClownX1511 I got a Google Wave invite!
38 seconds ago

MarceloPobleteT Ñañañaña....
Twitteando desde Google Wave :D
30 seconds ago

Butters78 Ok, what the hell is a google wave?
20 seconds ago

maxoxman1 Google Wave orgy at work.
12 seconds ago

11 new tweets

Julie_Cairns google wave isn't as cool once you try it. Just another

twitter   Join the conversation

Figure 7-36. Searching for "google wave"

Unless you specifically want a particular size, be sure to click the Dimensions option on the left and then click the "auto width" check box. This helps the widget fit into your blog page. See Figure 7-37.

Settings

Preferences

Appearance

Dimensions

Widget Dimensions

250

Width (in px)

OR

☑ auto width

300

Height (in px)

Note: Widget size won't update in preview.

Figure 7-37. Setting your widget dimensions

Then, when you're happy, click the Finish & Grab Code button:

Finish & Grab Code

This brings you to a screen where you can select and copy the code in the upper box, if you're comfortable working with code. You can also click the nice little Add to Blogger button at the bottom, as shown in Figure 7-38.

```
<script src="http://widgets.twimg.com
/j/2/widget.js"></script>
<script>
new TWTR.Widget({
  version: 2,
  type: 'search',
  search: 'google wave',
  interval: 6000,
  title: 'Social Networking Spaces',
  subject: 'Real-time tweets about
Google Wave',
  width: 250,
  height: 300,
  theme: {
    shell: {
      background: '#8ec1da',
      color: '#ffffff'
    },
```

Copy and paste this code into an HTML webpage

OR

Figure 7-38. The Add to Blogger option

Presto! You're taken to Blogger. (You may need to sign in. If Blogger doesn't take you to the screen shown in Figure 7-39 after you sign in, try going back to Twitter and clicking the Add to Blogger button again after you're signed in.) Then, select a blog, add a title, and click the Add Widget button.

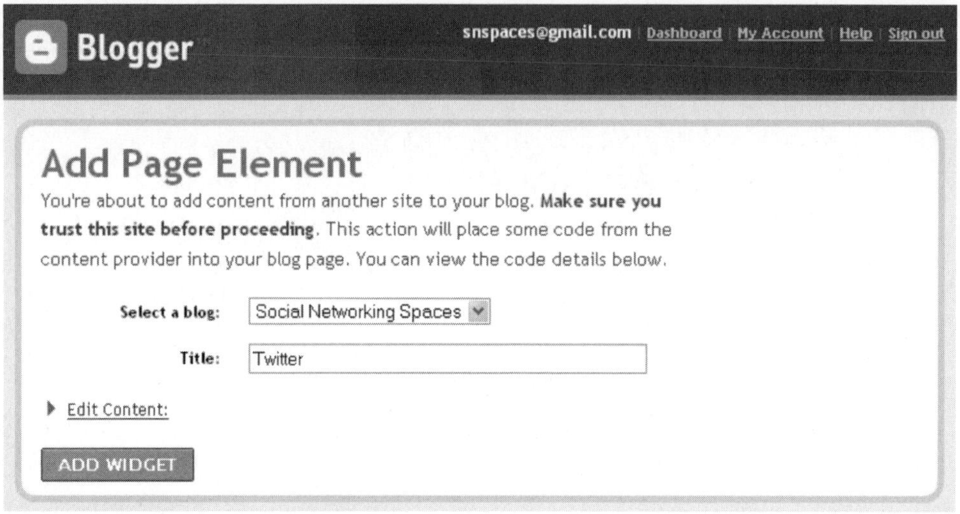

Figure 7-39. Adding a widget to your blog

You're taken to the layout section of Blogger, an easy-to-use visual space where you can click and drag things on your blog into different locations. In this case, you see that the widget has been automatically added, as shown in Figure 7-40.

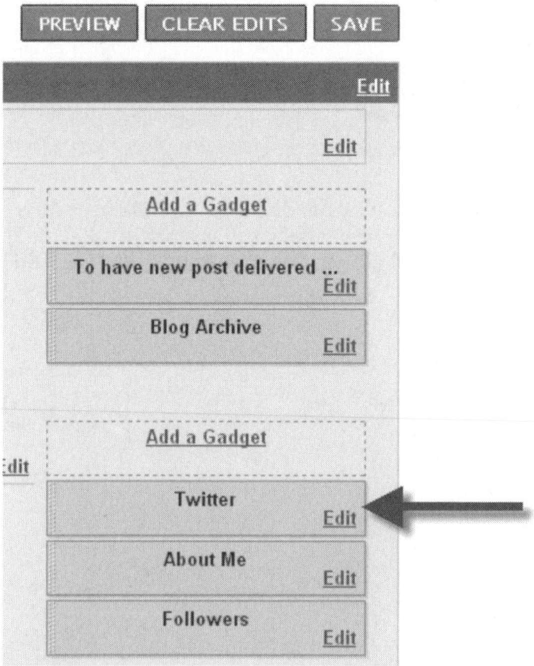

Figure 7-40. Your widget has been added.

So, you can click the Save button.

Then, you should see the widget appear on your blog, along with the live Twitter feed based on the search query you used. See Figure 7-41.

Figure 7-41. Pretty cool! Your widget appears on your blog.

Connecting Twitter to Facebook

Another cool widget is the Facebook widget, which allows you to send your tweets to your Facebook page. Fun!

Sign in, go down to the bottom of the page at Twitter.com, and then click Widgets on the left (see earlier in the chapter for how to get there). Then, click the Facebook option on the left, as shown in Figure 7-42.

Figure 7-42. Click Facebook to select the widget.

Click Facebook Application, as shown in Figure 7-43.

Figure 7-43. Click Facebook Application.

This leads to a screen where you can click the Install Twitter in Facebook button, as shown in Figure 7-44.

Add Twitter to Facebook

Figure 7-44. *Installing Twitter in Facebook*

And then you're taken to Facebook, where you need to sign in. You see a screen like that shown in Figure 7-45, where Facebook confirms that it's cool that you want to let a little blue bird (Twitter) access your Facebook account.

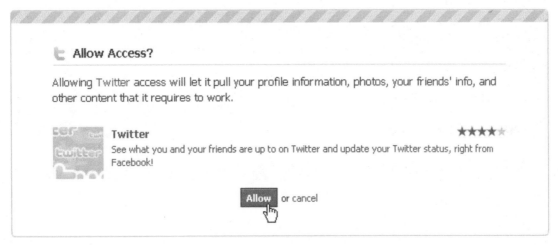

Figure 7-45. *Allowing Twitter to access your Facebook account*

From within Facebook, you need to give the application your *Twitter* login/password, and click Log in. See Figure 7-46.

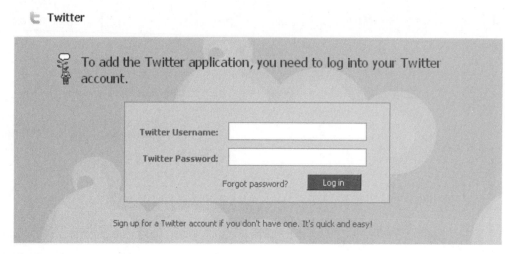

Figure 7-46. Type your Twitter username and password.

This is basically setting up a connection between Facebook and Twitter.

Now you can use Twitter within Facebook. In Figure 7-47, you see how you can enter a tweet in the familiar Facebook interface and click the Update button. This Twitter/Facebook application does allow you to do Twitter, without leaving Facebook.

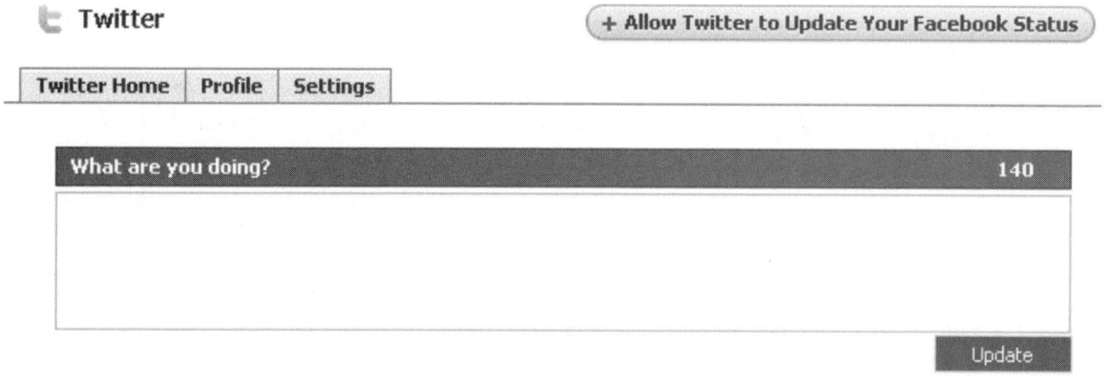

Figure 7-47. Tweeting without leaving Facebook

But I use it to update my Facebook status with Twitter; to enable that feature, you need to click the + Allow Twitter to Update Your Facebook Status button:

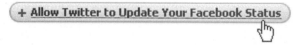

And you need to click Allow Status Updates so that it's approved, as shown in Figure 7-48.

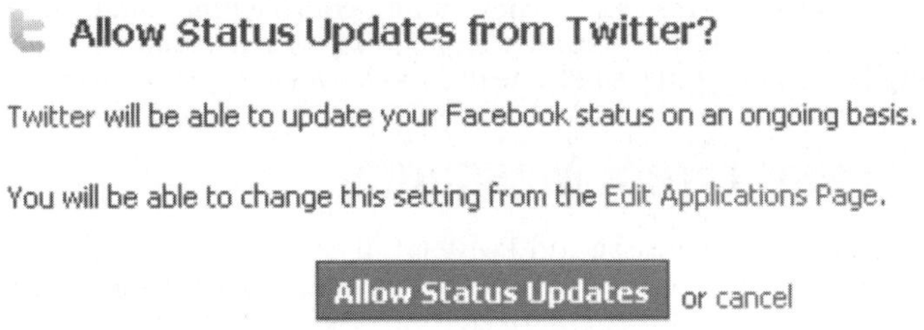
Allow Status Updates from Twitter?
Twitter will be able to update your Facebook status on an ongoing basis.
You will be able to change this setting from the Edit Applications Page.
Allow Status Updates
or cancel

Figure 7-48. Confirm that you want to allow status updates.

Then, you can add tweets in Twitter, as shown in Figure 7-49.

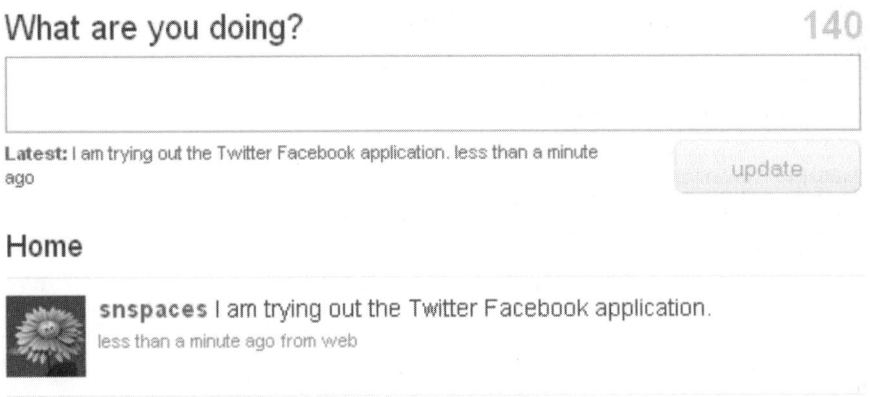
What are you doing?
140
Latest: I am trying out the Twitter Facebook application. less than a minute ago
update
Home
snspaces I am trying out the Twitter Facebook application.
less than a minute ago from web

Figure 7-49. Adding a tweet in Twitter …

Your tweets also appear in Facebook, as shown in Figure 7-50.

Jonathan Doe I am trying out the Twitter Facebook application. via Twitter
- 5 seconds ago clear
Wall
Info
Photos
Video
Notes
+
What's on your mind?
Attach:
Share
Options
Jonathan Doe I am trying out the Twitter Facebook application.
5 seconds ago via Twitter · Comment · Like

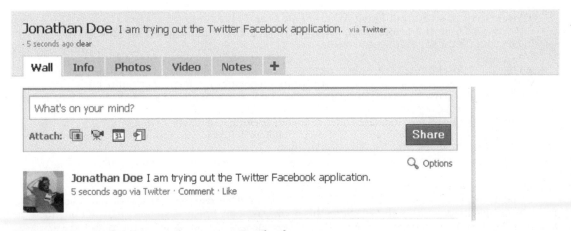

Figure 7-50. … and your tweet shows up on Facebook.

You can enter an update on Twitter, and it goes to both your Twitter followers and your Facebook friends. It's also an easy way to update everyone from a mobile device if you have it enabled in Twitter (see the section "Using Twitter on Your Cell Phone or Mobile Device" in this chapter).

Last but Not Least: Direct Messages

It's possible to send a direct, private message on Twitter, but only to someone who is following you. If you want to try this out and don't have any followers yet, you can follow snspaces (by visiting www.twitter.com/snspaces and clicking the Follow button), and I'll be sure to follow you:

1. Log in to Twitter, and in the Home section on the right side of your screen, click the Direct Messages link.

2. Look for "Send (menu) a direct message," and select a recipient on the drop-down menu.

3. Compose a message, and click the Send button.

Or:

1. Visit the profile page of the Twitter follower you want to send a message to (such as www.twitter.com/snspaces).

2. In the Actions area on the right side of the screen, click the "message" link (for example, "message" snspaces).

3. Compose a message, and click the Send button.

Q/A

Q: Is Twitter just a fad?
A: No.

Q: What do most people use Twitter for?
A: I don't think generalizations apply anymore, but there seems to be a strong theme of news, so people who like getting the latest news seem to be particularly interested. But it's so popular now that it's pretty much become a conversational medium for many, many people.

Q: I want to try something different. What should I use Twitter for?
A: Unless you're at your healthy weight, I invite you to join me and start going to the gym and working on your diet, and tweeting the results.

Q: I like this book, but there are only two chapters on Twitter. Where can I read more?
A: If you liked this book and this chapter or section, keep your eyes open for an entire book from CFTW Press on Twitter. If you want to keep posted about the book's progress, go on Facebook and search for (and join) the Social Networking Spaces Group, or search for (and become a fan of) the Social Networking Spaces Facebook page. I'll post messages once in a while to both, and maybe to the www.twitter.com/snspaces account too, if you'd like to follow it. Just as with this book, all author proceeds will be donated to CFTW. (See the Introduction to this book.) And don't worry if you don't know how to join a group or become a fan. You can learn by reading the Facebook chapters in this book!

Q: What's the difference between Google Buzz and Twitter?
A: Google Buzz has some features similar to Twitter, but it's integrated into Gmail, a free email program. Google Buzz was introduced just as this book was being finished, so there may not be much info in the book; but you can google Google Buzz on www.google.com and look for tutorials and

information (and maybe check Wikipedia). Basically, Google Buzz allows you to make Twitter-like posts with the convenience of being in the same interface as Gmail (which also includes some very helpful free tools like Google Documents, an online equivalent to Open Office and Microsoft Office; Google Sites; Google Calendar, and more). I like a definition of Google Buzz I just read, which called it a "mini-blogging" service (see the article at `http://www.linux-mag.com/id/7703`).

Unlike Twitter, it doesn't have a 140-character limit. But another interesting thing is that it's easy to connect sites you spend time on to Google Buzz, like Twitter, YouTube, Blogger. When you connect sites to Google Buzz, whenever you post something on those sites, Google Buzz automatically lets your Google Buzz followers know. At the time of writing, I haven't used Google Buzz long enough to really have an opinion – but I think it's nice.

Q: Wait! I have another question! Where can I ask it?
A: On `www.snspaces.com`.

Conclusion

Dear Reader,

In this chapter, you learned some of the cool things you can do in Twitter.

A whole world of techniques and things have evolved, so if you find yourself enjoying Twitter, I definitely recommend looking into some of the links and possibly picking up a copy of *Twitter Tips, Tricks, and Tweets* by Paul McFedries. (Or you're welcome to encourage me to write a book about Twitter.)

Best wishes, and happy tweeting!

Regards,

–Todd

P.S. If you've read Chapter 1, you may already know that the Life Story Suitcase is an experimental tool for gathering all your life media from Facebook, Blogger, and so on. The prototype can also help you back up Twitter; so if you like, you're welcome to come by `www.lifestorysuitcase.com`, try it out, and tell us how good or bad the experiment is.

snspaces.com

Come and visit the Social Networking Spaces companion web site at `www.snspaces.com`, where you can find more tips and updates and have an opportunity to share your thoughts or ask questions.

In Living Color: You can visit `www.snspaces.com/pics` to see full-color versions of all the pictures from this chapter.

Twitter Users: To follow Social Networking Spaces on Twitter, visit `www.twitter.com/snspaces` and click Follow.

■ ■ ■

CHAPTER 8

What the Heck Is a Blog?

In This Chapter:

- Introduction: An introduction to what blogs are and what they look like
- Creating your own blog with Google's Blogger: How to create your own blog using the free Blogger service from Google
- Blogger and Wordpress: How to make a blog post that you can share with friends

snspaces.com

Come and visit the Social Networking Spaces companion web site at www.snspaces.com, where you can find more tips and updates and have an opportunity to share your thoughts or ask questions.

In Living Color: You can visit www.snspaces.com/pics to see full-color versions of all the pictures from this chapter.

Praying Mantis Madness: If you'd like to see the blog that inspired the Kahonua "Mr. Mantis" character, visit http://mantisreport.blogspot.com. It was written when I was raising praying mantises. (If you like such things, search for "Mantis Report" on YouTube, and you'll find an amusing video.)

Introduction

A blog is basically a simplified way of sharing things, like an online journal or diary, in a format that can feel something like your own news column. Blogs are usually organized chronologically, containing news, thoughts, and reflections of various kinds, with the latest information showing up at the top, right where you can see it. However, they can be organized however you want.

More than anything else, for most people, a blog is a personal publishing platform. It makes it really easy to have a web site of your own. Blogs have started to catch on, and they offer competition for news web sites to the point that news organizations, politicians, and companies pay very close attention to blogs. The most popular bloggers have a significant influence—but anyone can be a blogger, and that's the point.

Some places let you make a blog for free, such as Google's Blogger (`www.blogger.com`). Wordpress (`www.wordpress.com`) starts free, but you can also add extra services for a charge. You can also go to these sites and just browse other peoples' blogs.

If you really get into it, you can also go to a place like Hostgator.com, get a web hosting account, and use a push-button feature like Fantastico to easily install your own Wordpress. This way, you can control every aspect of the blog.

■ **Note** Fantastico allows you to log into your web hosting account and click a few buttons to trigger the installation of a blog system like Wordpress (instead of having to manually install the software on your web hosting account). Basically, this saves a lot of time and means you can have your own fully-customizable Wordpress site without needing to have the technical skills usually required for installing such software.

Generally speaking, a free blog is fine for most people, and free blogs have a lot of additional features you can add. However, if you have the goal of making money with your blog, you may end up outgrowing the features that come with free blogs. For example, you may want to take advantage of one of the many advanced plug-ins for Wordpress, such as All in One SEO, which attempts to help you get listed closer to the top in Google search results.

Some people make a living blogging, while other people use a blog to share pictures, poetry, or even song lyrics, as shown in Figure 8-1.

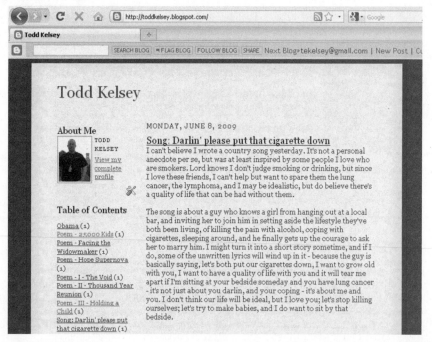

Figure 8-1. A personal blog with some poems and song lyrics. Blogs are so popular because they offer an easy way to express yourself. There's also a bit of magic: the idea that if people like your blog, they may tell other people—kind of like a distant cousin to a cross between a diary and the television show American Idol.

Blogs are a nice way to share pictures, stories, or reflections that contain pictures. It's important to note that a blog is usually public, but it doesn't have to be. You can make a blog and only share it with specific individuals.

■ **Tip** If you only have a moment, read this article about personal safety for bloggers: `http://tinyurl.com/` `safetyforbloggers` or `www.problogger.net/archives/2006/02/07/blog-stalkers-personal-safety-for-` `bloggers/`.

A SPECIAL NOTE FOR PARENTS (AND EVERYONE ELSE) ABOUT PRIVACY AND SAFETY

The nutshell is, if you're not sure, assume everything is public. Unless you learn how to make your blog private, keep in mind that the whole world can see it.

One reader who reviewed a draft of this chapter had this helpful suggestion: "Let people know that if their blog is public, they should be very careful about what kind of info they share. If someone can garner your full name, city, and the names of your kids from your blog, you could be putting your family at risk. My sister-in-law made her blog private after a random stranger made suggestive comments about her kids' pictures."

I do think it's important to make sure you remember the difference between something that is entirely public and something that is semiprivate or entirely private. For example, on Facebook, generally there is some level of privacy by default, yet you can make everything entirely public. In most cases, however, what you post only ends up going to your Facebook friends (unless you choose to set the privacy otherwise). But on Twitter, by default, anything you post is *entirely* public.

A blog is generally public, unless you make it private. (To make a private blog, see Chapter 9.) Some people choose to use only first names or never talk about their physical location. It all depends on what you want to do with your blog. But whatever you do, it's a really good idea to consider some kind of guideline for yourself and write it down. For example, if your blog is public, you may want to write something like, "Never mention x, y, or z," or "Only use first names."

Here is an example forum post offering a response to a query about blog safety: `www.blogsafety.com/topic/Family-Tools-For/Blogger-Safety/1200001134` or `http://tinyurl.com/blogsafety`.

Connectsafely.org shares information about safety on blogs, social networks, and mobile devices for parents and others. The following text is from their About page:

ConnectSafely is for parents, teens, educators, advocates—everyone engaged in and interested in the impact of the social Web. The user-driven, all-media, multi-platform, fixed and mobile social Web is a big part of young people's lives, and this is the central space—linked to from social networks across the Web—for learning about safe, civil use of Web 2.0 together. Our forum is also designed to give teens and parents a voice in the public discussion about youth online safety begun back in the '90s. ConnectSafely also has all kinds of social-media safety tips for teens and parents, the latest youth-tech news, and many other resources.

ConnectSafely.org is a project of Tech Parenting Group, a 501(c)3 nonprofit organization based in Palo Alto, Calif., and Salt Lake City, Utah. The forum is co-directed by Larry Magid of SafeKids.com and Anne Collier of NetFamilyNews.org, co-authors of MySpace Unraveled: What It Is and How to Use It Safely. *(Peachpit Press, Berkeley, Calif., July 2006).*

Now, Back to Our Show

In Figure 8-2, you see how I used a blog to show some pictures of my past life as a rock 'n' roll musician. This simple entry is known as a blog *post*. You'll learn more about how to make a post in the section "Creating Your Own Blog with Google's Blogger"—you're looking at the basics now.

At the time, it was heaven for me to travel around, playing shows. I loved life on the road. I thought to myself, "This is what I'm doing for a living, I don't need to finish that master's degree". But I did end up finishing my M.A. thesis on the tourbus.

And I'm glad I did.

This entry was posted on February 5, 2008 at 3:10 am and is filed under rocknroll, sister soleil. You can follow any responses to this entry through the RSS 2.0 feed. You can leave a response, or trackback from your own site. Edit this entry.

Leave a Reply

Submit Comment

Figure 8-2. A blog post consists of pictures, thoughts, and a spot where you can make a comment.

One of the features of blogs that makes them popular is that a blog provides a way for people to leave a comment, or reply, so blog posts can lead to social interaction. You don't have to enable comments on a blog, but you certainly can. A blog is basically a way to express yourself and to share adventures with your friends. Figure 8-3 is the blog of a friend who is using her blog to share her adventures on a trip to the Philippines, where she is studying to be a midwife.

Figure 8-3. Blogs can be used to share your personal and professional experiences.

Blog systems offer different templates or themes, which allow you to customize the look and feel of the blog (see Figure 8-4).

Figure 8-4. *Using templates, you can choose a visual style you like for your blog, and you can always change it later.*

The heart of a blog is a post. After you log in to a blog, you can type your thoughts, make a title for the entry, and publish it. Then, your blog post immediately goes live. Figure 8-5 shows the interface from the free Blogger service from Google. There's a spot to enter in a title, a larger blank area where you can type, some tools to format the text, and, at the bottom, the Publish Post button.

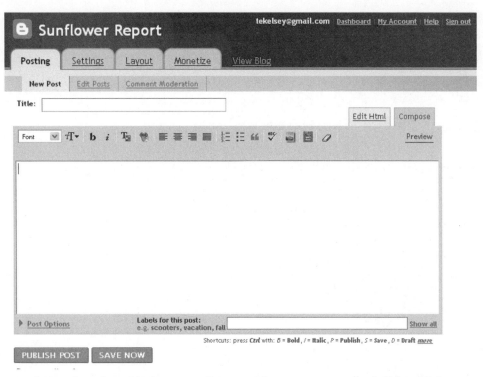

Figure 8-5. *This is where the magic happens. Choose a title, type some text, and click Publish Post.*

The process of making a blog post is similar to the user experience of a word-processing program. In essence, the system makes it a lot easier to make a web page because the system takes care of all the work for you.

It used to be that in order to put something on the Internet, you needed to know a code called HTML, upload the files, and have a monthly account with an Internet hosting company, which provides a place for you to put the files. It's not that traditional web sites have gone away. In fact, many companies and individuals need more than what a blog can do—but for many people, a free blog is just the thing for sharing thoughts and pictures of their lives.

Some blogs are very popular. To get a taste of the top blogs, try visiting Technorati.com and looking at the most popular blog list: `http://technorati.com/pop/blogs/`. As you can see in Figure 8-6, at the time of writing, the three at the tip-top of the top 100 list are the following:

- *The Huffington Post (www.huffingtonpost.com)*: Reports on political and social commentary

- *TechCrunch (www.techcrunch.com)*: Offers the latest news on technology

- *Mashable (www.mashable.com)*: A blog devoted to news on the world of social networking

Blogger Central / top 100 blogs

sort blogs by authority

1. **Breaking News and Opinion on The Huffington Post**

   Darryle Pollack called her first blog "I Never Signed Up For This" in honor of all the times she has said those words at some point in her life as a mother, breast cancer survivor, artist, chocoholic, former TV journalist ...

   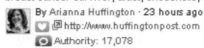 By Arianna Huffington · 23 hours ago
   http://www.huffingtonpost.com
   Authority: 17,078

2. **TechCrunch**

    By Michael Arrington · 32 minutes ago
   http://techcrunch.com
   Authority: 10,506

3. **Mashable!**

   Mashable is a leading tech blog focused on Web 2.0 and Social Networking news. With more than 5 million monthly pageviews, Mashable is the most prolific blog reviewing new Web sites and services, publishing breaking news on whatâ€™s new on the web.

    By Pete Cashmore · 3 hours ago
   http://mashable.com
   Authority: 10,196

Figure 8-6. You may enjoy visiting Technorati to take a peek at some of the most popular blogs. You can also go to any Blogger blog (including your own) and click the Next Blog link at the top of the blog page, which allows you to browse through blogs to see what other people are doing.

Blogs can be created in any language and are popular around the world. For example, the blog shown in Figure 8-7 is from one of the top bloggers in China (`http://blog.sina.com/sfskz`). The blog is on a news/blogging site called sina.com, which is popular in China (a country with hundreds of millions of Internet users). The blogger writes articles about well-known entertainment figures, cars, and other topics regarding popular culture.

Figure 8-7. This post, in Chinese, was written to commemorate the 60th anniversary of the founding of the People's Republic of China.

Creating Your Own Blog with Google's Blogger

OK, time to dive in. It's free, very easy—you can't break anything—and you may have fun doing it!

All you need to do is visit www.blogger.com. If you have a Gmail address, you can enter it and click the Sign In button. If you don't, no problem. Click the Create a Blog button, and Blogger helps you register, as shown in Figure 8-8.

Figure 8-8. *The main page at* www.blogger.com *where you can get started. It works especially nicely if you have a Gmail account, because you can use your Gmail address to log in, but it's not necessary. To start a free Gmail account, go to* http://mail.google.com. *There are also some helpful links on this page to keep in mind for learning more.*

As shown in Figure 8-9, the first step involves entering a display name. This is the name that appears on the blog, and it can be real, a nickname, or an imaginary name. After you've chosen a display name, click Continue. (If desired, you can later change the display name.)

■ **Note** You can create as many blogs as you like and delete them as well, but you may want to try making one for practice.

Figure 8-9. Step one in the sign-up process

Figure 8-10 shows that it's time to name your blog. You can enter a title; but like your display name, you can always change it later. The blog address requires a little more thought, however. Try entering a blog title that you like, and Google automatically suggests a blog address. Then, click the Check Availability link. If it's available, you're good to go. If it's not, try coming up with a different address. Next, click Continue.

Figure 8-10. Coming up with a name for a blog. The fun begins!

As shown in Figure 8-11, you also get to choose a template (which you can also change later). This is one of the fun parts because there are a number of templates that have different colors, backgrounds, and layouts. You can click the "preview template" link to get a closer look at any of them, and you can scroll down to see more. Just click the template you like to select it, and then click Continue.

Figure 8-11. *Choosing a template. There are a variety to choose from, and you can scroll down to see more. You can also click "preview template" to see what they look like.*

You just created a blog! It's as easy as that. Now, click Start Blogging (see Figure 8-12).

Figure 8-12. *Thanks, Google, for making it so easy to help people try these things out.*

Overall, all you really need to do in order to create a blog is: enter a title for your post in the Title field, type in some text, and click the Publish Post button. Clicking Save Now makes a draft, which you can come back and finish or publish later by clicking the Edit Posts link and locating the blog entry.

If you like, you can also enter a label in the "Labels for this post" field, such as "misc," as shown in Figure 8-13. Labels are kind of like categories and can help to keep your blog posts organized.

Figure 8-13. Making a post is as easy as entering a title, typing some text, and clicking Publish Post.

Woo-hoo! Your first blog post (see Figure 8-14).

Your blog post published successfully!

View Post ⊡

Need to change it? **Edit post** | **Create a new post**

Figure 8-14. The confirmation message

Now, you can click the View Post link to see what things look like on your fancy new blog. Figure 8-15 shows the results of the post that was just entered. It's now live on `http://snspaces.blogspot.com` for the whole world to see. Simple as pie.

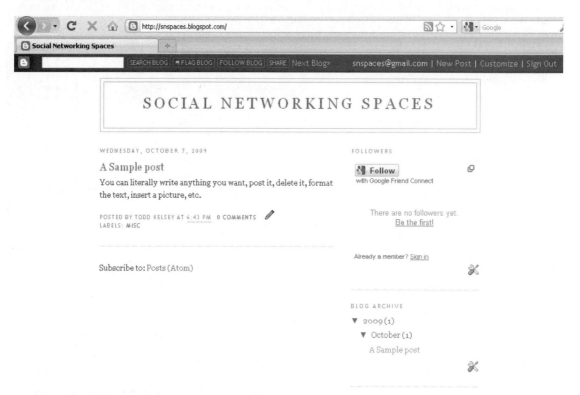

Figure 8-15. Voila! The finished project. Instant blog. Magnifique!

Whenever you like, you can come back to your own blog address/URL (for example, `http://snspaces.blogspot.com`). After you've created your blog, the address appears in the browser in the address bar, so you may want to make a note of it.

When you come back and sign in (either to Blogger.com or by going to your own blog directly), there is a small bar in the upper-right corner, where you can choose to make a new post or customize the blog (make it look different, and so on).When you're done, you can close the browser window or use the Sign Out link, as shown in Figure 8-16.

snspaces@gmail.com | New Post | Customize | Sign Out

Figure 8-16. Some helpful links appear in the upper-right corner of the screen. Go ahead, you won't hurt anything. Click away!

Figure 8-17 illustrates how the blog address appears in the browser and the very top row on the blog page.

Figure 8-17. *How cool: you have your own blog web address! You can copy and paste it into Facebook as a Wall post or into Twitter.*

Blogger and Wordpress

For extra credit, try visiting `www.wordpress.com` and creating a blog there. There are pros and cons to both Blogger and Wordpress. There are other blogging sites too, but these two are some of the best.

Blogger in general is a little easier to use, and it also allows you to use your own web site name for free, such as `www.myblogname.com`. Whenever you register a web site name (at a place like Hostgator.com), even if you don't get a full account to make your own web site, you have to pay a yearly fee for the web site name, also known as a *domain name*. It's usually less than 10 dollars USD. This is also known as a *domain-only account*. However, the nice thing about Blogger is that you can use your own domain name, and you can point it at Blogger. By comparison, you need to pay a yearly fee to have the same feature at Wordpress.

You can add a lot of powerful gadgets to Blogger (sign in ➤ Layout tab ➤ Add a gadget), but Wordpress seems to offer slightly more in the way of features. When you outgrow the capabilities of the free blogging services, Wordpress is the only one where you can have complete control and can use plug-ins like All in One SEO to help boost your web site on Google search results. When you get to that point, you end up needing to get the monthly hosting account at a place like Hostgator.com and then using software like Fantastico on the Hostgator web site to install your own copy of Wordpress. You also have to register your own web site name. For the person who wants more control and advanced features (generally speaking, when you want to try and make money), Wordpress as a hosting company makes sense (see Figures 8-18 and 8-19).

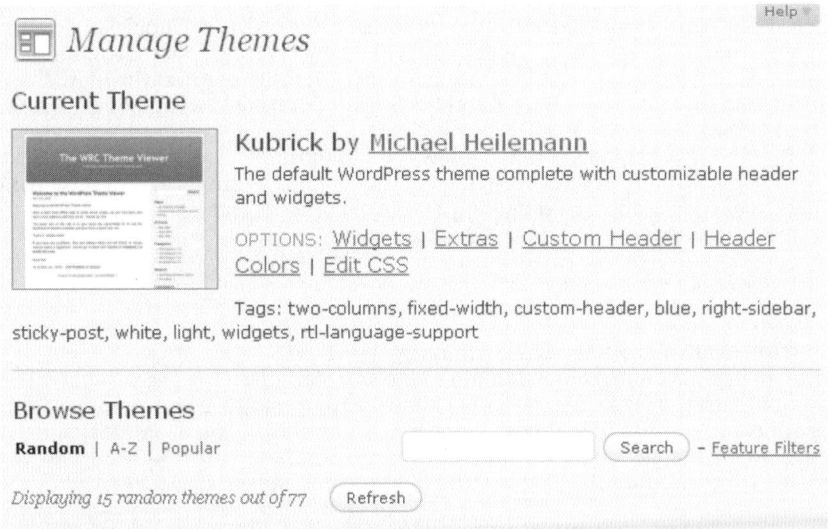

Figure 8-18. *Like Blogger, Wordpress has the ability to use templates, which are called themes.*

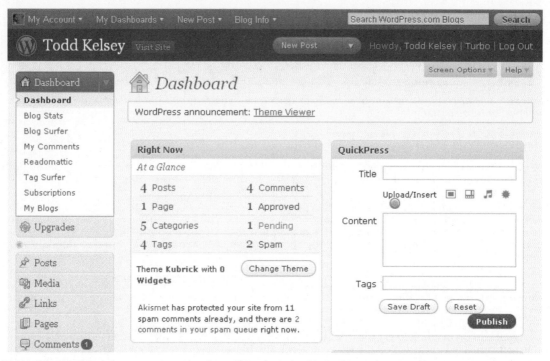

Figure 8-19. *Behind the scenes in a Wordpress blog, you find a dashboard and a place to manage your blog, just as in Blogger. Blogger seems a bit easier to use than Wordpress. The best thing to do is to try both.*

I personally recommend trying Blogger, trying Wordpress, and maybe even reading a book (or two). If you're curious about Wordpress, try entering "wordpress plug-ins" into Google and exploring a bit.

As mentioned, I find it easier to use Blogger, and I like how it's free. I also like being able to have a slightly more professional look and feel by pointing my own web site name at the blog. I've done this in a couple cases using www.sugaros.org, a blog about the Sugar operating system, but in some cases I've reverted back to the free blog.

One thing I like about Wordpress is that it allows you to more easily organize blog posts, like a table of contents, if you're more interested in arranging your blog posts by subjects rather than dates. In Blogger, you have to put some effort into making a table of contents (see http://toddkelsey.blogspot.com), but it can be done.

Q/A

Q: How do I use my own web site name with Blogger?

A: In general, to begin, you register a domain name at a place like Hostgator.com (you don't need a web hosting account, just the web site name, also known as a domain name). Then, you point the name at your blog by adjusting settings in your web site name account (at a place like Hostgator) and also adjust the settings in the Blogger account. For a tutorial example showing how to register and use your own web site name with your Blogger blog, see the Blog section on www.snspaces.com.

Q: How do I make a table of contents in Blogger?

A: In general, you add a label at the end of the post with the title you want to appear in your table of contents. Then, you add and customize the Labels widget in the Layout section of Blogger. For a tutorial, see the Blog section on `www.snspaces.com`.

Q: How often should I post to my blog?
A: As often as you like. You may enjoy making a post once a week to keep things fresh.

Q: How do I let people know about my new blog posts?
A: You can send an e-mail or post the link on Facebook (see Part 2 of this book) to share with your friends. You can also explore how to use Feedburner, which allows you to add a feature where people who want to be notified of new posts can subscribe by entering their e-mail address (instead of having to come back). This process is a little tricky and outside the scope of this book, but what the heck, may as well make a tutorial on `www.snspaces.com`.

Q: I like this book, but there are only two chapters on Blogger. Where can I read more?
A: If you liked this book and this chapter or section, keep your eyes open for an entire book from CFTW Press on Blogger. If you want to keep posted about the book's progress, go on Facebook and search for (and join) the Social Networking Spaces Group, or search for (and become a fan of) the Social Networking Spaces Facebook page. I'll post messages once in a while to both. Just as with *Social Networking Spaces*, all author proceeds for the book on Blogger will be donated to CFTW (see the Introduction to this book). Don't worry if you don't know how to join a group or become a fan. You can learn by reading the Facebook chapters in Part 2 of this book!

Q: Can I make money with a blog?
A: Sure. It takes effort, and it may not be realistic to earn a full-time (or even part-time) income, but there are people who do. My recommendation is, choose an area you have a passion about, and begin writing. To polish your craft, read books from the library about writing; and if you can afford it, take classes and workshops. There are also books on how to promote your blog, and so on. Personally, my perspective is that it all comes back to quality content.

Do your best to choose a topic or series of topics you're interested in, and if possible, think down the road of tying your blog to something that can be sold—in other words, a preexisting business that sells products you can write about and possibly that you could sell eventually (or gain a commission for referring sales). There are thousands and thousands of blogs, but that doesn't mean there's not room for some kind of niche.

Another way to think about making money with blogs is that it could help you to gain customers for some other kind of business—it may not make money itself, but it may serve as a valuable form of marketing, either for a home-based business or for someone's local business. In terms of making money from a blog directly, it's possible to use a product called Google AdSense—try googling it. If you happen to be interested in creating a home-based business, check out `www.digitalarchaeology.org`. If you like the idea of learning how to help local people to capture, preserve, and share their family stories, get in touch, and I'll put together an experiment. One of the next books I'd like to write is particularly in the area of helping people to do these things (including helping people set up related home-based businesses). I think something local with a blog could end up being fairly sustainable. Perhaps you won't make a fortune with it, but it may be a way to get by.

Q: Should I use notes on Facebook or make a separate blog?
A: Notes are a nice feature in Facebook. It's right there, easy to use, no muss, no fuss. It's also possible to share notes on Facebook or e-mail a link to someone to see them. You can include pictures, and notes have many blog-like features.

The nice thing about a blog is that you don't have to be on Facebook. Even though you can share notes outside of Facebook, a blog can potentially have a wider audience, and it also has its own web address (for example, `http://toddkelsey.blogspot.com`). You can even use your own web site name with it.

Q: Is there any way I can browse blogs?

A: You can go to any Blogger blog (including your own) and click the Next Blog link at the top of the blog page, which allows you to browse through blogs to see what other people are doing. Try going to `http://aboutrgb.blogspot.com` and clicking the Next Blog link.

Q: Wait, I have another question! Where can I ask it?

A: On `www.snspaces.com`.

Conclusion

Dear Reader,

In this chapter, you've taken a look at what blogs are, what people use them for, and how to create one. It's very easy to get started, it's free, and it's fun, so you may as well try it!

In the next chapter, you'll take a look at how to upload pictures and have other kinds of bloggery fun, including sharing your blog with other people on Facebook, Twittering about the blog, and so on.

Regards,

–Todd

P.S. If you've read Chapter 1, you may already know the Life Story Suitcase is an experimental tool for backing up your pictures and posts from Facebook, Blogger, Twitter, and so on. The tool helps you to weave the pictures and posts together, to capture and preserve stories from your life. The idea is to share the stories with your family and friends. If you like, when you've had a chance to try Blogger, you're welcome to come by `www.lifestorysuitcase.com` and tell us what you think of the experiment.

snspaces.com

Come and visit the Social Networking Spaces companion web site at `www.snspaces.com`, where you can find more tips and updates and have an opportunity to share your thoughts or ask questions.

In Living Color: You can visit `www.snspaces.com/pics` to see full-color versions of all the pictures from this chapter.

Praying Mantis Madness: If you'd like to see the blog that inspired the Kahonua "Mr. Mantis" character, visit `http://mantisreport.blogspot.com`. It was written when I was raising praying mantises. (If you like such things, search for "Mantis Report" on YouTube, and you'll find an amusing video.)

CHAPTER 9

■ ■ ■

Designing and Sharing Your Blog

In This Chapter:

- Uploading pictures to your blog
- Changing your blog's look and feel
- Sharing on Facebook

snspaces.com

Come and visit the Social Networking Spaces companion web site at www.snspaces.com, where you can find more tips and updates and have an opportunity to share your thoughts or ask questions.

In Living Color: You can visit www.snspaces.com/pics to see full-color versions of all the pictures from this chapter.

Praying Mantis Madness: If you'd like to see the blog that inspired the Kahonua Mr. Mantis character, visit http://mantisreport.blogspot.com—written when I was raising praying mantises. (If you like such things, there's also a mildly amusing video if you search for "Mantis Report" on YouTube.)

Introduction

In this chapter, you look at doing more with your blog, including adding pictures and customizing the way it looks. Then, you learn some ways you can share your blog, which is the best part of the process.

In case you're not quite sure where you'd upload pictures from, generally speaking, you get them on your computer by scanning them (you can buy a scanner at a retail chain that carries electronics, like Target or Walmart, or their web sites) or getting a digital camera (and then transferring photos from the camera to the computer). You may also have a camera phone, in which case your phone company may be happy to charge you a fee for transferring photos by e-mail to your own e-mail account (in some cases, you can buy a cable to transfer photos from the phone to the computer). Whichever way you go, the pictures wind up on the computer, and you need to learn how to locate them.

251

Aside from that, it can also be helpful to rename the pictures, especially if they come from a digital camera. There may be 10 pictures named 1004924.jpg or something like that—so it's a good idea to look at them and rename them so that you know which ones to upload.

One other suggestion: if you're taking a series of pictures, try separating the best ones for uploading to your blog. The great thing about digital cameras is being able to take as many pictures as you like—then you can pick the best pics. But that's also one of the problems with digital cameras—if you upload every single picture you take, it can bore people and distract them from the story you want to tell. There are no rules, and you should do what you feel like—it's *your* blog, not mine, not your audience's. But if you want the best effect, pick the best pictures.

Uploading Pictures

To upload pictures to your blog, start by signing in to the blog and clicking the New Post button, shown in Figure 9-1.

Figure 9-1. Click the New Post button.

Then, enter a title for your post, and click the little square Insert Image icon, as shown in Figure 9-2, which is to the right of the ABC/checkmark icon.

Figure 9-2. Insert Image icon

This starts the process of uploading the image. You first click the Browse button and locate the image you want (see Figure 9-3).

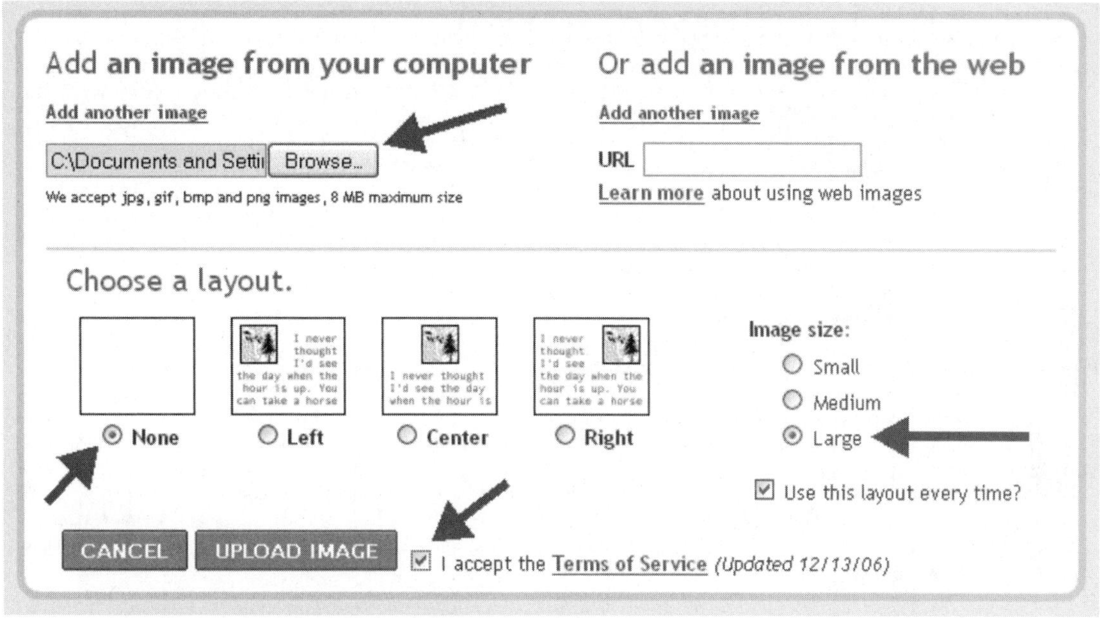

Figure 9-3. *Click Browse, and locate an image.*

Starting at the top of Figure 9-3:

- After you click the Browse button and locate the desired picture, you can click the "Add another image" link or move on.

- In the layout section, I prefer the None option. The other options place the image on the left (with text on the right of the image), center, or right, and so on.

- For the image size, I like going with Large.

- You need to click the "I accept the Terms of Service" check box.

- Then, you can click the Upload Image button.

You get a confirmation message after the image is uploaded, and then you can click the Done button (see Figure 9-4).

Your image has been added.

After clicking "Done" you can change your post and publish to your blog.

Figure 9-4. Click Done.

Your post ends up looking something like Figure 9-5.

Figure 9-5. Post after you add an image

Shuffling Pictures

For some reason, Blogger may insert your picture at the top of the blog post (even if you're writing and insert the picture at a certain point). If this happens, and you want to type some text before the picture, you can click the picture to select it (see Figure 9-6).

Figure 9-6. Click the picture to select it.

Then, press the left arrow on your keyboard to place the cursor to the left of the image. Press Enter a few times to move the picture down, and then use the up arrow key to move the cursor back to the beginning, as shown in Figure 9-7.

Figure 9-7. Move the cursor back to the top.

You can now type your introductory text, if you like (see Figure 9-8).

Figure 9-8. Type text before the photo.

You may choose to upload all your pictures and then type. Or, when you're uploading, you can use the layout option that places the pictures on the left and text directly to the right of the pictures. The best thing to do is to experiment. If you're looking for the easiest way to do things, here it is: when you're uploading pictures, choose the Left layout and the Small picture size, and be sure to leave a note in your post to let people know they can click pictures to see a larger version—something like "(Note: You can click pictures to see larger versions)."

Cutting and Pasting Pictures into Place

You can also overcome the issue of uploaded pictures appearing at the top of the post by cutting them and pasting them exactly where you want them, instead of fussing with the arrow key. First, upload a picture like the one in Figure 9-9.

Figure 9-9. *Upload a photo.*

When it appears at the top of the post, click it. Then, to cut the image, choose Edit ➤ Cut (or Ctrl + X key on Windows, or Apple key + X key on the Mac). Place the cursor where you want the picture to appear in the blog post. To paste the image, choose Edit ➤ Paste (or Ctrl + V key on Windows, or Apple key + V key on the Mac). Your image is now exactly where you want it, as shown in Figure 9-10.

Figure 9-10. *A cut-and-pasted image in its new location*

Now, you can click the Publish Post button. And when all's said and done, you have a complete blog post—with pictures (see Figure 9-11)!

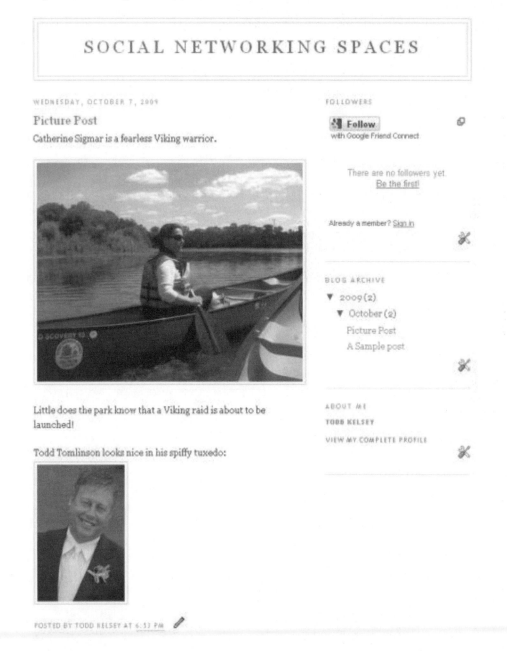

Figure 9-11. Blog post with pictures

Customizing Your Blog

One of the nice things about blogging is that you can customize how things look, to suit your needs. If you require the maximum amount of variety and specially designed templates, you can always go for a *paid* blogging service. (See the blog section on www.snspaces.com for some suggestions.) My personal recommendation for blogging is to start with one or more of the free blogging services, try them, concentrate on writing interesting relevant content and including interesting pictures, and then—when you have a significant number of people visiting the blog—explore paid blogging services.

But one nice thing about free blogging sites is that they're *free* and therefore very sustainable—they're also somewhat easier to manage, with fewer hassles. And free blogging sites like Blogger.com and Wordpress.com have a lot of options.

Changing the Profile Picture

One of the first things you may want to do is upload a profile picture (a picture of yourself, or your dog, or anything else) to give the blog a personal feel. To do this, log in to the blog, and click the Edit Profile link (next to the grey picture with the silhouette in it in Figure 9-12).

Figure 9-12. Click the Edit Profile link.

In the Photograph area of the Profile, click the Choose File button (see Figure 9-13), locate the desired picture, and double-click it.

Figure 9-13. The Choose File button

When you're done, you see a preview of the picture, as shown in Figure 9-14.

Figure 9-14. Profile picture preview

Click the Save profile button (see Figure 9-15).

Figure 9-15. The Save Profile button

Then, click the Dashboard link to go back to the Dashboard (see Figure 9-16).

Figure 9-16. The Dashboard link

Your profile picture appears in the Dashboard, as shown in Figure 9-17.

Figure 9-17. Profile picture in the Dashboard

It appears in a little box on your blog (see Figure 9-18).

Figure 9-18. Profile picture on your blog

Rearranging Elements on the Blog

Your blog allows you to reposition the way things appear. For example, by default, the About Me box may appear at the bottom, but you can place it at the top. To do this, first log in to the blog; on the Dashboard, click the Layout link (next to the New Post button in Figure 9-19).

Figure 9-19. Click the Layout link.

The Layout screen appears, with the About Me box in the lower-right corner (see Figure 9-20).

| Posting | Settings | **Layout** | Monetize | View Blog |

| **Page Elements** | Fonts and Colors | Edit HTML | Pick New Template |

Add and Arrange Page Elements
Click and drag to rearrange page elements on your blog.

PREVIEW · CLEAR EDITS · SAVE

| | **Navbar** | Edit |

Social Networking Spaces (H...
Edit

Blog Posts	**Add a Gadget**
	Followers
	Edit
	Blog Archive
	Edit
	About Me
	Edit
Edit	

Figure 9-20. *The Layout screen*

Click the About Me box (see Figure 9-21), and drag it into a new position, as shown in Figure 9-22.

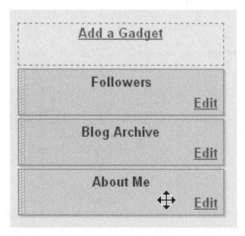

Figure 9-21. *The About Me box*

261

Figure 9-22. About Me, moved to a new position

Then, click Save (see Figure 9-23).

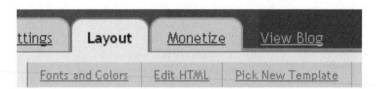

Figure 9-23. Click the Save button.

Changing the Template

Changing the template is like trying on a new outfit or seeing what something would look like if it were painted different colors. It's a fun way to try out a different look and feel for your blog. Remember, you can't break anything, and you may have fun!

To get rolling, go to your Dashboard, click the Layout tab, and choose the Pick New Template link (see Figure 9-24).

Figure 9-24. Pick New Template link

You end up with a screen with a lot of different options you can choose from, as shown in Figure 9-25.

The best thing to do is start clicking. The screen shows various templates that artists have created, and different versions of those templates. You can get a general idea of what they look like from the thumbnail images; and when you select a new option, you can click the "preview template" link to see what it looks like.

Select a new template for your blog.

Changing your template will discard any changes you made in Fonts & Colors. Your Page Elements will be retained.

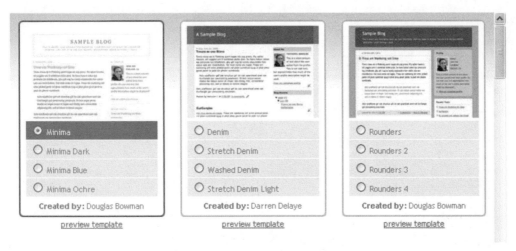

Figure 9-25. *Select a new blog template.*

Note that Figure 9-25 shows three templates, each with four different variations (indicated by the radio buttons—Minima, Minima Dark, and so on). And you can see more templates by using the scroll bar on the right to scroll down. Woohoo!

For example, you can click the Rounders option, shown in Figure 9-26.

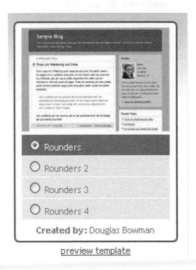

Figure 9-26. *The Rounders option*

If you click the "preview template" link, it opens a window that gives you a preview of how the blog will look with the new Rounders template, as shown in Figure 9-27 (try comparing this with the blog as it looked a few pages ago).

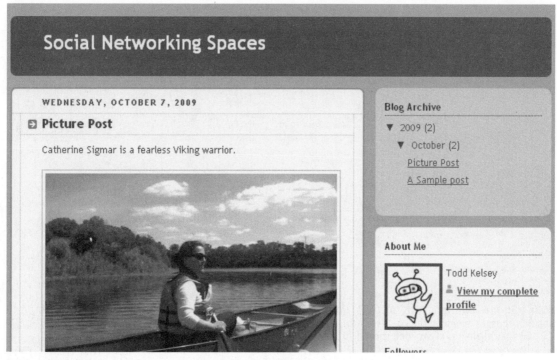

Figure 9-27. The blog with a new template

When you like how things look, click the Save Template button (see Figure 9-28).

Select a new template for your blog.

Changing your template will discard any changes you made in Fonts & Colors. Your Page Elements will be retained.

SAVE TEMPLATE

Figure 9-28. Click Save Template.

Fonts and Colors

If you didn't get enough of coloring with crayons in school, then you can play with colors on your blog. Try clicking the Fonts and Colors link under the Layout tab (see Figure 9-29).

CHAPTER 9 ■ DESIGNING AND SHARING YOUR BLOG

Figure 9-29. *The Fonts and Colors link*

As Willy Wonka would say, it's a world of pure imagination. Start clicking the options shown in Figure 9-30, preferably in a wild fashion.

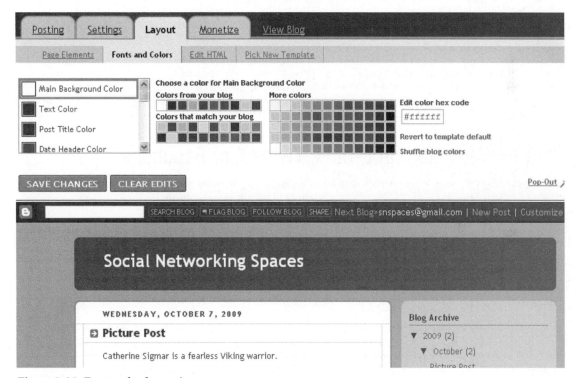

Figure 9-30. *Font and color options*

For example, you can click Text Color (see Figure 9-31).

Figure 9-31. *Text Color*

Then, click a color you like, as shown in Figure 9-32.

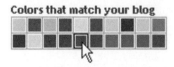

Figure 9-32. Click a color you like.

And then click Save Changes (see Figure 9-33).

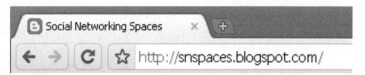

Figure 9-33. Save Changes

See how easy that was?

Ten points for creating the most nauseatingly disgusting color combination you possibly can, making a make-believe blog with a political tirade on it, and then deleting it.

Or ten points for creating the most ridiculous, brain-popping, psychedelic, headache-inspiring color scheme and writing a real or imagined blog about where you were and what you were doing in the 1960s or 70s (or posing as your parents, if you weren't born yet).

Sharing Your Blog on E-mail, Twitter, or Facebook

In the end, this is the really fun part. Of course, you can copy your blog address from the browser (for example, `http://snspaces.blogspot.com`, as shown in Figure 9-34), and paste it into an e-mail.

![Browser showing Social Networking Spaces with address http://snspaces.blogspot.com/]

Figure 9-34. Copy your blog address.

Or you can log on to Twitter and *paste your blog address into a tweet*! Woohoo! (See Chapters 5 and 6.)

But Facebook is also a very nice way to share, with a built-in audience. When you post a link about your blog, it automatically goes into your friends' News Feeds; and if you uploaded a picture, you can choose an image to display with the announcement that you've made a new blog post.

Note that the best thing to do is all of the above—including dropping an e-mail to people who you want to make sure get your latest blog post. Even though Facebook is a great way to share, not everyone reads their entire News Feed every day—and if a person has a lot of Facebook friends, your post may get buried in a lot of stuff. If you know they have an interest in hearing about the latest post (perhaps they're your close friends or family members), drop them an e-mail.

Begin by copying your blog address (see Figure 9-34), and then go to Facebook and look for the kind of box shown in Figure 9-35.

Figure 9-35. Look for a box like this on Facebook.

You can go about this two ways. The easy way is to click "What's on your mind?", type a comment, and paste the link into the box. The other way is to click the Link icon, as shown in Figure 9-36, and paste your blog address in the Link area.

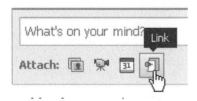

Figure 9-36. The Link icon

Either way, Facebook adds the link to your Wall post. If you have any pictures in your blog post, a thumbnail image also appears, as shown in Figure 9-37.

Figure 9-37. The link is added to your Wall post.

If you want, you can cycle through the thumbnail images by clicking the little arrows (see Figure 9-38).

Figure 9-38. *Click the arrows to cycle through the thumbnails.*

When you do, a different picture appears, as shown in Figure 9-39.

Figure 9-39. *A different image for the post*

Then, type something in the box, as shown in Figure 9-40, and click the Share button.

Figure 9-40. *Type a message in the box.*

Your Wall entry appears on your Wall (see Figure 9-41).

Figure 9-41. *The post appears on your Wall.*

Adding Your Blog Address to Your Facebook Profile

Another nice thing you can do is add your blog address to your Facebook profile, so that if someone looks at your profile, they see that you have a blog—and they may go look at it. To do this, log in to Facebook, and click Profile (see Figure 9-42).

Figure 9-42. *The Profile link*

Then, click the Info tab (see Figure 9-43).

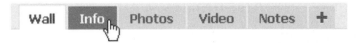

Figure 9-43. *The Info tab*

In the Contact Information area, roll the mouse over the area to the right, and click the little Edit icon, as shown in Figure 9-44.

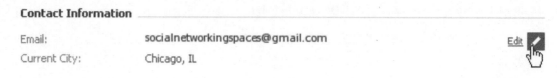

Contact Information
Email:
socialnetworkingspaces@gmail.com
Edit
Current City:
Chicago, IL

Figure 9-44. *The Edit icon*

Doing so allows you to add your blog address in the Website field, as shown in Figure 9-45. Then, click the Save Changes button.

Website:
http://snspaces.blogspot.com
Create a Facebook badge for your website
Save Changes
Cancel

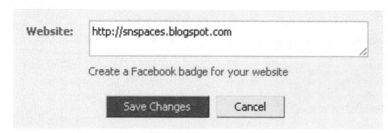

Figure 9-45. *Add your blog address.*

And when a friend looks at your profile, they can see your blog address, as shown in Figure 9-46.

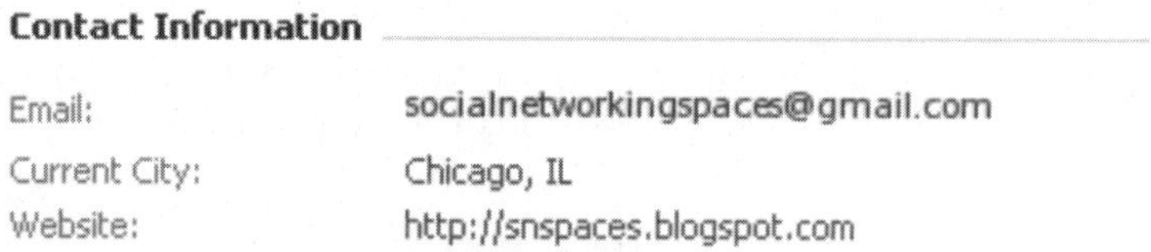
Contact Information
Email:
socialnetworkingspaces@gmail.com
Current City:
Chicago, IL
Website:
http://snspaces.blogspot.com

Figure 9-46. *The blog address appears in your profile.*

For additional fun, you can add more than one blog or web site address, or you're welcome to put the Sunflower Club web site address (see Figure 9-47).

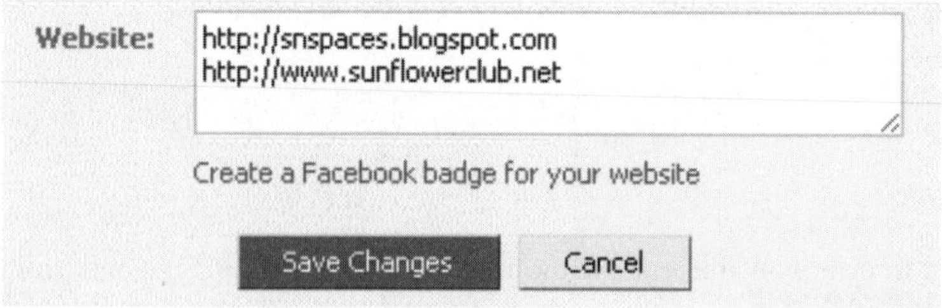
Website:
http://snspaces.blogspot.com
http://www.sunflowerclub.net
Create a Facebook badge for your website
Save Changes
Cancel

Figure 9-47. *Adding multiple web addresses*

Making a Private Blog

You can create more than one blog with .Blogger (just sign in and click "Create a blog"). And if you like, a blog can be private. (If you skipped over it, I definitely recommend reading the special note on privacy in the previous chapter.)

To make a blog private, choose the following: Settings ➤ Permissions ➤ Blog Readers ➤ Only people I choose OR Only blog authors ➤ type in e-mail addresses ➤ click Invite. Here are the steps:

1. Sign in to Blogger, click the Settings tab, and then click the Permissions link (see Figure 9-48).

Figure 9-48. Permissions link

2. Click the option "Only people I choose" or "Only blog authors," as shown in Figure 9-49. For example, "Only people I choose" may be friends or family (or no one). "Only blog authors" may be family members, if you're using Blogger to capture, preserve, and share private family stories; or may be multiple people collaborating on something that isn't public yet.

 Blog Readers Your blog can have up to 100 readers.

Figure 9-49. Choose who can view the blog.

3. Enter e-mail addresses, and click the Invite button (see Figure 9-50).

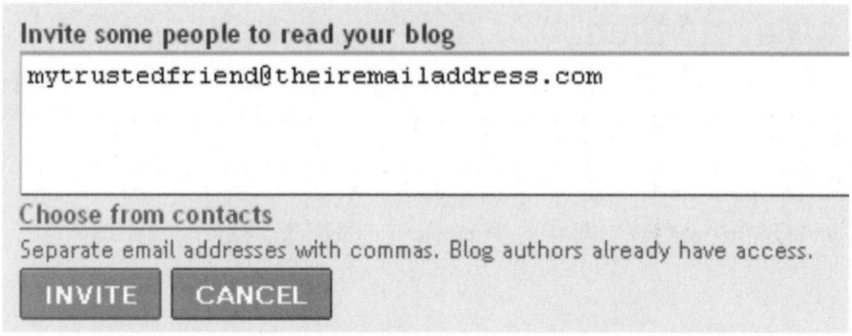

Invite some people to read your blog

mytrustedfriend@theiremailaddress.com

Choose from contacts

Separate email addresses with commas. Blog authors already have access.

INVITE   CANCEL

Figure 9-50. Enter addresses, and click Invite.

That's it!

Q/A

Q: What's the best way to manage my pictures?

A: Personally, I recommend using the free software Picasa from Google. I'm very impressed with the ease of use and the way it lets you edit things. One of my favorite features is the Fill Light effect, which does a very impressive job of brightening pictures without messing them up. In addition, some functions in Picasa let you automatically post pictures to your Blogger blog.

Q: How do I know what size to make my digital pictures?

A: The best thing to do is learn a bit about *pixels*. Try entering the word in Google and on Wikipedia and looking into *digital pictures, digital images, digital image basics*, and so on—but in a nutshell, pixels are the individual dots that make up a digital picture. As cameras get more powerful, they can take pictures with a greater number of pixels in them; this is the basis of the term *megapixels* (1 megapixel equals 1,000 pixels). A 5-megapixel camera may be able to take a picture that is 5,000 pixels wide.

It can get a bit confusing, but the basic rule of thumb is, if you want to be able to print your digital pictures, then the greater the number of pixels you use (cameras have different quality settings), the better quality the print will be. But if you only want 4 x 6 prints, 1 megapixel is fine; you can think of this as 1024 x 768 (1,024 pixels wide and 768 tall). In the end, the best thing to do is experiment.

As for me, in order to save on file size and how many pictures I can fit in the camera, and because I rarely ever print larger than a 4 x 6 print, I don't go higher than 1 megapixel, or 1024 x 768. When I need to resize pictures for the Web, I often make them about 600 pixels wide—to me, this is big enough to see easily. Experiment! And try www.picresize.com.

Q: I like this book, but there are only two chapters about Blogger. Where can I read more?

A: If you like this book and this chapter or section, keep your eyes open for an entire book from CFTW Press about Blogger. If you want to keep posted about the book's progress, go on Facebook and search for (and join) the Social Networking Spaces Group, or search for (and become a fan of) the Social Networking Spaces Facebook page. I'll post messages once in a while to both. Just as with *Social Networking Spaces*, all author proceeds for the book on Blogger will be donated to CFTW. (See the Introduction to this book.) And don't worry if you don't know how to join a group or become a fan. You can learn by reading the Facebook chapters in this book!

Q: Who is that handsome looking guy in the tuxedo in the picture examples? Wait a second, isn't he a Drupal expert?

A: Yes, that's Todd Tomlinson—and if for any reason you have the need of a Jedi master to make a web site for your library, local government, college, or large corporation, he's the man. He's a fellow Drupal enthusiast (my PhD dissertation is on making web sites in different languages with, among other things, open source content-management systems like Drupal—see `www.drupal.org`, or look it up on Wikipedia. Basically, it's a great way to do sustainable web sites—`www.recovery.gov` was launched on it, for example). He's VP of a company called ServerLogic, and they do great work. One unwritten chapter of this book would be making a social network–type site completely from scratch, so that unlike Ning, you control everything—Drupal would be a good platform for that, and Todd could help you out. Or read his forthcoming book, *Beginning Drupal 7*. Also, if you're interested in this digression (like, *really* interested), I'd be glad to send you a copy of my dissertation.

Q: Wait! I have another question! Where can I ask it?
A: On `www.snspaces.com`.

Conclusion

Dear Reader,

Thank you for reading this chapter. You've taken a look at how to upload pictures, change the template around, and experiment with colors. And, most important, you've looked at some of the ways you can share your blog posts.

So welcome to the world of blogging, and be sure to click everything! Learning about how to do it is all about exploration.

If you like, check out the `www.snspaces.com` site, and submit a link to your blog there.

And if you feel like it, please feel free to tell your audience about this book you read; or look at `www.snspaces.com` and, if you like it, make a little blog article about it, and encourage your friends to visit. If you go to `www.snspaces.com` and you don't see enough helpful information, then contribute some! Or just ask questions.

Don't forget, one of the best ways of learning is to teach someone, so I personally invite you to make a blog and then solidify your learning … by showing someone else how to do it. Woohoo! Try showing someone significantly older than yourself. Or significantly younger.

Regards,

–Todd

P.S. If you've read Chapter 1, you may already know the Life Story Suitcase is an experimental tool for backing up your pictures and posts from Facebook, Blogger, Twitter, and so on. The tool helps you to weave the pictures and posts together, to capture and preserve stories from your life. The idea is to share the stories with your family and friends. If you like, when you've had a chance to try Blogger, you're welcome to come by `www.lifestorysuitcase.com` and tell us what you think of the experiment.

snspaces.com

Come and visit the Social Networking Spaces companion web site at www.snspaces.com, where you can find more tips and updates and have an opportunity to share your thoughts or ask questions.

In Living Color: You can visit www.snspaces.com/pics to see full-color versions of all the pictures from this chapter.

Praying Mantis Madness: If you'd like to see the blog that inspired the Kahonua Mr. Mantis character, visit http://mantisreport.blogspot.com—written when I was raising praying mantises. (If you like such things, there's also a mildly amusing video if you search for "Mantis Report" on YouTube.)

■ ■ ■

CHAPTER 10

Using Flickr to Share Pictures

In This Chapter:

- Introduction to Flickr
- Creating an account
- Finding friends who are already on Flickr

snspaces.com

Come and visit the Social Networking Spaces companion web site at www.snspaces.com, where you can find more tips and updates and have an opportunity to share your thoughts or ask questions.

In Living Color: You can visit www.snspaces.com/pics to see full-color versions of all the pictures from this chapter.

Introduction

This chapter is dedicated to the Isdales, who have been a good influence on me, including: Chuck, who has encouraged me to take pictures and have fun; Christine; Rachael; and, of course, Jazmine (the family dog, who is patient with photographers and always up for a good romp around the block). Chuck has a good outlook on life and is an excellent example of a spirit of fun and adventure with photography. He exemplifies the spirit of Flickr and was my first exposure to it.

Flickr is a popular social networking site that enables you to share pictures and provides opportunities for connecting to other people who have similar interests. It's especially well suited for people who like photography.

In some ways, because of how many people are on Flickr, it's become like a search engine for pictures. Magazines, newspapers, and advertising agencies often use professional photographers or look in stock photography catalogs for images; but increasingly, even professional publications look at Flickr, and sometimes they ask for permission to license a photograph (and sometimes pay for the privilege). This chapter covers how to use Flickr to share photos and search for images.

Getting Started: Searching Flickr

The site has so many photos on it, there's a good chance that there will be a picture that corresponds to just about anyone or anything you type into the search box. Even before you create your own account, you may want to visit `www.flickr.com`, type something in the box, and click Search (see Figure 10-1).

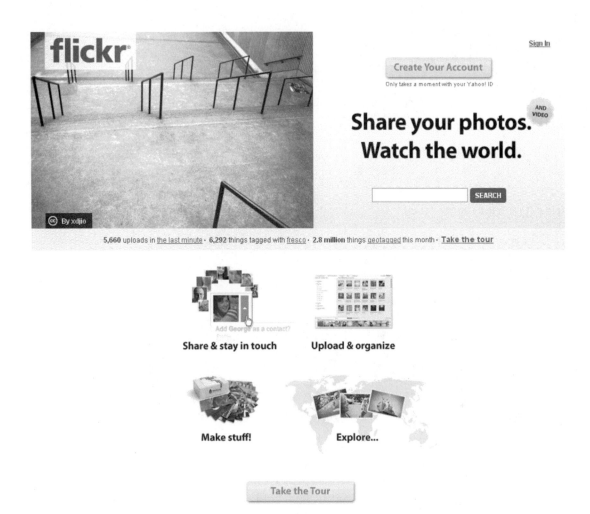

Figure 10-1. *Searching photos on Flickr*

Flickr provides standard online picture-sharing capabilities, as well as online tools for editing pictures, and easy ways to take pictures and print them in albums and on t-shirts, mugs, calendars, and the like.

For an example of a photo search, go to Flickr and type "Chuck Isdale" (see Figure 10-2).

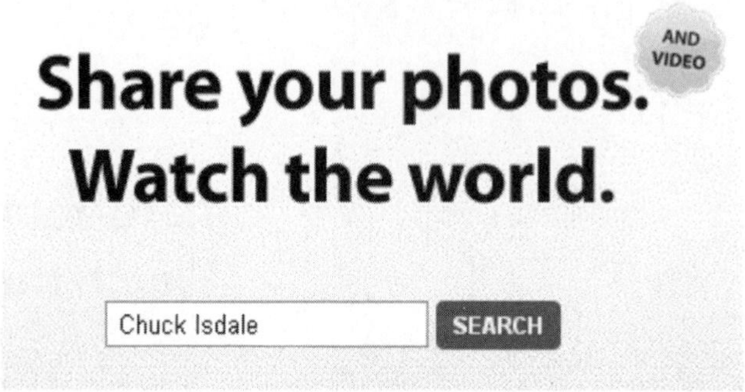

Share your photos. AND VIDEO
Watch the world.

Chuck Isdale   SEARCH

Figure 10-2. Searching for Chuck

Click Search, and you see several pictures of Chuck, taken by various photographers (see Figure 10-3), including my favorite, with Chuck sitting on a monstrously large chicken (see Figure 10-4).

Figure 10-3. Chuck through the lens of various photographers

Sirchuckles has a "chicken" moment

Figure 10-4. Chuck and his chicken

Chuck seems relaxed in the photo, whereas the chicken appears wide-eyed and entirely wired on caffeine. (Note: You have permission to put the book down and go on www.flickr.com and start searching for anything that interests you. The chapter will be here for you when you return.)

If you're ready to explore, you're also welcome to try searching for "Miss September 1864" (see Figure 10-5).

Photos | Groups | People

Miss September 1864 | SEARCH

Figure 10-5. Searching for Miss September

You get a list of results. Click the photo shown in Figure 10-6.

From sirchuckles

Figure 10-6. Isn't she lovely?

When you click the image, you come to the core of Flickr, which is a page just for the photo. It usually includes a title, the picture, any description the photographer writes, and the social opportunity for visitors to add a comment. See Figure 10-7.

Miss September 1864

This restored photo from a Cabinet card of Miss September 1864 published by "The Colonel" - like the Stereoview posted earlier in this stream, features the usual verbage about "for the Cause" on the verso of the card. However it does mention "delicately hand tinted for your viewing enjoyment." While I have not researched the genre of "upskirt" photography, this clearly is a rather early example of such photography - despite Wikipedia's suggestion that it is a relatively recent cultural phenomemnon (that I don't grok)

--sir"I captured this last week and fabricated this story"chuckles

Comments

 xxmachonexx pro says:

The "delicate tinting" does add to the photo.
Posted 17 months ago. (permalink)

Would you like to comment?

Sign up for a free account, or sign in (if you're already a member).

Figure 10-7. *A restored Miss September, complete with comments and a detailed description*

Flickr allows you to completely customize how you want pictures to display. You can make them public or private, and you can choose who can see them.

Taking a Tour

The best way to get to know Flickr is to explore, and one way is to click the Take a Tour link on the main page of www.flickr.com, shown in Figure 10-8.

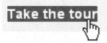

Figure 10-8. *Click here to start your tour.*

You see an introductory screen with a Start the Magical Feature Tour link at the bottom, as shown in Figure 10-9.

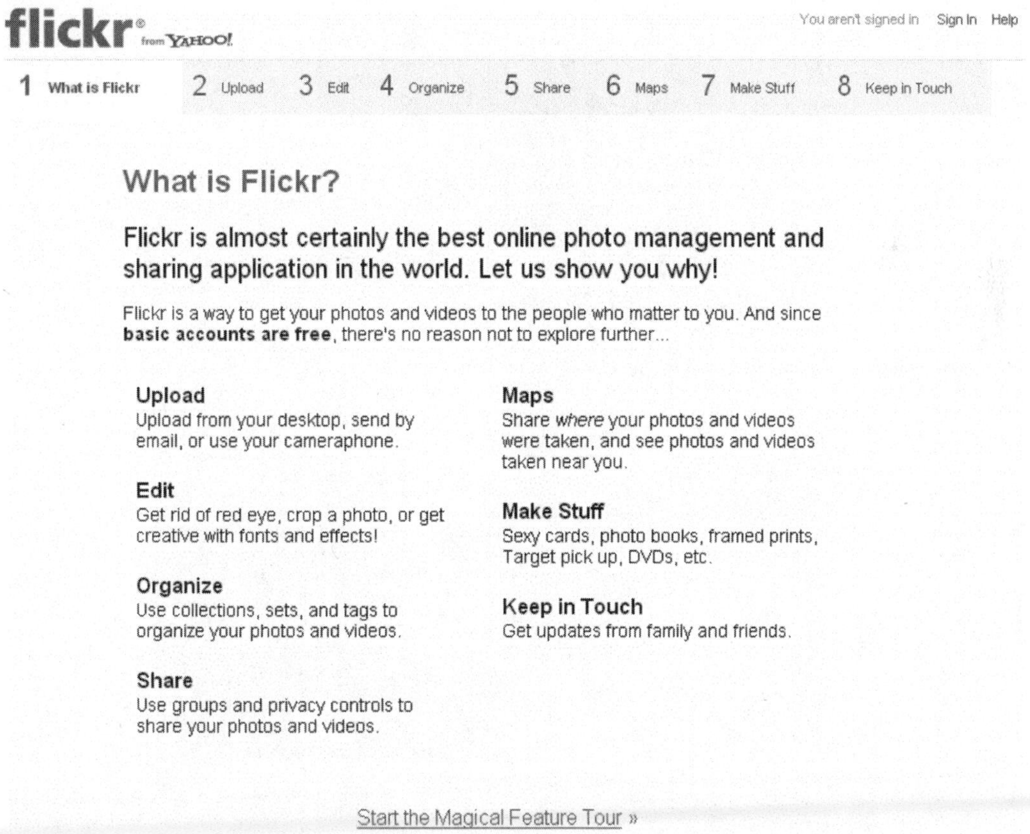

Figure 10-9. *Beginning the tour*

Another interesting feature of Flickr is the way you can *geotag* photographs, so that people can see photographs you've taken based on where they were shot.

There is a related map you can explore. Depending on which page you're on and whether you're logged in, you can get to it a couple different ways. You may see a sentence like the one in Figure 10-10 somewhere on the Flickr page, with a World Map link.

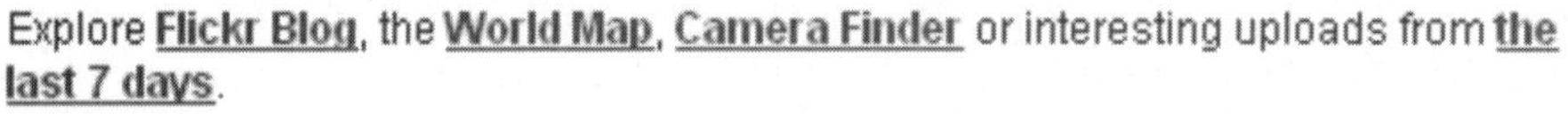

Explore **Flickr Blog**, the **World Map**, **Camera Finder** or interesting uploads from **the last 7 days**.

Figure 10-10. Depending on how often Flickr redesigns its page, you should be able to find a link like this.

On the World Map is a feature where you can type in a location:

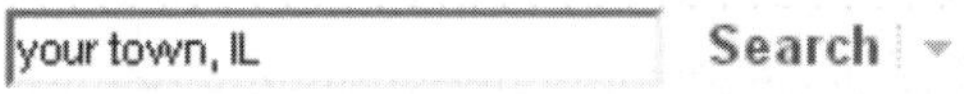

your town, IL   Search ▾

Pictures are marked by dots, which you can click. See Figure 10-11.

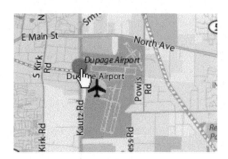

Figure 10-11. Click a dot to view an image based on location.

A picture pops up, as shown in Figure 10-12.

Figure 10-12. Ta-da! An image with a brief description.

If you click the picture, you go to the picture page, as you see in Figure 10-13.

A friend, with a sunset in the background

One evening my friend Todd (pictured) and I were driving to dinner discussing the fine sunset that was present that evening. During our conversation a comment along the lines of "take a photo of it" came up - So - I pulled over and did just that - putting him in front of it. (for me most sunsets are beautifull but they need another element to make the picture more interesting.)

Interestingly, this is the only time a police officer has pulled over to check out wheat I was doing. He was very cool about it - diodn't even get out of his car - and he agreed that the sunset was worthy of a picture. We were within 50 ft of the perimeter fence for an airport - so he might have been obligated to ask.

-- from the archives

Would you like to comment?

Sign up for a free account, or sign in (if you're already a member).

Figure 10-13. Click the image to be taken to the photo's page.

Creating an Account

Now that you've gotten a taste of the kinds of things you can find on Flickr, let's look at how to start an account of your own. First, click the Create Your Account button on `www.flickr.com`, as shown in Figure 10-14.

Only takes a moment with your Yahoo! ID

Figure 10-14. Your first step to creating your own Flickr account

If you have a Yahoo ID already, you can sign in. If you don't, you need to click the Sign Up link at the bottom of the window. See Figure 10-15.

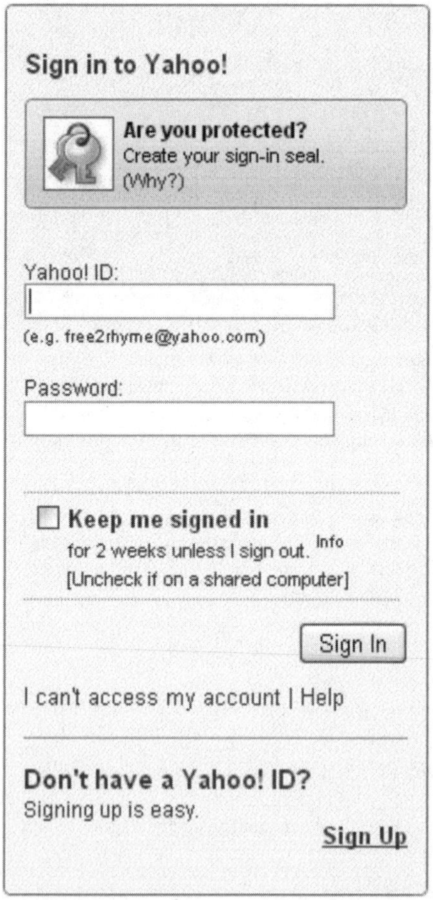

Sign in to Yahoo!

Are you protected?
Create your sign-in seal.
(Why?)

Yahoo! ID:

(e.g. free2rhyme@yahoo.com)

Password:

☐ **Keep me signed in**
for 2 weeks unless I sign out. Info
[Uncheck if on a shared computer]

Sign In

I can't access my account | Help

Don't have a Yahoo! ID?
Signing up is easy.
Sign Up

Figure 10-15. If you don't have one already, here is where you sign up for a Yahoo ID.

To create a Yahoo ID (after clicking the Sign Up link), enter your information and click Create My Account. See Figure 10-16.

1. Tell us about yourself...

My Name	Todd · Kelsey
Gender	Male
Birthday	January · 29 · Year
I live in	United States
Postal Code	

2. Select an ID and password

Yahoo! ID and Email	**snspaces@yahoo.com** Change
Password	●●●●●●●●●● Weak

Capitalization matters. Use 6 to 32 characters, no spaces, and don't use your name or Yahoo! ID.

Re-type Password	●●●●●●●●●●

3. In case you forget your ID or password...

Alternate Email	snspaces@gmail.com
1.Security Question	- Select One -
Your Answer	
2.Security Question	- Select One -
Your Answer	

Just a couple more details...

Type the code shown	◀) Need audio assistance ?

dppMyF

Try a new code

Do you agree? ☑	I have read and agree to the Yahoo! Terms of Service and Y important communications from Yahoo! electronically.
	I have also read and agree to the Mail Terms of Service.
	For your convenience, these documents will be emailed to yc

Create My Account   Cancel

Figure 10-16. Fill in the form to get an ID.

You're given an opportunity to choose an ID username, so try one, and click the Check button to see if it's available. See Figure 10-17.

Figure 10-17. *Testing your username for duplicates*

If your blood pressure goes up at having to create yet another online account, take a deep breath, think happy thoughts, and then, when you get something like the screen shown in Figure 10-18, click Continue.

Figure 10-18. *Congratulations! You have successfully created a Yahoo account.*

You may also be asked to verify the password you created for your Yahoo account. You can ignore the "Are you protected?" button. Just enter your password and click Sign In. See Figure 10-19.

Figure 10-19. *Test-driving your new Yahoo account*

Now, you get to choose your Flickr screen name. You still use your Yahoo ID to sign in (write it down, including the password), but your Flickr name can be something else.

Choose a name for Flickr, and click Create a New Account (see Figure 10-20).

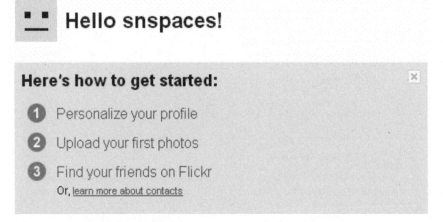

Make a new Flickr account

Choose your new Flickr screen name

snspaces

This can be different from your Yahoo! ID, you can change it later, and spaces are fine.

Note: Your use of the flickr.com site is subject to the Yahoo! Terms of Service and Privacy Policy.

CREATE A NEW ACCOUNT

Figure 10-20. Creating your Flickr account with your own screen name

Getting Started on Flickr

After you sign up for Flickr, a welcoming message on the site provides some suggestions about how to get started. See Figure 10-21.

Hello snspaces!

Here's how to get started:

1 Personalize your profile

2 Upload your first photos

3 Find your friends on Flickr
   Or, learn more about contacts

Figure 10-21. Ready to get started!

If you've made it this far in the book, you should know a thing or two about personalizing your profile. So, let's look at the process of uploading on Flickr. To get started, click "Choose photos and videos" (see Figure 10-22).

Figure 10-22. Preparing to upload

Locate your file, and choose your privacy settings. You can choose to make your images public or private. Within the Public option, you can choose to give family and/or friends permission to view your photos. See Figure 10-23.

Upload to Flickr

You've used **0%** of your 100 MB photo limit and 0 of your 2 video limit this month. Upgrade?

File	Size	Remove?
todd-kelsey.jpg	33.2 KB	🗑
grandpa-miller.png	97.7 KB	🗑

2 files   **Add More**   **Total: 130.9 KB**

Set privacy / Show more upload settings

○ Private (only you see them)

☐ Visible to Friends

☐ Visible to Family

◉ Public (anyone can see them)

[Upload Photos and Videos]

Figure 10-23. Locate your image, and choose your privacy settings.

When you're done, click Upload Photos and Videos.

Next, Flickr asks you if you want to add a description. And I must add, Flickr is friendly. It's probably the only web site I've ever visited that ends a sentence with "perhaps?" like a wise aunt who is guiding you along with a gentle suggestion (see Figure 10-24).

Finished! Next: <u>add a description</u>, perhaps?

Figure 10-24. A polite nudge from Flickr

Then, the fun begins. When you upload pictures, whatever the picture has for a filename is filled in for a title; you can click to change that if you like. You may want to write a few sentences of description; when you're finished, click Save. See Figure 10-25.

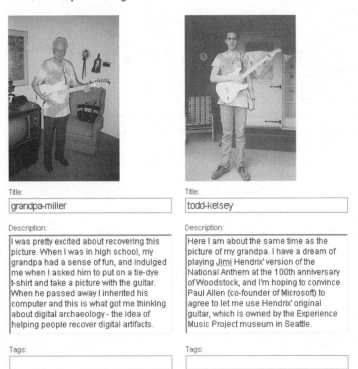

Figure 10-25. Click Save, and you're done.

You can enter *keywords* if you want people to be able to find these pictures more easily when they do a general search on Flickr. This may also help you find your own pictures, because it can be another way of organizing them.

After you enter the basic information and click Save, you see your *photostream*, which is simply a record of pictures you've uploaded. See Figure 10-26.

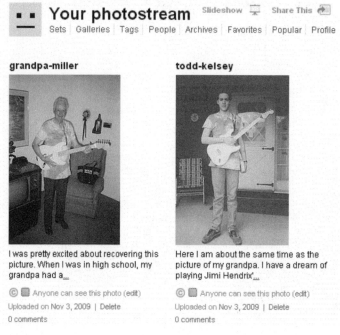

Figure 10-26. Your photostream

Flickr provides a welcome to your photostream, shown in Figure 10-27.

Welcome to your photostream. Your photostream is a visual history of everything you've ever uploaded to Flickr. In addition to your profile, your photostream is your public "face" on Flickr, though everyone enjoys a different view, depending on their relationship to you and your privacy settings. You might want to organize your photos or go to your home page.   OK, hide this ⊠

Figure 10-27. Flickr welcomes you to your photostream.

Getting Back Home

If you ever get lost, click the Flickr logo at the top of the screen to get home to the main screen (see Figure 10-28).

Figure 10-28. If lost, go home.

And when you sign in to Flickr, and you're new, Flickr greets you, as shown in Figure 10-29.

Aloha snspaces!
Now you know how to greet people in Hawaiian!
Here's how to get started:
1 Personalize your profile
2 Upload your first photos
3 Find your friends on Flickr
Or, learn more about contacts

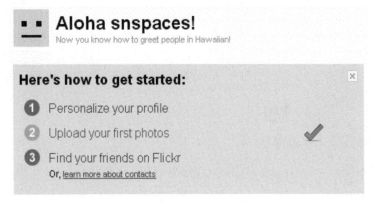

Figure 10-29. Well, aloha!

Notice that, in Figure 10-29, Flickr is helping keep track of things: it's suggesting that you personalize your profile. And if you followed along in the example, you have a green check mark to indicate that you did get as far as uploading some pictures. I recommend trying the "Personalize your profile" link or the "Find your friends on Flickr" link (chances are, you probably know someone who is already on Flickr).

If you click the "Find your friends on Flickr" link, a screen comes up with tabs on the left for Yahoo, Gmail, and Hotmail (see Figure 10-30).

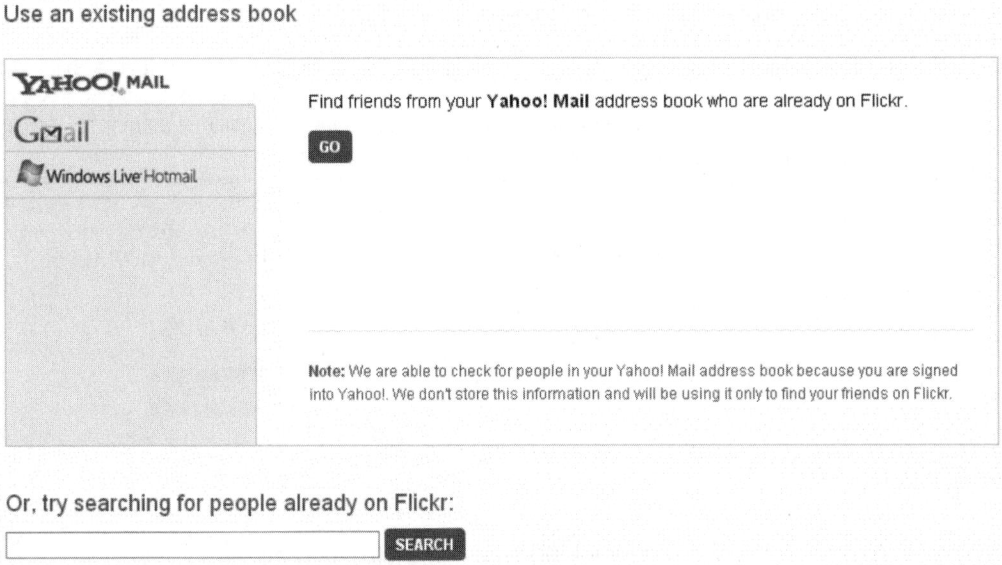

Use an existing address book
YAHOO! MAIL
Gmail
Windows Live Hotmail
Find friends from your Yahoo! Mail address book who are already on Flickr.
GO
Note: We are able to check for people in your Yahoo! Mail address book because you are signed into Yahoo!. We don't store this information and will be using it only to find your friends on Flickr.
Or, try searching for people already on Flickr:
SEARCH

Figure 10-30. Search for the friends you undoubtedly have on Flickr.

You can click one of the web mail tabs on the left and then click the Go button (see Figure 10-31).

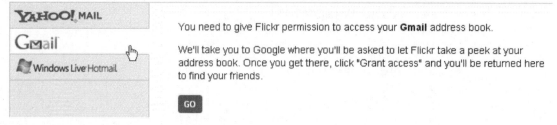

Figure 10-31. Searching by e-mail addresses

Flickr then leads you through a process during which it looks to see if anyone you know is on Flickr.

IN PRAISE OF GMAIL

If you've somehow made it this long without a Yahoo, Gmail, or Hotmail account, I'd recommend considering checking out Gmail. I've been around personal computers for a while, and I'm pretty impressed with Gmail, how easy it is to use, and a lot of the integrated features, such as:

- *Google Documents:* A free online equivalent to Microsoft Office
- *Google Sites:* A free, easy to use way to make a web site
- *Blogger:* A free blogging platform (see Chapters 8 and 9)

To sign up for Gmail, go to `http://mail.google.com`. (Note for AOL users: you can set up Gmail to check your AOL account. Check out `www.snspaces.com`, in the Flickr section; if there isn't a tutorial on how to do this yet, and you ask me nicely, I'll make one. My parents were both on AOL, and I finally convinced them to try Gmail. It's very good as far as searching old e-mails, and it has a lot of useful features.)

If you don't have any web mail accounts that Flickr can check, it's no big deal; move on. The feature for finding people also allows you to type in a person's name, as in Figure 10-32.

Or, try searching for people already on Flickr:

Chuck Isdale	SEARCH

Figure 10-32. You can also search by name.

This kind of search shows a list of people. If it looks like you've found who you're looking for, when you're signed in, you can click the "add as contact" link, shown in Figure 10-33.

Figure 10-33. *Adding a contact*

Then, you can add the person as a general contact, friend, and/or family, as shown in Figure 10-34.

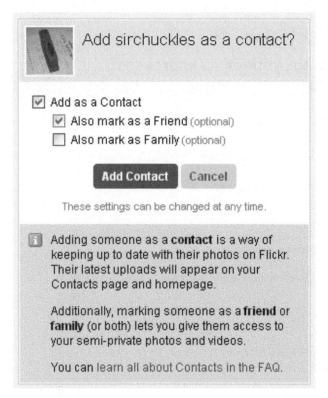

Figure 10-34. *Setting your contact type*

This setting allows you to share pictures with a person based on the type of contact they are. (If you remember, when you upload a picture, you have the opportunity to mark a picture as private or viewable only by friends or family. When you add someone as a contact, you're creating such a group of people.)

293

Yahoo

I'd rather not be forced by Yahoo to make a Yahoo ID in order to use Flickr. But what you can do is sign into your Yahoo account (at www.yahoo.com) and add another e-mail address, so that you never have to check your Yahoo e-mail if you don't want.

For example, until/unless Flickr changes things, your only option is to have a Yahoo ID associated with a Flickr account. In order to receive e-mail that Flickr may need to send you, you either need to check your Yahoo e-mail or add another e-mail address.

If you want to try this, log in to your Yahoo ID account, add an alternative e-mail address, and then come back and select that e-mail address as the one Yahoo uses to communicate with you. See Figure 10-35.

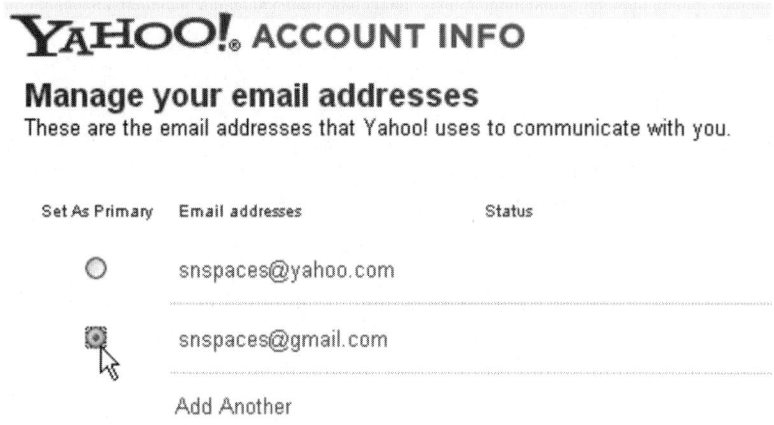

Figure 10-35. Managing your e-mail preferences

Then, think happy thoughts, and click Save, as shown in Figure 10-36.

Figure 10-36. Saving your e-mail preferences

Q/A

I asked Chuck Isdale, photographer and Flickr enthusiast, for his thoughts about Flickr. See www.flickr.com/photos/sirchuckles/ and the dedication at the beginning of this chapter.

Q: What do you like using Flickr for?

A: Flickr is the web site through which I have shared pictures and made acquaintances, both in the online and off-line world. There is the West Suburban Chicago Flickrers group that gets together to take pictures. There's the guy from California whom I met in front of the sign marking the beginning of Route 66 in downtown Chicago. (He is also a member of Flickr.) We both got a shot of the sign that day. I am sure there are many more people to meet as well as photos and techniques to share.

Q: What is one of your favorite things about Flickr?
A: Flickr has an agreement with Getty images (`www.flickr.com/help/gettyimages`), so it has options for people who like photography to have a potential market for their pictures. At the same time, it's very welcoming and easy for beginners to use.

Q: How many photos are on Flickr?
A: There are about 3.5 billion photos and counting on Flickr.

Q: How do you find inspiration?
A: I personally often find inspiration just looking at the "most recently uploaded" page (`www.flickr.com/photos`). Notice that thousands of pictures are uploaded every minute!

(And now … back to the regular Q/A.)

Q: Is Flickr free?
A: Yes, but you can also get a "pro" edition when you run out of space.

Q: Why should I bother going to `www.snspaces.com/pics`?
A: Because the picture Chuck took of me and the setting sun is amazing—and it's not me who is amazing—it's the colors. You *have* to see the spectrum of pastel sunset colors—very cool. And throughout the rest of the book, there are occasionally some pretty nice color pictures. Maybe if this book sells enough copies (nudge, nudge, wink, wink—tell your friends if you like it; all author proceeds are going to the non-profit CFTW, as mentioned in the book's Introduction), a future printing will be in color. There may even be electronic book editions either now or in the future that will be color (PDF, iPad, iPhone, Kindle color, and so on)—but for now, the only way to see full, living color is by visiting `www.snspaces.com/pics`. If you like color, check it out!

Q: Where should I put my pictures—Flickr or Facebook?
A: I think if you're just sharing them with friends and family, Facebook is fine. If you think you're interested in trying photography as a hobby, Flickr can be nice, because it's basically a community of photographers, so people will come by and make comments. I suggest trying both.

Q: You haven't mentioned the Life Story Suitcase in this chapter. (Thankfully! I was getting tired of hearing about it.) But I'm curious: why not?
A: Well, the LSS prototype is based on Blogger, Twitter, and Facebook—but if you think other sites should be added, let us know!

Q: Wait! I have another question! Where can I ask it?
A: On `www.snspaces.com`.

Conclusion

Dear Reader,

In this chapter, you learned about Flickr, which is a really great site that provides a lot of opportunities to connect with people. Chuck, for example, has spent time putting his pictures on Flickr and tagging them. And he's made a lot of fun connections with people who also like taking pictures.

Happy picture taking!

Regards,

—Todd

P.S. For you aspiring photographers: When I was looking at Chuck's comment about Getty Images in the Q/A, I remembered another interesting situation—when you put your photographs out on the Web, you never know who is going to come by. A friend, Greg Schreck, made a series of photos called "Bag Men" (see www.gregschreck.com, scroll down, and click the Bag Men link). Somehow, who knows how, Peter Gabriel, a famous pop singer, was out and about on the Net, wandered across the photos, and ended up contacting Greg and asking if he could use one on an album cover. If you like this story, let's figure out what the album was, interview both of them, and put it on www.snspaces.com as a bit of inspiration. Start with Flickr, and best of luck!

snspaces.com

Come and visit the Social Networking Spaces companion web site at www.snspaces.com, where you can find more tips and updates and have an opportunity to share your thoughts or ask questions.

In Living Color: You can visit www.snspaces.com/pics to see full-color versions of all the pictures from this chapter.

CHAPTER 11

Watching and Sharing Video on Youtube

In This Chapter:

- *Introduction*: What you can do on YouTube
- *Creating a YouTube account*: Browsing and watching popular videos.
- *Uploading videos on YouTube*: Uploading and sharing videos.

snspaces.com

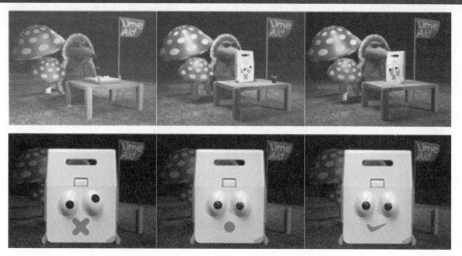

Come and visit the Social Networking Spaces companion web site at www.snspaces.com, where you can find more tips and updates and have an opportunity to share your thoughts or ask questions.

In Living Color: You can visit www.snspaces.com/pics to see full-color versions of all the pictures from this chapter.

The YouTube video corresponding to these pictures is at http://tinyurl.com/xoyoutube or www.youtube.com/watch?v=KPoynXO6FrA.

Introduction

YouTube, located at www.youtube.com, is a web site where you can upload and share videos. It began small, but over time it has become incredibly popular. Along with sites like Wikipedia, it's an example of how crowd-created content (made by the public) can make a site more popular than web sites with content made by large companies.

YouTube has a variety of features that make it *social*—if you like, you can visit and watch a video, but you can also make a comment. People like to make comments about other people's creations. This is the same principle that helps to make blogging popular because on a blog, you can leave a comment (see Chapter 8).

The other social thing about YouTube is that you can share your own videos. One of the reasons YouTube is so popular is that people have taken advantage of the show-and-tell opportunity. For example, when they come across a video they like (often a funny video), they share it with friends and co-workers.

YouTube often ends up providing an opportunity for someone who is relatively unknown to be catapulted into stardom, based on a simple video they did that was silly or completely stupid, hilarious, or crazy. This happens all the time.

This chapter looks at both the viewing side and the uploading/sharing side. To get started, sometimes the best way to understand something is to try it. If you'd like to jump right in, try visiting http://tinyurl.com/xoyoutube (or www.youtube.com/watch?v=KPoynXO6FrA if you want to get a headache typing all the letters). It's a simple video I made when I was doing some volunteer work for One Laptop Per Child (www.laptop.org)—an idea for a slightly silly commercial based on some 3D images that a friend Alexandra made (she created the little 3D characters that appear throughout the book). See Figure 11-1. It's very short, and it's not really even a traditional video because it displays a series of images. There's some sound, but it's simple and playful. The main point is, I enjoyed making it, and I particularly enjoyed uploading it and being able to share the link with people. Another point is, making the video itself was *social*—and that's another part of it. It's no problem if you go through life on YouTube never uploading a video, but it's fun!

Figure 11-1. A still image from a sample video

■ **Tip** These days, it's a lot easier to work with video. If you want to try making a video, you can pick up pretty inexpensive digital cameras with built-in video/audio recording. The Flip Video camera is also quite popular (and cheap); go to www.theflip.com.

■ **Note** Here's a Wikipedia article that gives background about YouTube: http://en.wikipedia.org/wiki/Youtube.

If you'd like to develop a deep head full of thoughts while you're exploring YouTube and want to understand more about the dramatic shift from professional-powered content to crowd-created content, there's a great book called *Wikinomics: How Mass Collaboration Changes Everything,* by Don Tapscott and Anthony D. Williams (Portfolio, 2006) that you may want to check out (look for it on Amazon or Wikipedia). It talks about Wikipedia, YouTube, Second Life, and some other sites.

If you look at the front page of YouTube.com, it's kind of like a newspaper for videos, as you can see in Figure 11-2.

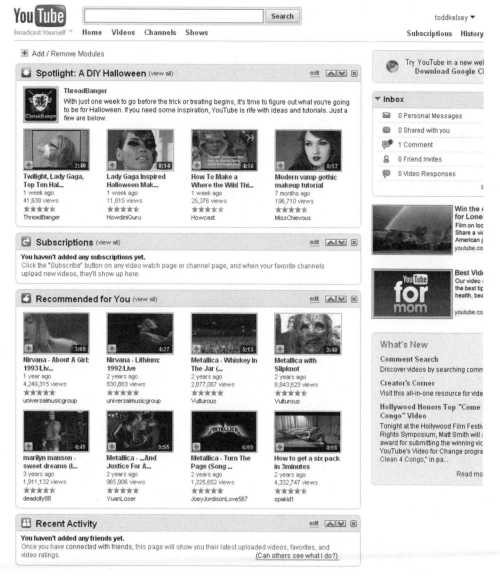

Figure 11-2. The front page of YouTube a snapshot in time. It's always subject to change.

The front page consists more or less of a series of thumbnail images of videos you may want to check out. Because this chapter was written around the time of Halloween, some seasonal things are being offered.

Some videos are featured in a spotlight, and other videos are recommended for you based on what you've watched on YouTube before. (The site has the capacity to remember and think about videos you've watched, but it's anonymous, so don't worry about anyone finding out that you looked for a video about the Muppets.)

One of the powerful things about YouTube is the search box. A lot of times, people share links with each other, and you may have already received a link from someone by instant message or e-mail. However, you can also go to the site and search for a video (see Figure 11-3).

Figure 11-3. You can search for a video.

If you go to the front page and click the Videos link right beneath the search box, you see a great number of video categories (see Figure 11-4).

Figure 11-4. Video categories

There's also a very cool, relatively new feature called YouTube EDU. One of my personal favorites is illustrated in the following image.

YouTube EDU lets you access a lot of free content developed at some leading universities, such as lectures by famous professors (or professors who aren't famous but who are teaching on interesting topics). Plus, you get to learn for free. There are also other videos about the colleges and what people are doing there. It's basically like a video university (see Figure 11-5). To see it, visit http://youtube.com/edu.

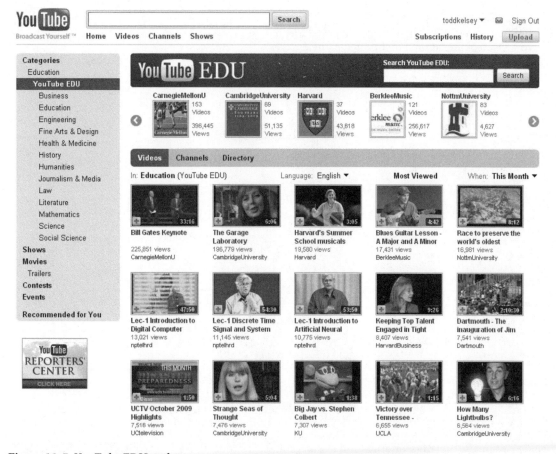

Figure 11-5. YouTube EDU rocks.

Figure 11-6 shows a close-up of the most popular videos on YouTube EDU at the time of writing.

Figure 11-6. Popular YouTube EDU videos

If you look closely, the number of views appears beneath the title of the video, which tells how many people have seen it and is an indicator of popularity. A lot more people have seen Bill Gates' keynote than the video of the laptop I mentioned earlier!

YouTube EDU, like other sections of YouTube, has its own categories, as shown in Figure 11-7.

Figure 11-7. YouTube EDU categories. Super cool!

It really is a good resource, and I highly recommend filing it away and exploring it. In some ways, YouTube is mostly about entertainment, but it also contains a lot of good learning material, and this will only continue to increase. You can find it in sections like YouTube EDU and also in the many videos people have made that offer tutorials and lessons about how to do things—anything from fixing a bike or learning how to speak a language to baking a cake. The search box at the top of YouTube is how you find it. Search away!

By way of introduction, another nice thing about YouTube is that it sometimes promotes special events by displaying icons around the page, as this image shows.

YouTube PRESENTS
U2
LIVE
FROM THE ROSE BOWL
10/25 8:30PM PT
YOUTUBE.COM/U2

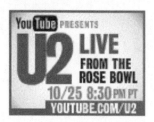

Music certainly is a part of YouTube; there are a lot of music videos, both independent and professional. You can see just about any band you can think of, including videos you may not have seen for a long time. Check them out!

Some Pointers on Watching YouTube Videos

In this section, you explore YouTube and try watching some videos. Visit YouTube.com, and type the phrase "mantis report" in the search box at the top (see Figure 11-8).

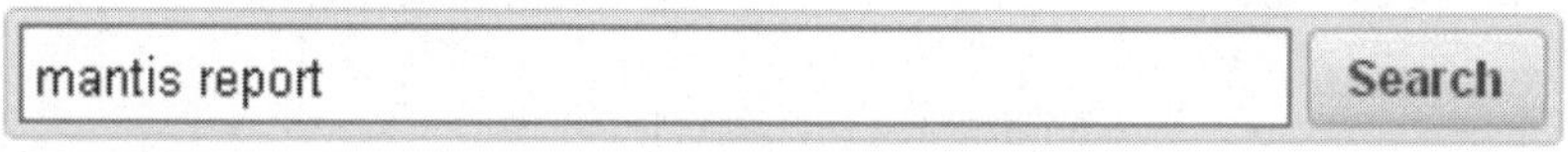

mantis report
Search

Figure 11-8. Searching for a video

When you search for videos on YouTube, the search results appear, including a small thumbnail image on the left, the title of the video, and a small blurb about the video (see Figure 11-9).

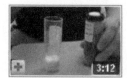

3:12
Dr. Fun - Mantis Report - Preparing Fruit Flies
When the fruit flies arrived in the mail, I had to go through the process of transferring them and starting a new culture. Starting a blog at...
1 year ago
455 views
toddkelsey

Figure 11-9. A video listing on YouTube

At the bottom of the listing are some stars (based on a five-star rating system, if anyone has rated the video). It also displays when the video was posted, how many views it has, and the username of the person who uploaded it (for example, toddkelsey).

In this type of listing, to watch the video, you can click the thumbnail image or the title of the video (for example, Dr. Fun - Mantis Report). When you do, it starts playing; so if you're at the office, you may want to turn down the volume on your computer (see Figure 11-10).

Figure 11-10. *Watching a video. I'm holding up the instructions for a scary maneuver I'm about to make in transferring fruit flies from one place to another. I got out the digital camera, shot the video, and uploaded it to YouTube. Fun!*

The following is one of the most useful buttons, which appears in the lower-left corner of the video.

This is the Pause button. To the right of the pause button, a solid red line represents the portion of the video that has played so far, along with a small circle to represent the exact part of the video you're on. If you want, you can click and drag the small circle back and forth to move around. To the right of the circle, a grey line represents the portion of the video that's still downloading from the Internet. If you're on a slower connection, you may want to wait for a significant part of the video to load before trying to watch it. You can click Pause, wait for the video to load, and then click Play again.

Toward the lower-right corner are some useful options and buttons, as shown in Figure 11-11.

1:07 / 3:12
HQ
How long you've been watching
Length
Volume
Switch to high-quality
Full-screen

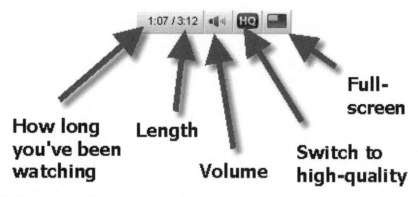

Figure 11-11. Info about a video

The numbers show elapsed time and the length of the video. You can click the small speaker icon to adjust the volume. If you don't hear anything, you may need to unmute or increase the volume on your computer or get some speakers.

The HQ symbol allows you to switch to a higher-quality version of the video (if you have a high-speed broadband connection), although most videos appear fine. The option on the far right is pretty cool because it lets you switch to full screen, so you can see a larger version of the video. (Press ESC to switch back to regular view.)

At the bottom of a video, you can see comments that people have made, as shown in Figure 11-12.

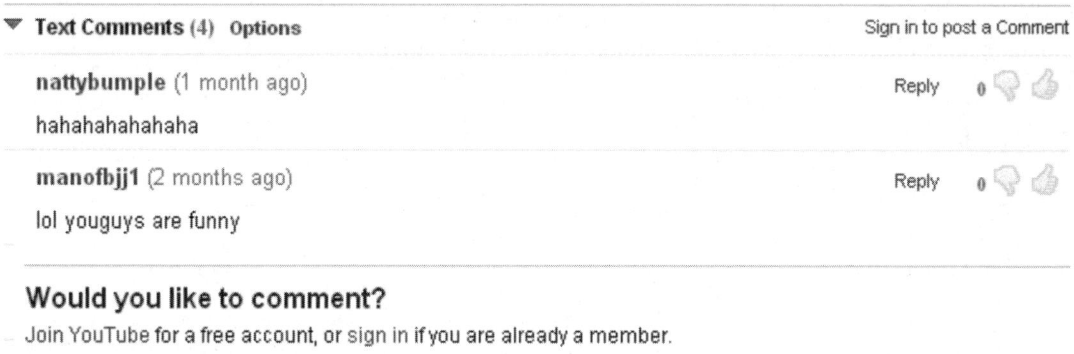

Text Comments (4) Options
Sign in to post a Comment
nattybumple (1 month ago)
hahahahahahaha
Reply 0
manofbjj1 (2 months ago)
lol youguys are funny
Reply 0
Would you like to comment?
Join YouTube for a free account, or sign in if you are already a member.

Figure 11-12. Comments are the social side of YouTube.

When you're signed in to YouTube, a form appears that allows you to easily make a comment (see Figure 11-13).

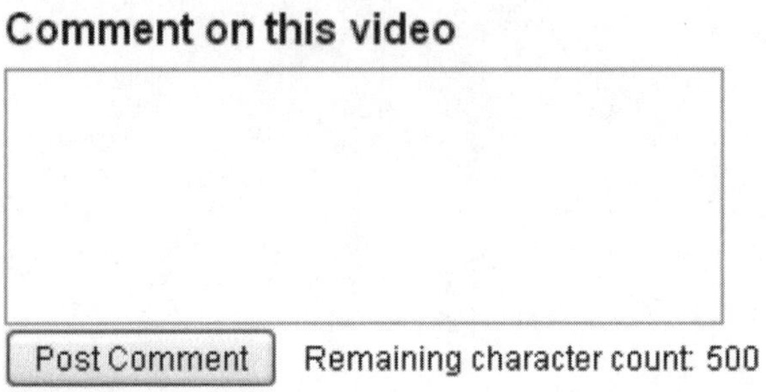

Comment on this video

Post Comment   Remaining character count: 500

Figure 11-13. A comment box

Another interesting thing about YouTube, which is part of the reason for its growth, is that it makes it easy to share videos elsewhere and to subscribe to someone's channel.

In the upper-right corner of the YouTube screen, when you're watching a video, is a small grey square. It contains some descriptive material and two fields labeled URL and Embed (see Figure 11-14).

Figure 11-14. One of the many panels in YouTube, with information and a "more info" link you can click

You can click the URL field or copy and paste it. This is the link to the video, so you can put it in an e-mail, a tweet, or on Facebook. And for those of you who are interested in promoting your video on a blog or elsewhere, the Embed field contains a piece of code that you can paste in a blog post. This actually allows you to embed a YouTube video in a web page (or blog). This requires learning a little about HTML, but if you want to get rambunctious, plan to read Chapters 8 and 9 on making a blog. In your blog, when you're writing a post for fun, try this: come to a YouTube video, copy the code from the Embed field, click the HTML tab in your post, paste in the code, and then click back on the Compose tab. Finally, publish the post. For an example of how an embedded YouTube video looks, see http://rgbgreen.blogspot.com: click Solar Power in the Table of Contents area and scroll down, and you see a YouTube video embedded part way down, similar to Figure 11-15.

Figure 11-15. *When I put this blog post together, it was really nice to be able to write about a topic and embed a video to help explain it. I first drafted the article in Blogger and then took the same code (HTML) and added the article to the main site at* www.rgbgreen.org. *The video makes it more dynamic. I searched for videos on YouTube and embedded ones I liked in the blog post as well as on* www.rgbgreen.org. *Cool!*

When a YouTube video is embedded in a blog post (you can embed anyone's YouTube video, including your own), it looks very similar to one that is on YouTube itself (see Figure 11-16). The same controls appear.

Figure 11-16. When you embed a video in a blog post or web page, it's like having your own YouTube.

I ended up using YouTube videos in a blog post because I was writing some articles to introduce people to renewable energy, and I thought it would be nice to include videos. I searched on YouTube, copied over the embed code as I described earlier, and put it in a blog post. It was very easy and made the blog post more engaging and interesting.

The moral of the story is, YouTube can be used in a variety of ways, and videos can easily be shared by using the URL feature in e-mails and instant messages. Using the Embed feature, you can share videos for education and entertainment in your own blog posts or in someone else's.

I hope you've gotten a bit distracted while exploring things on YouTube. But when you come back, go to the example video (or any video, for that matter). If you're not sure how to get back, search for "mantis report" in the search box at the top of www.youtube.com (see Figure 11-17).

mantis report	Search

Figure 11-17. Searching for a video

Then, look for the More From text on the right side of the screen, and click it. You see other videos that a person has uploaded, as shown in Figure 11-18.

▼ **More From: toddkelsey**

The Argonnauts - Sven the Tree Slayer
36 views
4:01

Pepsi King
55 views
0:51

See all 3 videos

Figure 11-18. Another thing you can explore is the More From area.

The More From area shows other videos by the same person. If you like what you see, you can click the other videos the person has uploaded.

Because you've been such a good reader, here are a few more videos you may enjoy exploring. If you haven't guessed already, I like having fun, and this is one of the popular fun videos on YouTube. Try typing "diet coke and Mentos" in the search box, as shown in Figure 11-19.

diet coke and mentos | Search

Figure 11-19. Worth watching.

It's a wonderful, wacky experiment that demonstrates what happens when you drop several Mentos candies in a bottle of Diet Coke. The experiment is quite ridiculous and interesting (see Figure 11-20).

Diet Coke + Mentos
Champagne

★★★★★ 3 years ago 10,262,070 views zorro103
2:57

Figure 11-20. Science can be fun!

Notice how many views the video has received. At the time of writing, over ten million views have occurred.

Here's another video to check out. Type the words exactly as they're spelled in Figure 11-21.

Hacki Tamas Strauss Polka | Search

Figure 11-21. One reason people like YouTube is because of all the humorous videos.

It doesn't sound like much, but I dare you to try to keep a straight face while watching the video (see Figure 11-22).

Figure 11-22. *Oh my gosh.*

Browsing on YouTube

There are a variety of ways you can look for videos on YouTube. One way is to go to www.youtube.com and click the Video link (beneath the search box), which takes you to the Categories area, where you can search for a category you may like, as shown in Figure 11-23.

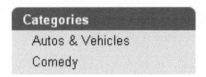

Figure 11-23. *Browsing categories*

After you click a category, YouTube shows a video in the Spotlight and other choices. One feature you should learn to click is the Most Viewed link (see Figure 11-24).

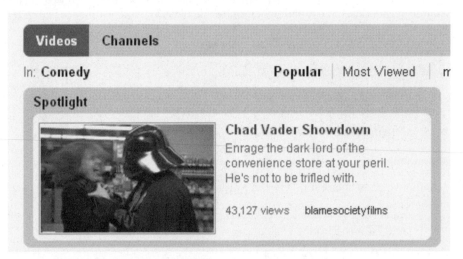

Figure 11-24. *YouTube can suggest popular videos. The Most Viewed link is important.*

After you click the Most Viewed link, in the When area, click the drop-down menu (where the text Today appears); then, choose the All Time link, as shown in Figure 11-25.

Figure 11-25. This is a nifty little feature in the Today drop-down menu.

This technique allows you to find the videos on YouTube that have been seen by the most people. It's also nice to see the videos that are the all-time favorites.

If you follow this example and click the Comedy category in YouTube, then the Most Viewed link, and finally the drop-down menu for All Time, you see something like in Figure 11-26.

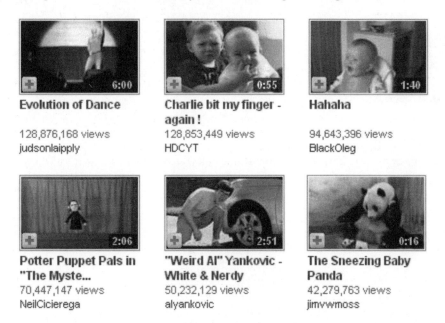

Figure 11-26. The hall of fame of YouTube, at least as far as number of views goes

The "Evolution of Dance" video has been viewed by more than 128,876,168 people. It's one of the most popular videos ever uploaded to YouTube. Then there's "Weird Al" Yankovic, a sneezing baby panda, and so on. Beware: it can be pretty addictive.

■ **Note** Technically, YouTube has restrictions on content that is uploaded—for example, there's not supposed to be any adult content. Although there's generally not anything worse than you'd see on television or in a PG-13 movie, be aware that some videos skirt the edges. My friendly editor also commented that "there are restrictions on copyrighted material, which explains why I have to use Netflix to see complete 'Doctor Who' episodes without having them cut into bits."

When you're browsing through videos, a nice feature allows you to add videos you'd like to see to a playlist, so you can come back and watch them. If you'd like an example video to try the playlist feature, try searching for "detholz," as shown in Figure 11-27.

Figure 11-27. d-e-t-h-o-l-z. Don't ask me why they named it that.

Scroll down to the Club Oslo video (see Figure 11-28).

Detholz! - Club Oslo video

Music video for "Club Oslo" from Chicago band **Detholz!** off of their 2006 album, "Cast Out Devils." Video directed by Micah Barber (www ...

★★★★★   2 years ago   1,444 views   hallameat

Figure 11-28. You can click the + sign on thumbnail images when you're browsing or searching.

Notice the + sign on the left side of the video thumbnail image. Whenever you're on YouTube, no matter what page or list of videos you're looking at, when you see the plus sign, it's a way to add the video to your playlist.

It's kind of like a shopping cart for video, but it doesn't cost anything. When you're browsing around, it's a way to gather videos (see Figure 11-29).

Figure 11-29. Clicking the + sign

To view the videos you've gathered, go to the QuickList link in the upper-right corner of YouTube, as shown in Figure 11-30.

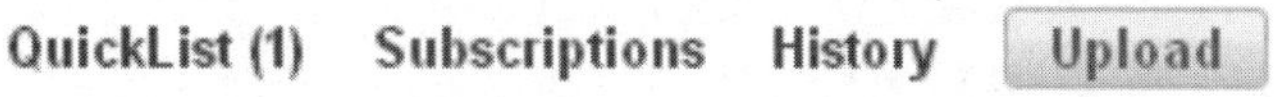

QuickList (1)   Subscriptions   History   Upload

Figure 11-30. QuickList

Creating a YouTube Account

You can watch videos on YouTube without signing in, but you need to have an account and be logged in if you want to comment, upload videos, or use other features.

If you have a Gmail account or a Google account, you can sign in with that (for example, your Gmail address and password). If you don't already have a Gmail account, you can get one at http://mail.google.com. I recommend that you get a Gmail account because you can use it not only for Gmail, but for logging into Blogger and to YouTube.

If you'd like to create a separate YouTube account for any reason, it's easy. To create an account, visit YouTube.com, and click the Create Account link in the upper-right corner of the screen, as shown in the following image.

Create Account or Sign In

YouTube offers some helpful general comments, as shown in Figure 11-31.

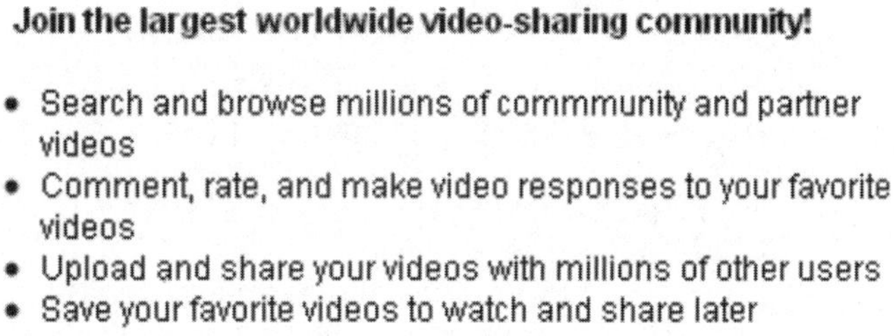

Join the largest worldwide video-sharing community!

- Search and browse millions of commmunity and partner videos
- Comment, rate, and make video responses to your favorite videos
- Upload and share your videos with millions of other users
- Save your favorite videos to watch and share later

Figure 11-31. Some comments from YouTube

On the sign-up page shown in Figure 11-32, enter a username, and click the Check Availability link until you come up with one that's available. Then, at a minimum, enter your date of birth. (You need to be at least 13 to be on YouTube.)

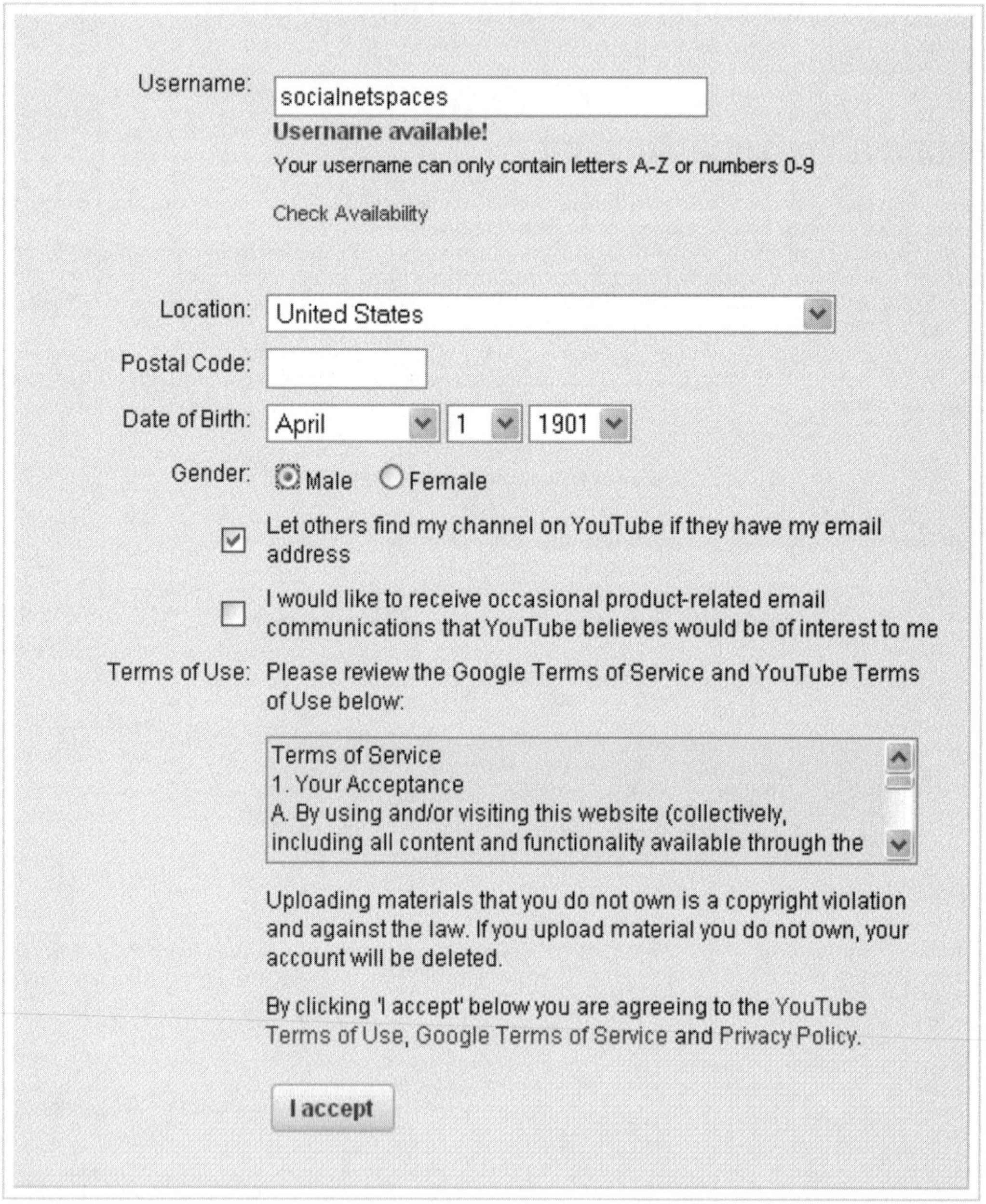

Username: socialnetspaces

Username available!

Your username can only contain letters A-Z or numbers 0-9

Check Availability

Location: United States ▼

Postal Code:

Date of Birth: April ▼ 1 ▼ 1901 ▼

Gender: ◉ Male ○ Female

☑ Let others find my channel on YouTube if they have my email address

☐ I would like to receive occasional product-related email communications that YouTube believes would be of interest to me

Terms of Use: Please review the Google Terms of Service and YouTube Terms of Use below:

Terms of Service
1. Your Acceptance
A. By using and/or visiting this website (collectively, including all content and functionality available through the

Uploading materials that you do not own is a copyright violation and against the law. If you upload material you do not own, your account will be deleted.

By clicking 'I accept' below you are agreeing to the YouTube Terms of Use, Google Terms of Service and Privacy Policy.

I accept

Figure 11-32. Entering initial information

Then, click the "I accept" button.

A nice feature that is tied in to your Gmail account appears, allowing you to connect with people you may have corresponded with, as shown in Figure 11-33.

Subscribe to your Google friends who are on YouTube already!

Figure 11-33. This is pretty cool.

Next, a list of names appears, and you can click the Subscribe button (see Figure 11-34). (You may need to click the bar.) YouTube displays notifications when the person adds new videos and keeps a list for you so you can go and see videos uploaded by people you know.

Figure 11-34. Youtube connects you with people automatically.

■ **Note** BJ Fogg is a cool Stanford professor who is doing a lot of interesting work at www.bjfogg.com. One of the fun things he worked on with his sister is some resources about Facebook for parents. If you like, go to the search box on YouTube, type in "Facebook for Parents," and look for their username and the videos they posted.

The set of links that appears after you create an account is also worth exploring, including the "account preferences" link shown in Figure 11-35.

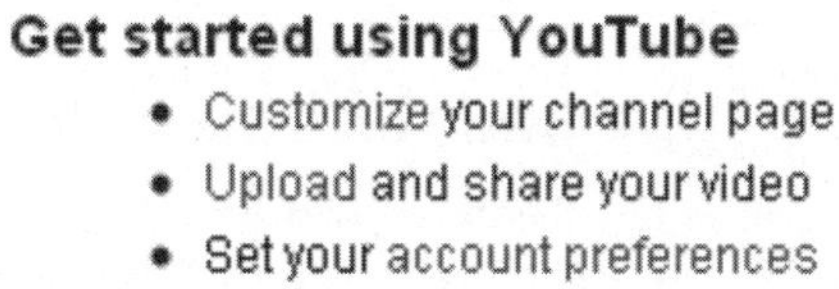

Get started using YouTube

- Customize your channel page
- Upload and share your video
- Set your account preferences

Figure 11-35. A helpful set of Getting Started links

Setting Your Age Not to Display

If you don't want your age to display on your profile in YouTube, then after your account is created and you're signed in, you can click your username at the upper-right corner of the screen, and click the Account link (see Figure 11-36).

Figure 11-36. Click your username at the top of the YouTube screen when you're signed in, and you can access several features.

Then, click Profile Setup, as shown in the following image.

Profile Setup

Next, click the Personal Details section.

Personal Details

Under Age, click the "Do not display my age" radio button.

Age:
○ Display my age
◉ Do not display my age

Finally, click the Save Changes button.

Save Changes

Help with Learning YouTube and Resources for Parents

YouTube has a good Help section. I definitely recommend exploring it, especially if you need some extra information to help you get going or if you're looking for information about how to deal with teen safety issues.

The Help links are always there at the bottom of the YouTube screen, including a helpful YouTube Handbook, as you can see in Figure 11-37.

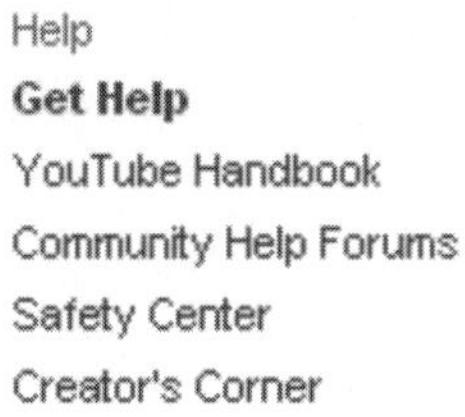

Help

Get Help

YouTube Handbook

Community Help Forums

Safety Center

Creator's Corner

Figure 11-37. *The YouTube Handbook. Helpful reading, now or later.*

To explore teen safety, click the Safety Center link, and then choose the Teen Safety radio button from the list of choices that comes up. Click the Continue button. A specialized Safety Center comes up and gives some helpful tips, as shown in Figure 11-38.

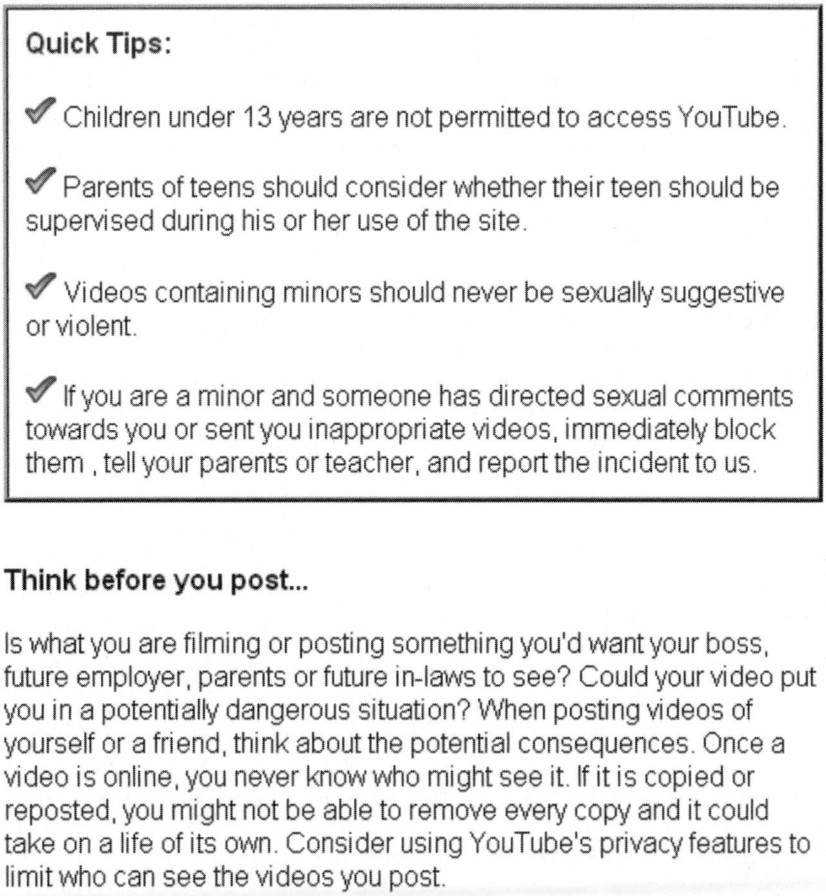

Quick Tips:

✔ Children under 13 years are not permitted to access YouTube.

✔ Parents of teens should consider whether their teen should be supervised during his or her use of the site.

✔ Videos containing minors should never be sexually suggestive or violent.

✔ If you are a minor and someone has directed sexual comments towards you or sent you inappropriate videos, immediately block them , tell your parents or teacher, and report the incident to us.

Think before you post...

Is what you are filming or posting something you'd want your boss, future employer, parents or future in-laws to see? Could your video put you in a potentially dangerous situation? When posting videos of yourself or a friend, think about the potential consequences. Once a video is online, you never know who might see it. If it is copied or reposted, you might not be able to remove every copy and it could take on a life of its own. Consider using YouTube's privacy features to limit who can see the videos you post.

Figure 11-38. *Some important things to keep in mind*

A couple of videos are worth watching with your children (or classroom), such as "Think before you post" and "Internet Safety PSA."

Some additional links are worth clicking, including the Parent Resources link, as shown in Figure 11-39.

Also check out...

Parent Resources

Blocking users

Figure 11-39. A set of helpful links

The link leads to a page with more information, including some good suggestions (see Figure 11-40).

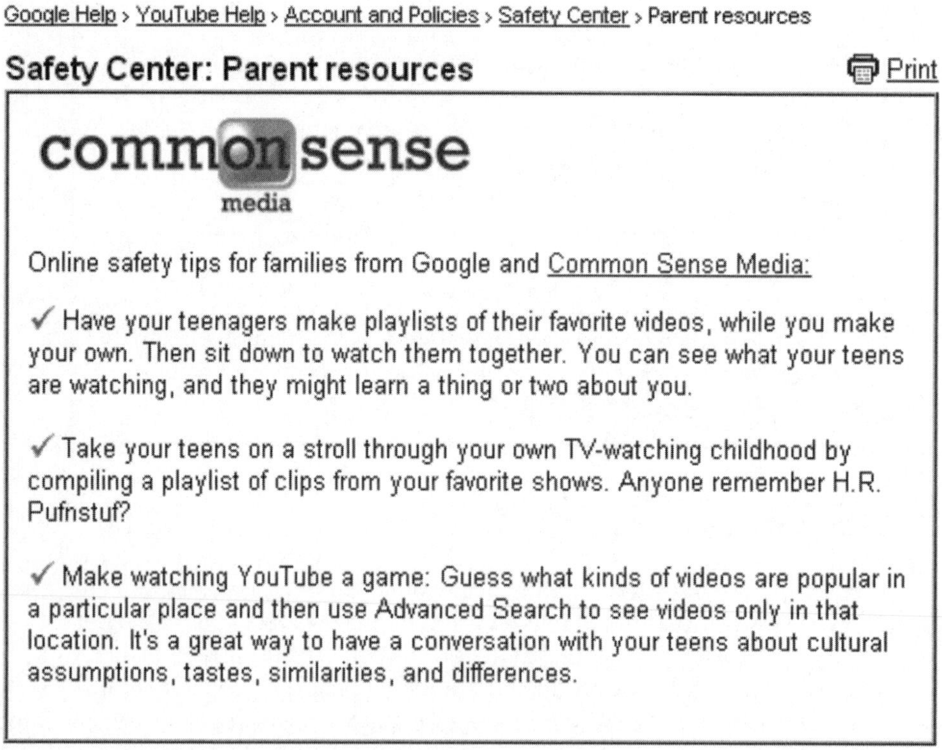

Google Help > YouTube Help > Account and Policies > Safety Center > Parent resources

Safety Center: Parent resources   🖶 Print

commonsense media

Online safety tips for families from Google and Common Sense Media:

✓ Have your teenagers make playlists of their favorite videos, while you make your own. Then sit down to watch them together. You can see what your teens are watching, and they might learn a thing or two about you.

✓ Take your teens on a stroll through your own TV-watching childhood by compiling a playlist of clips from your favorite shows. Anyone remember H.R. Pufnstuf?

✓ Make watching YouTube a game: Guess what kinds of videos are popular in a particular place and then use Advanced Search to see videos only in that location. It's a great way to have a conversation with your teens about cultural assumptions, tastes, similarities, and differences.

Figure 11-41. A good group with good information, worth exploring

Uploading Videos on YouTube

Ultimately, I hope at some point that you try uploading some videos on YouTube, either for public or private consumption. I'll explain how to set privacy settings in this section.

Facebook vs. YouTube

You can certainly upload videos to Facebook and share them with your Facebook friends. This could change, but at the time of writing, there's not an easy way to share videos with a wider audience on Facebook from a personal account. You can't have a direct link to a Facebook video like you can with a YouTube video. The only way to make video public is by including it on a Facebook page, and even then there may not be a direct linking capability. This could change in the future, but that's the way it is now.

On Facebook, it's nice to be able to upload a video to share with friends. When you upload, it appears in your News Feed. Then, there are some options for sharing, such as those shown in Figure 11-41.

Figure 11-41. Options for sharing a video that has been uploaded to Facebook. I didn't realize you could embed video; but I tried it, and it seems to work OK. (See http://toddkelsey.blogspot.com, and look for "Flying Dutchman." If you want to compare, invite me to be a friend on Facebook, and then look at the same video under my Videos tab.)

The Share button does allow you to easily send a message to a Facebook friend. You can also enter e-mail addresses for people who aren't on Facebook, but they have to sign up for Facebook. The Edit This Video link gives you easy access to privacy settings, so I think Facebook is a little easier and better for private video. Interestingly, the "Embed this Video" link allows you to take some code and put your Facebook video in a blog post, which could be public.

The best thing to do is try both Facebook and YouTube and see what works for you. Until Facebook makes some kind of YouTube-like section on Facebook, YouTube is the best place to share a public video that you'd like other people to see, especially if you want to try to share it with the widest possible audience.

If you're a band or have some other kind of business or thing you'd like to promote, YouTube is a good place to share it. A lot of people are on there; and if you strike the right chord, YouTube makes it easy for people to share the video with each other, and word can spread fast. At the time of writing, according to one study, YouTube (along with MySpace) also happens to rank above Facebook as a place where teens spend time. If you want to reach out to teens, make sure to be on YouTube.

Of course, you can always upload your video to YouTube and Facebook. If you're promoting things on Facebook, you can certainly upload video to a Facebook page or post the link to a YouTube video.

Getting Started

To get started, create a YouTube account (or sign in with your Gmail address), and click the Upload button, as shown in the following image.

Upload

■ **Note** You can upload just about any kind of video, in just about any format, but generally speaking, shorter is better. Try to record your video so that the best stuff you want to show appears in the shortest period of time. These days, it's easy to record video with a handheld digital camera that has video and audio capability, so you may find yourself recording video, transferring it to your computer, and uploading it directly without editing it. There are also options for recording video from a mobile device. For the best results, explore learning how to edit the video. On Macs, you can start with iMovie, and on PC, start with Windows Movie Maker; or there are a host of video editing programs you can grow into. Take a good look at the YouTube Handbook under the Help link at the bottom of YouTube if you want to learn more.

YouTube even has a way to edit videos online and to add subtitles! If you don't find what you're looking for on YouTube itself, feel free to go on www.snspaces.com and see if there's a tutorial that meets your needs. If not, ask nicely, and I'll write one or a whole book.

You may also want to try the options for automatically notifying via Facebook/Twitter when you add a video or do other things on YouTube (see Figure 11-42).

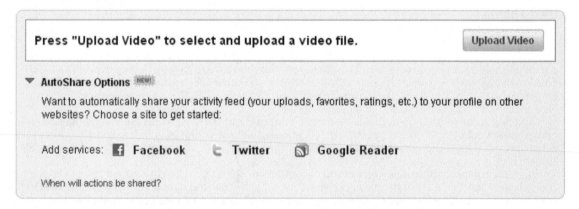

Figure 11-42. The Upload Video button is the important part, and the AutoShare options are pretty nice.

All you do is click the Upload Video button, locate the file, and wait for it to upload.

As part of the upload process, YouTube displays some notes, including a link to the YouTube Handbook, as shown in Figure 11-43.

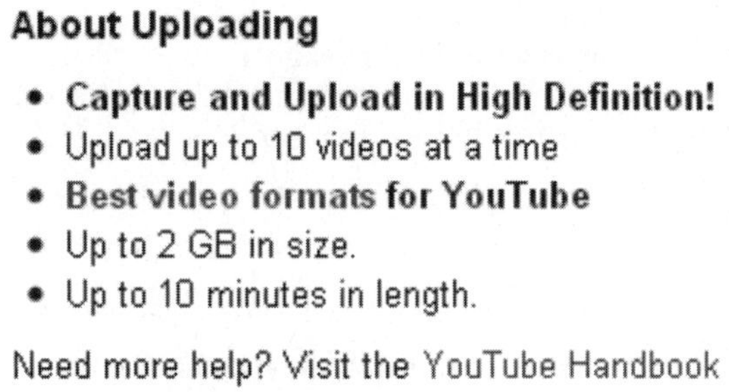

About Uploading
Capture and Upload in High Definition!
Upload up to 10 videos at a time
Best video formats for YouTube
Up to 2 GB in size.
Up to 10 minutes in length.
Need more help? Visit the YouTube Handbook

Figure 11-43. *Some important info to file away. I bet you 100 sunflower seeds you'll be happy if you bookmark this page in the book. One technique that can be helpful for longer videos is to break them into Part 1, Part 2, and so on.*

Figure 11-44 is an ad you may see for a useful device like a Flip Video, which is an increasingly popular handheld device that makes it easy to record video.

Flip video
ultra
as simple
as it is fun
now available in HD
Free Shipping
Order Now ▸
Flip

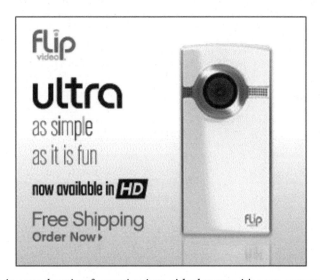

Figure 11-44. *The Flip is a good option for getting into videobecause it's easy, compact, and functional.*

■ **Tip** In my opinion, it's a really good idea to have some kind of device that shoots video with audio, which lowers the barrier as much as possible. You're more likely to capture some part of your life and be glad you did later, as will friends, relatives, and maybe even descendants. I think a Flip is one of the best investments you can make. And no, Flip didn't pay me to say that.

The length of time it takes to upload depends on how big the file is as well as the speed of your Internet connection. As a general rule, you want to probably keep the file size of your video in terms of megabytes, not gigabytes (by keeping it shorter and learning about file formats that aren't as large; see the YouTube Handbook). For perfectionists and filmmakers with high-speed connections, it's possible to upload as much as two gigabytes.

■ **Note** Digital cameras and things like Flip Video devices record in a high-quality mode but have relatively small file sizes. Most times, record in a format called mpeg-4 or mp4. This is a nice balance.

There are a world of video choices that you can get into (see the YouTube Handbook, and if it doesn't have what you need, look at www.snspaces.com). If you have a bigger video camera or video that you want to transfer online, then generally speaking, as a simple goal, aim to get it into MP4 format. Your video-editing program may allow you to do that, or you can download the relatively inexpensive QuickTime Pro software (google "quicktime pro") from Apple, which runs on both Windows and Mac. Then, open your video file and then save it into MP4. Another format you can try to get your video into is FLV. Also, for video buffs, please feel free to come on www.snspaces.com and make suggestions about programs you like.

As your video uploads, it gives you a time remaining—the shorter the video, the smaller the file size, the faster your connection, the less time it takes. See Figure 11-45.

Video File Upload

Figure 11-45. Video File Upload

While the video is uploading, there's a section on the screen where you can fill in information, including a title, description, and category, as shown in Figure 11-46.

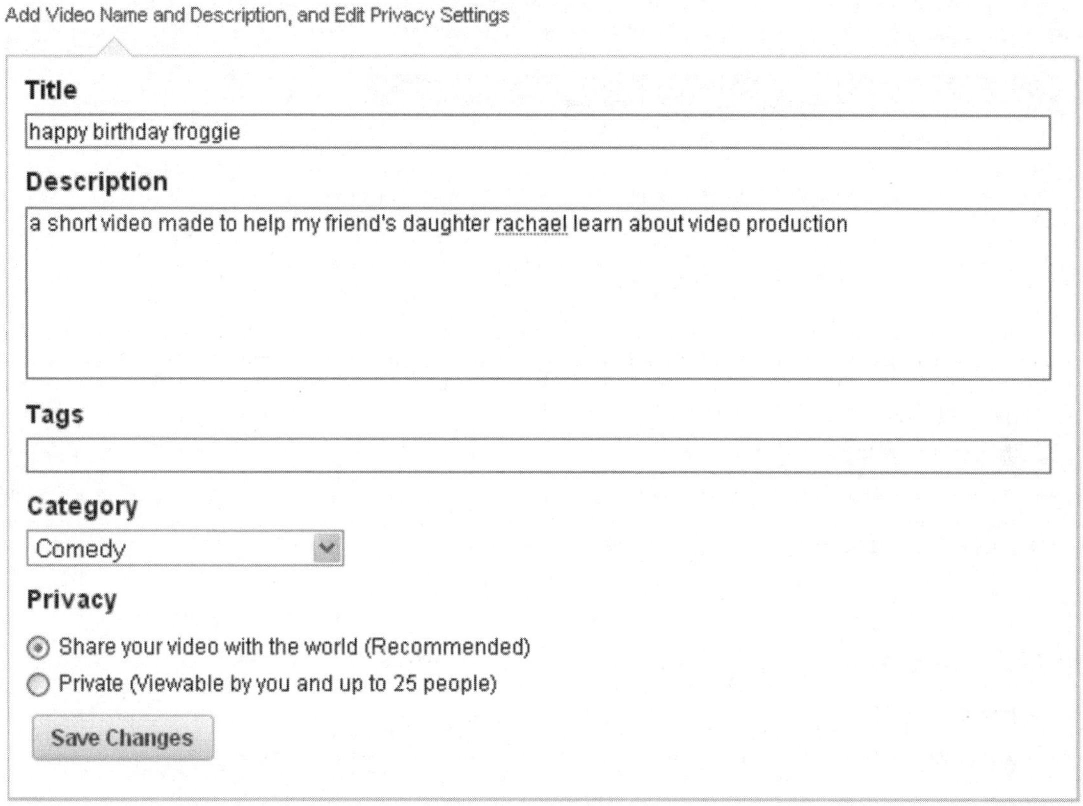

Add Video Name and Description, and Edit Privacy Settings

Title

happy birthday froggie

Description

a short video made to help my friend's daughter rachael learn about video production

Tags

Category

Comedy

Privacy

○ Share your video with the world (Recommended)

○ Private (Viewable by you and up to 25 people)

Save Changes

Figure 11-46. Entering the basic info

You can enter tags if you want people to be able to find the video more easily. They're phrases or words that have to do with the video, like "comedy" or "music video"—basically, whatever term or phrase a person may type in to find either your video in particular (such as the name of your band, your name, and so on), or your *type* of video. It's kind of like choosing the category, but more specific. Enter the words or phrases separated by commas.

You can leave the Privacy section set to the Recommended setting (public), but it's possible to make YouTube videos private. It's a little easier to make a video private in Facebook, but it's six of one and half a dozen of the other. Basically, when uploading, you can designate a video as private and then share it later.

If your video is still uploading after you've entered the basic information and clicked Save Changes, YouTube gives you a pending message, as shown in Figure 11-47.

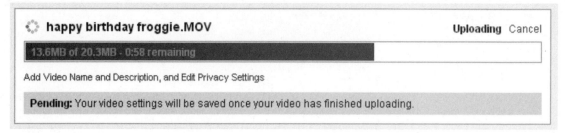

Figure 11-47. Waiting for the video to upload

When it's done uploading, you see a URL (link) that you can use to share the video, and a section with code you can use to embed your video in a web page or blog post (see Figure 11-48).

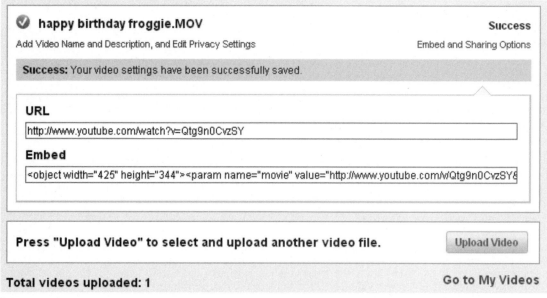

Figure 11-48. When the video is done uploading, YouTube gives you a link right away that you can use to share information about the video.

Sharing on Facebook

If you've uploaded a video on YouTube (or if you've found a video you like on YouTube and want to share it), you can share it easily on Facebook. In fact, this is a homework assignment: find a video you like on YouTube (or upload one), and share it on Facebook.

First, log in. Then, on your Wall, click the Link icon, as shown in Figure 11-49.

Figure 11-49. Back in Facebook and adding a link. See how these sites all fit together?

Next, paste your link in the Link field, as shown in Figure 11-50, and click Attach.

Figure 11-50. Attaching a link

Then, type in a comment, and click the Share button, as shown in Figure 11-51.

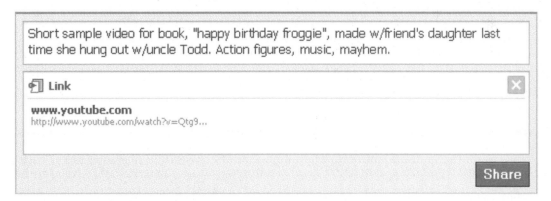

Figure 11-51. Sometimes, when you post YouTube video links, they show up with a thumbnail image, and sometimes they don't.

As Figure 11-52 reflects, you then have an entry that shows up in your News Feed on Facebook and on your friends' pages.

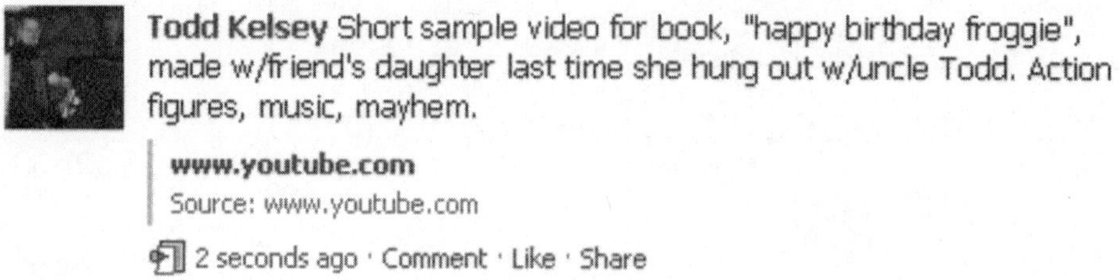

Todd Kelsey Short sample video for book, "happy birthday froggie", made w/friend's daughter last time she hung out w/uncle Todd. Action figures, music, mayhem.

www.youtube.com
Source: www.youtube.com

2 seconds ago · Comment · Like · Share

Figure 11-52. The way a YouTube link looks. If it doesn't pick up the title of your video or a thumbnail, you can always make a comment like "click the YouTube link below"; after you post your link, click it (for example, www.youtube.com), if that's what shows up, and it still should lead to your video.

Sharing on Twitter

Sharing a YouTube video on Twitter is similarly easy. This is also a homework assignment. Find a video you like on YouTube, or upload one, and share the link on Twitter.

Just log in to Twitter, paste in your link and comment, and click the Update button (see Figure 11-53).

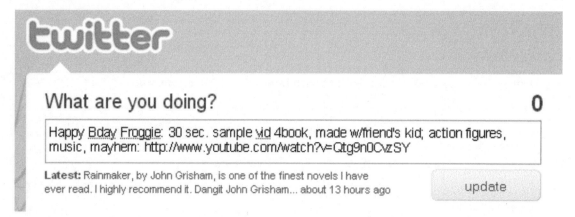

Figure 11-53. Are you having déjà vu? The social networks offer all kinds of ways to play show-and-tell.

To share on Twitter, I recommend pasting in the link first (or using a link-shortening service such as the one found at http://bit.ly or http://tinyurl.com to make the link shorter) and then typing in the description.

The tweet appears in your Twitter stream, and anyone who is following you on Twitter sees it, as does anyone who visits your Twitter page and looks through the posts (see Figure 11-54).

Home

 toddkelsey Happy Bday Froggie: 30 sec. sample vid 4book, made w/friend's kid; action figures, music, mayhem: http://bit.ly/1VF7xv

less than a minute ago from web

 toddkelsey Rainmaker, by John Grisham, is one of the finest novels I have ever read. I highly recommend it. Dangit John Grisham, you kept me up late!

about 13 hours ago from txt

 toddkelsey Finally. http://www.toddkelsey.com is up, sharing research concepts for digital archaeology, accessibility continuum, RGB. Simple; a start.

about 21 hours ago from txt

Figure 11-54. When you post a link to Twitter, remember that it's public and the whole world can see it. But that's how YouTube is, so the two go well together. For private videos, post them on Facebook and share only with those you want to see them.

Q/A

Q: Should I try to figure out how to share private videos on YouTube?

A: I'm going to specifically recommend that if you want to share private videos, you do so on Facebook, because at the present time, it's easier to control privacy with Facebook video. If for some reason you don't want to use Facebook, or otherwise want to know how to do it on YouTube, the YouTube Help section has some information.

Q: I'm interested in learning more about YouTube and the idea of *crowdsourcing*. Where I can I find more information?

A: I really enjoyed reading a book called *Wikinomics: How Mass Collaboration Changes Everything*, by Don Tapscott and Anthony D. Williams (Portfolio, 2006) about the rise of sites like YouTube, Wikipedia, and Second Life. These sites made the first serious inroads toward providing people with the tools to create content and a place to put it. This is a very interesting book and helpful for understanding that shift towards crowdsourcing, or enabling the crowd to create content. It's definitely an important aspect of social networking.

Q: How do I download a video from YouTube? How do I back it up?

A: There are programs that can do this. You also need to have a way to convert the video from YouTube format, because you may not just be able to watch it. Try googling "download YouTube video" or going on www.download.com and looking there.

As far as backing up is concerned, this is the kind of thing that got me thinking about the Life Story Suitcase, honestly. There are many places that you put pictures, notes, and video. Personally, I think it's a good idea to back it all up, especially if it's precious to you. Maybe you know where the original file is, maybe you don't. Services like www.backupify.com and www.socialsafe.net are starting to come around, but the idea of the Life Story Suitcase is this: don't just back it up, provide a way to put it together and put it somewhere else if you want. If you want to see YouTube capability in the Life Story Suitcase, tell us!

There's also a really interesting project at Google called Data Liberation Front (www.dataliberation.org), which was started internally by some Google engineers to make it easier for people to get their media and information off of Google. One reason you'll want to think about preserving your media is the very real possibility that it could get hacked. No site that is exposed to the Internet is 100% secure.

Q: Wait, I have another question! Where can I ask it?
A: Try posting it on Facebook, and see what happens. It's possible that one of your friends may know the answer. Sometimes people make videos to show people how to do things—there are billions of videos on YouTube.

Conclusion

Dear Reader,

In this chapter, you've learned how to upload YouTube videos and share them with friends. You've also seen various ways of exploring and sharing YouTube videos.

I am, of course, highly in favor of people getting comfy with recording video. Please consider playing around with it and trying to have fun. I recommend recording your family doing things and getting people to record you doing things. Even if you keep it private, I'm certain someday you'll be glad about (most of) the video you capture, so that your family, friends, and great-grandchildren have something interesting about your life.

If you have parents, grandparents, and especially great-grandparents who are still alive, I highly recommend getting something like a Flip Video or handheld digital camera with video/audio capability and going around and asking people to tell stories. Even if you don't put your video up on YouTube/Facebook publicly, you can still post some video on Facebook to share with other family members. And even if you don't want to post the video anywhere, I still urge you to at least capture some stories for yourself and your family.

If you're really interested in YouTube and dream of having your own YouTube, check out a thing called Google Hosted Apps. Basically, at some hosting companies, you can have your own YouTube, Gmail, Google Docs, and so on , for your personal use, your organization, or your business—all running off your own web site name. Technically, the YouTube part is called Google Video. See https://www.google.com/a/. And if you're looking for a hosting company, try Hostgator.com, and tell them Dr. Fun sent you. One of the reasons you may wish to try Google Video in this context is if you want to have your own niche site, whether private or for whatever reason.

Regards,

–Todd

snspaces.com

Come and visit the Social Networking Spaces companion web site at `www.snspaces.com`, where you can find more tips and updates and have an opportunity to share your thoughts or ask questions.

In Living Color: You can visit `www.snspaces.com/pics` to see full-color versions of all the pictures from this chapter.

The YouTube video corresponding to these pictures is at `http://tinyurl.com/xoyoutube` or `www.youtube.com/watch?v=KPoynXO6FrA`.

CHAPTER 12

■ ■ ■

What the Heck Is LinkedIn?

In This Chapter:

- Introduction: some general background about LinkedIn, an increasingly popular and important social network, used by 50 million people and counting

- Referrals (the power of LinkedIn): an introduction to one of the central features of LinkedIn and how they can help you, your colleagues, and your friends

- Help: a glance at the abundant learning material on the LinkedIn site that can help you get the most out of the site

- Creating an account: a walkthrough of how to get started

snspaces.com

Come and visit the Social Networking Spaces companion web site at www.snspaces.com, where you can find more tips and updates and have an opportunity to share your thoughts or ask questions.

In Living Color: You can visit www.snspaces.com/pics to see full-color versions of all the pictures from this chapter.

Introduction

LinkedIn is perhaps the most important business and professional social network in existence. Many people consider it a crucial tool that every worker can and should use to strengthen relationships and establish a network that can help them in their current job and to find a future job.

LinkedIn is increasingly used not only as a tool for maintaining a network of professional contacts, but also as a place to recruit and to find work. Roughly speaking, it's like a business convention, where you can meet new people, connect with colleagues from past and present jobs, and join groups for people who have similar interests (see Figure 12-1).

Figure 12-1. All the things LinkedIn offers you

Why Bother?

Taking the time to create and maintain a LinkedIn account can provide benefits in several ways, including helping you prepare for the future. One of the primary ways people find new jobs and sales leads is through referrals and introductions, and LinkedIn helps to automate this process, as you'll see in the next section. This ability alone is enough to warrant taking the time to have an account—it's also a way to help your friends and colleagues.

It's always a good idea to maintain a good-looking professional resume and profile, and LinkedIn provides several tools for doing this. And, similar to Facebook, LinkedIn provides a way to hear the latest about what's going with friends and colleagues in a professional sense, such as when someone finds a new job, is looking for a job, has created a new product, and so on.

There are also LinkedIn groups, which are a popular way of staying involved in a profession or interest area. (Group membership can look good on your profile, as well.)

But even if you never do anything more than create an account and connect with past and present colleagues, this can benefit your career and provide an easy way to help your friends and the people you work with. It takes very little time to add new connections; and once you're on LinkedIn, you'll find that other people who used to work at the same place will send you invitations.

One simple way to think of LinkedIn is a way to connect with someone after you get their business card or get to know them. You can say, "Hey, let's connect on LinkedIn," and people do—a lot. Then, you can check out their profile, their company, and so on, and also browse their connections. You may find that someday, that person can introduce you to another person they know, at a company you want to do business with or work at.

Referrals: The Power of LinkedIn

Let's take a closer look at one of the central, fascinating aspects of LinkedIn. My cousin is a lawyer, and I have friends who are lawyers, so I can get away with this next statement: LinkedIn referrals are kind of like lawyers—you may have mixed feelings about them, but you really appreciate them when you need their help.

Don't worry about how to use LinkedIn yet; just relax and enjoy the tour—you'll start an account later.

Suppose I'm on LinkedIn, and there's a particular person or company I'd like to get in touch with for some reason. I can search for them using the Search People or Search Companies feature, shown in Figure 12-2.

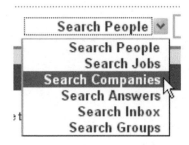

Figure 12-2. Searching on LinkedIn

Next, I enter the name of the company (see Figure 12-3).

Figure 12-3. Enter the company name.

LinkedIn may have some basic information about the company, as shown in Figure 12-4.

■ **Tip** If you have a company of your own, make sure you fill out the company profile.

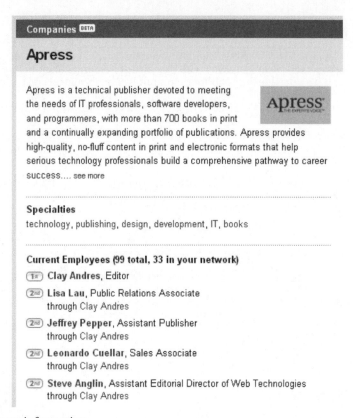

Figure 12-4. Company information

The search results include little blue numbers. 1 indicates that the person is a *first-degree contact*; that is, they're directly connected with you. In Figure 12-4, you can see that I'm directly connected to Clay Andres, who is a cheerful Jedi master editor who is wise in the ways of the Force, works on a lot of cool iPhone books, and also happens to be in the Sunflower Club.

Suppose the person I really want to get in touch with is Lisa Lau, because she is a public relations person at Apress. There's a 2 next to her name, which tells me she's a second-degree contact—even though I'm not directly connected to her, LinkedIn is telling me that someone I know *does* know her. And LinkedIn provides a way for me to ask my first-degree contact if they will introduce me to Lisa.

Take another look at Figure 12-4: if you notice, next to each second-degree name, it says "through Clay Andres." LinkedIn is saying that I'm connected to Clay Andres, who is a first-degree contact, and he can introduce me to Lisa—that is, if I ask nicely, if he's in a jolly mood, and if I bribe him by offering to send him some magic sunflower seeds.

This referral capability is important is because everyone is busy, and you're not going to give everyone an equal amount of time. But if someone you know says, "I know someone who'd like to meet you," then you're much more likely to give them the time of day. Maybe Clay will introduce me to Lisa, and maybe she'll be interested in connecting. LinkedIn makes this process a lot easier.

This is why 50 million people and counting are using LinkedIn. It's *helpful*. Even though it does a lot more, you can think of it like a matchmaking service for professional networking.

If I want to contact Lisa Lau, I click her name, as shown in Figure 12-5.

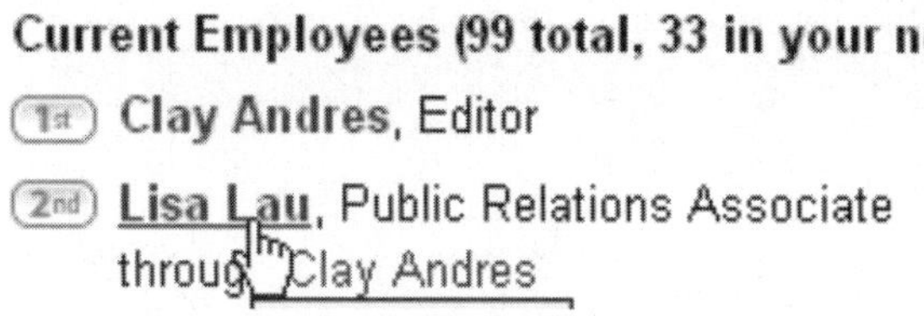

Current Employees (99 total, 33 in your network)

(1st) **Clay Andres**, Editor

(2nd) **Lisa Lau**, Public Relations Associate
through Clay Andres

Figure 12-5. Click the name of someone you want to connect with.

Her profile opens, as shown in Figure 12-6, and LinkedIn provides a variety of connection options.

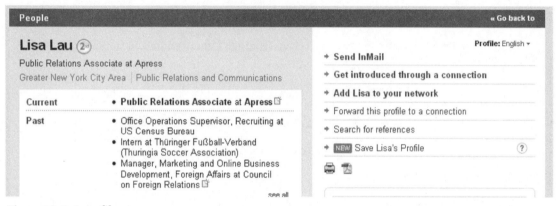

Figure 12-6. A profile

On the right, you see the option to send InMail. This is a paid service that LinkedIn offers, which lets you send a direct message without having to wait or rely on introductions. You can also use it if you have no way to connect to someone through your own network.

■ **Note** The price for InMail depends on the level of service. It currently ranges from $24.95 per month for Business level InMail to $499.95 per month for Pro level.

You can also ask to be introduced through a connection. Or in this case, if I already know Lisa, I can use the "Add Lisa to your network" link.

Further down on the profile page, LinkedIn provides a *social map*, which shows your path to the person whose profile you're looking at (see Figure 12-7. If you know someone who knows the person, LinkedIn plots it out (and this is the heart and soul of LinkedIn), showing you how you're connected.

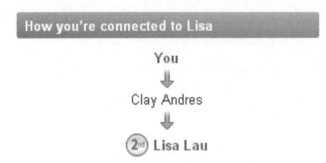

Figure 12-7. A social map showing your connection to another person

To connect to Lisa, I can click the "Get introduced through a connection" link at the top of the profile, as shown in Figure 12-8.

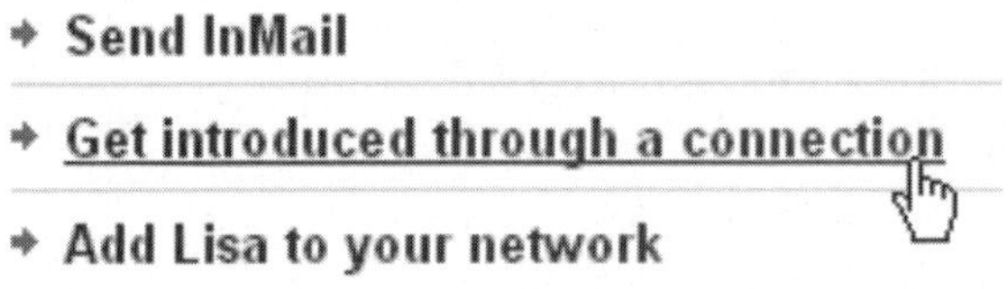

➔ **Send InMail**

➔ **Get introduced through a connection**

➔ **Add Lisa to your network**

Figure 12-8. Click to get connected.

LinkedIn helps me make the request. I fill out the Request an Introduction form shown in Figure 12-9 and hope for the best. (Hint: when you're on LinkedIn, pay attention to the little links that offer more information, such as the "How do Introductions work?" link.)

Introductions   ⑦ How do Introductions work? ◀━━━

Request an Introduction

To: **Lisa Lau**

From: Todd Kelsey

☑ Include my contact information

Enter the contact information you would like to share

Email: [▼]

Phone: [   ]

Category: [Expertise request ▼]

Subject: [Publicity for Sunflowers   ]

Your message to Lisa:

Lisa,

I wanted to ask if you would consider representing the global
sunflower community and helping to highlight their contribution
to reducing global warming, as well as their ongoing struggle
against vampire rabbits and visigothic squirrels.

-Todd

Lisa is interested in:
career opportunities,
expertise requests,
reference requests,
getting back in touch

**Lisa's contact
advice:**

Include a brief note for Clay Andres:

Clay,

Could you forward this to Lisa?

-Todd

Note: You have 2 Introductions en route. You can send 15 out at a time with your Business account. ◀━━━

[Send] or Cancel

Figure 12-9. The Request an Introduction form

LinkedIn provides a space for the message to the person you ultimately want to get in touch with, as
well as a spot to request the introduction. In this case, I want to get in touch with Lisa, and I'm asking
Clay if he can help me out.

■ **Note** There are various levels of LinkedIn accounts, and each has a limit on the number of introductions and InMail messages you can send. (InMail is the express message connection I mentioned earlier.) The more you use LinkedIn, the more you may find it useful to upgrade so that you can ask for more introductions, send more InMails, and so on. (See Figure 12-9 at the bottom.)

Exploring the Learning Center

Before you get started, let's look at the Learning Center. It's that good. Visit `http://learn.linkedin.com` (see Figure 12-10).

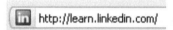

Figure 12-10. The Learning Center address

LinkedIn has unusually impressive help material, as you can see in Figure 12-11. It's organized well, tells you what you need to know, and can help you get up and running or expand your knowledge.

Figure 12-11. LinkedIn's impressive help materials

You may be thinking hesitantly about the idea of spending time learning about LinkedIn, as opposed to, say, watching the sixth season of the television show *24*. Fear not: you can legitimately learn LinkedIn at work—or at least over lunch break.

I definitely suggest spending some time at this web site, learning about the various features, looking at the user guide, and clicking the "Click here to learn the basics" link and every other link you see. Also check out the Resources section at left on `http://learn.linkedin.com`—it's got a lot of good links as well (see Figure 12-12).

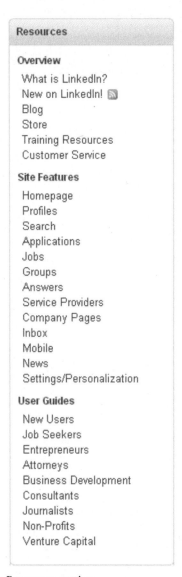

Figure 12-12. *The Learning Center's Resources section*

The more familiar you are with LinkedIn, the more helpful it can be to you, and the more you can help your friends.

If you're familiar with LinkedIn, or you consider yourself a beginner but have read an article or book that you found helpful, I invite you to visit `www.snspaces.com` and post links, tips, tricks, or anything else you think would be helpful.

Get a few Starbucks or a case of Jolt cola from eBay, and have at it!

Creating a LinkedIn Account

To begin, go to www.linkedin.com, and join LinkedIn. Enter your first and last name and your e-mail address, and come up with a password, as shown in Figure 12-13. Then, click Join Now.

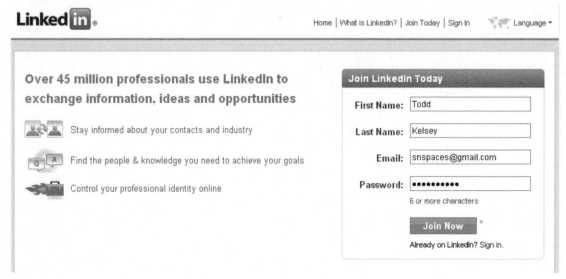

Figure 12-13. *Joining LinkedIn*

LinkedIn helps you to fill in your profile, as shown in Figure 12-14.

Figure 12-14. *Your profile*

■ **Note** One of the "I am currently" options is "Seeking work." There's no shame in that, it may help make your status clear to someone in your network (or a recruiter who is cruising LinkedIn looking for employees), and it may help you *find* work. Or, if you're seeking work, you may find a business or nonprofit organization you can help for cheap (or free) on a project, and then list yourself as a consultant or self-employed. But beware of putting "Seeking work" if you don't want your current employer to see it!

■ **Tip** If you're a job seeker, I'd like to take a moment to recommend exploring what I believe may be one of the most important books you can possibly read: *What Color Is Your Parachute?* This book has sold 10 million copies and offers very helpful advice not only for finding work, but also for figuring out what you really want to do. I highly, highly recommend it.

When you're entering a place of employment, LinkedIn explains the purpose of each field in the form. And when you start typing in a company name, it comes up with a list of potential matches, as you can see in Figure 12-15. Ideally, you'll be able to locate the specific company you work for.

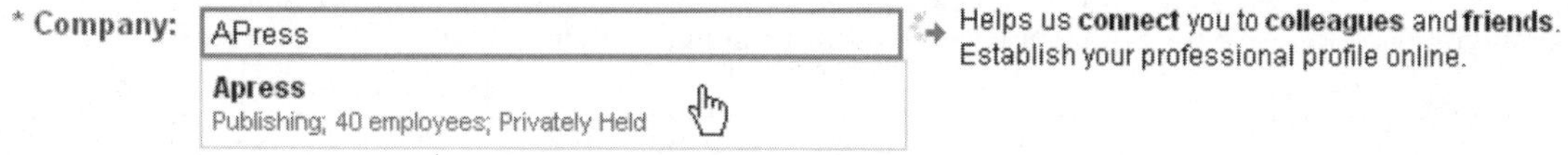

Figure 12-15. LinkedIn suggests possible company matches.

This is important because LinkedIn can help you locate colleagues at companies you worked for in the past or the one you currently work for—and this helps to build your network.

During the signup process, the main idea is to input the company you're working for now. But later, after you've signed up, you can expand your profile and add companies you used to work for—and this is a great way of connecting with past colleagues.

Next, enter your job title, as shown in Figure 12-16.

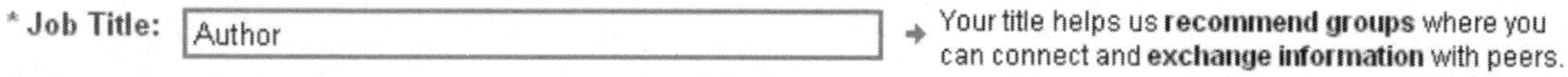

Figure 12-16. Enter your job title.

Notice how the job title can help you on LinkedIn as well, including helping LinkedIn know what groups it can suggest that you may like to join. (Don't worry too much about the title if you wear more than one hat—like anything else on LinkedIn, you can always change it later.)

Now, enter your zip code (see Figure 12-17).

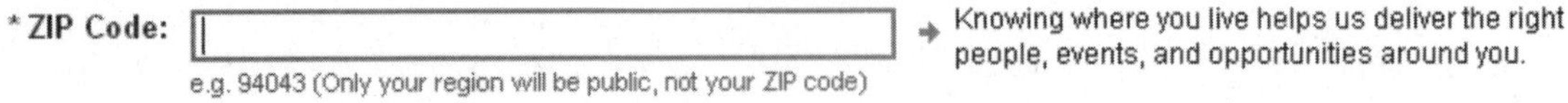

* ZIP Code:

e.g. 94043 (Only your region will be public, not your ZIP code)

→ Knowing where you live helps us deliver the right people, events, and opportunities around you.

Figure 12-17. Enter your zip code.

Click the Continue button, and LinkedIn may display a screen like the one in Figure 12-18, depending on what type of email address you have. I'm a big fan of Gmail and all the tools Google provides, so I personally recommend using a Gmail address for your professional (and personal) e-mail, but you don't have to.

Confirm Your Email Address

A confirmation email has been sent to **snspaces@gmail.com**. Click on the confirmation link in the email to activate your account.

Go to Gmail now

Figure 12-18. LinkedIn asks you to confirm your e-mail address.

The purpose of this screen is to indicate that LinkedIn has sent you a confirmation e-mail (which you need to go and check). Depending on what e-mail system you use, the button says "Go to Gmail now" or "Go to AOL now," and so on. When you check your e-mail and click the link in the message, it brings you back to LinkedIn, where you see the screen shown in Figure 12-19. Click Confirm.

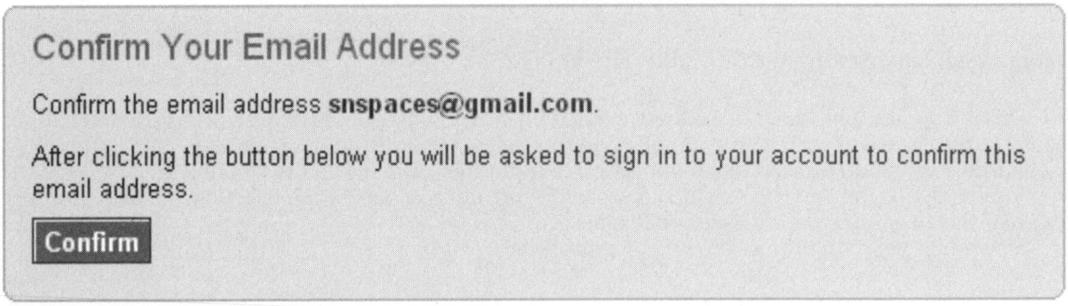

Confirm Your Email Address

Confirm the email address **snspaces@gmail.com**.

After clicking the button below you will be asked to sign in to your account to confirm this email address.

Confirm

Figure 12-19. Click Confirm.

You may need to sign in to LinkedIn using the e-mail address and password you entered earlier. Alternatively, you can click the "Forgot password" link (see Figure 12-20).

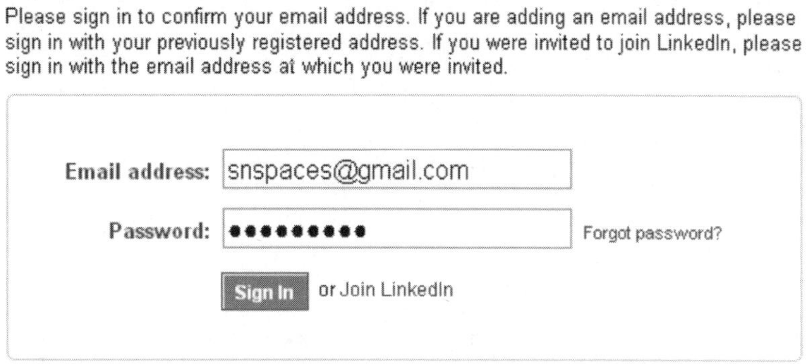

Please sign in to confirm your email address. If you are adding an email address, please sign in with your previously registered address. If you were invited to join LinkedIn, please sign in with the email address at which you were invited.

Email address: snspaces@gmail.com

Password: ●●●●●●●●●   Forgot password?

Sign In   or Join LinkedIn

Figure 12-20. If necessary, click "Forgot password."

Now you get to the really fun part: if you have a Gmail, Yahoo, AOL, Windows Live Hotmail, or other kind of e-mail account, LinkedIn can check your contacts and see if any of them are on LinkedIn (see Figure 12-21).

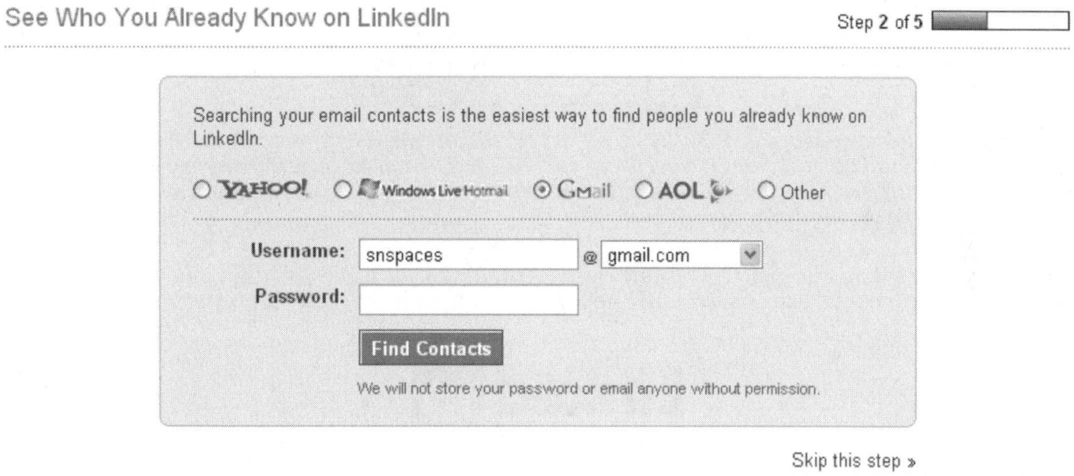

See Who You Already Know on LinkedIn   Step **2** of **5**

Searching your email contacts is the easiest way to find people you already know on LinkedIn.

○ **YAHOO!**   ○ *Windows Live Hotmail*   ● Gmail   ○ AOL   ○ Other

Username: snspaces   @ gmail.com ▾

Password: [   ]

Find Contacts

We will not store your password or email anyone without permission.

Skip this step »

Figure 12-21. Checking your contacts

On this screen, you enter the password for your e-mail account, not your LinkedIn account (unless they're the same). LinkedIn logs in to your e-mail and checks the contact list. I *definitely* recommend doing this.

If you're not on one of the featured web mails, the Other radio button allows you to choose from a list of popular web mail options, as shown in Figure 12-22.

AOL
Other
gmx.at
gmx.at
gmx.ch
gmx.de
gmx.net
googlemail.com
indiatimes.com
libero.it
live.com
mac.com
msn.com
rediffmail.com
t-online.de
web.de
yandex.ru
gmail.com

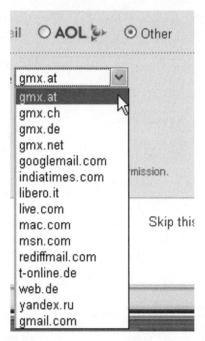

Figure 12-22. *Other e-mail options. By the way if you're still on AOL (I was, from about 1990–2005), you can start a free Gmail account, and it can check your AOL account so you can transition over. Gmail offers a lot of helpful stuff. I didn't used to like it, but now I do—and this isn't a paid announcement, it's just really useful. I even got my dad to switch over.*

LinkedIn chews on this for a few minutes (see Figure 12-23), as it checks your e-mail contacts to figure out which ones are also on LinkedIn (see Figure 12-24), to make it easier for you to connect.

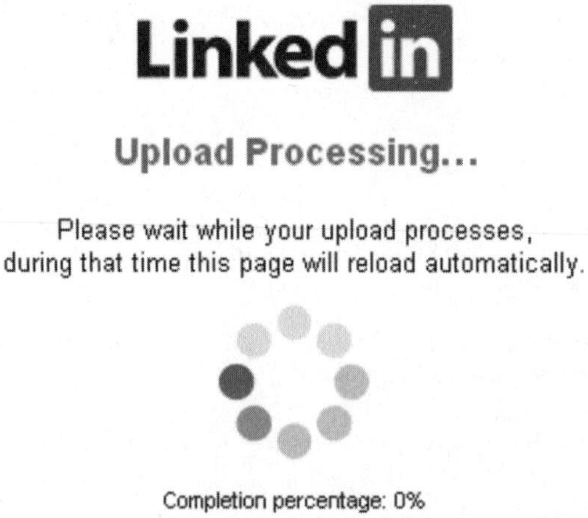

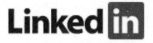

Linked in
Upload Processing...
Please wait while your upload processes,
during that time this page will reload automatically.
Completion percentage: 0%

Figure 12-23. *Looking for contacts*

You can check the box next to a person and then click Add Connection(s) to see if they want to connect.

Because I entered Apress as my company, LinkedIn shows me all the people who currently work there who are on LinkedIn (see Figure 12-25)—and there's Lisa Lau! I can click her name, too.

Do You Know These People?   Step 4 of 5

Select people you know and trust, and connect with them to stay in touch.

☐ Select All   1 Selected

☐	**Laurike De Lange** Owner	☐	**Laura Esterman** Production Editor | Project Manager
☐	**Susan Glinert** Senior Compositor	☐	**Alan Harris** Author
☐	**Matthew Kennedy** Marketing Associate	☐	**Damon Larson** Associate Copy Editor
☑	**Lisa Lau** Public Relations Associate	☐	**Lynn L'Heureux** Freelance textbook compositor

Add Connection(s) or Skip this step »

Figure 12-25. LinkedIn shows you other people who work at your company.

If LinkedIn shows you this list and you don't know anyone on it or don't want to connect with them, you can click the "Skip this step" link.

As the final step of the sign-up process, you can enter the e-mail addresses of anyone you know who you figure is on LinkedIn, as shown in Figure 12-26.

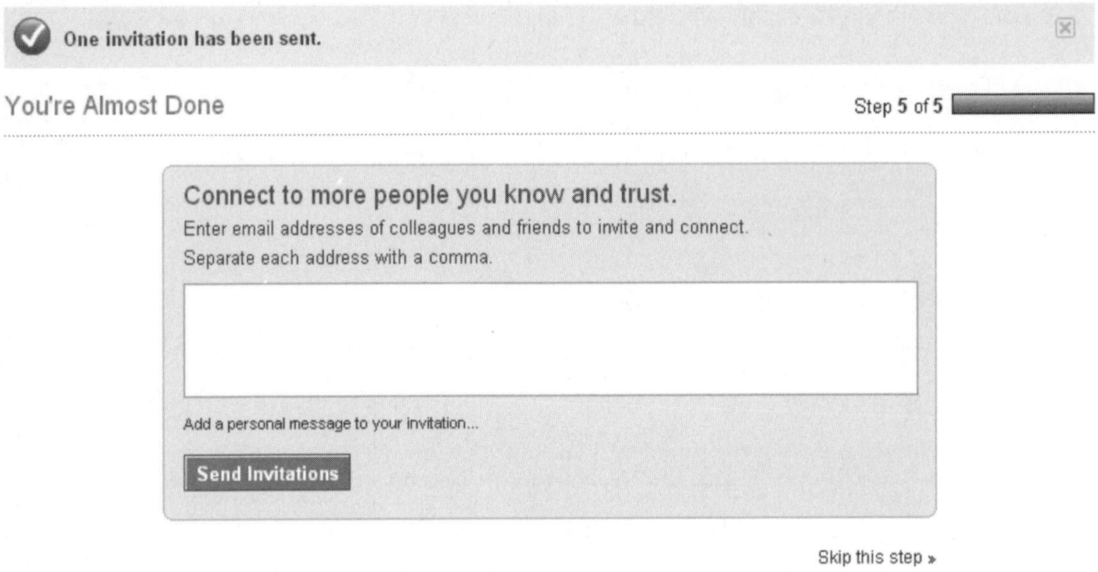

✓ **One invitation has been sent.**   ⊠

You're Almost Done   Step **5** of **5** ▬▬▬▬▬

Connect to more people you know and trust.

Enter email addresses of colleagues and friends to invite and connect.
Separate each address with a comma.

Add a personal message to your invitation...

Send Invitations

Skip this step »

Figure 12-26. Enter the e-mail addresses of other people you know.

After you complete Step 5, you probably see the full LinkedIn screen and something like Figure 12-27 in the center.

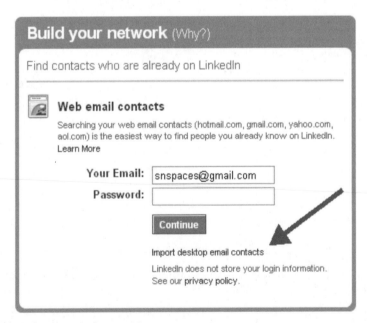

Figure 12-27. The box that opens after you sign up

This box is a reminder that you can dig in to your web mail contacts to add people. It contains two important links. I've highlighted one with an arrow: "Import desktop e-mail contacts" can be really helpful if you use Outlook.

And 10 points if you can guess the other important link. Look around Figure 12-27 and see if you can guess.

Why?

You got it! The Why? link. It's important to explore LinkedIn's links, help, and so on—exploration can be fun, and you can probably learn something.

At some point, you should receive a welcome e-mail, which looks something like the one in Figure 12-28.

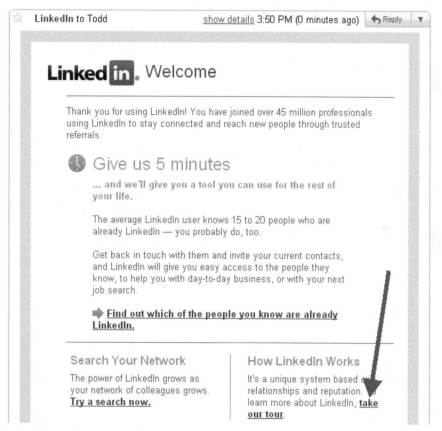

Figure 12-28. Welcome e-mail message

Be sure to explore the links from this e-mail message—in particular, the "take our tour" link, which leads to good information, as shown in Figure 12-29.

Figure 12-29. *The LinkedIn tour leads to helpful spots.*

Q/A

Q: Why should I bother using LinkedIn? I can't afford it.

A: LinkedIn is free. The only reason you have to pay is if you use InMail. You should consider using LinkedIn because having a stronger career network may be helpful to you someday (for example, if you're searching for work). You can used LinkedIn to get an inside connection by requesting an introduction to someone at a company you're interested in working for. It's been shown that in addition to regular job techniques, proactively finding companies you're interested in working for, and seeking to make contact through things like informational interviews, increases your chances of finding work. You also increase your chances of finding work when you collaborate with others.

For more information about these proven techniques, read *What Color Is Your Parachute?* It rocks. Even if you're not searching for a job at the moment, in my opinion, you may want to read this book if you don't find your current job fulfilling; *WCIYP* isn't just for people who are unemployed—it's a great book to help you consider what work you'd find truly fulfilling.

Q: What's InMail?

A: InMail is for situations when you want to send someone a message but they aren't in your network. Say, for example, that you read an article that mentions someone at a particular company or organization. If you want to get in touch with that person, you may not be able to find their e-mail address on the Internet, but you may be able to find them on LinkedIn. If they have their account set so that they accept InMail, then you can send them a message (but doing so costs you—in part to make money for LinkedIn, and also to cut down on the number of frivolous e-mail people receive). The more famous/influential a person is, the less likely they are to have InMail activated.

Q: Why do you keep promoting the Social Networking Spaces site? Enough already!

A: I'm sorry if the repetition is annoying. Sometimes, people forget about opportunities until you mention them a few times. And part of the point of this book is to serve as the beginning of a conversation; no offense if you're not interested in participating, but I hope a few people will visit the site, ask questions, benefit from the tutorials, and contribute their thoughts. Ultimately, what this book is about, and what CFTW is about (the nonprofit organization to which the author proceeds are going), is trying to help people learn about things they're interested in.

Q: I like this book, but there are only two chapters about LinkedIn. Where can I read more?

A: If you liked this book and this chapter or section, keep your eyes open for an entire book from CFTW Press about LinkedIn. If you want to keep posted about the book's progress, go on Facebook and search for (and join) the Social Networking Spaces Group, or search for (and become a fan of) the Social Networking Spaces Facebook page. I'll post messages once in a while to both. Just as with *Social Networking Spaces*, all author proceeds for the book on LinkedIn will be donated to CFTW. (See the Introduction to this book.) And don't worry if you don't know how to join a group or become a fan. You can learn by reading the Facebook chapters in this book!

Q: Do you own Google stock or something? You sure seem to like Google.

A: Nope. Google doesn't need my help. Facebook is already likely to be getting their attention in a serious way, given that 400 million people are on there. (Source: recent *Economist* report on social networking. It's an excellent report and may still be available for free—go to www.economist.com, look in the Special Reports section for the one on social networking, and then either read it or click Buy PDF. If you're a business type, I highly recommend it.) But Google is pretty strong.

The thing I really appreciate about Google is how it has made my life easier, as I've explored the various free tools and introduced friends to them to help them with their projects. Time and time again, I've been pleased with the ease of use and power of the tools Google provides and the quality of the functionality compared to other tools, including ones you have to pay money for.

I also particularly appreciate how Google supports communication when crossing the language gap—see Chapter 18. And that's something I appreciate about LinkedIn, too: it's one of the first entities I've come across that makes it possible for a person to have a profile in more than one language. Pretty cool. Not even Google does that (yet).

I'm sorry to bore everyone else, but if you're interested in this type of thing, feel free to ping me, and I'd be glad to share a copy of my PhD dissertation with you; it's a sort of tour through sustainable, multilingual web sites and various tools and approaches from open source content-management systems to tools from Google.

Q: Wait! I have another question! Where can I ask it?

A: On www.snspaces.com.

Conclusion

Dear Reader,

Thank you for reading this chapter. It was a pleasure to write, as this whole book has been. In it, you've taken a look at what LinkedIn can do and how to get an account going, which I encourage everyone to do, regardless of employment status, age, or any other factor.

Personally, it feels to me as though LinkedIn is one of the most important social networks during a time of economic change. As far as I'm concerned, the more we can do to help each other develop our careers, the better.

Learning by helping someone else is a proven way to enhance your own understanding. You don't have to be an expert—it's OK to explore.

Be sure to buy a copy of *What Color Is Your Parachute?* if you don't already own this book. I wish you the best in your journey of developing your career and connecting with people.

And one special note: if I happen to have the honor of addressing any retirees (especially if you're retired), or someone who isn't technically a senior and isn't retired, but feels too old, you should join LinkedIn, too. You have *valuable wisdom*—and if you desire to be active, there are many ways you can share that wisdom, especially with nonprofit organizations. Lest you still think you're too old for LinkedIn: you're not old until you hit your nineties. If you need convincing that you're young, take a good look at this next picture.

Life Story News

Everyone has a life story.

This is my Grandpa Kelsey, who lived from 1898-1998. In 1918, in November, he was on his way to Europe to join World War One. Then, on Nov. 11th, they declared the Armistice, which ended the War. It was also his birthday, which coincided with Veteran's Day ever since. Below is his Draft card.

REGISTRATION CARD

So, please join LinkedIn! And feel free to invite me to be a connection!

Regards,

–Todd

snspaces.com

Come and visit the Social Networking Spaces companion web site at www.snspaces.com, where you can find more tips and updates and have an opportunity to share your thoughts or ask questions.

In Living Color: You can visit www.snspaces.com/pics to see full-color versions of all the pictures from this chapter.

CHAPTER 13

Using LinkedIn to Strengthen Your Career Support Network

In This Chapter:

- How to build your network: it's important for everyone; help yourself and help your friends.

- How to find a job: unless you're in the extreme minority (like my dad, who had a single employer for 40 years), chances are you'll need to find a job at some point.

- How to join a group: LinkedIn groups can be a good way to develop contacts, find out about job opportunities, and keep abreast of the latest information in your field.

- How to benefit from LinkedIn as a retiree.

snspaces.com

Come and visit the Social Networking Spaces companion web site at www.snspaces.com, where you can find more tips and updates and have an opportunity to share your thoughts or ask questions.

In Living Color: You can visit www.snspaces.com/pics to see full-color versions of all the pictures from this chapter.

Introduction

There are 50 million people on LinkedIn. It's important.

LinkedIn provides really powerful tools that you can use to help yourself and help your friends career-wise. It's an increasingly popular tool for developing business contacts and finding work. Just about anyone who has a career and wants to continue working or is currently seeking a job should invest the time to build and maintain their network.

Even if you're currently working and believe you'll be in this position for the rest of your life, I'd caution you to consider that things could change. What LinkedIn provides you, in some ways, is a safety net: by investing the time to build your network, you're maintaining contacts that could become crucial when and if you do look for a job. And even if you're 100 percent certain you'll always be in your current job, you can provide a valuable service for your friends by being connected online and helping them to "link in" to other people.

One of the best ways to find a job is through referrals, and that's what LinkedIn provides. It's also a great tool for developing existing businesses. I can't really think of a good reason why anyone shouldn't use LinkedIn, only reasons why you should, for the sake of your own career/business/non-profit organization, as well as for the sake of your friends and colleagues.

In fact, I think LinkedIn is so important that I want to suggest that you consider spending some time with it on a regular basis. For example, perhaps you might spend Monday lunches on LinkedIn.

A NOTE FOR RETIREES (AND EVERYONE ELSE)

There is at least the possibility that you may get bored in retirement, so you may want to use LinkedIn to keep connected with your field. And learning to use LinkedIn and helping others to learn it (and mentoring younger folk, especially very young folk) could be an excellent way to help other people who are entering the workforce. Plus, you may find it interesting to join LinkedIn groups and either offer to mentor upstarts (and startups) or earn a bit of money doing some consulting, based on your expertise. See the Q/A section at the end of this chapter.

So don't skip this chapter! I want to encourage you to share your vast, precious wisdom on LinkedIn.

All I'm asking is please, don't write yourself off for *any* reason. Society needs you!

Case in point: At the time of writing, I visited a fine library that had a really interesting program where they were reaching out to retirees in the area, to help them capture and convert historical items into digital format for the benefit of preserving community heritage. How cool! People got some training and provided a valuable service. If your library doesn't have a program like that but you like the idea, perhaps you can ask them to start one!

Or if you want to mentor but don't know where to start, begin by asking for some help at the library to learn enough to capture your story, put some of it up on Facebook, and start a LinkedIn account. Then, if you feel so led, you may want to go back to the library and tell them that if any younger folk need a mentor or some encouraging wisdom, you're there. And come on www.snspaces.com and tell us about it! Or if you don't find any takers locally, come to www.snspaces.com and announce that you're available for mentoring. Carpe diem!

Let's Connect Everyone Who Wants To

If you're not a retiree but are reading this section, I invite you to consider filing these thoughts away or at least keep an open mind in the immediate term. You may come across someone, such as a relative, and find yourself thinking, hmmm, maybe I could help this person to get on to LinkedIn and find some way of keeping active (which they probably desire to do). And maybe you'd like to help them discover some empowering or even fun things they can do online, and help them get to the point where they can use something like Facebook or even LinkedIn. Why the heck not? That's what I say.

The point is, everyone will retire someday, and anyone who wants to should be able to connect with other people on social networks—and some people may need a bit of encouragement and help. That's what this book is all about. And the reality is, some people will be excluded unless you help them. Conversely, some people will feel included when you help them. It doesn't necessarily mean that everyone needs an Internet connection—there's a thing called sunnygram that can print and mail a copy of Facebook activity to someone (www.sunnygram.com, or see the CNN article "How to e-mail Grandma if she doesn't have a computer" at http://tinyurl.com/sunnygram).

Yes, I chose to put this note in a LinkedIn chapter, but it applies in various ways to just about every social network mentioned in the book. My dream is for you, the reader, to learn a lot from this book and be so encouraged and inspired that you take the time to help someone else learn some of the skills you acquire, or at least buy the book for a relative, a friend, or your local library.

Build Your Network

To get started with LinkedIn, first get familiar and comfortable with adding people to your network. In Chapter 12, you saw how LinkedIn allows you to check your web mail contacts as part of the sign-in process, and this automatic checking is something you can *continue* to do on a regular basis. I review this technique in this section. But you can also invite people whom you interact with at work and whom you meet; and when you build your profile and list the names of companies you've worked for, LinkedIn can help you find people at those companies whom you may know.

Get in the habit of asking yourself whether there is anyone you've interacted with recently whom you would do well to invite to connect on LinkedIn.

■ **Tip** If you need a good system of reminding yourself to do things, I suggest getting a Gmail account (http://mail.google.com), learning how to use the Calendar feature, and setting a reoccurring appointment to e-mail you a reminder or send a message to your phone. Gmail has pretty good help, but feel free to look on www.snspaces.com for a Google Calendar tutorial; if you don't find one, feel free to ask me nicely, and I'll be glad to put one up (tekelsey "at" gmail "dot" com).

Adding Contacts

There are a variety of methods for building your network, but the simplest and most straightforward way is to add more contacts. Log in to LinkedIn, and click the Contacts link at left, as shown in Figure 13-1.

Figure 13-1. Click Contacts.

A few tabs appear, and you can click the Add Connections link at right (see Figure 13-2).

Figure 13-2. Click Add Connections.

You can use the See Who You Already Know feature by entering your e-mail address and the password for your e-mail account to automatically display a list of people you can invite. You can also enter e-mail addresses.

Then, you may want to explore the Colleagues and Classmates tabs, shown in Figure 13-3.

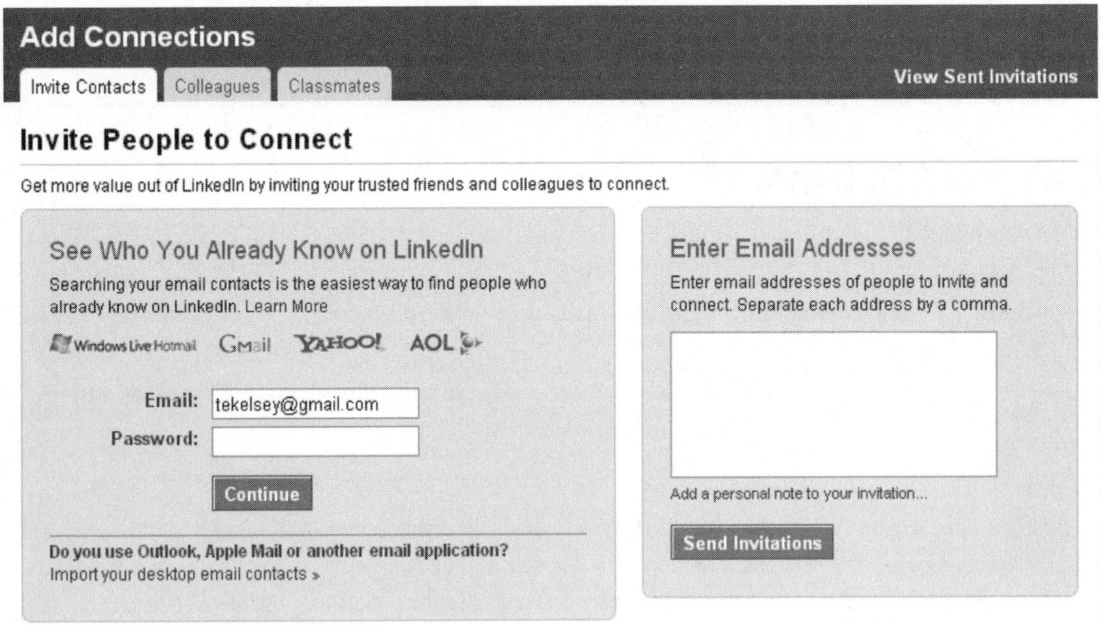

Add Connections

Invite Contacts | Colleagues | Classmates   View Sent Invitations

Invite People to Connect

Get more value out of LinkedIn by inviting your trusted friends and colleagues to connect.

See Who You Already Know on LinkedIn

Searching your email contacts is the easiest way to find people who already know on LinkedIn. Learn More

Windows Live Hotmail   Gmail   YAHOO!   AOL

Email: tekelsey@gmail.com

Password:

[Continue]

Do you use Outlook, Apple Mail or another email application?
Import your desktop email contacts »

Enter Email Addresses

Enter email addresses of people to invite and connect. Separate each address by a comma.

Add a personal note to your invitation...

[Send Invitations]

Figure 13-3. The Colleagues and Classmates tabs

The Colleagues tab displays people you may know based on the company names you've listed in your profile (which is a good reason to complete your profile). The Classmates tab is a handy tool that can help you find alumni of the school you went to, whom you may know.

And don't forget that you can "Import your desktop e-mail contacts" with the link at the bottom.

Searching for Colleagues

In this section, you look at the search function and see some of the ways LinkedIn works and thinks. Go to the search box, choose the Search People option from the drop-down menu to the left of it, type the name of a person, and click Search. See Figure 13-4.

Search People ✔	Clay Andres	Search

Figure 13-4. Searching for people you know

Even though this technique looks easy and comes in handy, I recommend going through the process of checking your web mail contacts, importing addresses from desktop e-mail, and using the Colleagues and Classmates tabs on a regular basis.

When you search for someone, you see a list of results; do your best to find the right person. (So many people are on LinkedIn, there are often many people with the same name. If you're not sure who is who, click their profiles.) When you're sure you have the right person, click the "Add to network" link. See Figure 13-5.

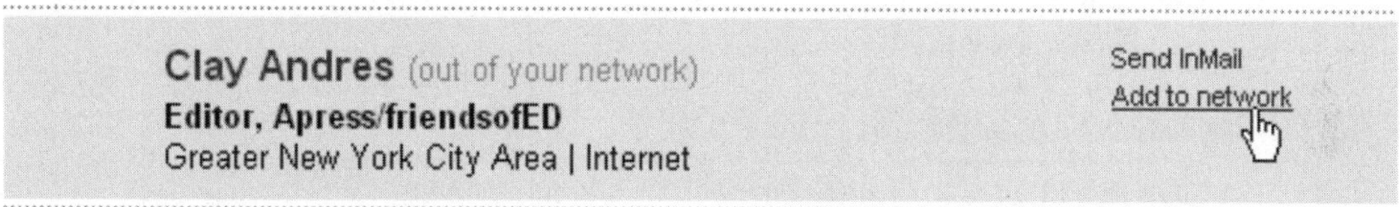

Clay Andres (out of your network)
Editor, Apress/friendsofED
Greater New York City Area | Internet

Send InMail
Add to network

Figure 13-5. Adding a contact

■ **Tip** The Send InMail function is a way to send a message to someone who isn't on your network. You have a limited number of InMail credits, so it's better to use those for reaching out to someone to propose a business deal, contacting a recruiter, and so on.

Next, you see an invitation screen, which is how you ask your contact to join your network. See Figure 13-6.

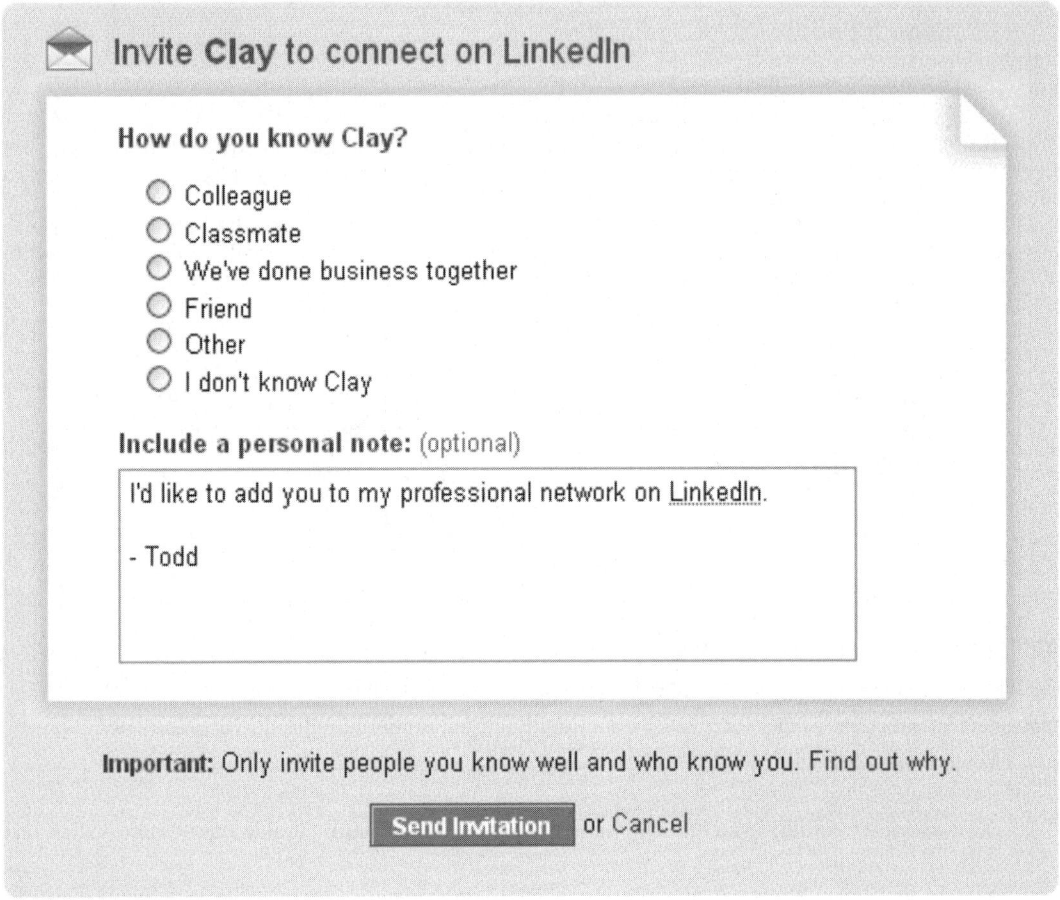

Figure 13-6. *The invite screen*

You can choose how you know the person, enter a note if you like, and click the Send Invitation button. You may also want to click the "Find out why" link to learn about the value of inviting people you know.

If you choose the Colleague option, you see a drop-down menu that may have a suggestion of a company, as shown in Figure 13-7.

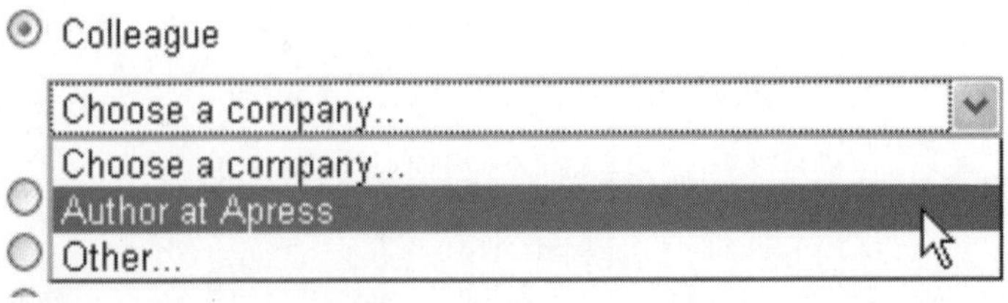

Figure 13-7. *How do you know this person?*

You can include a note if you like, as shown in Figure 13-8.

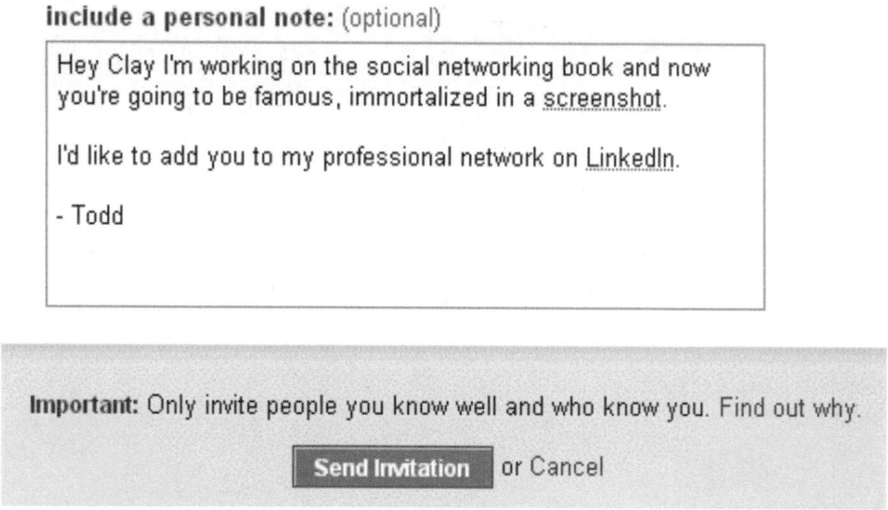

include a personal note: (optional)

> Hey Clay I'm working on the social networking book and now you're going to be famous, immortalized in a screenshot.
>
> I'd like to add you to my professional network on LinkedIn.
>
> - Todd

Important: Only invite people you know well and who know you. Find out why.

Send Invitation or Cancel

Figure 13-8. Including a personal note

Adding Connections by Company

You can use the Colleagues tab in the Add Connections screen to easily find colleagues based on the companies you've listed in your profile. To start, click the Contacts link, shown in Figure 13-9.

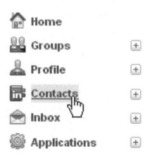

🏠 Home

👥 Groups   ⊞

👤 Profile   ⊞

📇 Contacts   ⊞

✉️ Inbox   ⊞

⚙️ Applications   ⊞

Figure 13-9. The Contacts link

Then, click the Add Connections link, shown in Figure 13-10.

Add Connections | Remove Connections

Figure 13-10. Click to add a connection.

You're directed to the Add Connections screen, shown in Figure 13-11.

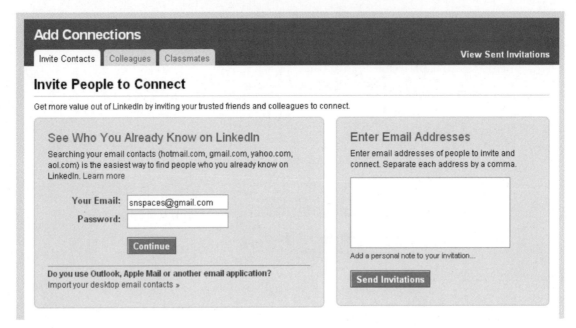

Figure 13-11. *The Add Connections screen*

On the Add Connections screen, click the Colleagues tab, shown in Figure 13-12.

Figure 13-12. *Click here to find past and present colleagues.*

LinkedIn guides you through the process of finding people whom you may know at companies where you've worked. (Remember, this feature depends on your having filled out your profile.) See Figure 13-13.

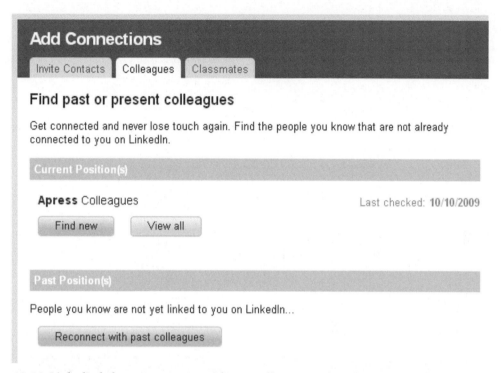

Figure 13-13. LinkedIn helps you reconnect with past colleagues and stay connected with current ones.

Exploring Your Contacts' Connections

LinkedIn generally frowns on people trying to add connections by asking people they don't know to join their network. So it's probably a bad idea to go around randomly reaching out to people you don't know. (That is, except in the case of InMail, which is a contact tool. In that case, you aren't trying to add a person as a connection, but are just contacting them. To learn more about InMail, look in the Help section on LinkedIn.)

But you can click your contacts' profiles and see if they're connected with anyone you know by doing the following:

- Looking at your connections' profiles
- Clicking their Connections link
- Looking for people you know, clicking their profiles, and using the "Add (person) to your network" link

Searching for a Job on LinkedIn

LinkedIn is a great tool for building your career and helping you find work. According to the well-known career guide *What Color Is Your Parachute?* (Ten Speed Press), sending out resumes in the traditional way is one of the *least effective* techniques for finding work. But the good news is that when you combine multiple job-search techniques, including *working on your job search with others*, your chances of finding work increase significantly.

LinkedIn is all about working with others and connecting with people. So you connect with people, and build your network; and then, for example, when you do want to contact someone about a job (such as a recruiter), you may know someone who has valuable leads.

■ **Tip** Use the general job search function, and also keep your eyes open in the "LinkedIn updates" e-mails, in case someone is posting a job.

To search for a job on LinkedIn, you can click the Jobs link shown in Figure 13-14.

Figure 13-14. The Jobs link

Then, type in keywords, and click Search, as shown in Figure 13-15.

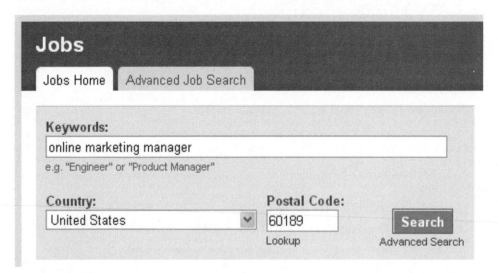

Figure 13-15. Begin your search.

LinkedIn displays listings that may relate, as shown in Figure 13-16.

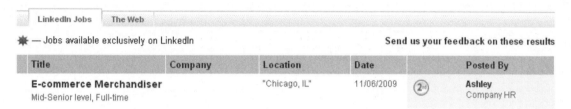

Figure 13-16. LinkedIn's search results

This is where LinkedIn differs from other job boards. In the job listing shown in Figure 13-16, there's a 2 in the Posted By column. Basically, LinkedIn tells you how far removed you are from the recruiter, and whether someone you know is a direct or indirect contact. The 2 means that someone in your network is directly connected to the recruiter. It's still worth applying even if it's not a 2, but this demonstrates one reason why it's good to get in the habit of building your network.

For those retirees and independently wealthy people who are still paying attention: one thing you can do for others is to maintain your network, because you may be able to make an introduction sometime that could make a difference. There are also groups in LinkedIn that you may want to participate in, so keep reading.

If you click a job listing, it comes up, and you can click Apply Now, or you can click Request Referral. See Figure 13-17.

Figure 13-17. Apply or request a referral here.

Requesting a referral is an option for getting introduced through your network, which could make a difference in getting the attention of the recruiter and getting the job.

■ **Tip** Visit the resources in the Learning Center (http://learn.linkedin.com), including the ones on looking for jobs.

After you click a job listing, in addition to the section where you can click Apply Now and Request Referral, there's also a section that mentions who posted the job. See Figure 13-18.

Figure 13-18. *This screen lets you know who posted the job.*

This is important, because you can click the "See who connects you" link. When you click this link, a little map comes up and shows who connects you, as shown in Figure 13-19.

Figure 13-19. *A connections map shows you how you're linked to another person.*

In this example, Ashley posted the job, so it's possible Robin may be willing to pass my resume long. (LinkedIn does show full names, but I erased the last names for the sake of privacy.)

If you have a second-degree connection (indicated by the blue circle with the 2 in it), LinkedIn shows whoever you know who knows the person you want to get in touch with (including if there's more than one person you know who is connected to them). And if it's a third-degree or higher connection (meaning no one you know knows the person directly), LinkedIn can still plot a path.

With LinkedIn, whether with job searching or if you're a sales or business development person trying to connect or propose a new venture, when you ask for an introduction, basically the question is, will the person you know forward the introduction to the person they know?

Let's say you want to get in touch with Bill Gates. And you know Tom, but he doesn't know Bill Gates directly. But Tom knows Andy Grove, the founder of Intel, who probably knows Bill Gates. So if you request the introduction, the question is, will Tom forward a note to Andy, and will Andy forward the note to Bill Gates?

It's partly a question of social capital. In this scenario, Andy Grove doesn't know you, so if he gives your resume to Bill Gates, it's not a direct referral, but it has been passed along a series of trusted relationships. In principle, with job searches, it's stronger to have some kind of connection. That's why LinkedIn is a helpful tool.

You may notice some additional information, such as LinkedIn groups, on the page of the person who has posted a job. So (ding, ding, ding!) one reason why it's a good idea to join LinkedIn groups is that the hiring manager at a company, or the HR person, or the recruiter, may be a part of the LinkedIn group, too, and this provides more opportunities. See Figure 13-20. (For more information about LinkedIn groups, see the "LinkedIn Groups" section later in this chapter.)

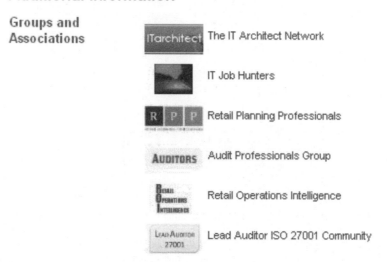

Figure 13-20. A contact's Groups and Associations

The point is, align yourself with what you're interested in and your profession, and chances are, at some point it will help you to connect with other people in your profession—which may help you land a job. Not only may the recruiter notice you're in a group when you're applying for a job, because they may look at your profile, but recruiters may look on LinkedIn and notice that you're in a group, or post a job opportunity to a specific group. You may also want to see what groups particular recruiters are members of, and potentially join them. It makes sense all around.

WHAT COLOR IS YOUR PARACHUTE?

In addition to getting on LinkedIn, I believe that one of the best things you can do to help in your job search (and for generally developing a sense of what kind of job would be a good fit)—is to read the book *What Color Is Your Parachute?*

LinkedIn and this book work well together. For example, one of the principles in *What Color Is Your Parachute?*, based on strong evidence and the expertise of the author, is that your chances of finding work increase significantly when you work on the process with others. This is exactly what LinkedIn is about.

I wish I had enough money to buy a copy of *that* book for every reader of *this* book.

It's that good. It's sold bazillions of copies, because it's a really helpful tool, not only in the practical side of job hunting, but also for thinking about what kind of work you're best suited to do.

I have a special affection for writing these two chapters on LinkedIn, in part because of some of the surprises and transitions in my own career, including being downsized for economic reasons (I empathize with anyone reading who has been laid off). And what I'd say about *What Color Is Your Parachute?* is the same thing I'd say about LinkedIn: the ideal way to go through them, to use these tools—is *with others*.

I definitely recommend reaching out to connect with others:

1. Put an ad up on the bulletin board at your local grocery store or library or on `www.craigslist.org`.

2. Reach out on Facebook or Twitter.

3. Look for a Meetup in your area (see the chapter on Meetup) that is focused on job-hunting or *What Color Is Your Parachute?*

4. Create a new Meetup group.

While writing this book, I started going through the latest edition of *What Color Is Your Parachute*; if you like, you're welcome to visit a blog I created at `http://wciyp.blogspot.com` that offers my thoughts about the book. I'm going to use it as a place to offer encouragement and reflection based on reading the book and, I hope, get people interested in reading it.

LinkedIn Groups (and Jobs)

I didn't understand the value of LinkedIn *until I discovered groups. While some groups are chock-full of spam and self-promotion, others are places where you can learn from your peers, participate in interesting discussions, and meet great people. Some even host virtual events. For example, the* LinkedIn *.NET User Group (LIDNUG)* *holds periodic webcasts with people like Scott Guthrie from Microsoft. It's pretty cool to be able to ask questions and interact with a large audience from around the world, all of whom share an interest in a particular topic with you.*

—Ehren von Lehe, Creative Engineer: http://vonlehecreative.com

LinkedIn Groups are a great way to connect with people who have similar professional interests, for exchanging information, for finding out about jobs, and for asking questions. You can learn more about groups by looking at your connections' profiles to see what groups they're in, or by searching for people and seeing what they're involved with (see Figure 13-21).

Search People ✔ | todd kelsey | Search

Figure 13-21. Search for your contact.

Click the name of your contact when you know it's the right person (feel free to request me as a LinkedIn contact to practice and/or permanently). See Figure 13-22.

Todd Kelsey 🔲 (YOU)
Online Marketing Manager at Cradle.org
Greater Chicago Area | Information Technology and Services

Figure 13-22. Click the name to see your contact's profile.

Then, you can always scroll down to a person's Groups and Associations section, which lists what groups they're part of (see Figure 13-23).

Groups and Associations

Drupal   Drupal

Professional Second Lifers

Figure 13-23. Your contact's Groups and Associations

One technique for learning about groups is to browse around the profiles of people you're connected with. You can even learn things by looking at the profiles of people you don't know; for example, you can search for "architect" or "computer programmer," look at the profiles of the people who appear, and see the groups they have joined. Then, you can click the group names to learn more about them, and perhaps join those groups.

A benefit of joining a group is that you often receive e-mails with career-related news and even job openings. For example, Figure 13-24 shows a typical message in my inbox.

☐ ☆ **Drupal Group Members**   **From Eisenstein Michael and other Drupal group member**

Figure 13-24. A message from one of my groups

The message has news about Drupal (an open source content-management system; see www.drupal.org). Sometimes these messages have job postings as well, as shown in Figure 13-25.

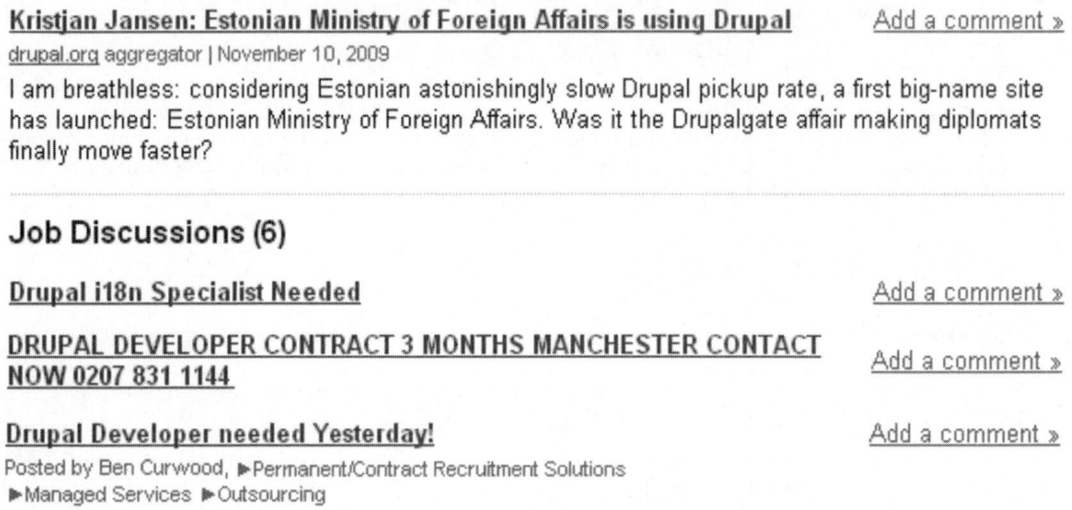

Kristjan Jansen: Estonian Ministry of Foreign Affairs is using Drupal
Add a comment »
drupal.org aggregator | November 10, 2009
I am breathless: considering Estonian astonishingly slow Drupal pickup rate, a first big-name site has launched: Estonian Ministry of Foreign Affairs. Was it the Drupalgate affair making diplomats finally move faster?
Job Discussions (6)
Drupal i18n Specialist Needed
Add a comment »
DRUPAL DEVELOPER CONTRACT 3 MONTHS MANCHESTER CONTACT NOW 0207 831 1144
Add a comment »
Drupal Developer needed Yesterday!
Add a comment »
Posted by Ben Curwood, ▶Permanent/Contract Recruitment Solutions
▶Managed Services ▶Outsourcing

Figure 13-25. *News from one of my groups*

When you connect on the group page, it may very well have a Jobs tab, which you can browse proactively. See Figure 13-26.

Groups
Drupal
Overview
Discussions
News
Jobs
Subgroups
More

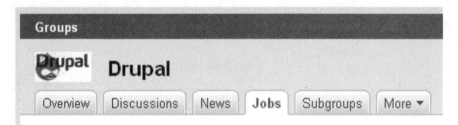

Figure 13-26. *Some groups include Jobs listings.*

Accessing LinkedIn Groups

To get to the Groups feature, click the Groups link at left on the LinkedIn screen, as shown in Figure 13-27.

Home
Groups
Profile

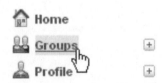

Figure 13-27. *Accessing the Groups feature*

Any groups you're part of show up, and you can click their names to access the Group page. See Figure 13-28.

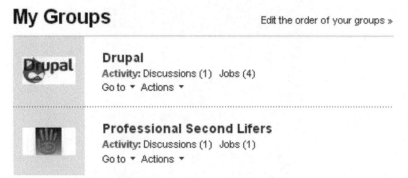

Figure 13-28. *A listing of all my groups*

When you click the Groups link, the resulting screen also has a Find a Group link, which you can use to search for groups, and a Create a Group link (if you don't find what you're looking for). See Figure 13-29.

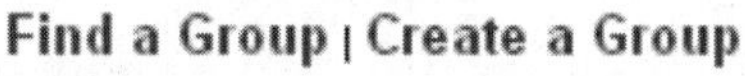

Find a Group | Create a Group

Figure 13-29. *Here you can find or create a group.*

Encouragement for Career Changers, Job Seekers, and Anyone in Career Transition

In this section, I share a bit about some transition in my own career, as an attempt to encourage you to keep on going. I also figured you may expect a chapter on LinkedIn to be the least interesting and most boring—so I'm trying to spice things up a bit.

A few moons ago, I joined a band called Sister Soleil, and we started playing locally in Chicago for tiny audiences. Here's the poster from our very first gig:

As a musician, the first time I played in a coffeehouse on my own, I was nervous. Later, in this band, it was through practice that I gained confidence. Through rehearsals, everything became second nature. And it was tremendously fun to put on a show, and to *share*.

I see sharing knowledge/skills the same way: it is tremendously fun. If you try sharing things you learn about LinkedIn, and enjoy the experience, keep on trying! Not only will you be in a better position yourself, but you can also be in a position to help others. This can help you find a job, and you can help others.

Sister Soleil was the beginning of my musical career. We practiced a lot and played shows, and I went from being very quiet and swaying back and forth timidly like a tree, to being a little more active and feeling more comfortable playing in front of larger audiences.

Eventually, things grew. The largest audience we played in front of was 14,000 people, at a wonderful outdoor summer concert. Here's the poster:

At upper left is Everclear, to the right are the lads in Slipknot, and beneath them is Stella, the lead singer of the band I was in. (You can find this page on www.last.fm by searching for "Sister Soleil" and looking at the Events tab, or by visiting http://tinyurl.com/dotfest2.)

At the time, the biggest name on the bill was Everclear (Slipknot had not yet been on Conan O'Brien nor risen to stardom), and we went on right after them. The noise of the cheering crowd was so loud it was unbelievable. It was a wonderful experience. A *lot* of people.

Another reason I'm mentioning this story is because of career transitions.

You may think your job is stable, but it's a really good idea to prepare for the possibility of things not working out. For example, let's consider my own situation. Playing in front of 14,000 people, touring around the country in a bus, living the dream.

No reason to read *What Color Is Your Parachute?* or go on LinkedIn. I mean, why bother, right? But the world of rock 'n' roll did come abruptly to a halt; we made some good music, but Sister Soleil didn't end up with a hit radio single.

And this is why you'll find the following entry on my LinkedIn account:

Past
- Consultant at McDonalds Corporation
- Global Learning Advocate at Hostway
- Language Learning Coordinator (Volunteer) at One Laptop Per Child
- Featured Guest and Co-Writer at TechTV
- Contractor at United Loyalty Services
 • Producer at MyPoints

see less...

After the rollercoaster of rock 'n' roll, I needed to consider other options, and I ended up at a company called MyPoints.com.

So yeah, it was rough. Transitions are rough. But I'm still standing, and part of the reason I'm relating this is that I want readers who are going through transition to know that you aren't alone, and that you *can* get back on your feet again. Even if the rug has been pulled out from under you, like it was for me, and even if you find yourself needing to look in new directions like I did, you've got *transferrable skills.*

As for me, over time, I slowly learned how to find my bliss, which seems to be encouraging people to capture, preserve, and share their life stories, and helping other people learn and try new things.

What were my transferrable skills? I suppose being a producer, and learning how to draw things together. I used these skills working on my own little music projects when I was supporting Stella (who was a solo artist, under the name Sister Soleil). Ironically, even though I wasn't a record producer, I did end up as an official "producer" at Mypoints, working on web content.

Another lesson I learned is this: do your own thing. You don't have to pin *all* your hopes and dreams on making it big. You can find a lot of satisfaction in doing your own thing, even if the dream doesn't work out quite like you wanted it to.

For example, I have some fun stories to share. Yes, it was fun to be in Sister Soleil. And yes, it was delightful to record an album at Peter Gabriel's studios in England. (See http://tinyurl.com/sistersoleil for pics.) And yes, it's cool that Peter Gabriel made a little cameo vocal on our album (you can find the album on Amazon.com and listen to a preview of the song, "Blind," if you like.)

However, it was actually more satisfying to do my own music and to finish a project called "Neocelt," which was all me. It wasn't even released commercially. Not even live. But it's very dear to my heart. (You can find it at www.cftw.com/music/neocelt/.) The really ironic thing is, years after Sister Soleil evaporated, I went backstage at a Slipknot show, and I saw the drummer Joey Jordison. The first thing he said to me, after not seeing me for many years, was, "I listen to the 'Neocelt' CD every night."

As for me, I survived. At the time of writing, 1 in 10 readers will be out of work, so this encouragement is especially for you. It was hard for me to go from playing on stage and going on tour to getting thrown off the rock 'n' roll rollercoaster and finding myself in a dotcom cubicle; and it was harder still to get thrown off the corporate rollercoaster when the dotcom bubble burst and I found myself out of a job.

But I survived, and here I am. Apologies if you get squeamish about personal notes, but there's at least one other person out there who cares: me.

In my own career path, on the way from Real World Studios to LinkedIn, I will admit I was pretty discouraged about music. So I'm going to try to put my money where my mouth is: I think that fully bouncing back will involve getting back into music again. By the time this book is printed, I pledge to put some tunes up on www.snspaces.com and to give an update about me dusting off the guitar and flute and trying it again. Maybe, just maybe, I'll actually write a song again, and if I do, it will be for you.

One final note for those of you who need encouragement. It's kind of surprising to me, but I guess I'm easily amused. Today, as I revisited this chapter before passing it on to the editors, it so happens that I made the post below to Twitter and Facebook about my career. It doesn't look like much, only 140 characters, but it represents the first time since things came crashing down with the band that I've found a way to make peace with it.

Todd Kelsey 30m ellip. I read "Hammer of Gods" Led Zeppelin biog, realized I grew up,rock'n'roll's fun but I only need a wife,guitar,typewriter 2b happy

8 hours ago via Twitter 🔒 · Comment · Like

"30m ellip." refers to my practice of posting to Twitter/Facebook about my exercise, for accountability as I work on getting down to my healthy weight. The rest is a sequence of events: last night I was reading about Led Zeppelin, an incredibly successful band that in some ways was my prototype for a rock 'n' roll dream. I still think Led Zeppelin made great, magical music, but I realized on the way to the gym this morning that I have a life I can be happy in, and it doesn't necessarily depend on the dream I once had of being famous. It made me happy to be onstage, and it also makes me happy to write this book for you.

This doesn't mean I advocate giving up dreams; it means that I'm living proof that you can go through transitions in your career, and survive, and make peace with how things are.

I still have dreams. One of them is to find someone to spend my life with, and save up enough money to record a few songs that have been rolling around my head at Real World Studios, and make a special trip there. Maybe if you and I make friends on Facebook, when that dream is finally realized, you'll enjoy listening to these songs.

I have another dream (which you're welcome to share), which is represented by the "30m ellip." above, and it's also mentioned in Chapter 1. Now that you've read this section and know more about my musical history, this dream may be a little more meaningful to you. I want to live to be 100 and play at the 100th anniversary of Woodstock in 2069. In order to make it, I need to change my health, and I've discovered that having a goal like that has been good; going to the gym has had an impact on just about everything, including my energy levels for working on my career.

If this all sounds crazy to you, please forgive me; I'm hoping that at least some readers will find some encouragement and motivation to spend time in LinkedIn (and in reading *What Color Is Your Parachute?*, and visiting http://wciyp.blogspot.com).

If you're like me and need to make some positive changes in your health, I also encourage you to set some goals and then tweet about them, or send messages on Facebook to your friends. Even if you don't want to live to be 100, you may still benefit from going to the gym (and having some accountability, as well as some cheerleaders). If it would encourage you to hear updates about how I'm doing in my quest for sustainable health and in my dreams, visit http://twitter.com/toddkelsey; please feel free to follow me (see the Twitter chapters) or to add me as a friend on Facebook.

Q/A

Q: What is the Recommendations feature on LinkedIn, and how do I use it?

A: The Recommendations feature provides a way for people to have a strong career-supporting page on LinkedIn. You can request an endorsement/recommendation, and it shows up on your profile. This can come in handy when you're job searching or interacting with other people. Again, if you think your job will last forever, and that's the reason you're dismissing the idea of putting any effort into Linkedin, I say think again: there may come a time when you find yourself looking for work, for a variety of unforeseen reasons. Even if you're independently wealthy, the Recommendation feature is another way you can give back. It's a two-way street: people may request a recommendation from you, and it can be a simple way to give a friend or colleague a (legitimate) boost. If someone requests a recommendation, the request appears in your e-mail. Just write a few sentences telling something positive you noticed about the person's impact, abilities, and/or character.

Q: How do I request a recommendation?

A: If you want to request a recommendation, go to the Profile Menu, choose the Recommendations link, enter the name of a LinkedIn connection, select any additional options, and click Send.

Q: Can I recommend someone?

A: Yes. You can also visit a person's profile and click the Recommend link to fill out a recommendation. It doesn't automatically appear; a person has to review/approve. Conversely, it's a good idea once in a while to go to the Profile menu and select the Recommendations option to see if there are any recommendations that people have given you (which you haven't requested); you can review them and publish them to your profile if you like. In fact, I had five recommendations that I found waiting for me because I never received an e-mail letting me know they were there!

Q: LinkedIn seems like it would require a lot of effort. Is it really worth it?

A: Yes, it is. Don't be alarmed if you feel intimidated by how many options there are. I built my LinkedIn profile over time, adding things now and then, going on there once in a while. If you'd like a suggestion of how to space it out, I suggest getting a free Gmail account at http://mail.google.com, clicking the Calendar link at the top of the Gmail screen, learning how to use Google Calendar, and setting up a monthly reminder via e-mail to "log onto LinkedIn and poke around a bit."

Q: I'm retired. Why should I bother?

A: Well, you have a wonderful amount of wisdom and experience up in that noggin of yours, and there are people who appreciate wisdom, including me. I'm convinced there are people out there who could benefit from your experience, regardless of the type of job or career you had. You may think I'm crazy for suggesting this, but even though you're retired, I encourage you to consider not only joining LinkedIn, but reading *What Color Is Your Parachute?* You may find some fulfilling things to do in your retirement and also discover how some of your skills translate into new industries and jobs; and this may provide an opportunity to mentor and offer wisdom. Also, you may still have contacts at some companies or organizations that could benefit a person just getting started, and that's partly what LinkedIn is about. As for mentoring, there are initiatives specifically designed to help connect the wisdom of retired expertise with younger people who are in need of it. I don't have a laundry list, but you're more than welcome to come on www.snspaces.com to request some links to be added; or if you find any good ones on Google or know of any, please feel free to post them!

Q: I like this book, but there are only two chapters on LinkedIn. Where can I read more?

A: If you liked this book and this chapter or section, keep your eyes open for an entire book from CFTW Press on Linkedin. If you want to keep posted about the book's progress, go on Facebook and search for (and join) the Social Networking Spaces Group, or search for (and become a fan of) the Social Networking Spaces Facebook page. I'll post messages occasionally to both. Just as with *Social Networking Spaces*, all author proceeds for the book on LinkedIn will be donated to CFTW. (See the Introduction to this book.) And don't worry if you don't know how to join a group or become a fan. You can learn by reading the Facebook chapters in this book!

Q: Wait! I have another question! Where can I ask it?

A: On www.snspaces.com.

Conclusion

Dear Reader,

To me, LinkedIn exemplifies a spirit of collaboration: the whole is greater than the sum of the parts, and when you're actively collaborating, you're better for it. Even if you don't think you need help at the moment, I'd like to mention this story: when I was in the band Sister Soleil, when it was getting started, I remember someone saying to me something like, "Remember the people that you interact with on the way up are the ones you interact with on the way down." And it did end up being a rollercoaster, like any job or career can be (see http://tinyurl.com/sistersoleil for some pictures and more thoughts). My purpose in sharing the story of my experience with Sister Soleil is to highlight one of the most valuable uses of LinkedIn: building a career support network. There may come a time when you go through transition as I did, taking you in totally new directions. That's one time when a career-support network certainly comes in handy.

When you're pursuing a job based on being motivated (because you're interested), this is a great combination. The point of *What Color Is Your Parachute?* is to identify transferrable skills: things you're good at, things you like doing, skills that can be transferred from one position to another, if times or situations change. The book can help you to consider what you really find fulfilling—so even if you have a job, it's important to read to consider your overall fulfillment. My belief is simple: you may not necessarily have the opportunity to do what you want, but it's certainly worth trying, using all the tools you have available, and LinkedIn, and *What Color Is Your Parachute?*—and doing it with friends.

You're most welcome to visit www.snspaces.com and sound off any way you like, with stories, questions, concerns, complaints, compliments, suggestions, or feedback of any kind. All are welcome.

I wish you the best in your career, and I relay the words that my grandfather that which were so encouraging to me: Keep on going!

Regards,

–Todd

snspaces.com

Come and visit the Social Networking Spaces companion web site at www.snspaces.com, where you can find more tips and updates and have an opportunity to share your thoughts or ask questions.

In Living Color: You can visit www.snspaces.com/pics to see full-color versions of all the pictures from this chapter.

CHAPTER 14

■ ■ ■

What the Heck Is MySpace?

In This Chapter:

- Explore MySpace: creating a MySpace account
- Uploading songs
- Uploading photos/video to MySpace

snspaces.com

Credits and links to explore: www.myspace.com/nuno23, www.myspace.com/killlizziemusic, www.myspace.com/thedetholz, www.myspace.com/aph0rism (with a zero), and www.myspace.com/freakygerbils. Comic art courtesy http://tinyurl.com/gerbilfront, and glf music video stills courtesy of glf "she's my gerbil"; YouTube video at http://tinyurl.com/glfvideos or high-quality video at www.cftw.com/tk/glf.

Come and visit the Social Networking Spaces companion web site at www.snspaces.com, where you can find more tips and updates and have an opportunity to share your thoughts or ask questions.

In Living Color: You can visit www.snspaces.com/pics to see full-color versions of all the pictures from this chapter.

Introduction

MySpace is another social network. Although it isn't as popular as Facebook overall, it still has tens of millions of users. At one point in the recent past, it was the most popular network; because it invested early on in going international, it still has some popularity there. A youth-oriented virtual world called Habbo did a recent study and maintained that MySpace (and YouTube) were more popular than Facebook among teenagers (see http://tinyurl.com/habbostudy).

It's generally accepted that MySpace is popular with teens and also is a popular place for bands to have pages. If you're trying to decide whether to make a personal profile on Facebook or MySpace, I suggest that if you're a teenager, you may want to do both. If you're older, you may find more of your peers on Facebook. If you have a band, you probably want to make a MySpace page. If you're interested in doing business on social networks, or advertising on them, then it may depend on your audience.

MySpace and Facebook are fairly similar. At the time of writing, MySpace pages are a bit more customizable (in terms of being able to access the underlying code called the HTML, which stands for Hypertext Markup Language). You can find more general information on MySpace at http://en.wikipedia.org/wiki/Myspace.

Exploring MySpace

This chapter looks at how to create a MySpace account as if you're a band. You also upload a few pictures.

If you'd like to get to know more about MySpace before signing up, one of the best ways is to visit the Today on MySpace section on the front page of Myspace.com, and click the "Take the full tour" link, as shown in Figure 14-1.

Today on MySpace

Welcome	Featured	Videos	Music	Celebrity Updates	

Get Started On MySpace!

Join for free, and view profiles, connect with others, blog, rank music, and much more!

- Join now and be a part of the MySpace community
- Tell us about yourself and upload photos and videos
- View profiles and add friends to your network
- Discover new bands, filmmakers and comedians

Take the full tour »   Sign Up

Figure 14-1. Today on MySpace

Even if you decide not to sign up, you can also learn a few things by reading the rest of the chapter and seeing the kinds of things you can do.

Creating an Account

Creating an account is easy and (surprise) similar to other social networks. Visit www.myspace.com, and click the Sign Up tab, as shown in Figure 14-2.

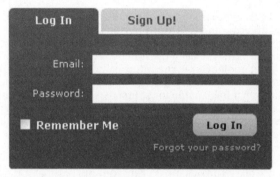

Figure 14-2. Go to www.myspace.com, and click the Sign Up tab to get started.

Enter your e-mail address, come up with a password, enter your other information, and click the Sign Up button (see Figure 14-3).

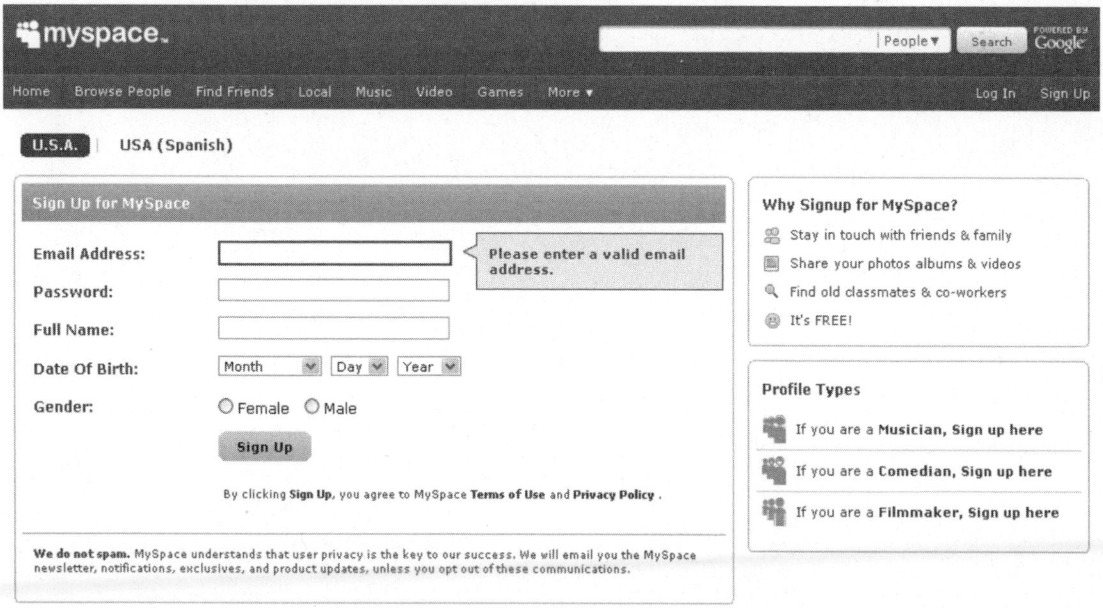

Figure 14-3. Sign Up page on www.myspace.com

That's pretty much it. Depending on what type of MySpace account you create, you're asked for additional information and given the opportunity to upload a photo and add friends.

For the purpose of this chapter, you're creating a band account. On the screen shown in Figure 14-3, you look in the Profile Types box and click the "Musician, Sign up here" link.

If you're an independent/professional musician, comedian, or filmmaker, you may very well wish to make a MySpace page. I'd also like to make the point that if you'd enjoy becoming any of these things— or desire to pretend to be one— maybe you'd like to try making a musician, comedian, or filmmaker profile. In other words, play, make believe, try a new identity. When you express yourself online, you never know where things will go. Case in point: on YouTube, sometimes a silly random thing can become huge. So, it pays to play.

If you like, you can make an alternate identity for yourself by signing up for different Gmail addresses (`http://mail.google.com`) and creating different accounts. Dream, that's the important thing. For example, consider a television show like *American Idol* for singers, or *Saturday Night Live*, where they have bands or comedians, or maybe even the Independent Film Channel. It's fun to be on TV in front of a world-wide television audience. On the Internet, however, there are a billion people. If you explore, dream, and try different things such as MySpace and Facebook, you can try different identities. For example, you could make up a stage name for yourself as a singer (or karaoke singer for that matter), a line dancer, an artist, or a hobby you like. In short, you can do just about anything you like or can dream of, publicly or anonymously (through a fictitious name).

Of course, you can keep things private. Look in the help sections of MySpace and Facebook, and learn how to share things with a few people. Then, when you get some confidence, share with more.

Regardless of what type of account you start, you need to choose a MySpace URL. Usually, this will be your username; in the case of a band, it's most likely your full band name. I didn't want a really long address, so I put a shorter abbreviation.

After you choose a URL, depending on the type of MySpace profile you're starting, you have other choices to make. In this case, choose the genre the band is in, as shown in Figure 14-4.

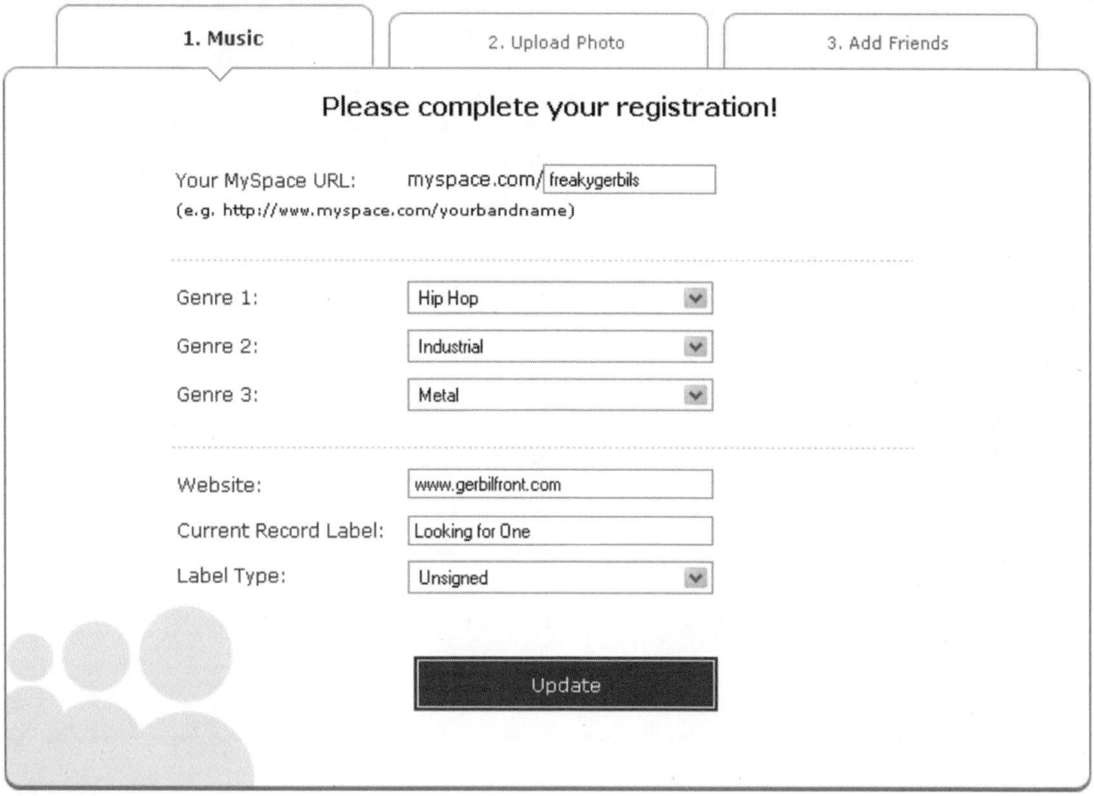

Figure 14-4. *Choose a home URL (for example, www.myspace.com/freakgerbils), and enter your basic information. The choices vary depending on what kind of MySpace page you're making. In this case, it's a music page.*

For a band profile, you can put a web site address, record label, or label type. When you're done with the page, click the Update button.

Figure 14-5 shows the page where you're given the opportunity to upload a photo. Click the Browse button to find it, and then click the Upload button. (You can always change it later.)

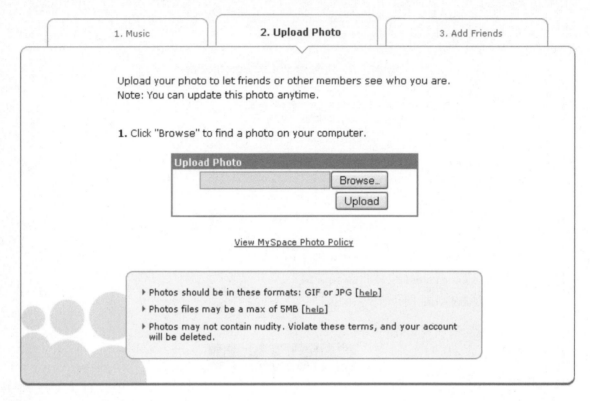

Figure 14-5. Upload photos

The Add Friends option allows you to enter your e-mail information and have MySpace check your address book (see Figure 14-6). However, you can also click the "Skip this step" link.

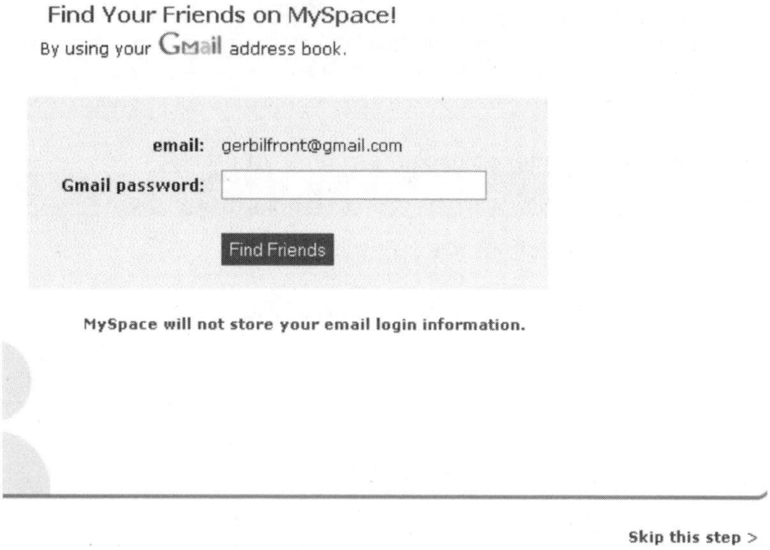

Find Your Friends on MySpace!

By using your Gmail address book.

email: gerbilfront@gmail.com

Gmail password: [   ]

[Find Friends]

MySpace will not store your email login information.

Skip this step >

Figure 14-6. Check your web mail to see who is already on MySpace that you know.

Uploading Songs

You're given an opportunity to edit your profile, and you can also choose Manage Featured Songs, as shown in Figure 14-7.

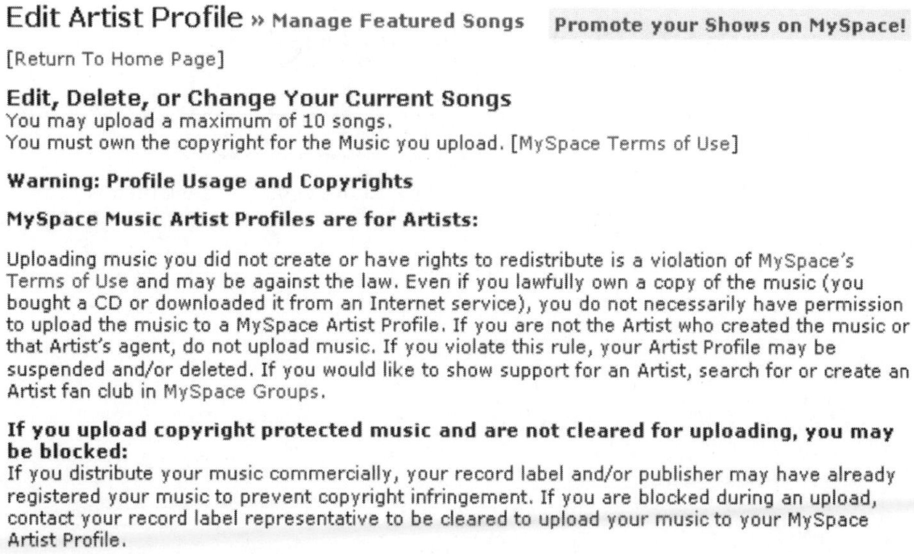

Edit Artist Profile » Manage Featured Songs   Promote your Shows on MySpace!

[Return To Home Page]

Edit, Delete, or Change Your Current Songs
You may upload a maximum of 10 songs.
You must own the copyright for the Music you upload. [MySpace Terms of Use]

Warning: Profile Usage and Copyrights

MySpace Music Artist Profiles are for Artists:

Uploading music you did not create or have rights to redistribute is a violation of MySpace's Terms of Use and may be against the law. Even if you lawfully own a copy of the music (you bought a CD or downloaded it from an Internet service), you do not necessarily have permission to upload the music to a MySpace Artist Profile. If you are not the Artist who created the music or that Artist's agent, do not upload music. If you violate this rule, your Artist Profile may be suspended and/or deleted. If you would like to show support for an Artist, search for or create an Artist fan club in MySpace Groups.

If you upload copyright protected music and are not cleared for uploading, you may be blocked:
If you distribute your music commercially, your record label and/or publisher may have already registered your music to prevent copyright infringement. If you are blocked during an upload, contact your record label representative to be cleared to upload your music to your MySpace Artist Profile.

Figure 14-7. Edit Artist Profile page

At the bottom of the page, you can adjust the song settings. You may want to let users add your songs to their profile or have the first song automatically play when someone visits your profile. When you're finished, click Update Settings, as shown in Figure 14-8.

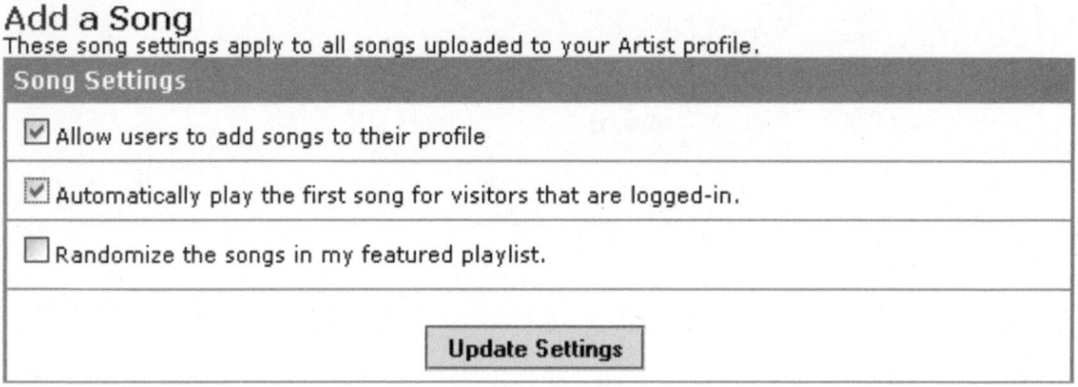

Add a Song
These song settings apply to all songs uploaded to your Artist profile.

Song Settings
☑ Allow users to add songs to their profile
☑ Automatically play the first song for visitors that are logged-in.
☐ Randomize the songs in my featured playlist.
Update Settings

Figure 14-8. Add a Song page

When you're ready to add a song, click the word Add in the title, as shown in the following images.

Now, click the "Add a song to your profile: link.

Enter song information as you like (or make up information), and click the Update button. Remember, make sure you only update what you have the rights to, as shown in the Warning message in Figure 14-9.

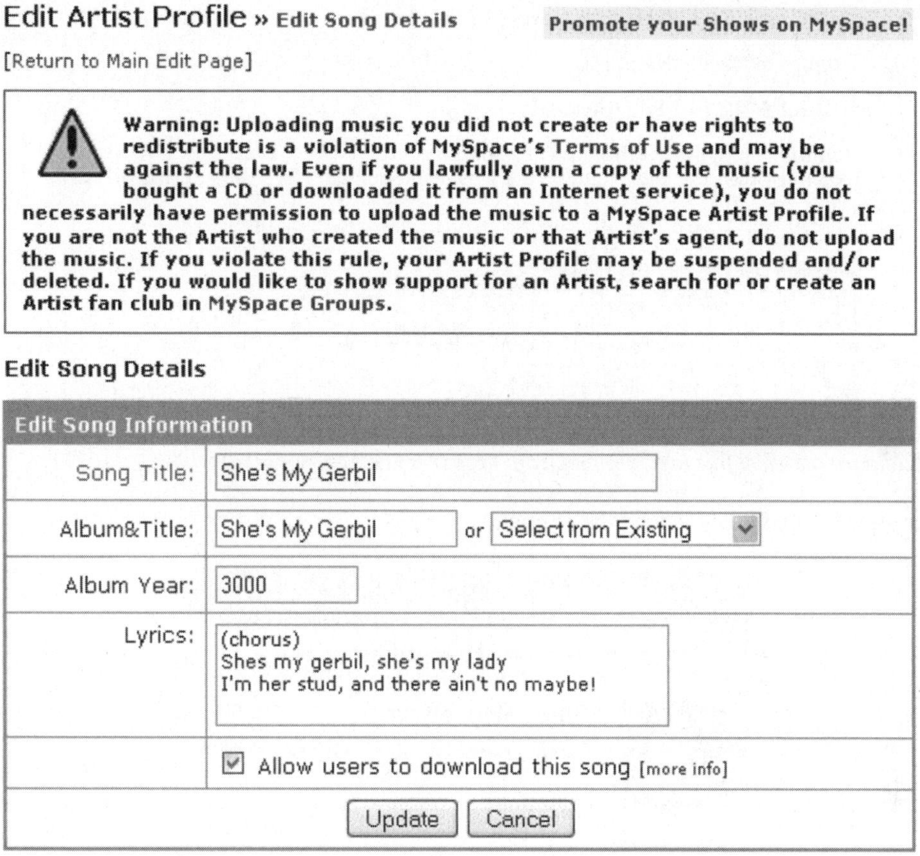

Edit Artist Profile » Edit Song Details

[Return to Main Edit Page]

> ⚠ **Warning: Uploading music you did not create or have rights to redistribute is a violation of MySpace's Terms of Use and may be against the law. Even if you lawfully own a copy of the music (you bought a CD or downloaded it from an Internet service), you do not necessarily have permission to upload the music to a MySpace Artist Profile. If you are not the Artist who created the music or that Artist's agent, do not upload the music. If you violate this rule, your Artist Profile may be suspended and/or deleted. If you would like to show support for an Artist, search for or create an Artist fan club in MySpace Groups.**

Edit Song Details

Edit Song Information	
Song Title:	She's My Gerbil
Album&Title:	She's My Gerbil or [Select from Existing ▾]
Album Year:	3000
Lyrics:	(chorus) Shes my gerbil, she's my lady I'm her stud, and there ain't no maybe!
	☑ Allow users to download this song [more info]
	[Update] [Cancel]

Figure 14-9. Edit Song Information page

■ **Note** If you want to make your song/poem/story downloadable, so that people can listen to it at their own convenience on their computers/iPods/MP3 players, check the option to "Allow users to download this song."

Click the Browse button to locate the file you want to upload, and then click the Upload button, as shown in Figure 14-10.

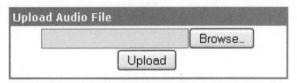

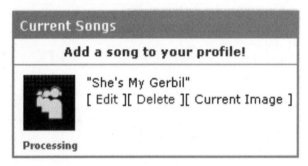

Figure 14-10. Click the Browse button to find a file, and then click Upload. (If you need a sample file to play with and upload, feel free to download from http://cftw.com/music/glf.)

Figure 14-11 shows how the new song appears.

Figure 14-11. *Current Songs shows the uploaded tune and indicate that it's processing.*

When the song is finished processing, if you like, you can upload an image to represent the particular song (see Figure 14-12).

Figure 14-12. *"Upload an image for this song" link*

You can continue to use the "Add a song to your profile" link to add new material, such as songs, as shown in Figure 14-13. You can also upload just about anything else involving audio, such as poems, thoughts, tirades, readings of a play, interviews, and so on. Try getting a voice recorder, go wild, and put together a MySpace page.

Figure 14-13. *A list of current songs with thumbnail images*

If you like, click the Return to Home Page link, shown in the following image.

Edit Artist Profile » Manage Featured Songs

[Return To Home Page]

MySpace brings you back to your profile page, as shown in Figure 14-14.

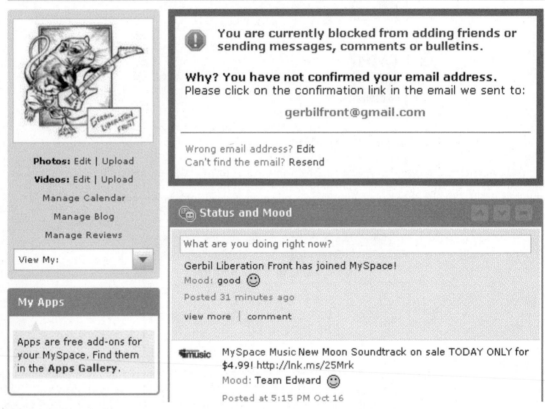

Figure 14-14. MySpace profile page with a vivid warning about needing to confirm your e-mail address. If you get a message like this, check your e-mail.

You may have a message like the one shown in Figure 14-14, indicating that you need to go check your e-mail to verify that you're a live person instead of a software program trying to send spam to people.

After you verify your e-mail address, you get a confirmation message like this one:

Email address verified!

Your email address has been verified. You will now
be able to send messages, add friends, and more!

Return to Home.

RECOGNIZING SPAM E-MAIL

Not every e-mail you get claiming to come from MySpace is necessarily legitimate. This also applies to Facebook. Sometimes, hackers send out genuine-looking e-mails that ask you to click links that lead to genuine-looking web pages. The key is to make sure you're looking at the right *address*. For MySpace, make sure the address starts with `www.myspace.com`. Be aware that some hackers even go so far as to make the link in the e-mail correct (for example: `myspace.com/greatoffer`), but then they program the link to wind up at an alternative site (for example: `myspaceoffers.ru`).

To be safe, first check the link in any e-mail you receive; if you're using Gmail, you can roll over the link and look at the bottom of your browser window to verify where it's going. If it seems OK, then make sure the address starts correctly, with the main address of the site—`www.myspace.com`, `www.facebook.com`, `www.ebay.com`, `www.paypal.com`, and so on. If you'd like more info about computer safety, check out `www.keepthewebsafe.com`, and look for the web comic book on phishing scams.

Generally speaking, the safest way to deal with e-mails from web sites is never to click them unless you're expecting them. In other words, you can always go to the site yourself—sometimes when you're invited to a site, the invitation may come from a hacker. When you're signing up for a new account, and the site indicates you should receive a confirmation e-mail, then it's you who initiated contact. Otherwise, the safest route is to be careful. The following image is an example along these lines in the context of MySpace:

Always make sure you're visiting the real myspace.com!

1. Check the URL in your browser.
2. Make sure it begins with http://www.myspace.com/
3. If ANY OTHER PAGE asks for your info, DON'T LOG IN!

After the sign-up process, your profile page looks something like Figure 14-15, if you created a band profile. Remember, though, a band profile can be used to share anything you've recorded. For example, you can upload spoken words recorded with a voice recorder or an interview with a relative or friend.

Figure 14-15. A basic MySpace page. In the bottom right, MySpace automatically adds a MySpace staff member (in this case, Tom) as a friend.

Uploading Photos/Video to MySpace

To add photos (or videos) to a MySpace profile, log in. Then, in your Profile area, click the appropriate Upload link (see Figure 14-16).

Figure 14-16. The Photos and Videos sections under a MySpace profile pic allow you to edit what you have and to upload more files.

You can also come back and click the Edit link to change things later. Also, notice that there are Calendar and Blog features. Explore both.

When you try to upload something for the first time, you may get a message like the one shown in Figure 14-17 (the upload function uses Java software, which you may need to authorize). If you get this message, click the Run button.

Figure 14-17. You may get this message when you try to upload something for the first time. It's OK to click through because the program needs to install software to help the upload process.

Next, locate the folder where your photos are on the left, and select photos on the right (see Figure 14-18). The small + and – signs allow you to open/collapse folders.

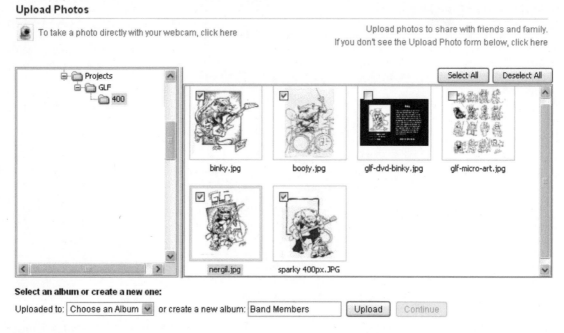

Figure 14-18. *Choose pictures to upload*

If you've already created an album on MySpace, you can choose that album and directly upload more photos into it, or you can choose a name for a new album. After you've made your choices, click the Upload button. MySpace lets you add captions, as shown in Figure 14-19.

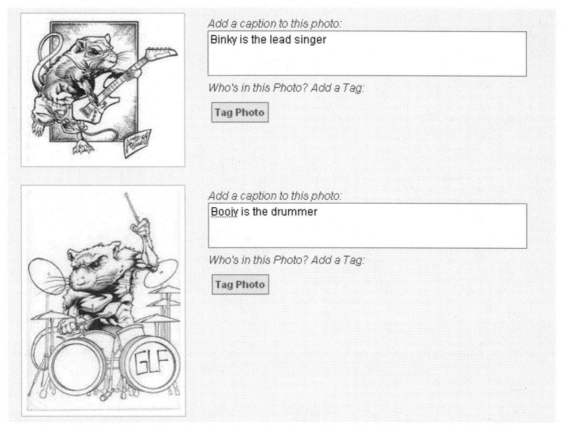

Figure 14-19. *Add captions. If you have MySpace friends and they're in a photo, you can also click Tag Photo.*

The Tag Photo button allows you to choose MySpace friends who are in the picture. This is like Facebook, where you can tag friends and then they get a notification that they're in a picture you've uploaded. Depending on the settings, the picture may show up on their profile, too.

When you're done adding captions, click the Done Editing button as shown in the following image. (If you don't want to add captions, you can also click "Skip this step.")

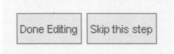

You're taken to the album page, as shown in Figure 14-20.

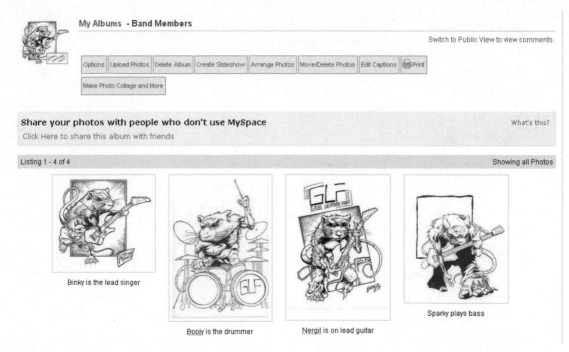

Figure 14-20. *Photo album page showing thumbnail images along with captions. If you'd like to see what all of these MySpace features look like, go to* www.myspace.com/freakgerbils *and see how the live page corresponds to the pictures in the book.*

You can also share a MySpace photo album with people, even if they're not on MySpace. To do so, click the link "Click here to share this album with friends." Then, click the Next button, as shown in Figure 14-21.

Figure 14-21. *Sharing albums*

You can import contacts to make albums easier to share with people, or you can click the Skip Import button (see Figure 14-22).

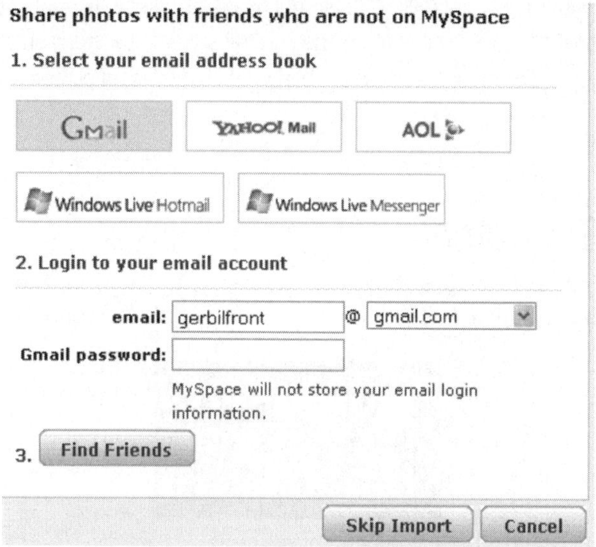

Figure 14-22. *Connecting with web mail contacts makes it easier to reach out to people. If you don't have a web mail account and would like one, visit* http://mail.google.com.

MySpace allows you to enter e-mail addresses of people you'd like to share the album with, along with a message (see Figure 14-23).

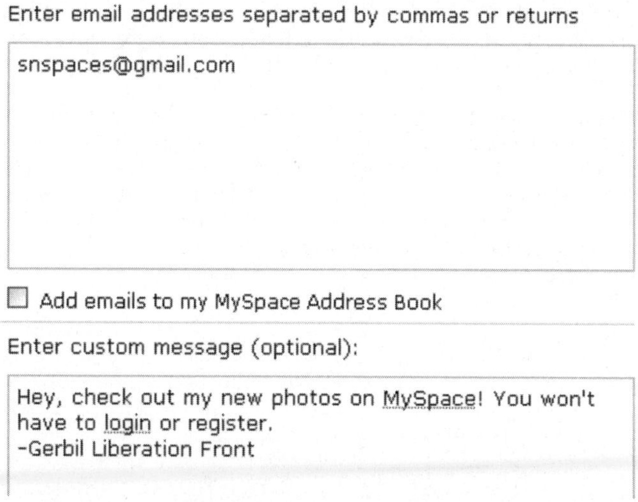

Figure 14-23. *You can also share if you want to copy and paste or type peoples' e-mail addresses.*

■ **Note** If you don't see a button at the bottom of the form, don't be alarmed. At the time of writing, a bug made this window appear at the bottom of the screen. If the button is cut off, press the Tab key on your keyboard (when you're filling out a form online, the Tab key can move the cursor between the areas on a form). When the selection moves beyond the custom message area, try pressing Enter; you should see a screen where you can click the Send Mail button.

Lost? How to Get Home

As you explore MySpace, if you ever get lost or want to get back to where you started, you can always click the Home link. It always appears in the upper-left corner of the screen:

Q/A

Q: Should I use MySpace or Facebook?

A: I recommend trying both. If you have a band or any kind of creative enterprise, and you want to promote something, especially if teens may be in the audience, I definitely recommend creating a MySpace page. I talked to one guy the other day who said, "I like MySpace better because it feels more personal to me," and some people feel that it offers more customization. Others prefer Facebook. As far as the number of people using them, it seems as though Facebook is growing more than MySpace, but it's not like MySpace has disappeared—it hasn't. Try both, and see how you like them.

Q: Who are all the bands in the pictures at the beginning and end of the chapter?

A: Various friends who have music projects and MySpace pages. I've provided a collection of links you may want to visit, to experience some of their music; they range from a DJ to electronic and rock. MySpace isn't just for musicians, but it's a good place for them to have a presence.

Q: Wait, I have another question! Where can I ask it?

A: On www.snspaces.com.

Conclusion

Dear Reader,

Thank you for reading this chapter. You learned how to create a MySpace account, how to upload files, and how to share with friends.

Best wishes, and remember to keep exploring!

Regards,

–Todd

P.S. If you're curious about what the heck the Gerbil Liberation Front is, there are some pictures and links in a Facebook album at `http://tinyurl.com/gerbilfront`, and you can find a couple of the music videos on YouTube. A total of five or six songs were produced. If you want to hear all of them, ask nicely, and I'll be glad to post all the MP3's. Very, very silly. I primarily blame the influence of Monty Python.

snspaces.com

Credits and links to explore: `www.myspace.com/nuno23`, `www.myspace.com/killlizziemusic`, `www.myspace.com/thedetholz`, `www.myspace.com/aph0rism` (with a zero), and `www.myspace.com/freakygerbils`. Comic art courtesy `http://tinyurl.com/gerbilfront`, and glf music video stills courtesy of glf "she's my gerbil"; YouTube video at `http://tinyurl.com/glfvideos` or high-quality video at `www.cftw.com/tk/glf`.

Come and visit the Social Networking Spaces companion web site at `www.snspaces.com`, where you can find more tips and updates and have an opportunity to share your thoughts or ask questions.

In Living Color: You can visit `www.snspaces.com/pics` to see full-color versions of all the pictures from this chapter.

▪ ▪ ▪

CHAPTER 15

Meetup: The Original Social Network

In This Chapter:

- Some general background about what Meetup is and a few things that it does
- Finding and joining a Meetup group
- Creating a Meetup group

---

snspaces.com

Come and visit the Social Networking Spaces companion web site at www.snspaces.com, where you can find more tips and updates and have an opportunity to share your thoughts or ask questions.

In Living Color: You can visit www.snspaces.com/pics to see full-color versions of all the pictures from this chapter.

Introduction: The Original Social Network

Even though social networks provide nice ways for people to become very connected, some people end up feeling that they have a lack of meaningful, significant relationships. I think the answer is simple. I believe that the best way to connect with people and form relationships is through the *original* social network: hanging out in person with people who have similar interests.

Meetup.com provides an opportunity to find and join local groups who are interested in meeting to discuss common interests. It's a great way to spend time with people who have similar interests, and it's a really nice way to get geographic, physical, and local—meaning, connecting *in person*.

With all the hoopla and opportunities that social networks offer for "getting connected," one of the drawbacks of spending so much time online is that you're not spending it *with* people. Some may argue that you're with a person when you're chatting online; but for me, it's not the same as talking to them in person or being in a group setting.

So I think Meetup is a great resource. In some ways, it seems like the most important social network of all, because it's an excellent way to spend time with people.

Some will undoubtedly think I'm crazy for suggesting this in a book about social networking, but I'm OK with that. I can point to my own experience: I've gotten so caught up in using computers and spending time online that sometimes I've missed opportunities to spend time with people in person.

On a related note, I ended up participating in a contest called the Knight News Challenge, which challenged me to think about local, physical, geographic communities. This experience helped me to see that I'd been so caught up in thinking "globally" and "online" that, to a certain extent, I was ignoring the people in my own town (including people who don't spend *any* time online).

For me, one element of achieving balance is continuing to do things online, and especially to develop a sense of being a global citizen and learning about other countries. Another element of balance is working to find ways of getting involved locally.

Meetup.com is a helpful reminder of all the ways you can meet people and be social when others share your interests. That can be truly enjoyable and affirming and can bring more energy and vitality to your life—it's not a solution for everything, but inasmuch as humans are social creatures, it's a good thing.

In my own humble opinion, if you feel isolated or disconnected at all, I suggest starting by finding something you enjoy, for the fun of it, through a Meetup group, or taking a class, or both. That's like training wheels, in a way. You'll find that there can be meaning and significance simply in having fun.

But it doesn't have to stop there. If you're looking for meaning and significance, I suggest continuing to explore and searching for a group where you can pursue deeper meaning, whatever that means for you. For example, you may develop an interest in seeing what it's like to volunteer for an organization that helps the community, or visiting a spiritual organization or church. The idea is, find a community of people of like mind and heart who are seeking to grow.

If you're seeking meaning and significance in relationships, you may want to go from spending time with others purely for entertainment toward spending time with others for the purpose of *growing*. (I guess this is the gardener in me speaking.) One of the best ways to develop a sense of community is to spend time with other people, with the focus on a common goal of growth and service. This isn't utopianism—it's an opportunity for meaning and significance that is right outside your door, and right down the street. The point is ultimately that you're *not* alone. Get to know your neighbors!

What the Heck Is Meetup?!?

The concept of Meetup is simple, but it's quite powerful. Meetup.com (see Figure 15-1) is basically an online social network that helps you to find local groups of people, who meet in person to discuss topics of interest.

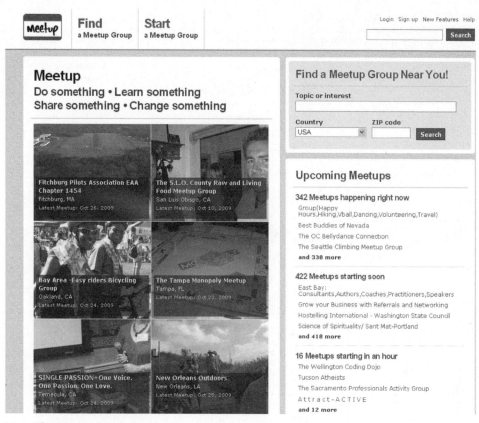

Figure 15-1. The Meetup home page

At the time of writing, Meetup has the numbers shown in Figure 15-2 proudly displaying on the site.

Figure 15-2. Meetup's current numbers

That's a lot of people using the site!

It's pretty interesting to see the most popular types of groups (see Figure 15-3). There are many types, both for personal (and professional) development.

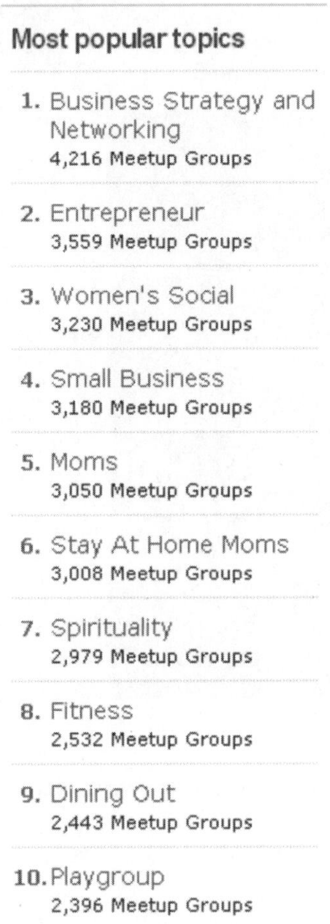

Most popular topics

1. Business Strategy and Networking
   4,216 Meetup Groups

2. Entrepreneur
   3,559 Meetup Groups

3. Women's Social
   3,230 Meetup Groups

4. Small Business
   3,180 Meetup Groups

5. Moms
   3,050 Meetup Groups

6. Stay At Home Moms
   3,008 Meetup Groups

7. Spirituality
   2,979 Meetup Groups

8. Fitness
   2,532 Meetup Groups

9. Dining Out
   2,443 Meetup Groups

10. Playgroup
    2,396 Meetup Groups

Figure 15-3. The most popular types of groups

And at a high level, Meetups are arranged by categories, as shown in Figure 15-4.

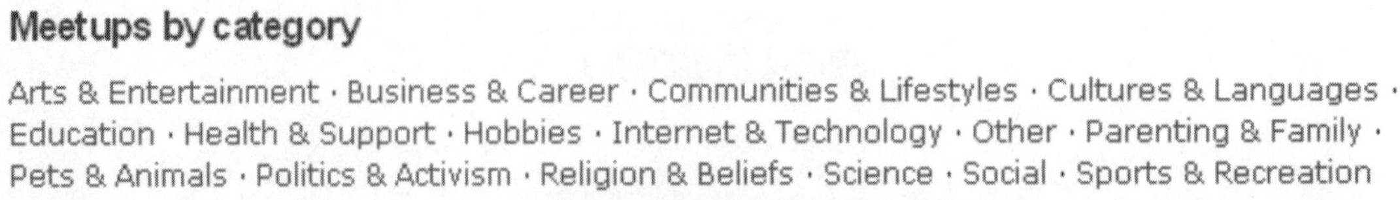

Meetups by category

Arts & Entertainment · Business & Career · Communities & Lifestyles · Cultures & Languages · Education · Health & Support · Hobbies · Internet & Technology · Other · Parenting & Family · Pets & Animals · Politics & Activism · Religion & Beliefs · Science · Social · Sports & Recreation

Figure 15-4. Meetup categories

Registering and Exploring

You don't need to register at Meetup in order to explore, but I'd recommend it. It's easy to sign up; and if you're logged in while you're browsing, it makes it a bit easier to connect when you find a group you'd like to join.

To be clear, *joining* a Meetup group simply means indicating you're interested. It's not a commitment of any kind—you don't *have* to go to any meetings. It's about exploring.

To register, click the "Sign up" link anywhere you can find one on the page you're on (there's always a "Sign up" link in the upper-right corner of the screen); see Figure 15-5.

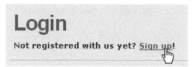

Figure 15-5. Click the "Sign up" link.

Then, enter a name, an e-mail address, and your location information, click the "I agree" check box, and click the Submit button, as shown in Figure 15-6.

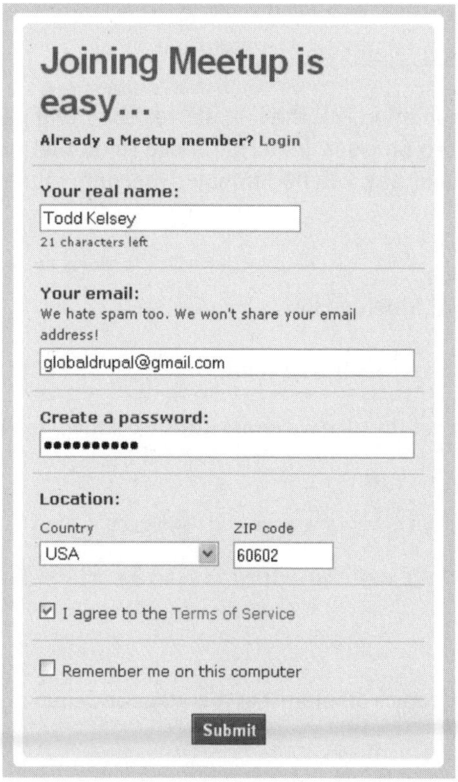

Joining Meetup is easy...

Already a Meetup member? Login

Your real name:

Todd Kelsey

21 characters left

Your email:

We hate spam too. We won't share your email address!

globaldrupal@gmail.com

Create a password:

●●●●●●●●●●

Location:

Country

USA

ZIP code

60602

☑ I agree to the Terms of Service

☐ Remember me on this computer

Submit

Figure 15-6. Joining Meetup

You end up getting a message about a confirmation e-mail (see Figure 15-7).

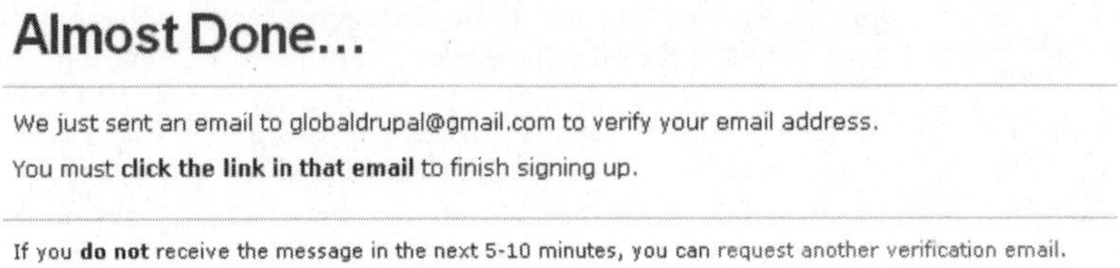
Almost Done...
We just sent an email to globaldrupal@gmail.com to verify your email address.
You must click the link in that email to finish signing up.
If you do not receive the message in the next 5-10 minutes, you can request another verification email.

***Figure 15-7.** Meetup tells you that it has sent a confirmation e-mail.*

When you receive the confirmation e-mail, click the link in the message to verify your account (see Figure 15-8).

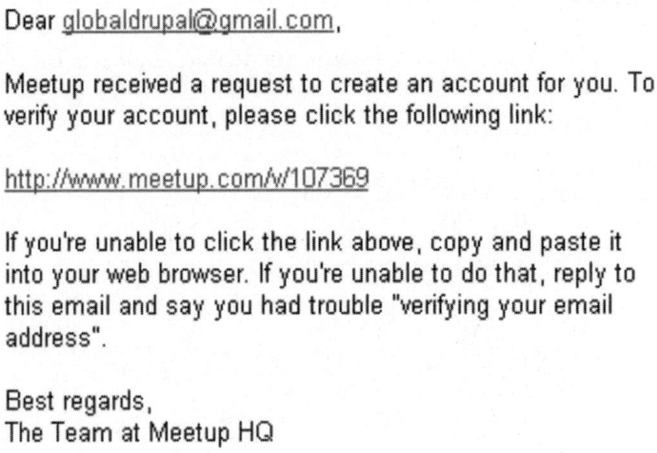
Dear globaldrupal@gmail.com,
Meetup received a request to create an account for you. To verify your account, please click the following link:
http://www.meetup.com/v/107369
If you're unable to click the link above, copy and paste it into your web browser. If you're unable to do that, reply to this email and say you had trouble "verifying your email address".
Best regards,
The Team at Meetup HQ

***Figure 15-8.** Click the link in the confirmation e-mail.*

When things work out, you get the nice welcome message shown in Figure 15-9.

Welcome to Meetup!
Your email address has been verified.

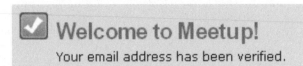

***Figure 15-9.** Welcome message*

If you like, you can indicate topics of interest at this stage and upload a picture, but you can also just click the Submit button (see Figure 15-10).

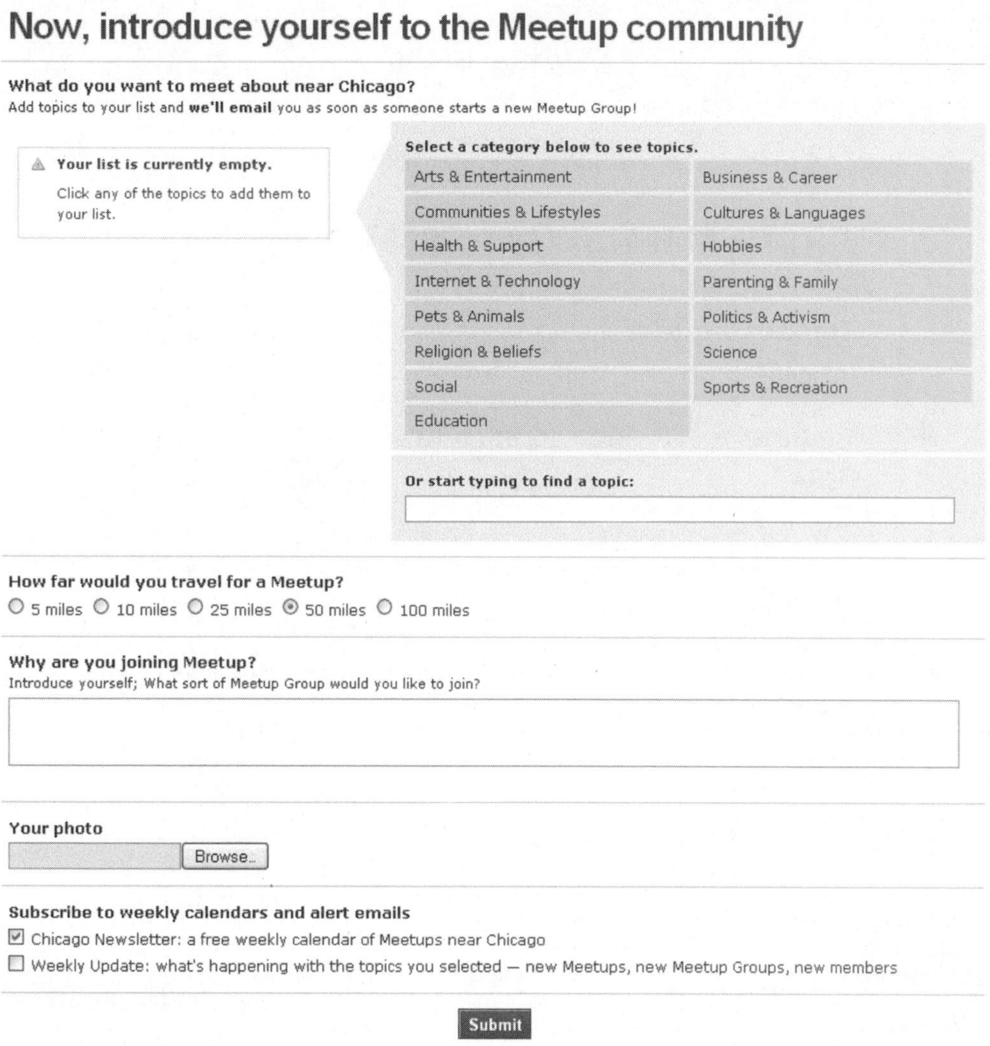

Now, introduce yourself to the Meetup community

What do you want to meet about near Chicago?
Add topics to your list and **we'll email** you as soon as someone starts a new Meetup Group!

⚠ **Your list is currently empty.**
Click any of the topics to add them to your list.

Select a category below to see topics.

Arts & Entertainment	Business & Career
Communities & Lifestyles	Cultures & Languages
Health & Support	Hobbies
Internet & Technology	Parenting & Family
Pets & Animals	Politics & Activism
Religion & Beliefs	Science
Social	Sports & Recreation
Education	

Or start typing to find a topic:

How far would you travel for a Meetup?
○ 5 miles ○ 10 miles ○ 25 miles ◉ 50 miles ○ 100 miles

Why are you joining Meetup?
Introduce yourself; What sort of Meetup Group would you like to join?

Your photo
[Browse...]

Subscribe to weekly calendars and alert emails
☑ Chicago Newsletter: a free weekly calendar of Meetups near Chicago
☐ Weekly Update: what's happening with the topics you selected — new Meetups, new Meetup Groups, new members

[Submit]

Figure 15-10. The window you see when you begin using Meetup

That's it! You're ready to find a group.

Finding a Group

To find a group, you can go to Meetup.com, look for the Find box (or click the Find a Meetup Group icon shown in Figure 15-11), and enter a topic you're interested in, like sunflowers, or stay at home moms, or St. Bernard owners, or just about anything. Then, enter your country and postal code, and click Search, as shown in Figure 15-12.

Find
a Meetup Group

Figure 15-11. Click the Find a Meetup Group icon.

Find a Meetup Group Near You!

Topic or interest

    drupal

Country   **ZIP code**

    USA ▾   60602   **Search**

Figure 15-12. Enter the topic you're interested in.

Meetup displays a list of groups, along with some basic information (see Figure 15-13).

2 Meetup Groups
within 25 mi ▾ of Chicago, IL

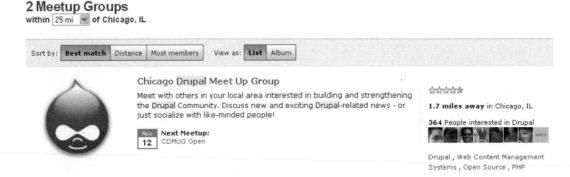

Sort by: **Best match** Distance Most members   View as: **List** Album

Chicago **Drupal** Meet Up Group

Meet with others in your local area interested in building and strengthening the **Drupal** Community. Discuss new and exciting **Drupal**-related news - or just socialize with like-minded people!

Nov 12 **Next Meetup:**
CDMUG Open

☆☆☆☆☆

1.7 miles away in Chicago, IL

364 People interested in Drupal

Drupal , Web Content Management Systems , Open Source , PHP

Figure 15-13. Search results

If you like, you can adjust the distance of the search, as shown in Figure 15-14.

Figure 15-14. Adjusting the search distance

When you find what you're looking for, you can read the basic description, as shown in Figure 15-15.

Figure 15-15. Each group has a basic description.

And if you want to, you can click the title of the description to visit the group page (see Figure 15-16).

The Fox Valley Drupal Meetup Group

Meet with others in your local area interested in bu

Figure 15-16. Click the title to visit the group page.

Meetup pages vary, but in general, the page provides some information about the group, including basic statistics (see Figure 15-17).

Home
About
Calendar
Members
Photos
Mailing List
Message Board
Polls
Files
Promote!
Welcome, Chicago-West Fox Valley Drupal users
Location
Saint Charles, IL
Meetups
13 so far
Members
72 People interested in Drupal
Rating
Meetup topics
Drupal , PHP , Open Source , Web Content Management Systems
Founded
January 7, 2009
Organized by
Bob Snodgrass
email me
Asst. Organizers:
Chris Calip, Hans, Jason Bell, Kevin Thull, Kirk Clawes
Other nearby Meetup Groups
Meet with others in your local area interested in building and strengthening the Drupal Community. Discuss new and exciting Drupal-related news - or just socialize with like-minded people!
Our Meetups are open to anyone interested in developing and operating sustainable websites and applications. Our focus will be to offer opportunities for our group members grow their understanding and appreciation of the Drupal framework and create a cooperative community in the far western suburbs of Chicago.
We will focus on:
*Site Presentations and Special Guests
*Hands-On Coaching on Modules, Theme, and API uses
*Questions and Answers
Typically we will try to meet on the fourth Thursday of the Month at McNally's Traditional Irish Pub! (schedule dependent)

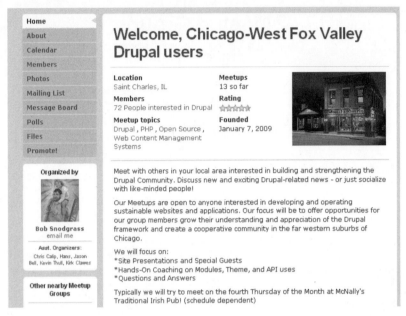

Figure 15-17. A group page

The page may have a section that gives information about the next meeting, as shown in Figure 15-18.

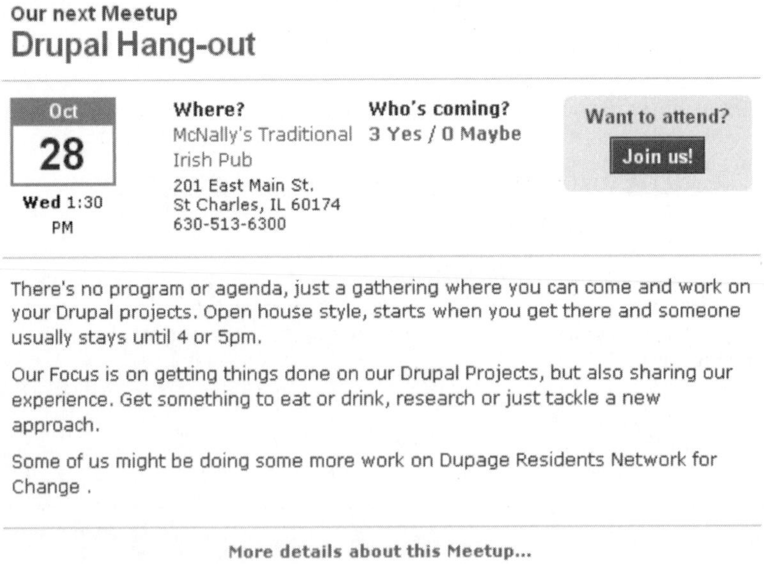

Our next Meetup
Drupal Hang-out
Oct
28
Wed 1:30 PM
Where?
McNally's Traditional Irish Pub
201 East Main St.
St Charles, IL 60174
630-513-6300
Who's coming?
3 Yes / 0 Maybe
Want to attend?
Join us!
There's no program or agenda, just a gathering where you can come and work on your Drupal projects. Open house style, starts when you get there and someone usually stays until 4 or 5pm.
Our Focus is on getting things done on our Drupal Projects, but also sharing our experience. Get something to eat or drink, research or just tackle a new approach.
Some of us might be doing some more work on Dupage Residents Network for Change .
More details about this Meetup...

Figure 15-18. Meeting information

There's also likely to be a box that lets you join the group. If you aren't registered and logged in to Meetup, the box looks like Figure 15-19.

Figure 15-19. The Join box if you aren't a registered, logged-in Meetup member

If you *are* logged in, the box just has a "Join us" button, as shown in Figure 15-20.

Figure 15-20. The Join box if you're registered and logged in

■ **Note** I recommend registering and logging in to Meetup before you browse groups because if you don't, and you register on a group page, the result may be confusing. When you get your confirmation e-mail, Meetup may not return you to that group page—you have to find it again. You may find it easier to register for Meetup and then go exploring.

When you've successfully joined a Meetup group, you get a confirmation message like the one shown in Figure 15-21.

Figure 15-21. Confirmation message when you join a group

If you like, you can fill in some introductory information and adjust your settings (see Figure 15-22). To bypass this window, click Save—but there are good reasons to look through it.

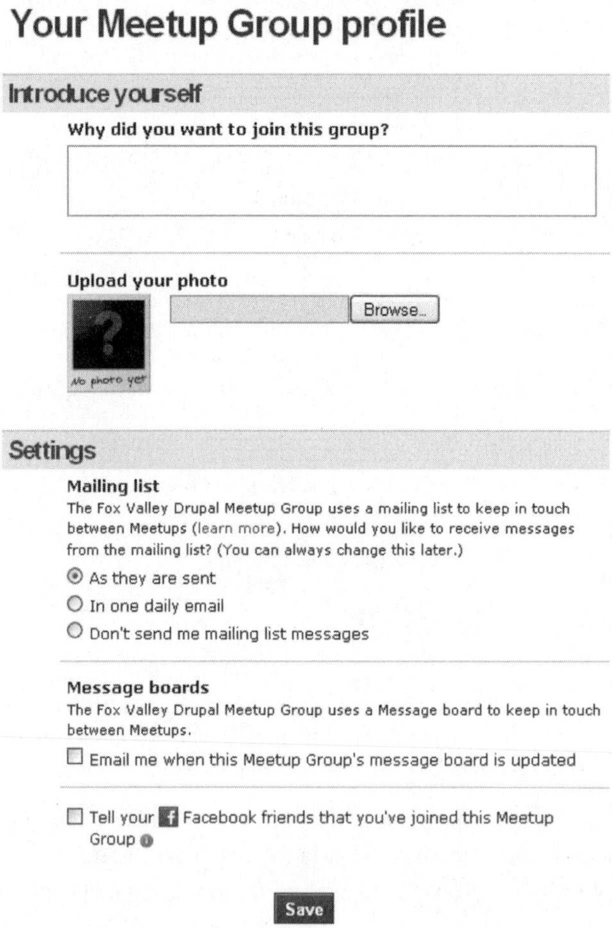

Your Meetup Group profile

Introduce yourself

Why did you want to join this group?

Upload your photo

Browse...

No photo yet

Settings

Mailing list

The Fox Valley Drupal Meetup Group uses a mailing list to keep in touch between Meetups (learn more). How would you like to receive messages from the mailing list? (You can always change this later.)

⦿ As they are sent

◯ In one daily email

◯ Don't send me mailing list messages

Message boards

The Fox Valley Drupal Meetup Group uses a Message board to keep in touch between Meetups.

☐ Email me when this Meetup Group's message board is updated

☐ Tell your 🅕 Facebook friends that you've joined this Meetup Group ⓘ

Save

Figure 15-22. Your group profile

The "Introduce yourself" field is a nice way to say hello (so much easier than speaking in a room in front of people!), as shown in Figure 15-23.

Figure 15-23. Introducing yourself to the group

If you haven't registered before with Meetup and haven't uploaded a photo, you can do so now. To upload a photo, click Browse (see Figure 15-24) and locate the photo you want to use on your computer.

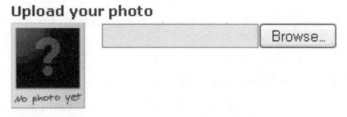

Figure 15-24. You can upload a photo to your profile.

The main thing to pay attention to is the mailing list settings, shown in Figure 15-25. Unless you like getting a lot of e-mail, I recommend choosing the "In one daily e-mail" setting.

Figure 15-25. Let Meetup know how often to send you e-mail.

You have an opportunity to receive other notifications, including a simple option for telling people on Facebook what you're up to (for example, that you've joined a study group for basket weaving—actually, I did get a basket-weaving kit from a Native American museum recently, so stop laughing).

When you're done, click Save (see Figure 15-26).

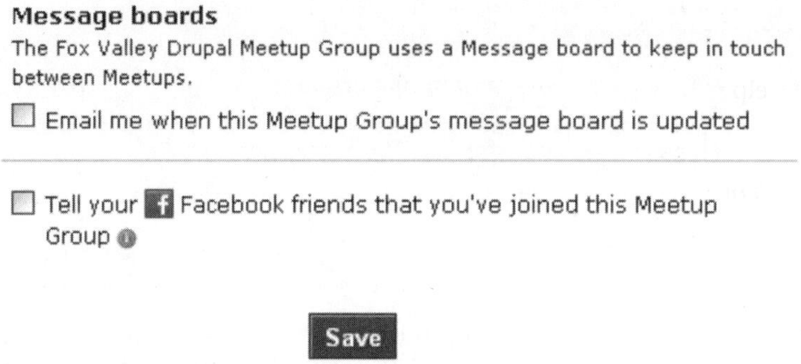

Message boards

The Fox Valley Drupal Meetup Group uses a Message board to keep in touch between Meetups.

☐ Email me when this Meetup Group's message board is updated

☐ Tell your 🇫 Facebook friends that you've joined this Meetup Group ⓘ

Save

Figure 15-26. Specify any other updates you want to receive.

You may want to bookmark the page of the group you've joined or are thinking about joining. If you join a group, Meetup also keeps track of it for you.

Accessing Your Profile/Account

If you want to come back and change anything, log in to Meetup.com, and, in the upper-right corner, click the Profile or Account link (see Figure 15-27).

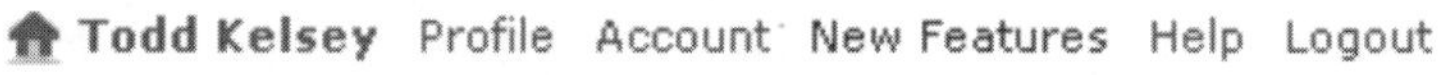

🏠 **Todd Kelsey**   Profile   Account   New Features   Help   Logout

Figure 15-27. Click Profile or Account to go back to your profile page.

Just as with other social networks, there's a lot you can add—but you don't *have* to. It's all up to you. Strictly speaking, you don't even have to upload a picture—and you certainly don't have to use your own picture (see Figure 15-28).

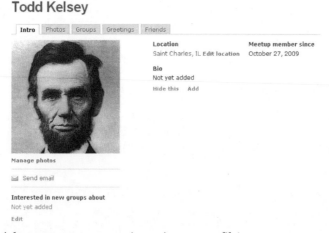

Figure 15-28. You don't have to use your own picture in your profile!

Getting Help

Meetup has a good Help section. Look for the Help link in the upper-right corner of the screen, as shown in Figure 15-29.

Todd Kelsey Profile Account New Features Help Logout
Search

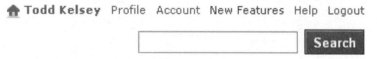

Figure 15-29. *The Help link is in the upper-right corner.*

There's a good section called New to Meetup, along with other links that are worth exploring to help you get acquainted (see Figure 15-30).

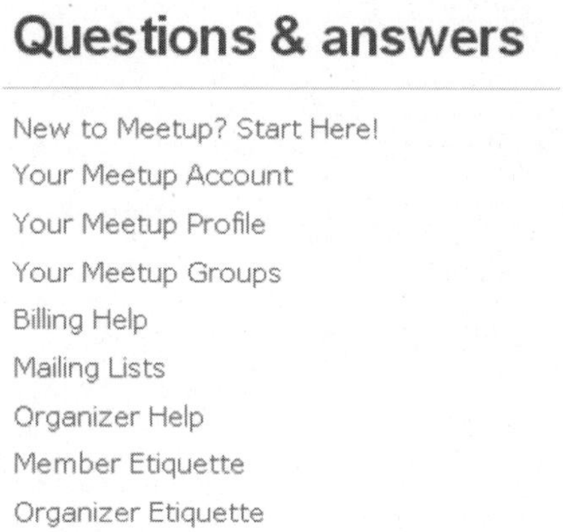
Questions & answers
New to Meetup? Start Here!
Your Meetup Account
Your Meetup Profile
Your Meetup Groups
Billing Help
Mailing Lists
Organizer Help
Member Etiquette
Organizer Etiquette

Figure 15-30. *Meetup's Help section*

The Help area also has some links on the left side of the screen, including the Organizer Center (see Figure 15-31). This is a very good resource for people who want to start a Meetup group.

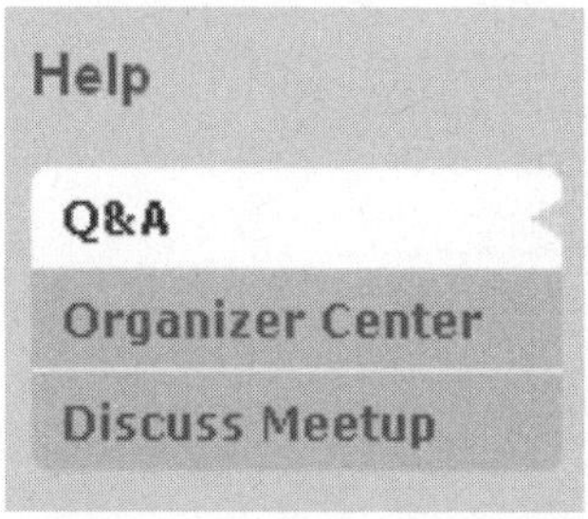
Help
Q&A
Organizer Center
Discuss Meetup

Figure 15-31. *Links on the left side of the Help section*

As you can see in Figure 15-32, the Organizer Center provides a lot of good information (it's part of the Meetup blog)—so much that it's difficult to read!

Figure 15-32. The Organizer Center contains a lot of material.

If you're thinking of starting a Meetup group, it's in your best interests to visit the Help link ➤ Organizer Center and review the links in the first few sections, shown in Figure 15-33.

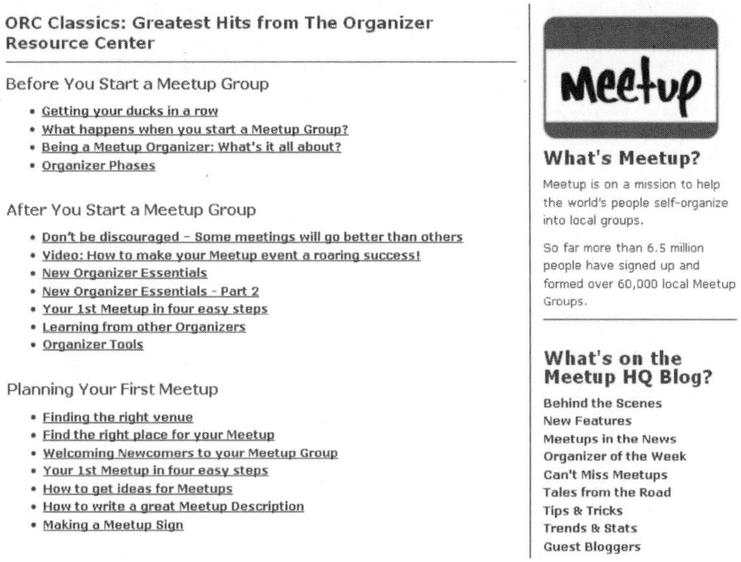

ORC Classics: Greatest Hits from The Organizer Resource Center

Before You Start a Meetup Group

- Getting your ducks in a row
- What happens when you start a Meetup Group?
- Being a Meetup Organizer: What's it all about?
- Organizer Phases

After You Start a Meetup Group

- Don't be discouraged – Some meetings will go better than others
- Video: How to make your Meetup event a roaring success!
- New Organizer Essentials
- New Organizer Essentials - Part 2
- Your 1st Meetup in four easy steps
- Learning from other Organizers
- Organizer Tools

Planning Your First Meetup

- Finding the right venue
- Find the right place for your Meetup
- Welcoming Newcomers to your Meetup Group
- Your 1st Meetup in four easy steps
- How to get ideas for Meetups
- How to write a great Meetup Description
- Making a Meetup Sign

Meetup

What's Meetup?

Meetup is on a mission to help the world's people self-organize into local groups.

So far more than 6.5 million people have signed up and formed over 60,000 local Meetup Groups.

What's on the Meetup HQ Blog?

Behind the Scenes
New Features
Meetups in the News
Organizer of the Week
Can't Miss Meetups
Tales from the Road
Tips & Tricks
Trends & Stats
Guest Bloggers

Figure 15-33. Useful Organizer Center links if you're thinking about starting a group

Starting a Meetup Group

At the present time, starting a Meetup group costs money—this is how Meetup makes the business sustainable. It's free to browse and participate, but there is a charge for starting a Meetup group. However, the cost is small, and it can be shared. My general recommendation is to try joining and participating in a Meetup group to see what it's like. Then, if you or some friends or people who are already in a group think "Hey, we should do this," all the better! Creating a way for people to connect locally is a great thing.

The first step may be to see if there's already a group of people in your area who have similar interests. You may be surprised. Then, if you're interested in starting your own group, more power to you. (You may want to start the group with a friend.)

To start a Meetup group, click the Start a Meetup Group icon in the upper-left corner of the screen (see Figure 15-34).

Start
a Meetup Group

Figure 15-34. The Start a Meetup Group icon

You're presented with a series of numbered steps for the process, as shown in Figure 15-35.

413

Set up your new Meetup Group!
The basics
2 Pick a theme
3 Find the right members
4 Plans and pricing
5 Between Meetups...
6 Schedule your first Meetup
Did you know? Organizers pay a subscription fee. Learn more

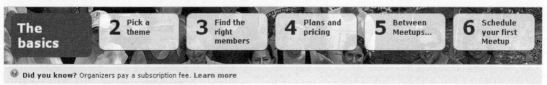

Figure 15-35. Follow these steps to start a group.

The basic information, shown in Figure 15-36, includes an opportunity to name the group, which affects the group's address. I like the pledge at the bottom. How cool—there should be more pledges like that. Go Meetup! When you're finished, click the Next button.

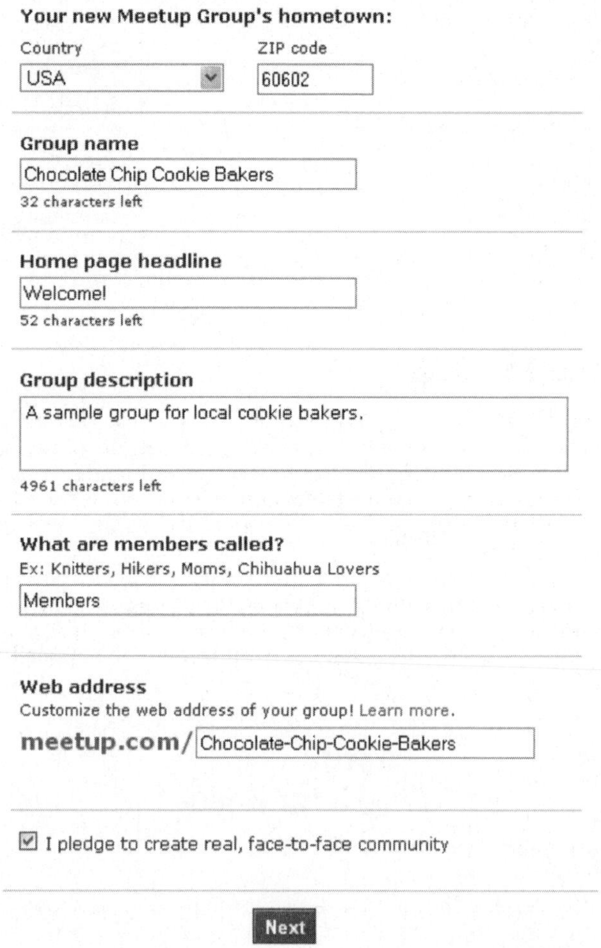

Your new Meetup Group's hometown:
Country
USA
ZIP code
60602
Group name
Chocolate Chip Cookie Bakers
32 characters left
Home page headline
Welcome!
52 characters left
Group description
A sample group for local cookie bakers.
4961 characters left
What are members called?
Ex: Knitters, Hikers, Moms, Chihuahua Lovers
Members
Web address
Customize the web address of your group! Learn more.
meetup.com/ Chocolate-Chip-Cookie-Bakers
I pledge to create real, face-to-face community
Next

Figure 15-36. Basic group information

Then, you can pick a theme for your group (or make your own), as shown in Figure 15-37. When you've chosen, click Next.

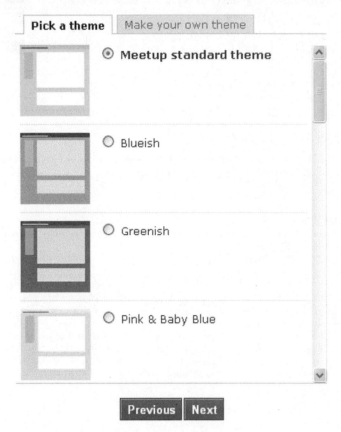

Figure 15-37. Choose a theme for your group.

The topics area allows you to indicate more about what your group does (see Figure 15-38). Meetup suggests topics based on the group title, and you can enter your own as well. A group can have up to seven topics. When you're ready, click Next.

Pick a few topics

Topics **categorize** and **describe** what your Meetup Group is about in a word or two.

Pick up to **7 topics** for your Meetup Group.
Learn more about topics.

> Enter a topic... (required)
> Up to 50 characters.

Why are topics important?

🔖 Well-picked topics help **the right members** find your Meetup Group.

📖 Your Meetup Group will be **listed in our directory** under each topic you choose.

Suggested Topics

Suggestions are based on your Group's info and/or what other topics Meetup Groups like yours have added.

Baker
Add as topic

Cookie Swap
Add as topic

Social Networking, Chat, Chew and Chocolate
Add as topic

Bakers Square Alum's
Add as topic

Dark Chocolate
Add as topic

Wine , Cheese and Chocolate Socials
Add as topic

Chocolate
Add as topic

Dining, Sushi, Desserts&Wine Tastings & Chocolate
Add as topic

Cookie Decorating
Add as topic

Healthy Chocolate 101
Add as topic

Previous Next

Figure 15-38. Select your group's topic(s).

Then—the pricing information. Doh! It's similar to a magazine subscription, but it can allow you to make a difference in peoples' lives and to have fun in the process. (And you can share the cost.) At the time of writing, the pricing is as shown in Figure 15-39.

Choose a subscription plan:

Need to enter a coupon?

● **6 months for only** $12/month	**SAVE 37%**	Billed in one payment of $72.00
RECOMMENDED		
○ **3 months for only** $15/month	**SAVE 21%**	Billed in one payment of $45.00
○ **1 month for only** $19/month		

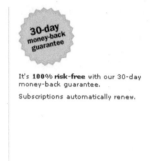

30-day money-back guarantee

It's **100% risk-free** with our 30-day money-back guarantee.

Subscriptions automatically renew.

Figure 15-39. Group pricing at the time of writing

■ **Note** Don't be discouraged if you want to form a group but can't afford to. Number one, maybe someone at Meetup will read this sentence and raise the idea of a scholarship program that lets people make the case that they can have an impact in their community with a Meetup group but can't afford it; you never know, the Meetup wizard may grant this wish. Number two, until you can afford to create a group (remember: share costs, or go to your local government—who knows, they may sponsor it), there are free alternatives. For example, try Ning.com, or go on `www.google.com` and google "google groups," and consider making a local group with one of those tools. The free alternatives may not be as flexible as Meetup, and not as many people may browse themselves into your group, but the other sites can get you started.

Remember, there is a *very useful Help section* on Meetup.com, which is specifically designed to support Meetup organizers. Go to the top of any Meetup page, click the Help link, and then explore the Organizer Center and the Discuss Meetup area.

Q/A

Q: Is there a free alternative to Meetup?

A: The distinctive thing about Meetup is that it's a fairly large community of users, and there are a lot of groups that you can explore. Participating in Meetup is free; it only costs if you want to create a new Meetup page. As a free alternative to using Meetup, you can explore Google groups, Facebook groups (see the Facebook chapters), Facebook events, or Evite—they don't do the same thing, but they can help you to get a group of people together. (Try entering these names into Google.) Also, see Chapter 16—Ning can be used to gather people together locally.

Q: How do I keep safe when I go to a Meetup group?

A: Go with a friend, and/or go only to meetings that are in public places.

Q: Where can I read more about Meetup?

A: Keep your eyes open for an entire book from CFTW Press about Meetup. If you want to keep posted about the book's progress, go on Facebook and search for (and join) the Social Networking Spaces Group, or search for (and become a fan of) the Social Networking Spaces Facebook page. I'll post messages once in a while to both. Just as with this book, all author proceeds will be donated to CFTW. (See the Introduction to this book.) And don't worry if you don't know how to join a group or become a fan. You can learn by reading the Facebook chapters in this book!

> Q: Wait! I have another question! Where can I ask it?
> A: On www.snspaces.com.

Conclusion

Dear Reader,

Thank you for reading this chapter.

In this chapter, you learned about exploring Meetup, how to find a group, and how to start one.

And now, because I personally consider it to be so important, I invite you to go back and re-read the "Introduction: The Original Social Network" section at the beginning of this chapter. I invite you to read it or read it again, blog about it, discuss it with your neighbor, challenge it, ask questions about it, discuss it on www.snspaces.com—whatever you like.

Regards,

–Todd

---

snspaces.com

Come and visit the Social Networking Spaces companion web site at www.snspaces.com, where you can find more tips and updates and have an opportunity to share your thoughts or ask questions.

In Living Color: You can visit www.snspaces.com/pics to see full-color versions of all the pictures from this chapter.

CHAPTER 16

■ ■ ■

What the Heck Is Ning?

In This Chapter:

- How to create your own social network on Ning
- How to share a post
- How to invite people to visit your Ning site

Introduction

The increasingly popular and free Ning makes it easy to create your own social network for your organization, group, club, business, and so on. Ning came to be by tapping into the same interest that Facebook and Twitter do: the desire to be social and form groups around common interests. And what Ning allows you to do, for free, is to make *your own* social network.

Why bother?

On Facebook, you can create a Facebook group; the tremendous value of Facebook is how interconnected it is. So many people are on Facebook that it's easy to find people who are interested in the same thing, easy to create a Facebook group, and easy to advertise it. But there are limitations on Facebook groups, and sometimes it's nice to have your own space.

You can find features on Ning that are similar to Facebook, such as discussions, shared photos, and so on. But there are some options that you don't have in Facebook, like being able to customize how things look, and giving people their own blogs.

For example, Figure 16-1 shows a nice example of a Ning site, which provides a personal space for Dancing Ink Productions. There are several groups based on the mutual interests of the creator and people who came along, such as Second Life and virtual business.

Figure 16-1. An example of a Ning site

If you compare what you can do with a Ning site and a Facebook group or a Facebook page, it looks more like a web site. It's just as easy to work with as Facebook, perhaps even a little easier, and it's "your" site.

It's an especially good, sustainable option for any situation where you want to gather some people together around a common interest or cause, or for an organization. It's sustainable because it's free, yet you can make it look reasonably good. It may be the best tool for a situation where you already have some people in a group of some kind, such as employees or volunteers with a particular organization, or members of a club, and there's a natural draw for people to participate in the site.

But it doesn't have to be a group. For some, Ning may be the easiest, cheapest way to get a web site launched. Perhaps you have a product you want to sell, or a home business of some kind, and you need something that makes it as easy as possible to get going. There's nothing wrong with making it social, right?

How is Ning different from a blog? A blog is generally a forum for personal expression and for sharing articles and information; the social component is generally focused around comments. Pretty straightforward. Something like a column in a newspaper. A Ning site is more like a clubhouse or storefront, a place where people can hang out.

That's it. Compared to a Facebook group, a Ning site can allow you to make things a little more *personal*. It takes more effort, but for a situation where you want your own space, it can be nice.

Another thing about Ning is that you can access an increasing number of Ning apps (applications), which allow you to add features to your group site that you can't necessarily do on a Facebook group. See Figure 16-2.

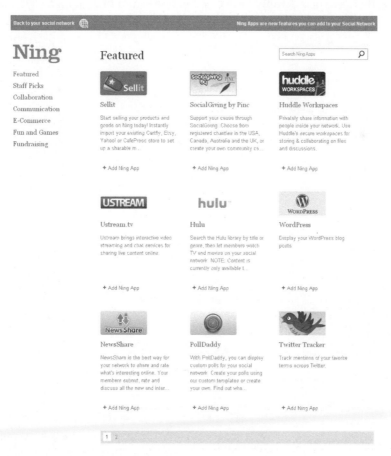

Figure 16-2. Ning applications

If you create a Ning network (some people use Ning to access an existing network that someone has already created), you can sign into your Ning network and click the Ning Apps icon in the Manage page.

If you're out there daydreaming, the best thing is to imagine what you like doing, and play around with things like Facebook groups, Facebook pages (including Facebook applications for pages), a blog, or a Ning site (including Ning applications). Just play and explore.

Help

I recommend diving right in; but remember, there's always the Help link on the Ning site in the lower-right corner. It's not just for when you get in trouble: there's a lot of good information that explains what you can do with Ning.

Help   Privacy   Terms of Service

For example, there's a good Getting Started section (see Figure 16-3). It's a really good idea to read the Getting Started articles and maybe click the Learn More link.

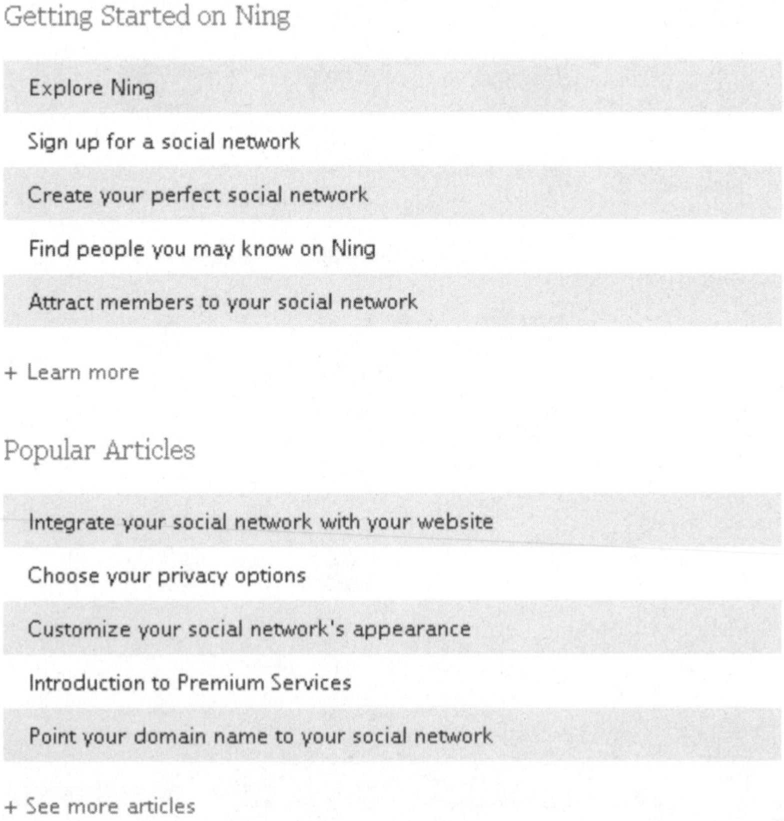

Getting Started on Ning

Explore Ning

Sign up for a social network

Create your perfect social network

Find people you may know on Ning

Attract members to your social network

+ Learn more

Popular Articles

Integrate your social network with your website

Choose your privacy options

Customize your social network's appearance

Introduction to Premium Services

Point your domain name to your social network

+ See more articles

Figure 16-3. Getting help in Ning

You may wish to browse in the Popular Articles section, to get a taste. It's always a good idea to pay attention to popular articles in help areas on web sites. They can be a good clue to things people are interested in, like some of the nicest features. The first article, for example, mentions that you can use a Ning site in conjunction with an *existing* web site. This is likely to become more popular as organizations and businesses look for ways to engage, create, and support online communities of members and customers.

And if you have a question, the Help link supports that, too, as shown in Figure 16-4.

Ning Help

How can we help you?

Enter search terms above, like "upload a video" or "use my domain"

Figure 16-4. You can ask questions in the Help section.

The right side of the Help screen has some nice content as well, including announcements and more helpful learning material, such as a workshop (see Figure 16-5).

Announcements

Update to email verification on Ning Networks

Ning Apps are live on your Ning Network!

The Status feature is now available on your Ning Network

Ning Workshop
Read our tips and tricks for setting up, running, and promoting your social network.

Premium Support
Get more guidance and support on growing and customizing your social network.

Safety Tips & Resources
Check out some simple guidelines to keep your online experience safe and fun.

Figure 16-5. Announcements and other info in the Help section

Create a Ning Site

To create a Ning site, start by visiting www.ning.com, shown in Figure 16-6. There's a place at the top where you can get started. You can also browse *existing* networks to see how other people are using Ning or to join in the fun.

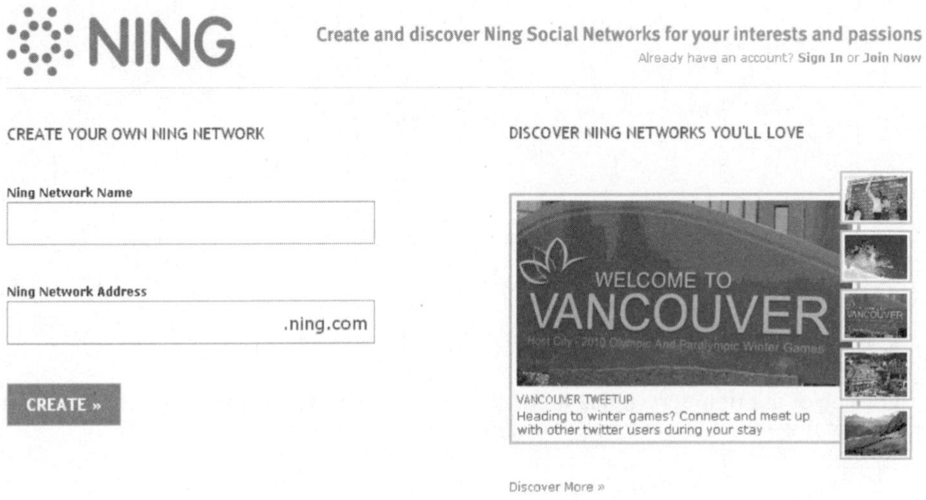

Figure 16-6. Getting started with Ning

To begin creating a network, choose a name, an address, and click the Create button, shown in Figure 16-7.

Figure 16-7. Click Create to start building your site.

You also need to pick a URL. This means coming up with a name of at least six letters, which will appear before `.ning.com`. For example, the social networking spaces Ning site is at `http://snspaces.ning.com`. Generally speaking, you want to strike a balance between short and meaningful. If a particular name is taken, try using dashes or numbers between letters.

If you don't already have a Ning account, you can create one. See Figure 16-8. If you already have one, then you can sign in.

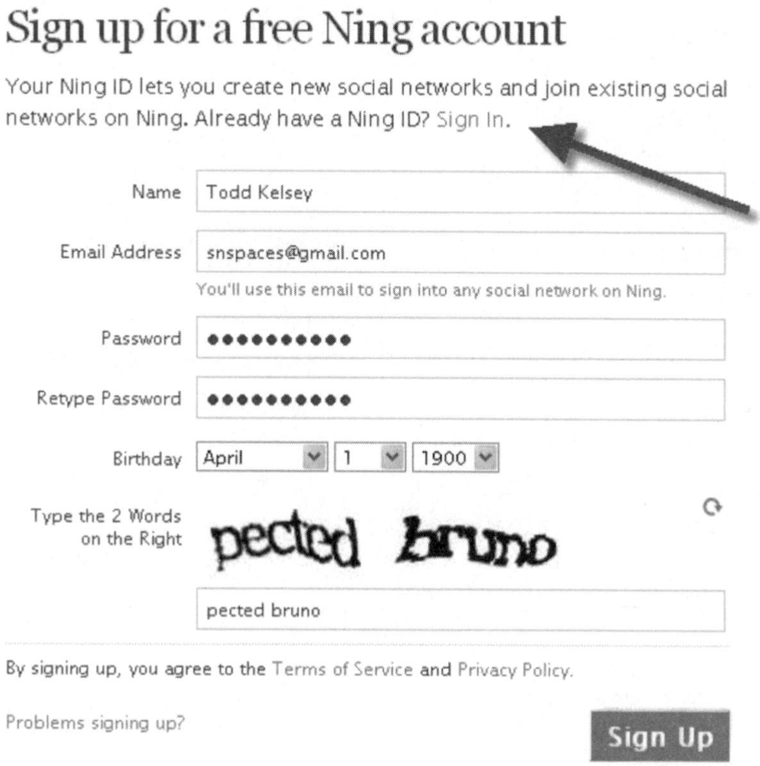

Sign up for a free Ning account

Your Ning ID lets you create new social networks and join existing social networks on Ning. Already have a Ning ID? Sign In.

Name	Todd Kelsey
Email Address	snspaces@gmail.com

You'll use this email to sign into any social network on Ning.

Password	••••••••••
Retype Password	••••••••••
Birthday	April ▾ 1 ▾ 1900 ▾
Type the 2 Words on the Right	pected bruno
	pected bruno

By signing up, you agree to the Terms of Service and Privacy Policy.

Problems signing up?

Sign Up

Figure 16-8. Sign up for an account.

When you're ready, click the Sign Up button.

Next, Ning asks you to verify your e-mail address. Depending on which system you use, it may have a button like Go to Gmail, which can take you directly there. See Figure 16-9.

Verify your email address

We now need to verify your email address. We've sent an email to snspaces@gmail.com. Please click the link in that email to continue.

Go to Gmail

Figure 16-9. Verify your e-mail address.

You'll get confirmation e-mail with a link you can click, as in Figure 16-10.

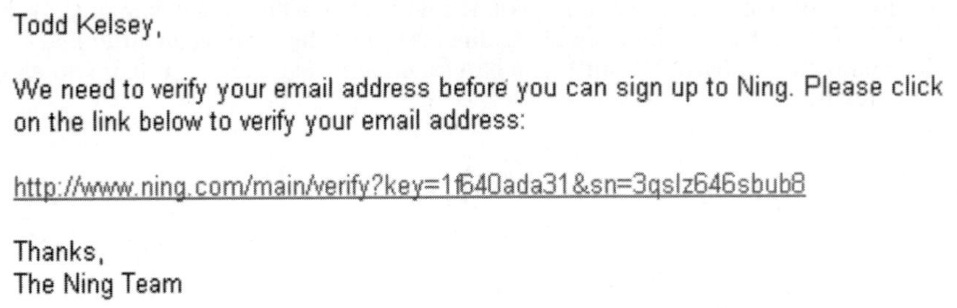

Todd Kelsey,

We need to verify your email address before you can sign up to Ning. Please click on the link below to verify your email address:

http://www.ning.com/main/verify?key=1f640ada31&sn=3qslz646sbub8

Thanks,
The Ning Team

Figure 16-10. E-mail confirmed!

You're asked to enter more information (which you can change later). If you want, you can click the Launch link, but I recommend at least coming up with some simple temporary information, as in Figure 16-11.

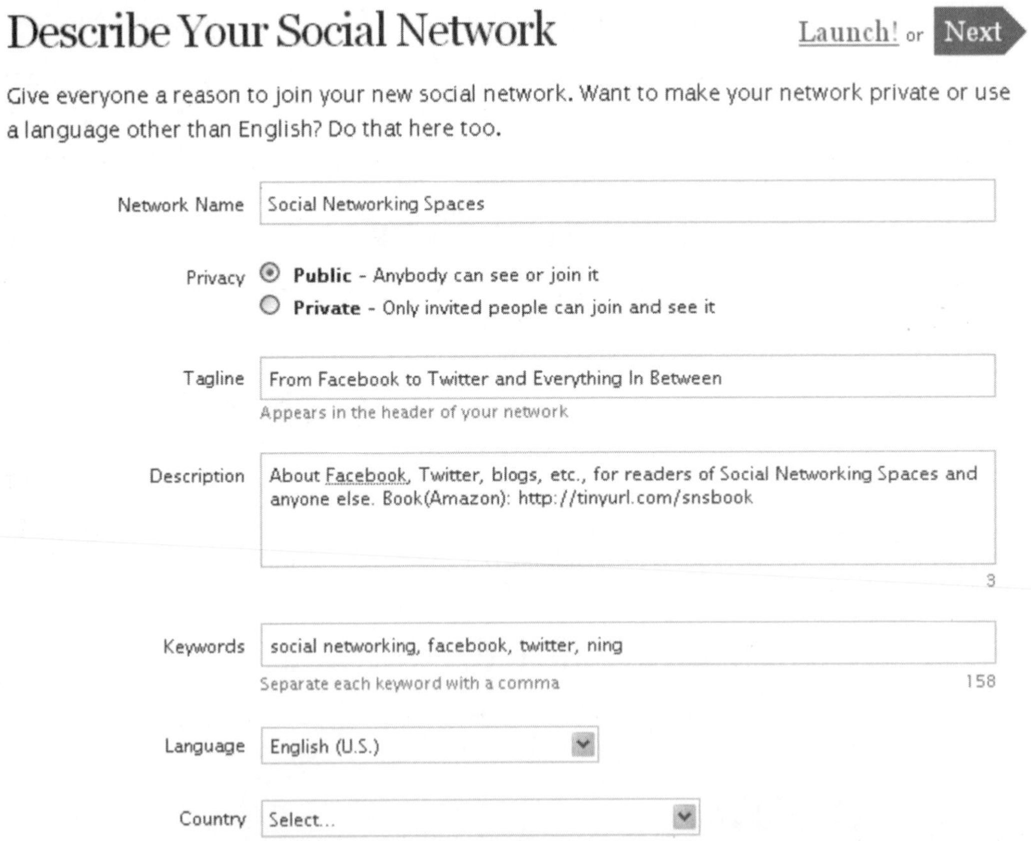

Describe Your Social Network
<u>Launch!</u> or **Next** ▶

Give everyone a reason to join your new social network. Want to make your network private or use a language other than English? Do that here too.

Network Name   Social Networking Spaces

Privacy   ◉ **Public** - Anybody can see or join it
           ○ **Private** - Only invited people can join and see it

Tagline   From Facebook to Twitter and Everything In Between
           Appears in the header of your network

Description   About Facebook, Twitter, blogs, etc., for readers of Social Networking Spaces and anyone else. Book(Amazon): http://tinyurl.com/snsbook

3

Keywords   social networking, facebook, twitter, ning
            Separate each keyword with a comma   158

Language   English (U.S.)

Country   Select...

Figure 16-11. Describe your network.

426

The Keywords section allows people who are searching for Ning groups to more easily find your group. The Country setting is optional. When you're ready to move on, click the Next button.

The next screen demonstrates how powerful and easy-to-use Ning is (hats off, Ning, for a good user experience). My Ph.D dissertation is on how open source content-management systems like Drupal can make it easier and more sustainable for nonprofits to have their own web sites, and I'm coming to believe that, like Google sites, Ning is also a valid and powerful option in many cases. Basically, as in Figure 16-12, you can drag things around to play with features that you may like to have on the site.

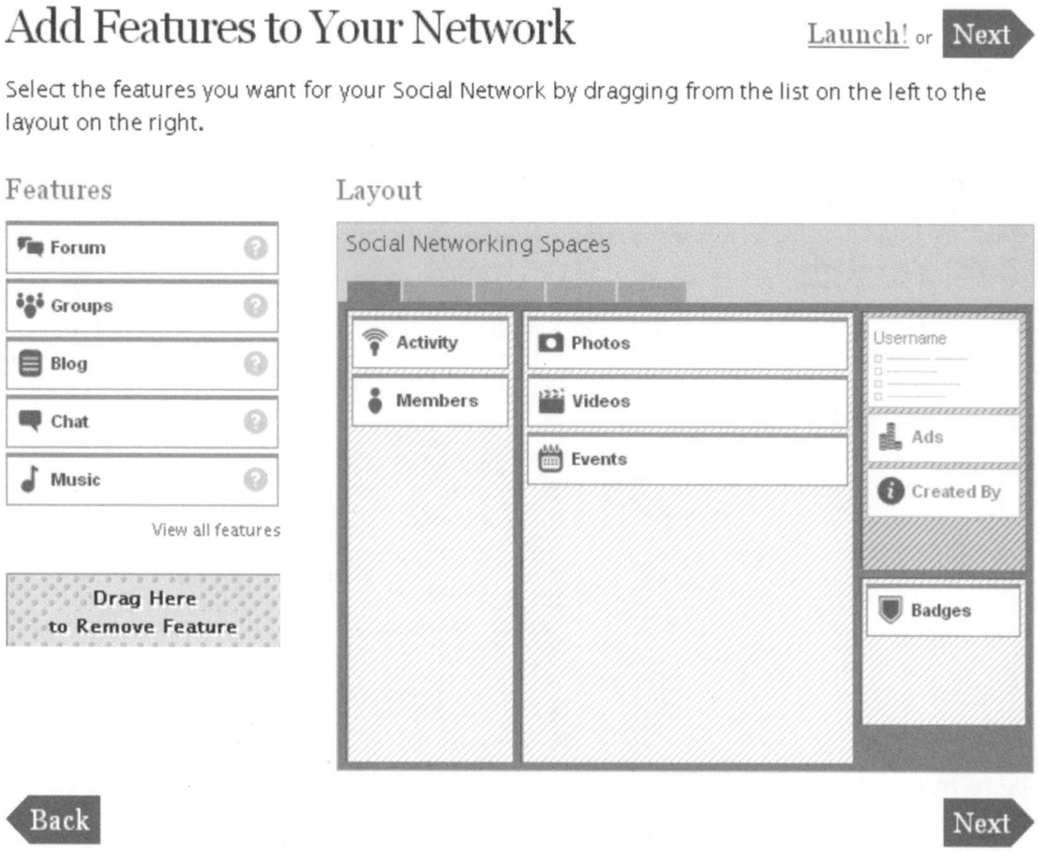

Figure 16-12. *Select features you'd like to include.*

To enable a feature, roll your mouse over a block on the left, until the mouse pointer turns into a four-sided arrow thingy (see Figure 16-13).

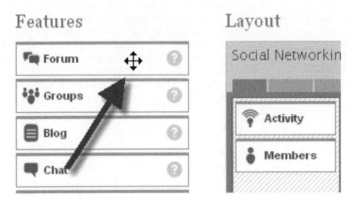

Figure 16-13. *The mouse pointer changes when you roll over a feature.*

Then, click and drag the feature into position in one of the columns on the right, in the Layout section (see Figure 16-14).

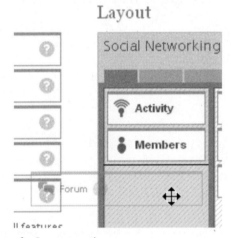

Figure 16-14. *Drag the feature to the Layout section.*

The feature has now been added, as shown in Figure 16-15. How cool is that. Go Ning!

Layout

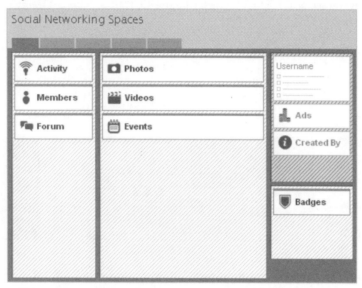

Figure 16-15. *The feature is added.*

You can also drag things from one column to another. For the Social Networking Spaces site, I dragged everything out of the middle column, and dragged the Blog feature in, as shown in Figure 16-16.

Layout

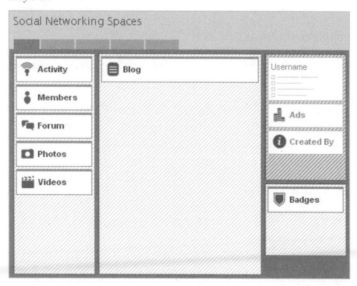

Figure 16-16. *I added the Blog feature.*

When you're ready (you can always change things later), click the Next button.

The next screen you see is also a lot of fun (see Figure 16-17) and includes many templates you can choose from that determine how the site looks.

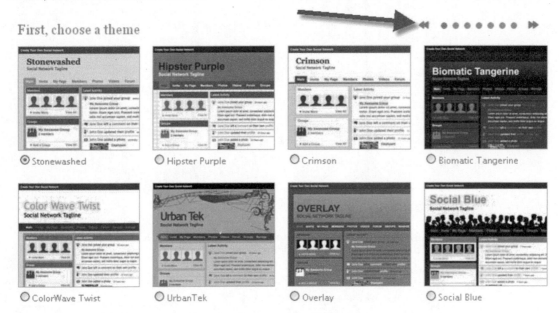

Figure 16-17. Determining your site's appearance

Click the little set of left-pointing arrows (<<) or right-pointing arrows (>>) to see more templates:

More themes are shown in Figure 16-18.

First, choose a theme

Figure 16-18. Choosing a theme

Have fun, but don't over-think it. You can come back later and change the way your site looks. When you're ready to share, click the Launch button:

Launch!

You may even want to count down from 10 and say "Launch!", especially if you've been drinking too much Starbucks or Caribou, or if you have a child nearby with a sense of fun and adventure, or if you yourself are a child with a sense of adventure. Wait a second, everyone has a child inside!

Your site appears, all ready for you to add content. See Figure 16-19.

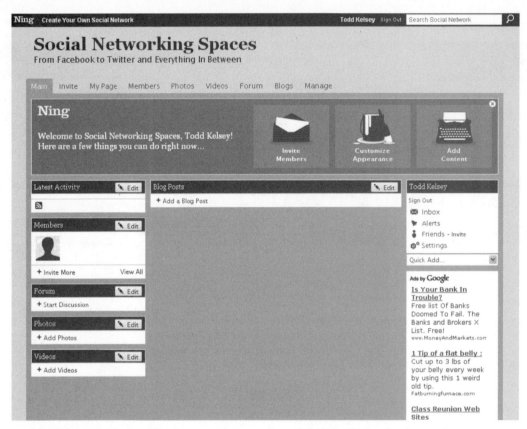

Figure 16-19. Congratulations! You've created your own social network! Facebook, watch out!

After you launch, you get another e-mail from Ning, which has some links to help you get started enhancing your site or inviting visitors. You may want to save the e-mail for reference. See Figure 16-20.

Dear Todd Kelsey,

Congratulations on creating Social Networking Spaces, your new social network on Ning.
Now that you've created your social network, there are four simple things you can do to get started:

1. Invite your friends or your first set of members http://snspaces.ning.com/main/invitation/new

2. Customize your social network's appearance http://snspaces.ning.com/main/appearance/edit

3. Add features to your social network http://snspaces.ning.com/main/feature/add

4. Add Content http://snspaces.ning.com/main/index/addContent

Thanks!
The Ning Team

Figure 16-20. Save this helpful e-mail.

Also, if you created a new Ning account, the next time you sign in, you may have an opportunity to load a picture if you want and to include some basic information about yourself for your public Ning profile, as shown in Figure 16-21 (you can also click the Skip link):

Ning   ✕

Welcome, Todd Kelsey!

Add Your Photo
[   ] [Browse...]

Country
[Choose...   ▼]

Gender
[Choose... ▼]

About Me
[   ]
[   ]

                                          [Done]   Skip

Figure 16-21. You can add a picture if you like.

Add Content: Create a Blog Post

The type of content you can add depends on what features you added in the site-creation process. You can always go to the Manage tab if you don't have the Blog feature but would like to add it. (Choose Manage tab ➤ Features.)

If you added the Blog feature, you can make a post by clicking the + Add a Blog Post link (see Figure 16-22).

Blog Posts   ✎ Edit
+ Add a Blog Post

Figure 16-22. The Add a Blog Post link

Then, you can enter a title and some text, as shown in Figure 16-23. Roll your mouse over the little icons directly under the word *Entry*. They're for formatting text, adding links or a picture, and so on:

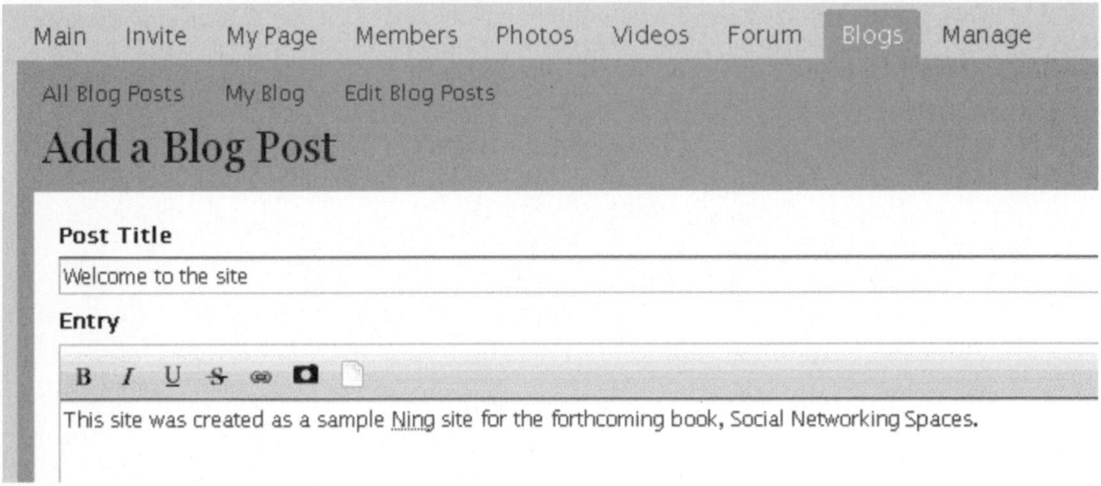

Figure 16-23. *Enter your blog post.*

You can publish the blog post now, or you can set it to appear in the future. Sometimes, bloggers work on several posts ahead of time and set them to appear at different intervals (instead of all at once). This helps to keep a steady stream of content going.

At the bottom, you can adjust additional settings, as shown in Figure 16-24. When you're ready, click the Publish Post button. If you like, you can click Preview to see what your post looks like. The Save as Draft button can save it if you've started a blog post and want to come back to it later.

Figure 16-24. *Additional blog settings*

When you click the Publish Post button, you're taken to the Blogs section of the site, as shown in Figure 16-25. This section has several blog-related links, some of which only appear to you, because you're managing the site.

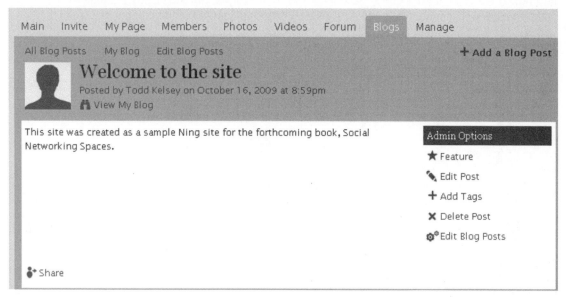

Figure 16-25. The Blogs section

You can click the Main tab (all the way on the left, at the top), to get back home (see Figure 16-26).

Figure 16-26. The Main tab

And because the Blog feature had been added to the middle column, when a blog post is added, it appears there. Pretty cool.

Remember, you can always go back and change things (and I encourage you to explore and play around). There's a lot of stuff under the Manage tab. For example, you can go into Manage ➤ Appearance and try a different outfit on for your web site (see Figure 16-27).

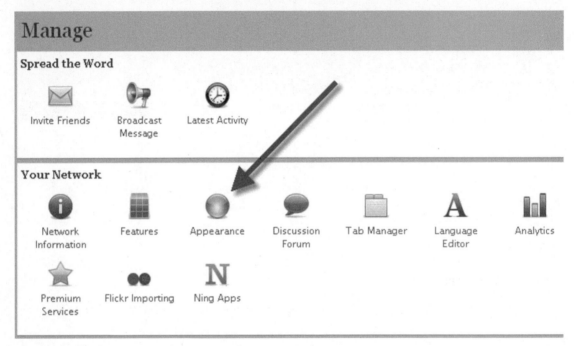

Figure 16-27. *Options under the Manage tab*

Inviting People

To invite people, click the Invite tab at the top of the Ning screen (see Figure 16-28). If you still have the green bar at the top, you can click the Invite Members icon. If you want to get rid of the green bar, click the X in the upper-right corner.

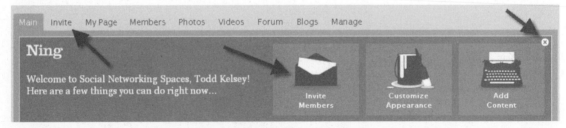

Figure 16-28. *Click the Invite tab to invite people. To close the green bar, click the X.*

The Invite feature allows you to import addresses from your e-mail account (see Figure 16-29).

Figure 16-29. Importing e-mail addresses

Or, you can click the Enter E-mail Addresses Manually link, enter one or more e-mail addresses with a message, and click Send Invitations (see Figure 16-30).

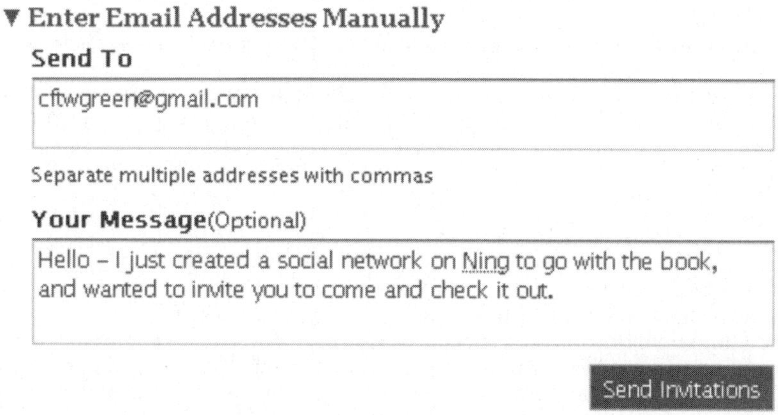

Figure 16-30. You can invite people by entering their e-mail addresses.

You can also send someone an e-mail or instant message with the address of the site (for example, http://snspaces.ning.com).

Consider Making a Family Site in Ning

You may want to try creating a site for your family. In fact, a Ning social network can be *private*. You can also have more than one Ning site.

If you like, create a family site. Make it private, if you want to (I recommend that, in part for safety, and also to respect privacy and to have a place where people can speak their minds). To make it private, click the Private radio button during the sign-up process, as shown in Figure 16-31.

Network Name | Social Networking Spaces

Privacy ◉ **Public** - Anybody can see or join it
         ○ **Private** - Only invited people can join and see it

Figure 16-31. You can make a site public or private.

You may wish to prepopulate your private Ning site by gathering stories from people via e-mail or by phone—maybe one from each person, but aiming for something interesting (your first date, a time you got in trouble, an important event in your life, where were you when such-and-such happened, and so on). And put the stories up on the Ning site!

Then, invite people to come and check it out and see what others have posted, to hear about the time Uncle Bob went on a road trip through Montana and met his wife when she pulled him over doing 90 in a 70 mph zone, or whatever. Don't feel shy about using marketing techniques in your invitation, listing little inviting blurbs when you ask people to join the network. And don't feel shy about being creative with the site's name: The Kelsey Family Ranch, Secret Story Vault, or Family Hall of Fame. You can make the address family focused (http://kelsey.ning.com), and you can always change the name if you'd like to experiment.

Most important, come on www.snspaces.com and share how it goes. That may help someone else to see how fun it can be.

If you invite people to contribute recollections of an event or story or something, I *100 percent guarantee* you'll be glad you did. It's possible that some family members will groan, and some of the groaning may come from younger family members. But someday, even if that day is very far off, they'll come around.

Q/A

Q: What if I already have a domain name? Or how do I register one?

A: If you have a domain name already, such as www.myname.com, you can point it at a Ning site. See the Help section I mentioned earlier in this chapter, and look carefully at the screenshots. Also, be aware that if you don't have a domain name, you can register one at a place like Hostgator.com. If you're using your main domain name already (such as www.websitename.com), be aware that you can create something like social.websitename.com and point that at Ning. That's called a *subdomain*. When you own a domain, such as snspaces.com, it gives you the ability to control whatever appears to the *left* of the domain name. I could create blog.snspaces.com and point it at a blog, or I could create ning.snspaces.com and point it at the Ning site, and so on.

Q: Which should I use, Ning or Facebook groups?

A: I suggest trying both. If you're evaluating for a group or organization, get a few people to try out the features, and compare the two. For some, a Facebook group may be good enough; it has the advantage of being in the context of Facebook, where people may be signing on anyway, so it makes it easy to get to. Ning has more customization capability, including the ability to use your own web site name.

Q: Wait! I have another question! Where can I ask it?
A: On www.snspaces.com.

Conclusion

Dear Reader,

Ning is a good example of a site you may come across as a browser (where someone may invite you to participate as a member of a group or organization) and where there's also an opportunity for you to create your own site.

Facebook and other mass sites are good for some things, and they have features for making your own groups. But in some cases, it may be nice to have your *own* social network, and Ning makes this possible.

Ning makes it significantly easier for people to have their own fully-fledged online community. (Thanks, Ning!) This allows you to do basically whatever you want, and instead of following Facebook's guidelines and rules, you can make your own guidelines.

I hope you enjoy exploring Ning, either as a browser, taking a look at one of the many networks people have created, or as a creator.

Best wishes!

Regards,

–Todd

---

snspaces.com

Come and visit the Social Networking Spaces companion web site at www.snspaces.com, where you can find more tips and updates and have an opportunity to share your thoughts or ask questions.

In Living Color: You can visit www.snspaces.com/pics to see full-color versions of all the pictures from this chapter.

■ ■ ■

CHAPTER 17

Exploring 3D Virtual Worlds: Second Life

In This Chapter:

- How to sign up and use Second Life
- World heritage: virtual tourism and adventure
- Things to try

snspaces.com

Come and visit the Social Networking Spaces companion web site at www.snspaces.com, where you can find more tips and updates and have an opportunity to share your thoughts or ask questions.

In Living Color: You can visit www.snspaces.com/pics to see full-color versions of all the pictures from this chapter.

Visual Introduction: Why Try Second Life? Virtual Tourism, Taking Life Story Pictures, and More

Second Life is a free, user-created virtual and social three-dimensional world. It's basically like a 3D game where you create your own character and interact with other people. People use it for a lot of different things, such as socializing and even recreation. This section is an *extended* visual introduction to Second Life. If you want to start an account, please feel free to skip ahead to the "Getting on to Second Life" section.

A fair number of people are using Second Life as a platform to facilitate meetings of one kind or another, including corporate meetings as well as educational seminars. In a typical webinar, you might look at a presentation and hear someone talk. However, wouldn't it be interesting to be in a virtual auditorium and have the opportunity not only to listen to the presentation but also maybe interact with people afterward? Second Life has this educational/convention/conference kind of dimension. See `http://en.wikipedia.org/wiki/Second_life` for more information.

In addition to the preceding, I happen to think Second Life is particularly fun as a way to go someplace new and take pictures. For example, Figure 17-1 is picture of me in a 3D re-creation of Dublin.

Figure 17-1. *This is my 3D avatar. In effect, it's "me," posing for a picture.*

Figure 17-2 is picture I took with my friend Phil.

Figure 17-2. *My friend Phil and me*

Have you ever visited a museum or a historical place and taken pictures of you and your friends? Or, have you ever visited somewhere new, made new friends, and then taken pictures? You can do this in Second Life. If nothing else, you can end up with some interesting pictures to put in your photo album.

■ **Tip** This chapter in particular is one where I recommend taking a peek at the full-color pictures on www.snspaces.com to get the full experience, because black-and-white doesn't do the pictures justice.

Overall, it's fun to try flying around and taking pictures. Later in the chapter (see the section "Virtual Tourism"), you see how to sign on to Second Life and visit re-creations of famous places like downtown Dublin.

You can also go *dancing* on Second Life (see Figure 17-3). And you don't need any special skills, either.

Figure 17-3. Wandering into a dance club on Halloween

One of the things people like doing in Second Life is going to dance clubs. You can click a feature and do very realistic dance moves as an individual; or sometimes, the dancing is synchronized. It's quite a sight to see everyone dancing. In fact, it's rather surreal.

Just like at parties in real life, people go up to each other to socialize, flirt, or dance. A few dancers doing their thing are shown in Figure 17-4.

Figure 17-4. People with various costumes

You can walk up to people and communicate with them. The most common way is via text messages, but there is some capability for voice chat as well. You can customize your character, also known as an *avatar*, with whatever kind of body and clothing you'd like.

You can also walk around a location to explore it. Here I am in Korea (see Figure 17-5).

Figure 17-5. Walking down the street in a re-creation of a Korean city

Of course, it's interesting to walk around a virtual world and interact with people. But why just walk down a street in Korea if you can fly down it, instead (see Figure 17-6)?

Figure 17-6. *Flying is more fun than walking. It feels like you're in a movie, like The Matrix.*

Ever had a dream in which you were flying? In a sense, Second Life provides a way to help you explore (some) dreams or fantasies, or parts of your imagination that the real world doesn't allow you to because of things like the laws of physics.

You explore Second Life through a series of interfaces such as maps, and you walk around using your keyboard's arrow keys. When you're on Second Life, flying is as easy as pressing the Page Up key (using the arrows), whereas the Page Down key can bring you back to the ground. It's fun!

Exploring Second Life

One way to explore Second Life and understand more about virtual worlds before installing the software is to visit www.secondlife.com (see Figure 17-7).

Figure 17-7. These are some videos you can watch on www.secondlife.com.

A number of videos give a good description of the kinds of things people like doing on Second Life, and what it ends up looking and feeling like. In addition to exploring the videos, you may also choose to click the link at the top of the screen, as shown in Figure 17-8.

What Is Second Life?

Figure 17-8. A helpful link

The Quick Start guide can be helpful if you think you want to try Second Life (see Figure 17-9).

Figure 17-9. Quick Start Guide

In a nutshell, Second Life is a piece of free software available for Windows/Mac/Linux. You register and sign up, and then you can check it out.

Virtual Tourism: Going on an Adventure and Taking Pictures

To try to inspire your imagination a bit, I suggest that because of the interesting places people have created in Second Life, even if you don't see yourself having an ongoing interest in virtual worlds, you may enjoy thinking of them like an excursion. Maybe take some pictures and include them in your life-story suitcase either on Facebook or by printing them out. It may be an interesting thing for your relatives or descendants to look back on.

For example, tonight, while working on this chapter I thought, what the heck—may as well upload some pictures to Facebook to show some of the virtual places I've been in Second Life. You may even enjoy looking at the photo album yourself, because this book will be in black and white, whereas the photo album is in color: www.facebook.com/album.php?aid=116940&l=a6fa9cf3f7&id=773814569.

I'd be impressed if you typed that link without spraining your fingers. I'll put it on www.snspaces.com along with all the other links so you don't have to type in anything from the book; that way, you have an easy way to click to sites and then bookmark them. Here's the shortened URL if you do want to type something in and go directly: http://tinyurl.com/vhalloween.

My point is, in real life you'd most likely buy a plane ticket to go to Ireland. The entire world hasn't been created in Second Life, but some friendly souls re-created downtown Dublin. To find it, when you have the software installed (and to search for just about anything else), you type it in (see Figure 17-10).

Figure 17-10. *Type a place in the search box. Whether it exists in Second Life depends entirely on whether someone has created it.*

When you use the search feature, you can find a lot of places to go. In order to go somewhere, you click the Teleport button (see Figure 17-11).

Place: Dublin 3 - Christchurch Cathedral

Category: BUSINESS

Region: Dublin 3

West Dublin in SL

Owned by: Dublin in SL Managers (group)

Teleport

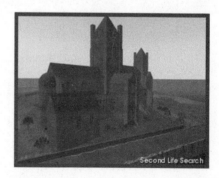

Figure 17-11. *A re-creation of a historic cathedral that you can visit without a plane ticket. You can meet people there, even if in "real" life the person is on the other side of the world.*

After you click teleport, poof! You're there. You explore by walking (or flying) around. In Figure 17-12, like a real-world tourist, I'm looking at a welcome poster.

Figure 17-12. Standing in the 3D world, looking at some basic welcome information

In Second Life, when you go to a different location, it's called *teleporting*, something like what happens in classic science fiction shows like *Star Trek* and *Dr. Who*. Not only can you transport yourself *wherever*, you may also go *whenever*, depending on what people have created (or depending on what you create).

Zooming to Dublin is an example of the kind of thing people are doing—taking the opportunity to go to a location, and maybe back in time as well.

Virtual Picture Taking

Second Life has other features to help you have fun and take photos. Camera controls allow you to adjust things around so you can get the right shot (see Figure 17-13).

Figure 17-13. Try clicking and dragging to see what happens.

I'm not much of a photographer, but it's fun to snap pictures. If you're going to go visit Dublin, you may as well take some pictures and put them on Facebook or in a photo album, right?

■ **Tip** When you're on Second Life, to take a picture, go to the File menu and choose the Take Snapshot option. Save the photo somewhere you can find it, such as your desktop, and name it something memorable, as if you were labeling any other picture. Then, you may wish to read Chapters 2–5, which focus on Facebook, to learn how to put together a photo album. You can amaze your friends by travelling somewhere and filling the Facebook photo album with virtual pictures. Please feel free to post a link to your Facebook virtual photo album on www.snspaces.com or share it on the Social Networking Spaces Facebook group. It would be fun to see and may inspire others to have some fun.

Virtual Heritage

Although I've only been on Second Life a few times, I've enjoyed it, and I think it would be fun to develop more projects so as to explore the learning side of the site. I'd especially like to think about exploring how people could have a family reunion when separated by geographic distance. That's another dimension of something like Second Life: it allows people to interact in ways they otherwise couldn't, because it transcends distance. I'm particularly intrigued by the international ramifications. How cool is it when there's a tool that lets students from different parts of the world interact virtually? Maybe they can explore a virtual historical site together. Maybe they know the same language, maybe they don't—but that's what things like Google Multilingual Chat are for.

Is Dublin the only place people can meet? No, there are a lot of other places. Try visiting this helpful web page for a few samples: http://nmsua.edu/tiopete/sl-world-heritage-international-sites/ or http://tinyurl.com/vheritage.

■ **Note** The links you see on the pages that follow are SLURLS. To visit these places, you need to install Second Life. If you click them, most likely your browser will help guide you toward getting going on Second Life. Otherwise, you may want to continue reading, including the section on installing Second Life, and keep your eyes open for the section "Exploring with SLURLs."

This should be enough to keep any teacher busy for a while, thinking about the pedagogical value of virtual world tourism. Each of the places mentioned below represents a virtual re-creation of a place that has been deemed in the real world to be a common heritage and world treasure. In Figure 17-14, the professor has captured some cool things, including such gems as Historical Preservation in Second Life for those who may like to go adventuring around the world.

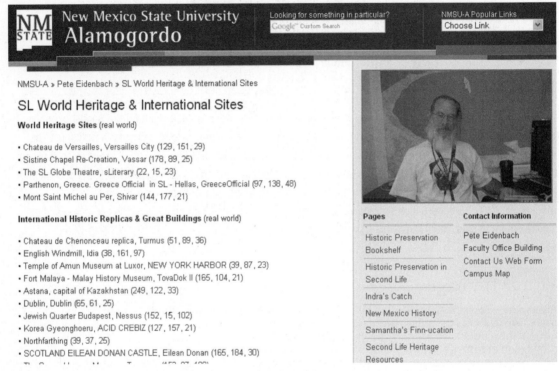

Figure 17-14. A nice web page with a collection of helpful links

Vacations can be a nice way of getting people together who don't normally see each other. What would be wrong about learning how to do these things and connecting in Second Life by going to visit Ireland or the Louvre? (There are technical limitations of what can be done in Second Life, but architecture and especially art are where Second Life excels.)

A classroom of students may yawn at *some* things, but what about travelling halfway around the world in 3D (and maybe being able to do a bit of flying as well?). You can walk around a virtual city, check it out, and realize that you can take pictures.

Figure 17-15 shows me inside the Dublin cathedral.

Figure 17-15. Going inside a building can be fun too.

Another thing that can make virtual tourism fun is flying. How many times have you been able to share a picture with a friend where you've flown to the top of a building? (See that little speck at the top of Figure 17-16? It's me on top of the cathedral!)

Figure 17-16. *With camera controls, you can set up different perspectives for interesting pictures.*

Figure 17-17 is another rooftop picture in Dublin. How fun!

Figure 17-17. *Anywhere you can fly, you can take a picture.*

Music in SL

Another thing people do sometimes on Second Life (or SL, as it's sometimes referred to) is have virtual concerts, such as classical music. Musicians and artists, you may have fun presenting your works via Second Life and advertising them, as in Figure 17-18.

Figure 17-18. A virtual concert poster. Second Life goes beyond a live web cast by providing an opportunity for people to gather socially and virtually to listen to a live performance, even if they're dispersed geographically.

Getting on to Second Life

The general process of getting on Second Life involves registering on the site and then downloading and installing the software. Overall, Second Life is free; but as with some other virtual worlds, you can pay a small fee to get credits to spend on things. In this case, a virtual currency called Linden Dollars is used, which has actually developed *real* value. An entire economy has evolved in Second Life, where people design, sell, and buy virtual goods such as houses and cars. They even get their own land, on an existing island or by buying their own island. However, you don't have to spend a dime in order to explore. You can visit popular places.

Registering on the Site

As software goes, it's fairly processor intensive and memory hungry because it's an immersive 3D world with animation. There are versions for Windows, Mac, and Linux. For more information, see `http://secondlife.com/support/system-requirements/`. In general, if you have a fairly recent computer, you're probably fine to run the program. However, you may wish to close down most or all other software before you run the Second Life software.

To register for Second Life, visit `www.secondlife.com`, and click Join Now, as shown in Figure 17-19.

Join Now >>
It's fast, free and easy!

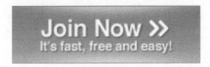

Figure 17-19. *Join Now*

Enter your basic information in the top section (see Figure 17-20).

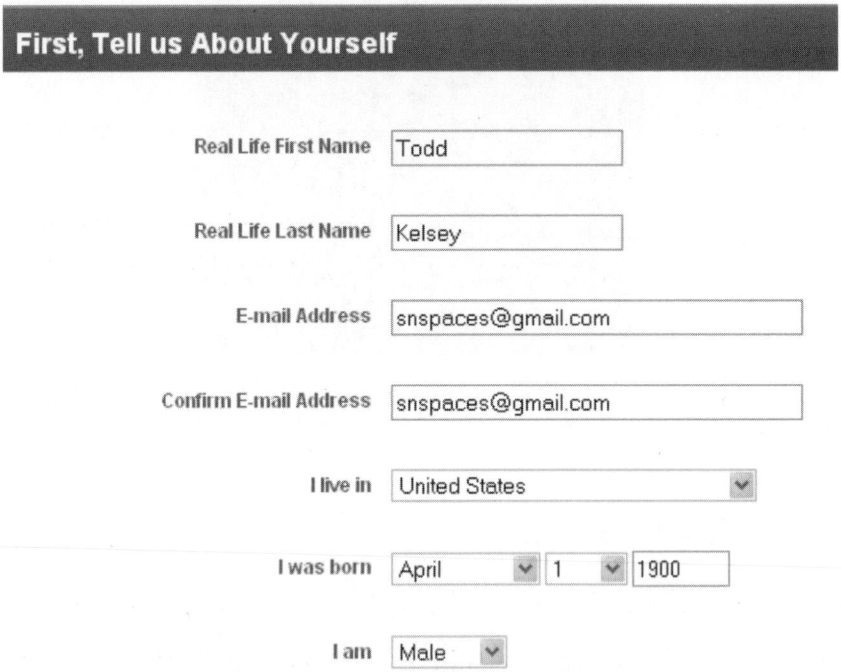
First, Tell us About Yourself
Real Life First Name
Todd
Real Life Last Name
Kelsey
E-mail Address
snspaces@gmail.com
Confirm E-mail Address
snspaces@gmail.com
I live in
United States
I was born
April
1
1900
I am
Male

Figure 17-20. *Filling in basic information*

Figure 17-21 shows the helpful FAQ link on the right, if you need it.

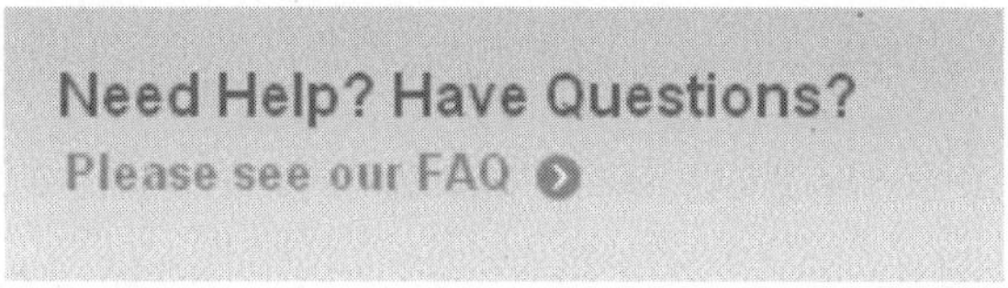

Need Help? Have Questions?
Please see our FAQ ❯

Figure 17-21. FAQ. Worth remembering that it's there, and worth browsing through.

Next, you choose your Second Life username in the window shown in Figure 17-22. It's similar to picking a name for web mail or instant messaging. You choose a first name, and then the page gives you a list of available (imaginative) last names. Some people like to use their real first name or pick a random name or prefix. You can try different combinations before you register—but after you register, you can't change your username (although you can create a new account). Then, you choose a password.

Next, Create your Second Life Personality

Create your user name and password

Your username includes a first and last name. Each last name is available for a limited time. Choose a first name to see which last names are available now!

| Create a First Name | | Find Last Names |

| Create a Password | |

| Confirm Password | |

Figure 17-22. This is where the fun begins.

■ **Note** After you choose your username and password, make sure you write them down, because you need both to log in to Second Life. Case matters, so if your username contains both, remember to note whether you chose uppercase or lowercase.

Figure 17-23 shows a note from Second Life.

Note: Your username is both your screen name in Second Life, and your login ID. Once you register, your username cannot be changed

Figure 17-23. Choose a username

As shown in Figure 17-24, I tried Todd.

Create a First Name | Todd | **Find Last Names**

Length: 2–31 characters. Letters or numbers only. Case matters.

Figure 17-24. Start by typing in a first name. It doesn't have to be your real name.

Click Find Last Names, and Second Life comes up with the list of First Name, Last Name combinations (Todd Bardenboar, and so on). You can click the arrows to page through various combinations, and then click a name combination that you like, as shown in Figure 17-25.

Figure 17-25. Think theatrically, as though this is your stage name.

You can also click the Change button to change the first name (see Figure 17-26).

Change

Figure 17-26. Change button

In certain cases, typing a certain username may bring the result that all possible last name combinations are already being used. Figure 17-27 shows me typing in DJ, but all the last names were taken.

DJ | **Find Last Names**

Length: 2–31 characters. Letters or numbers only. Case matters.

Figure 17-27. Keep on trying.

However, when I typed in "Captain" as a first name, it worked. I liked the ring of "Captain Kalamunda," so I chose that one (see Figure 17-28).

Choose your Second Life name by clicking
on one below

Captain Kalamunda
Captain Kaufmat
Captain Kerang
Captain Kolonimann

Figure 17-28. Keep trying until you find something you like.

In the following section, you choose a look for your Second Life character, also known as your avatar. You can change it later (extensively, if you like), but at this point choose one. Notice in the signup process that your real-life name and gender are asked for, but sometimes men create female avatars and vice versa (see Figure 17-29).

Choose a starting look

Click on images below to select a starting look. Once in Second Life, you can change your appearance, or shop for a whole new look.

Figure 17-29. All the different basic looks

Figure 17-30 shows how Second Life gives you a little preview of your avatar.

Captain Kalamunda

You in Second Life

Figure 17-30. A basic starter avatar. You can find a plethora of other outfits in Second Life, either free or by buying them with some of the Linden Dollars you get when you start your account.

At the bottom of the page, fill out the security information shown in Figure 17-31.

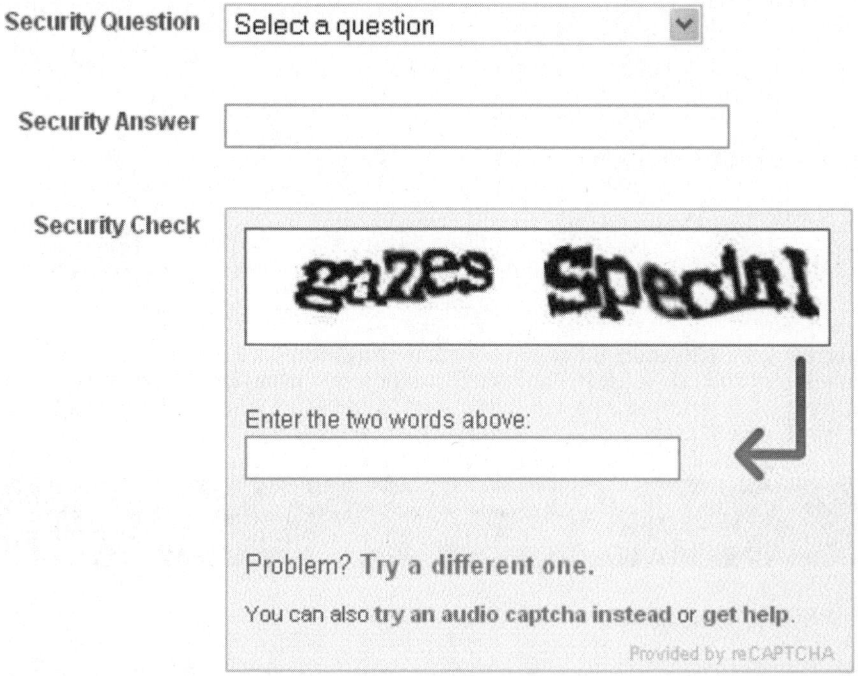

Security Question Select a question

Security Answer

Security Check

gazes special

Enter the two words above:

Problem? **Try a different one.**

You can also **try an audio captcha instead** or **get help**.

Provided by reCAPTCHA

Figure 17-31. Choose a security question and answer, and prove that you're a human and not a spam robot by looking at the image and typing its contents in the box. If you can't get it, click the "Try a different one" link.

Finally, click the Create Account button (see Figure 17-32).

Figure 17-32. Create Account button

Second Life then sends you an activation e-mail like the one in Figure 17-33.

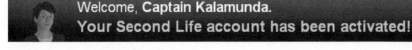

Account activation email sent to:

snspaces@gmail.com

In the e-mail click on the activate link to confirm your registration

Figure 17-33. Check your e-mail to confirm the account. Check your spam folder if you don't see it after a few minutes.

When you click the activation link in the e-mail, it brings you back to the Second Life page. You still have to install the Second Life software, but you can choose a starting location on this page. Unless you've used Second Life before, it's best to start out on Help Island, where you can learn to move around and so forth (see Figure 17-34).

Welcome, **Captain Kalamunda.**
Your Second Life account has been activated!

Choose a starting location

Help Island

- Learn tips & tricks to get you started in Second Life
- Get help from volunteers
- View demos and tutorials
- Browse galleries and freebie stores
- Created by Second Life

Go to Help Island

Community Gateways

- Visit themed locations built for specific interest groups, languages and cultures
- Created and run by community members
- Get help and learn tips on how to explore Second Life
- Meet people who speak your language

Browse Community Gateways

Figure 17-34. You can visit a variety of locations. I recommend Help Island initially.

Installing Second Life

Registering is the first step. Next, you actually download and install the software. Then, a screen indicates the final steps to get going. This involves downloading and installing the Second Life viewer and then launching and logging in, as shown in Figure 17-35.

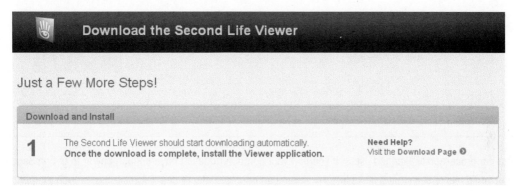

Figure 17-35. Download screen

Depending on your operating system, the download may start automatically. You may see a window like the one in Figure 17-36 appear.

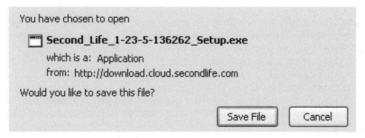

Figure 17-36. A download message may appear, asking you to save the file.

The window shown in Figure 17-37 indicates that after you install the software, you double-click the icon to run the program. Then, log in to begin.

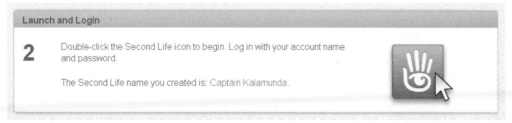

Figure 17-37. When you have the software installed, you can double-click the icon on your computer. This step reminds that you can log in with your username and password.

On the part of the screen shown in Figure 17-38, you may want to click Quick Start Guide and bookmark it. The Quick Start Guide provides some of the basics of getting around.

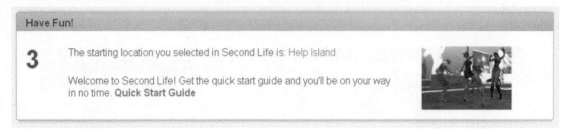

Figure 17-38. *The last step in getting started*

■ **Note** For processor-challenged users: If you find your computer doesn't have enough power to get on Second Life, but you'd like to see what it looks like, try visiting an Internet Café, or see if you can go through the process of getting your local library to install it.

Exploring Second Life with a SLURL

After you have Second Life installed, a common way to give people links to get to a certain place in Second Life is by using a SLURL. This stands for Second Life URL, whereas URL is a standard way of saying web address.

A SLURL is a link you can click in an Internet browser, which then jumps to the Second Life software and takes you to a particular place. For example, when you log in to Second Life for the first time after registering, it takes you to the start location. However, you can always go somewhere else.

If you enter the following link into your Internet browser, you jump to an IBM island for a project where they're developing a tool to create written descriptions so visually impaired people can also participate in the virtual world: http://slurl.com/secondlife/IBM%20Event/215/42/23. Figure 17-39 is a picture of me on the island.

Figure 17-39. *Visiting a new location*

If you remember from earlier in the chapter, Figure 17-14 shared a really cool site with a bunch of SLURLs for exploring world heritage sites. The following are a few more:

- Chateau de Versailles, Versailles City
  `http://slurl.com/secondlife/Versailles City/126/4/30`

- Sistine Chapel Re-Creation, Vassar
  `http://slurl.com/secondlife/Vassar/128/128/0`

- The SL Globe Theatre
  `http://slurl.com/secondlife/sLiterary/22/16/24`

- Parthenon, Greece
  `http://slurl.com/secondlife/GreeceOfficial/97/139/49`

- Mont Saint Michel au Per, Shivar
  `http://slurl.com/secondlife/Shivar/144/178/22`

After installing Second Life, you may want to visit that web page and explore some of these places as well as take some pictures! You can use either `http://nmsua.edu/tiopete/sl-world-heritage-international-sites/` or `http://tinyurl.com/vheritage`.

A Note for Parents and Teachers

There are some technical requirements for Second Life because people express themselves in different ways, and some of those ways aren't particularly suitable for people under 18 years of age. From my perspective, Second Life is like the Internet: everything is out there. You can go where you want to go, so if you don't want to go somewhere—don't go there.

To help navigate, some places in Second Life are 18 and over, and others are teen-friendly areas. There are tools to set up access so that you can ask people not to use language or engage in activity that would be offensive. When a virtual area is created, you can indicate it's basically a family-friendly area; then, if people come along and violate those rules, they can get banned from Second Life. Safeguards do exist.

In a school context, I'd suggest that Second Life is worth exploring as an educational tool. I see some wonderful promise in the idea of leveraging virtual worlds as places to connect students who wouldn't otherwise have any way to connect to each other in real life.

My suggestion for parents and teachers is, try a shared experience: a *guided* experience. Explore how you can set preferences to restrict things to what you consider appropriate.

In a classroom, for example, you may initially experiment carefully by visiting Ireland on a projector, but then invite individual students to come up and run the mouse, and let everyone have a turn. This way, you can keep an eye on things.

If you're a teacher grappling with these issues at a school, but you want to explore how to integrate Second Life or social networking, there are resources out there, including teachers who have been experimenting with this. I'm not an expert but have seen some discussions. My personal suggestion is, try to find a couple of supportive teachers, and look at some of the cases where teachers have chosen to embrace the new technologies successfully to see if you can get at least one computer in for some research.

If you need some hard data to help make your case, check out the "Creating and Connecting" study by the National School Boards Association, which has some pretty interesting insights and recommendations about social networking for schools: `www.comminit.com/en/node/283231/307` or `http://tinyurl.com/socialschools`.

Best wishes with your parental or educational adventures, and please feel free to ask questions, post links, or sound off on `www.snspaces.com`.

Q/A

Q: Is there a Second Life for teens?
A: Yes, it's kind of a separated area that has some safeguards as far as adult content, and so on. See `http://teen.secondlife.com/`.

Q: I've heard you can buy virtual land and that there's currency on Second Life. What's that all about?
A: It's pretty interesting, because there's an entire economy on Second Life. For example, users can own virtual land. Second Life also provides easy-to-use tools so you can create your own building, or anything else for that matter, for free without any prior experience. Advanced users started building more sophisticated things and selling them. There are places in Second Life that offers free plots of land, or you can buy other places, even your own island. Of course, there are places where you can buy a house someone designed, and so on. It's fun having a space for people to gather virtually. You start out with some free currency, and then you can always buy more.

Q: What is a virtual business?
A: There are a variety of virtual businesses on Second Life, usually involving things like virtual houses, objects, vehicles, or clothing. After learning Second Life, people end up creating a 3D location and putting the virtual goods in the location. Then, if they like something, they can buy it.

Q: Are there other virtual worlds? What's IMVU?

A: IMVU is another virtual world, especially popular with younger people, which is similar to Second Life, but more based around chat rooms. Instead of a large connected space with a lot of different regions, IMVU allows people to have private and public chat rooms. They are 3D chat rooms that have a great deal of detail with different themes, and the graphics are pretty impressive. It's worth exploring if you're interested in 3D. Try googling it, and look at it on Wikipedia.org.

Q: I'm a parent, and I'm freaking out about my teenager spending what seems like an endless amount of time on _____ (fill in the blank with a 3D game/virtual world of some kind).

A: I'm not a parenting expert, but I'd recommend treating the virtual places that your child is visiting like any other place. Stay engaged, and ask them about it. If you're struggling to find an alternative for something you can do together, perhaps first try learning about the game world. Install the game, learn enough to be dangerous, and ask your kid if they can take you on an adventure either on that game or another if that's their "private space." It's also remotely possible that some teens who like the adventure-type virtual games may be drawn into an interest in real history, such as going to a museum or art exhibit. By all means, if you have suggestions or thoughts (or you're a teen with suggestions or thoughts), please post on www.snspaces.com.

Q: Wait, I have another question! Where can I ask it?

A: On www.snspaces.com.

Conclusion

Dear Reader,

Thanks for reading this chapter.

If you're not convinced yet about visiting a virtual world heritage site, then when you have the opportunity, I highly recommend visiting a United Nations World Heritage site. They've set aside special places, to preserve them for the world's enjoyment. One of my favorite places that I recommend anyone consider visiting is the Northwest coast of Ireland:

(The lovely colors of the sunset on the northwest coast of Ireland are worth seeing on www.snspaces.com or in person, if you can.)

It's a wonderful place, and because of some of the past troubles in Ireland and economic challenges, a stretch of coast has gone relatively undeveloped. The United Nations had the good sense to get hold of it. Generally speaking, the area is known as the Giant's Causeway.

While writing the section about heritage and world heritage and tourism, I recalled a visit to this place in Ireland. If you like, you can go and visit this blog entry, see some of the pictures, and read my thoughts using http://olpc.wordpress.com/2007/09/08/the-last-hurrah/ or http://tinyurl.com/causewaytrip.

If you get to the point of getting your toes wet, please do share some things on www.snspaces.com. I can't tell you how encouraging it can be for others when you step out and do something, and tell them how important it was. I'm talking about skills you acquired, but also the *story* of what you're doing in your life. If it's private, cool. If you don't mind sharing, please do.

Regards,

—Todd

snspaces.com

Come and visit the Social Networking Spaces companion web site at www.snspaces.com, where you can find more tips and updates and have an opportunity to share your thoughts or ask questions.

In Living Color: You can visit www.snspaces.com/pics to see full-color versions of all the pictures from this chapter.

■ ■ ■

Going Global: Connecting with People in Other Countries and Languages, with Google Translate and Google Multilingual Chat

In This Chapter:

- A brief tour of social networks around the world

- Free Google tools that can help you carry on a conversation with someone in a different language

- How a multilingual Web can make the world better

snspaces.com

Come and visit the Social Networking Spaces companion web site at www.snspaces.com, where you can find more tips and updates and have an opportunity to share your thoughts or ask questions.

In Living Color: You can visit www.snspaces.com/pics to see full-color versions of all the pictures from this chapter.

Introduction

There has been a rapid growth of social networks around the world—for example, at the time of writing, *The Economist* reported that there are 400 million people on Facebook (see `http://economist.com/specialreports`, and look for the report about social networking). But there's still a tendency for people to keep to their own language groups—except for the small number of people who are bilingual.

Wouldn't it be great to cross this language gap and get to know people who have common interests, yet happen to speak a different language? As you see in this chapter, Google has brought this exciting capability to anyone around the world who has a free Gmail account, through *translation bots*.

Most people enjoy visiting other countries in person. And when you read an article about another country, that may be interesting; but it seems like the next best thing could be to explore the citizens of another country, and the country itself, through the eyes of people from that country in conversation with them. As far as I'm concerned, it's the next great frontier of exploration, and it's within your grasp *right now*.

This chapter gives you a brief introduction to some of the things that are going on around the world in social networking and looks at some tools from Google that can help you communicate using computer-based translation. These tools have their limits, but for the vast majority of people who speak a single language, they're better than nothing.

People from different national and language backgrounds have an increasing number of opportunities to interact online. Typically, this is possible when someone has learned enough of another language to communicate. I celebrate that and believe very strongly that learning a language is a wonderful thing—so I've been delighted to see web sites like `www.livemocha.com` and others, which are specifically designed to give people opportunities to practice speaking another language by using the Internet to connect in a phone conference session. I think it's wonderful when people have either casual or formal training and go on language-study travel, on a long-term or short-term basis—it seems to me that total immersion is one of the best ways to learn, because you *have* to speak the language.

I also think it's fun that Google has created tools to help try to cross the language gap, and in this chapter you look at how you can try them. Google uses its massive computing power and some special techniques to do computer translation. Although there are some definite limits, it can provide an opportunity for people who speak two different languages to have at least some communication—and I think that's wonderful.

Social Networking around the World

If you go to `www.google.com/trends` and use the fascinating Trends tool, you can type in "facebook" or "bell bottom jeans" or any other phrase and get a sense of whether something is increasing or decreasing in popularity, and how quickly. Google provides this free tool based on data it gets from people searching for things. Figure 18-1 shows what happens if you type the phrase "social networking"; this chart, in a broad sense, gives some indication of the growth of social networking around the world.

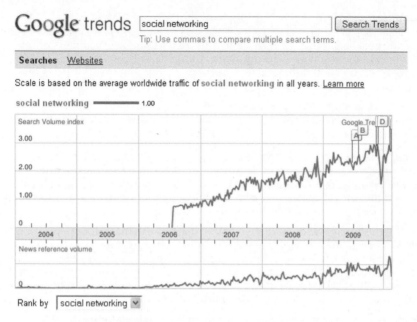

Figure 18-1. Social networking, on the rise

There are a variety of resources about social networking in different parts of the world, and if you're interested in the topic, the best way to learn about it is probably to go on Google and start searching. Personally, I recommend starting with the *Economist* report mentioned earlier, doing some searching on Google, looking to see if anyone has posted something interesting on www.snspaces.com, and posting any links you find that are interesting.

To get you started, you can find a fascinating map (which I wasn't able to get permission to use at the time of publication) that shows various social networks in relation to each other, at the following URL: http://tinyurl.com/globalsocialmap or www.vincos.it/wp-content/uploads/2009/06/wmsn-06-09.png. The map shows which social networks are the most popular in various parts of the world. Generally speaking, as you may expect, Facebook is very popular in many countries. Certain networks are strong in particular countries; for example, Orkut (from Google) is particularly popular in Brazil.

You can also read a good related article from the popular blog site TechCrunch at http://tinyurl.com/topsocialnetworks or www.techcrunch.com/2009/06/07/a-map-of-social-network-dominance/.

Asia

You may be interested in exploring Google for companies like the following in Asia or other parts of the world, which have expertise and insight about particular regions and can offer some fascinating perspective. (If you have such a company or would like to contribute an article or links to existing resources that your company or organization has, please visit www.snspaces.com.)

- *Social networking in China:* Nanjing Marketing Group (NMG), `www.nanjingmarketinggroup.com`. NMG was founded by Tait Lawson with the specific goal of helping Western companies reach Chinese consumers online. It's involved in the social networking side of things as well. In a recent conversation, Tait mentioned, not surprisingly, "Social networking in China is a huge topic; the social networking scene is always changing and growing."

  NMG has some interesting free resources available on their site, in the Knowledge section. Also, keep your eyes open for a special article from NMG on social networking in China, which I'll post on `www.snspaces.com`.

- *Social Networking in Asia:* ComScore Asia, `www.comscore.com`. Joe Nguyen of ComScore is representative of the kind of people who are gathering information and helping companies and individuals to understand what's going on in other parts of the world. ComScore is a large company that gathers information about Internet behavior, and Joe focuses on Asia.

  Joe had this to say: "With more than half of the Asia-Pacific online population active on social networking sites, competition between global and local brands continues to intensify in the battle for visitors and their time. As Facebook increases its dominance across the globe and relative newcomers such as Twitter bring novel utility to users, the social media landscapes of many markets are in a critical state of flux and growth."

Some nice reports are available. You can read them at the following URLs:

`http://tinyurl.com/asianetworks` or

`www.comscore.com/Press_Events/Presentations_Whitepapers/2010/`
`The_State_of_Social_Networks_in_Asia_Pacific_with_a_Focus_on_Hong_Kong`
(click the Download Slides link).

Additional presentations are available at `http:`

`//tinyurl.com/comscoreasia` or

`www.comscore.com/Press_Events/Presentations_Whitepapers`.

Keep your eyes open for a special article from ComScore about social networking in Asia, which I'll post on `www.snspaces.com`.

Brazil: Orkut

There's not enough space in the chapter to go over every social network in the world (but if you'd like to go on such a tour, try viewing the map mentioned earlier and then typing in the names of the networks in Wikipedia). But here's some perspective on one social network, Orkut, from Enzo Silva, a native of Brazil (Orkut is available anywhere but is especially popular in Brazil):

> *Orkut was released in January 22, 2004, and is the brainchild of Orkut Büyükkökten, a Google employee who developed the social network as an independent project. Initially, users could join by invitation-only after receiving invites from their friends who were already part of the trusted community.*

I remember when I still lived in Brazil in 2005 and first got my invitation to join the community in its beta phase of development. At the time, it was the most talked about (if not the only one) social networking website in Brazil as the buzz started to spread in workplaces, school and wherever friends would gather. It was an innovative concept that helped with finding old high school classmates, childhood friends and coworkers. But although Orkut remains the dominant social network especially in Brazil and India, the service now seems to be playing catch-up with sites like Facebook and Twitter.

As of May 2009, 51.09% of Orkut's population was from Brazil, followed by India at 20.02% and the United at 17.29%. The social network's presence in the rest of the world adds up to 3.15% of its population. The social networking site doesn't seem to be significantly losing territory to other social networking sites that are popular elsewhere, such as Facebook and Hi5. In recent years, Orkut revamped its website by adding the "applications" feature and "status updates" similar to what Facebook has had since its infancy stages.

What can be seen as an advantage of this social network over others is the fact that it is a service maintained by Google, therefore making it possible for easier integration with one's Google account, Google applications and services such as Gtalk.
Out of the box, Orkut offers services one would expect to see in a social network: profile information, photo and video sharing, public messages (which Orkut users call "scraps"), private messages, events and testimonials.

My Own Experience

My own experience with the international dimension of Facebook came from creating the Sunflower Club Facebook group (search for "A sunflower club")—I found that people from different countries started signing up (in part because I ran an advertisement globally as an experiment, which would theoretically display anywhere in the world, in English, for someone who liked sunflowers). That kind of interaction was generated because of the people in other countries who spoke English, so there isn't really a significant language gap. That's been fun. (If you like, see the Facebook chapters to learn about Facebook groups. And try searching on Facebook for "A Sunflower Club," and look at some of the sunflower pictures that people have contributed from around the world.)

In another experiment, I participated in an international contest to submit ideas, and someone from Colombia somehow came across my entry and perhaps knew enough English to have some sense of what it was about. They contacted me—but their communication was all in Spanish. They didn't speak any English, I didn't speak any Spanish. It was an example of a situation where Google Translate helped to provide some basic communication ability.

Google Translate

Computer-based translation has some definite limitations and isn't really a substitute for human translation; but it still goes a long way, especially where there's no alternative. When you make very simple sentences, with as little slang as possible, you can get better results.

Google Translate (`www.google.com/translate`) is easy to use; you can just visit, paste in some text, and click Translate (see Figure 18-2).

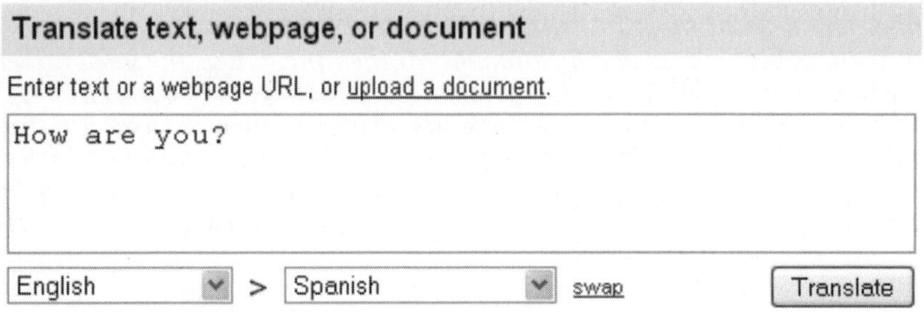

Translate text, webpage, or document

Enter text or a webpage URL, or upload a document.

> How are you?

English > Spanish swap Translate

Figure 18-2. Type in some text, and click Translate.

It does its best to give you the result you're looking for (for example, "Como estas?" for "How are you?" as shown in Figure 18-3), which you can then select, copy, paste, and use if you like:

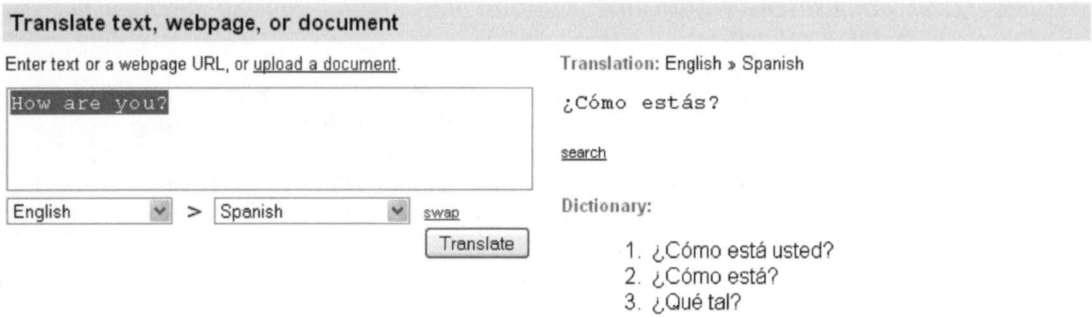

Translate text, webpage, or document

Enter text or a webpage URL, or upload a document.

> How are you?

English > Spanish swap
Translate

Translation: English » Spanish

¿Cómo estás?

search

Dictionary:

1. ¿Cómo está usted?
2. ¿Cómo está?
3. ¿Qué tal?

Figure 18-3. The translation appears at right.

Google Multilingual Chat

At the time of writing, the ability to have Google translate a group chat conversation is limited to chat within Gmail. I think it's tremendously exciting that Google finally connected its computer translation system to let people try to chat. Basically, you end up adding a translator bot as a contact in Gmail; then, when you're chatting with someone, you invite the translator bot into the chat room, and it looks at whatever people are saying and translates for you. The wild thing is that you can invite more than one translator bot—you could have a little United Nations going on, with people speaking English, Spanish, Chinese, Arabic, or whatever. It could get pretty chaotic on the one hand—or it could be glorious.

To try it, the easiest way is to visit this help article: `http://tinyurl.com/gchatbots` or `www.google.com/support/talk/bin/answer.py?hl=en&answer=89921#r`. Then, when you're at the article, click one of the bot links (see Figure 18-4).

Google Help > Google Talk Help > Google Talk Client > Using the Google Talk client
> Talking to Friends > Translation bots

Translation bots   🖶 Print

Google Talk can help you with quick translations, or even translate
your chats in real-time! All you need to do is chat with one of our
Translation Bots. The bots are named using two-letter language
abbreviations formatted as '[from language]2[to
language]@bot.talk.google.com,' and all available combinations are
listed in the table below.

To use a bot, add it to your Friends list and send it the message
you want translated. For example, if you send "Hello" to
en2es@bot.talk.google.com (English to Spanish), it will respond
with "Hola." If you're using the Google Talk Gadget, you can also
get your conversation translated by inviting a bot to a group chat
with a friend.

You can send a chat to these bots to get your messages
translated:

Languages	Bots	
Arabic - English	ar2en	en2ar
Bulgarian - English	bg2en	en2bg
Czech - English	cs2en	en2cs
Danish - English	da2en	en2da
German - English	de2en	en2de
German - French	da2fr	fr2da

Figure 18-4. Choose a translation bot.

For example, if you go to the article in Figure 18-4 and click the en2de link, Google creates a
sample "Guest chat" window and invites the en2de (English to German) translation bot. If you type in
something, the bot translates it to German, as shown in Figure 18-5.

Figure 18-5. The bot translates your chat messages.

If you want to try making a multilingual chat with someone who has a Gmail account, you create a chat window and then invite the bot. But first, you need to add the bot as a contact. For example, to add a German bot as a contact, you add en2de to @bot.talk.google.com, which gives you en2de@bot.talk.google.com. You then add this contact in Google chat.

To do so, sign in to Gmail, and click the Contacts link (see Figure 18-6).

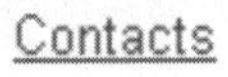

Contacts

Figure 18-6. The Contacts link

Then, click the Add a Contact button (see Figure 18-7).

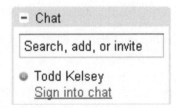

Figure 18-7. The Add a Contact button

Based on the chart in Figure 18-4 and the instructions you saw previously, you add the appropriate e-mail address, as shown in Figure 18-8, and then click Save.

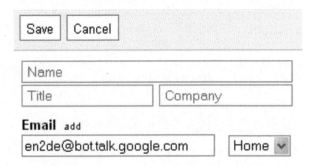

Figure 18-8. Enter the e-mail address for the translation bot.

Now, sign in to chat in the Gmail window (on the left side), as shown in Figure 18-9.

Figure 18-9. Sign in to chat.

Double-click the name of the friend you'd like to chat with (see Figure 18-10).

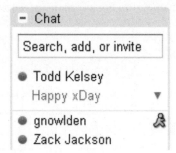

Figure 18-10. Double-click a friend's name.

A chat window opens. Type something to start the conversation, as shown in Figure 18-11, and press Enter.

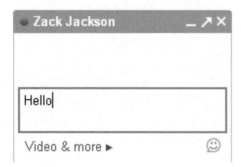

Figure 18-11. Start your conversation.

Then, click the "Video & more" link at the bottom of the chat window, and select "Group chat," as shown in Figure 18-12.

Figure 18-12. Choose the "Group chat" option.

Type the first few letters of the translation bot's contact information (you added the bot as a contact earlier). Google suggests the full address, as shown in Figure 18-13, and you can click it to select it.

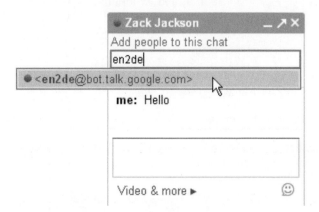

Figure 18-13. *Click the full address when Google suggests it.*

Click the Invite link to invite the translation bot to the chat room (see Figure 18-14).

Figure 18-14. *Click Invite.*

Google indicates when the translation bot has joined the conversation, as shown in Figure 18-15.

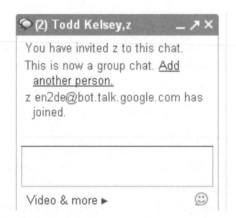

Figure 18-15. Google tells you when the bot joins in.

You may want to click the little arrow that points to the upper-right (see Figure 18-16), to "pop out" the chat window so it's bigger.

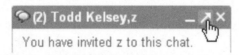

Figure 18-16. Click this arrow to enlarge the chat window.

Now, when you type a message, the translator bot translates it, as shown in Figure 18-17.

Figure 18-17. The bot translates for you.

You can use Google group chat to invite people who have Gmail accounts into a group chat situation—and regardless of the language they speak, you can have basic communication. It's like your own private United Nations, with a set of professional interpreters; each person gets their own interpreter so they can understand what's being said.

Pretty amazing stuff—and it's especially nice for connecting with people you meet on social networks.

Here are the original instructions from the Google help page, along with the full list of translation bots (source: `www.google.com/support/talk/bin/answer.py?hl=en&answer=89921#`):

Google Talk can help you with quick translations, or even translate your chats in real-time! All you need to do is chat with one of our Translation Bots. The bots are named using two-letter language abbreviations formatted as '[from language]2[to language]@bot.talk.google.com,' and all available combinations are listed in the table below.

To use a bot, add it to your Friends list and send it the message you want translated. For example, if you send "Hello" to en2es@bot.talk.google.com (English to Spanish), it will respond with "Hola." If you're using the Google Talk Gadget, you can also get your conversation translated by inviting a bot to a group chat with a friend.

You can send a chat to these bots to get your messages translated:

Languages	Bots	
Arabic - English	ar2en	en2ar
Bulgarian - English	bg2en	en2bg
Czech - English	cs2en	en2cs
Danish - English	da2en	en2da
German - English	de2en	en2de
German - French	de2fr	fr2de
Greek - English	el2en	en2el
Spanish - English	es2en	en2es
Finnish - English	fi2en	en2fi
French - English	fr2en	en2fr
Hindi - English	hi2en	en2hi
Croatian - English	hr2en	en2hr
Italian - English	it2en	en2it
Japanese - English	ja2en	en2ja
Korean - English	ko2en	en2ko
Dutch - English	nl2en	en2nl
Norwegian - English	no2en	en2no
Polish - English	pl2en	en2pl
Portuguese - English	pt2en	en2pt
Romanian - English	ro2en	en2ro
Russian - English	ru2en	en2ru
Swedish - English	sv2en	en2sv
Chinese - English	zh2en	en2zh
Traditional Chinese - English	zh-hant2en	en2zh-hant
Traditional Chinese - Chinese	zh-hant2zh	zh2zh-hant

Don't forget to add @bot.talk.google.com (for example, en2de@bot.talk.google.com).

Gmail Translation

Another nice feature Google is experimenting with is e-mail translation—again, there are some definite limits to computer translation, but it's a nice tool for communicating with someone you met on a social network. It's part of Gmail Labs, which is a set of features that are experimental but that you can add and try out. (If e-mail translation doesn't appear as described in this section, it may be that Google has promoted it to being an active Gmail feature, in which case it's probably somewhere in Settings—you can go on `www.google.com` and type n something like "gmail e-mail translation" to see what the status is.)

In Gmail, click Settings (in the upper-right corner):

Click Labs, as shown in Figure 18-18.

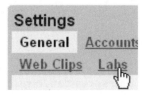

Figure 18-18. *Click the Labs link.*

Next, click the Enable radio button (see Figure 18-19).

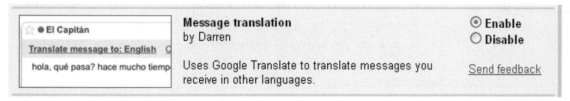

Figure 18-19. *Click Enable.*

Then, click Save Changes:

From this point on, if you get an e-mail containing text in a language other than English, the message will contain a special menu in which you can click a "Translate message" link, as shown in Figure 18-20.

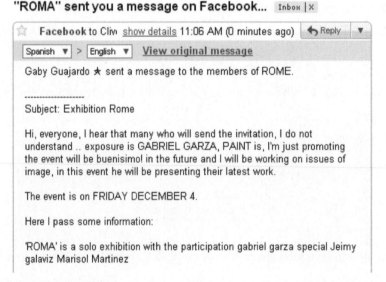

"ROMA" sent you a message on Facebook... Inbox | X

☆ **Facebook** to Cliv show details 11:06 AM (0 minutes ago) ↩ Reply ▼

Spanish ▼ > English ▼ **Translate message**

Gaby Guajardo ★ sent a message to the members of ROMA.

Subject: Exposición Roma

Hola, a todos, oigan creo que muchos a los que les mande la invitación, no
me entendieron.. la exposición es de GABRIEL GARZA, es de PINTURA, yo
solo estoy promocionando el evento que va a estar buenisimo! en un futuro
el y yo estaremos trabajando en cuestiones de foto, en este evento el estará
presentando su última obra.

El evento es el VIERNES 4 DE DICIEMBRE.

Aquí les paso algo de información:

Figure 18-20. Click the "Translate message" link.

Google does its best to translate. It never hurts to repeat: computer translation has its limits, as you can see in Figure 18-21. But if the phrases are relatively simple, it can help. I think this is incredibly cool.

"ROMA" sent you a message on Facebook... Inbox | X

☆ **Facebook** to Cliv show details 11:06 AM (0 minutes ago) ↩ Reply ▼

Spanish ▼ > English ▼ **View original message**

Gaby Guajardo ★ sent a message to the members of ROME.

Subject: Exhibition Rome

Hi, everyone, I hear that many who will send the invitation, I do not
understand .. exposure is GABRIEL GARZA, PAINT is, I'm just promoting
the event will be buenisimo! in the future and I will be working on issues of
image, in this event he will be presenting their latest work.

The event is on FRIDAY DECEMBER 4.

Here I pass some information:

'ROMA' is a solo exhibition with the participation gabriel garza special Jeimy
galaviz Marisol Martinez

Figure 18-21. An example translation

Figures 18-22 and 18-23 are based on a real communication I received. Figure 18-22 is further evidence of the kind of thing that is increasingly happening, as people cross the language gap. I have a former student who was in a web design class and who is now in Mexico. Most of the people he communicates with are Spanish-speaking, so even the Facebook page for the event—a gallery opening for his art, which is quite good; see www.gabrielgarza.net—is in Spanish.

Figure 18-22. Facebook page in Spanish

I hope that someday Facebook gets with the program and offers the option of tapping into Google or some other service to see a preview of translation. In the meantime, you have to make do. It's nice when you can share visual imagery that requires no translation, like that in Figure 18-23.

Figure 18-23. A picture that requires no translation

■ **Note** If you like fine art or are an artist, be sure to come and see these last couple of figures on www.snspaces.com and to visit Gabriel's site at http://gabrielgarza.net. Not only is his art very good, but it may give you some ideas about promotion, either in your native country and language or another. Notice Gabriel's use of Facebook messages, events, and photo albums, for example.

Q/A

Q: Can you use translation bots in Google Talk? What's the difference between Google Talk and Google Chat?

A: Google Talk is a separate application: it allows you to chat with Google contacts, and it runs in a separate window. I like it because I don't have to keep going back to the Gmail window to chat there—I can use a small window just to see who is online. (Technically, you can pop out chat from Gmail; but for me, the ability to control the window isn't as nice as having the separate application.)

As far as translation goes, technically you can invite a translator bot as a friend in Google Talk; but at present, all you can do is talk to the bot. Theoretically, you could open a window with the person you want to talk to, and post their replies into a new window that you open with the translator bot. But it doesn't do group chat, especially if you have more than one language and several people talking. The great thing about multilingual chat in Gmail is that you can add translator bots for whatever language combinations you want (English to Chinese, Chinese to English, English to Italian), and it's like having interpreters in the room.

Q: How do I get Google Chat? Can I download it?

A: You can access Google Chat within Gmail, which you use online. To start a free Gmail account, visit http://mail.google.com.

Q: Where can I read more about translation bots and other Google tools?

A: Keep your eyes open for an entire book on the topic from CFTW Press. If you want to keep posted about the book's progress, go on Facebook and search for (and join) the Social Networking Spaces Group, or search for (and become a fan of) the Social Networking Spaces Facebook page. I'll post messages once in a while to both. Just as with this book, all author proceeds will be donated to CFTW. (See the Introduction to this book.) And don't worry if you don't know how to join a group or become a fan. You can learn by reading the Facebook chapters in this book!

Q: Wait! I have another question! Where can I ask it?

A: On www.snspaces.com.

Conclusion

Dear Reader,

Thank you for reading this chapter.

The moral of the story is, the world is getting smaller, and even though learning languages and experiencing human contact are best, social networks provide a way to transcend distance. Some really interesting tools from Google can help you cross the language gap. If you want to have some adventures, I recommend getting comfortable with Google tools (and signing up for a Gmail address if you don't have one already—http://mail.google.com). Then, seek out people from a different country (search on Facebook for people who live in another country, or join a Facebook group like "a sunflower club," which has international members).

I certainly hope a few teachers are reading, because it feels to me like some rich opportunities are available to connect kids and classrooms, or college students. (For example, they could talk via chat or Gmail, or using a tool like Google Chat in conjunction with an international meeting in Second Life, or during a group visit to a world heritage site in Second Life.)

If you have anything to say about this—especially if you've had any interesting experiences interacting with people online in a different language (or, ideally, if you use Meetup, Skype, and so on, for language practice)—please go on www.snspaces.com and tell the story (or make a blog, and post a link to your blog post).

Regards,

–Todd

snspaces.com

Come and visit the Social Networking Spaces companion web site at www.snspaces.com, where you can find more tips and updates and have an opportunity to share your thoughts or ask questions.

In Living Color: You can visit www.snspaces.com/pics to see full-color versions of all the pictures from this chapter.

∎∎∎

Kahonua and RGB

If you are interested in any of the themes from this appendix, please take an opportunity to explore how exchanging information and collaborating through social network sites can change the world. You don't necessarily need any prior experience—just *interest*.

Kahonua is the name for a project that comprises all the 3D characters seen at the beginning and end of many chapters in this book. It means "globe of the earth" in Hawaiian.

It would be great to hear what you think, especially if you'd like to collaborate or support the idea in some way. Sometimes negative feedback is the most valuable! It's an open door.

This Appendix is a review of the project idea, and an invitation to participate by coming on to snspaces.com and providing feedback, expressing interest in trying it out, or sharing anything you like. At the time of writing, conversation has revolved mainly around creating a children's e-book (the book that could be part of a gift set illustrated in one of the last slides of the RGB presentation, shown in and viewable at http://tinyurl.com/aboutrgb).

Kahonua is a CFTW project of CFTW, a nonprofit organization, so the project is likely to be nonprofit itself, but it could also be a way to generate revenue for some of the activities CFTW is embarking on (see Appendix B). It could also be a way to provide learning opportunities and employment for people.

Kahonua is an idea that came out of volunteer work for One Laptop Per Child (www.laptop.org). I thought it would be nice to have an "open source *Finding Nemo*," a project that could develop into a movie for kids, which would help them learn about living in a community. As I worked with the volunteer community of One Laptop Per Child, which spanned multiple continents and languages, I was struck by the feeling of how important it is to support education and collaboration that crosses gaps in culture and language. I was also struck by the efforts of One Laptop Per Child in the area of environmental responsibility and going green—not only was the laptop the "greenest" laptop ever made in terms of environmental responsibility (low power consumption, etc.), it was also green in color.

As these ideas were rolling around, a very talented 3D artist named Alexandra Constantin agreed to help me develop some character concepts into 3D images. Ken Bado of Autodesk donated a couple copies of a software program called 3D Studio Max, which Alexandra used to begin creating some characters. If you are as impressed by Alexandra's ability as I am, please consider hiring her to do freelance 3D or Web design. See http://www.cgadvertising.com.

The Kahonua and related RGB ideas are described in two Facebook photo albums:

- *Act One*, *Kahonua*: http://tinyurl.com/kahonua1 explains the characters and concepts behind Kahonua.

- *Act Two*, *RGB*: http://tinyurl.com/aboutrgb is a simple idea for a color coded way to balance causes such as red (health), green (environment), and blue (community), also known as RGB. I developed the concept out of a desire to try and be helpful in thinking of a way you could help make the world better without pursuing one thing to the exclusion of another. The presentation, which also appears on the following pages, touches on some of the concepts and characters found in the Kahonua album.

On the following pages, the Kahonua idea appears followed by the RGB presentation.

We are dreaming of finding a way to make a film someday, but are thinking of taking the next step by developing a simple children's e-book. If you are interested in either set of ideas (even if you just want to learn 3D design!) or have thoughts of any kind, you are most welcome to join the conversation at snspaces.com.

Kahonua

The idea appears in a question/answer format that Google created for their 10tothe100th contest.

What one sentence best describes your idea?

The Kahonua Islands have just been discovered near Hawaii; they contain treasure the world urgently needs: peace, jobs, conservation, health, and hope.

Describe your idea in more depth.

The Kahonua Island Chain is an idea for a series of online spaces for people to explore, as a form of entertainment and education. Each island symbolizes a worldwide community of organizations that are making the world better in a particular area, and the organizations can be featured on respective islands. The islands represent places for having fun and learning about organizations that people can get involved with.

The island names, their Hawaiian meaning, and what they symbolize:

- *Kahonua Island*: globe of the earth in Hawaiian (environment)
- *Laulauna Island*: friendly, sociable (peace)
- *Hanaola Island*: job, life, livelihood (jobs)
- *Lonopuha Island*: the art of healing (health)
- *Lehopulu Island*: earth clinging rainbow (hope/inspiration)

Hawaii is beautiful, and I think the Hawaiian language is also beautiful. I am not Hawaiian, but like many others, I sometimes dream about visiting a beautiful island and meeting new people. The Kahonua Islands are also meant to be a set of virtual islands designed for both kids and adults, with friendly animals from RGB, like Mr. Green. The Islands are designed to be accessible to as many people as possible, using various devices: computers, mobile phones, etc. This is possible using an adaptive approach: 1D (text), 2D (text/graphics, web pages, animated 2D avatars), and 3D (conventional virtual worlds). This approach also makes it easier to access the islands in various languages.

When you visit the Kahonua Islands, you will be invited to learn Hawaiian, which I hope the whole world will learn. Many people in the world have visited Wikipedia and know one Hawaiian word already: wiki, which means, to run.

What problem or issue does your idea address?

I was trying to think in terms of categories that represent the most critical and urgent problems. Basically, peace, jobs, conservation, and health. However, these problems are significantly harder to deal with if you don't deal with the problem of paralysis (i.e., feeling overwhelmed), so inspiration is the fifth category. On these islands, many other causes can find a home.

If your idea were to become a reality, who would benefit the most and how?

The whole world could benefit, because the islands would be a virtual world heritage site, created by the world, for the purpose of making the world better. Like a 3D virtual world equivalent of Wikipedia.org, but a land specifically for kids. Open source, free, and available to everyone, on new computers, older computers, and mobile devices in the language of their choice.

What are the initial steps required to get this idea off the ground?

Existing virtual worlds might support this, such as Second Life, or it might be possible to use a game engine like Unity3D, or ask IBM to help, using the Torque game engine that they used in the beyondspaceandtime.com project. The first step would be to assemble the 1D text/story, as well as resources to help people discuss and participate who are interested in collaborating, including individuals, schools, colleges, etc. This could involve building 2D wiki pages, inviting people to participate, and establishing a presence on social networks. Then, with adequate resources, it would be possible to build 3D islands (including 2D interactive animated spaces for computers that can't display 3D), and integrate multilingual instant messaging (see Chapter 18). The intention would be to establish a safety/privacy system, and work to include "amusement park" areas for kids, with friendly animal avatars, using live people to "act," for kids to learn about the environment, health, and peace. It might be possible to use a Club Penguin model. It would then be nice to begin an undersea world, where kids and adults can take on the role of sea creatures and learn about community. Sea creatures are asked to perform undersea tasks that symbolize roles for maintaining a wiki like Wikipedia, so when you return to the web you can try editing the Kahonua wiki.

Describe the optimal outcome. How would you measure it?

It would be measured in the number of people who visited the islands, shown in statistics, and the crowning achievement would be to inspire a generation of creative media designers to grow up and make the first full-length open source 3D film, based on the story, as it evolves, with peoples' input.

It would also be measured in the support, traffic, and resources that are generated for the ideas and causes featured on the islands. These are shown in the following:

Kahonua Island: Globe of the earth (environment)

Problem: Environment | *Need*: Conservation | *Solution*: Green/blue community

Potential partners: rgbgreen.org, rgbblue.org, or possibly green.org/blue.org (and your school/class/college/organization)?

Laulauna: Friendly, sociable

Problem: Conflict | *Need*: Peace | *Solution*: Cross-cultural friendship community

Potential partners: Friendly Language (and your school/class/college/organization)?

Hanaola: Job, life, livelihood

Problem: Economy | *Need*: Alternative economy | *Solution*: Vocational community

Potential partners: joblife.org (and your school/class/college/organization)?

Lonopuha: The art of healing

Problem: health | *Need*: healing | *Solution*: health community

Potential partners: rgbred.org (and your school/class/college/organization)?

Lehopulu: Earth clinging rainbow

Problem: Individual paralysis | *Need*: Hope/inspiration | *Solution*: Catalyst community

Potential Partners: A group on Facebook (and your school/class/college/organization)?

RGB

Here are the slides from the RGB presentation. They give an idea of some of the background to Kahonua, plus the colors are nice. I encourage and invite you to see the presentation online, in full color, at `http://tinyurl.com/aboutrgb`. It's also located at `http://aboutrgb.blogspot.com` (where you can leave comments if you like).

RGB

health | environment | community

Welcome! We hope you enjoy this short presentation. It represents ideas and concepts that are still evolving. It is not meant to be definitive, but simply captures a portion of the RGB story, with a focus on exploring green and blue.

Special thanks to:
- Griffin deLuce, for the sublime RGB logo
- Alexandra Constantin, for the wonderful 3D images
- Chuck Isdale, for the photograph of the sunflower and bees and the incredible picture of the sunflower and the mantis
- to Sunflower Club members, for pictures of sunflowers

Introduction: The RGB Color Model

- RGB is a simple creative approach for color-coding charitable concepts, based on the way that computers represent colors.
- Computers use the RGB color model, representing colors using varying levels of red, green and blue.
- RGB offers a simple way to make the world better, by appealing to the imagination, and inviting people to explore the various colors.

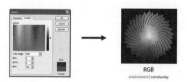

RGB

environment | community

The Origins of RGB
Sunflowers = environment = green

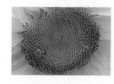

$r = c\sqrt{n}.$
$\theta = n \times 137.5°.$

The G in RGB is "Green", the first color to take shape.

It all started with sunflowers. A core influence on RGB was the Sunflower Club, where kids of all ages have tried growing sunflowers, and have learned about the environment.

The Origins of RGB
Sunflowers = environment = green
2007 - Sunflowers take over the back yard.
2008 - Sunflower Club forms, sunflowers start to take over the world.

Sunflowers + OLPC = Green

Volunteering for One Laptop Per Child led to the idea of kids growing sunflowers as a way to learn about the environment. And interestingly, it turned out that one of OLPC's founders had himself been influenced by sunflowers when he was a child:

"My first recollection of science was when, in third grade, we planted sunflower seeds and began logging their growth, keeping track of weather, and then trying to do some rudimentary statistical analysis . . . I was hooked-on math and science and on gardening – ever since." – *a blog post on sunflowerclub.net from Walter Bender, MIT*

Walter Bender directs Sugar Labs, the makers of Sugar OS for the XO laptop. He also gardens.

OLPC founders Walter Bender (left) and Nicholas Negroponte.

Environment + Education = rgbgreen.org

- Mission: simple site to help people explore how to play an active role in the ecosystem, with information on recycling and renewable energy, fun learning activities, and stories about individuals and organizations that are making a difference.
- Philosophy/Scope: Open, transparent, apolitical, friendly. Emphasis on education and personal responsibility. Draw visitors with creative learning content. Don't re-invent the wheel; refer people to existing projects and sources of information.

More Inspiration from OLPC and Sugar Labs: Make It Child-Friendly, Environmentally-Friendly

- "In developing the XO laptop, OLPC had the goal of creating a child-friendly educational tool that inspires creativity and learning for children all over the world," said Mary Lou Jepsen, chief technology officer at OLPC.
- "But equally important for us was to produce a laptop that could be used in remote areas with unreliable or limited energy sources. The result is a laptop computer that has more than 10 times less environmental impact than the average laptop computer. It's the greenest laptop ever made, and that's not just its color."

rgbgreen.org: Child-Friendly Education

rgbgreen.org dreams of learning activities that are both child-friendly and environmentally-friendly. Mr. Green and a series of friendly characters take kids on adventures in the Sunflower Kingdom.

Mr. Green is searching for knowledge, and loves to capture it in song and dance.

Grondlet joins the club, a sunflower scientist who explains solar energy, and how flowers grow.

Mr. Grishnak joins them, a mantis mathematician who speaks in rhymes and shares his silly mantis math.

Kahonua: A Parallel Universe to Encourage Young Minds

Wouldn't it be cool . . . kids can pick up where the stories leave off, trying suggested club-based activities at home or school: growing sunflowers, measuring their height, making statistics; raising praying mantises, and so on. These science and math activities could also be in a *free* virtual world, so more could join in the fun.

rgbblue.org - serving an Ocean of Communities

Working together to conserve water is important. And the ocean itself can serve as an excellent metaphor for learning how to work together in community. A fascinating, undersea world, full of symbiotic relationships, showing how we rely on each other.

- rgbblue.org, a simple site to help individuals, organizations and educational institutions to consider water in new ways.

rgbred.org - health for the world (under development)

PROBLEM: Every day, an estimated 4100 men, women and children die in sub-Saharan Africa from HIV.

SOLUTION: rgbred.org provides a cost-effective, multilingual, scalable platform for delivering educational content:

- introduce people to organizations and efforts around the world that are working to improve the world's health
- affirm and encourage a balanced approach: paying attention to the humanitarian crisis *and* the environmental crisis
- invite people who are interested in the environment to also learn about global health issues: physical and financial. (Debt Aids Trade Africa)
- •explain how organizations like the Global Fund are fighting AIDS in Africa, and explain how people can get involved
- •help people to understand how money flows to the Global Fund when they choose (RED) products

Seeding the Market

Some "seed" ideas to help generate interest and/or revenue.

RGBTea - color-coded, anti-oxidant teas:
Red - pomegranate
Green - green tea
Blue - blueberry

Gift Set: Story booklet and sunflower seeds, in mini box. Aims to inspire kids to plant their "magic seeds" and bring the story to life.

Join the Sunflower Club: free seeds to grow interest in the environment and renewable energy.

A concept for an mp3 player (Codenamed "iPod Green"), where a portion of the sales could go to support green causes. It could feature music by artists such as Peter Gabriel and ReaWorld Records.

RGB

health | environment | community

*Thanks for viewing this presentation - I'd be **very** interested to hear any thoughts you might have - please consider emailing me at tekelsey@gmail.com - good, bad, indifferent, something you liked, something you thought was wacky, didn't quite "get" it, whatever it is, it's valuable feedback, and will help me revise the presentation. - Todd*

▪ ▪ ▪

CFTW: A Personal Invitation to Join the CFTW Conversation

If you are interested in any of the themes from this appendix, please read on to take an opportunity to explore how exchanging information and collaborating through social network sites can change the world. You don't necessarily need any prior experience—just *interest*.

As part of my PhD research, I started the organization Communication for the World (CFTW), a nonprofit organization. For more information, see cftw.com.

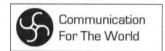

In general, the mission is to simply explore how to make the world better, especially with free learning material. All author proceeds from this book and from various CFTW projects support this mission. This appendix contains a series of ideas, and includes a question and answer format adapted from a contest called the Knight News Challenge.

The ideas represent a series of conversations involving various people, on ways that the CFTW could help to make the world better. If I've learned anything over the last several years of the PhD program, it's the value of collaboration. I used to think that in order to get anything done, I had to do it myself, but I'm convinced that we need to work together to make the world better, and that collaboration is the only answer.

No matter what your background, age, or experience level, I'd greatly value any feedback you might like to give, as well as any questions you might have. If any of these ideas interest you, you are most welcome to participate in the conversation and community at snspaces.com. These projects and CFTW are not mine, but ours. Ours means anyone who is interested.

▪ **Note** Keep in mind that some of the language is quite promotional. It's used in the context of seeking funding. I think in various ways that some of the ideas would require funding, either from a grant or an investor. Some projects could result in forming businesses whose purpose could involve making the world better, generating revenue to support CFTW and other nonprofits, and rewarding investors. I believe in nonprofits and business working together. Also, some ideas could be developed without any funding at all, but I can't do it alone. This is why I'm sharing this invitation in the context of a book on social networking. It's an opportunity to provide feedback and get involved. Remember, you don't necessarily need any prior experience—just *interest*.

Sunflower Club

The Sunflower Club is a group with members in various countries and locally in the Chicago area. It has been a partnership between a set of local residents and the news media. The club's premise is an invitation for residents of all ages to try growing sunflowers, blog about them, and then share the seeds with others. Each year, this organic network grows, as people share their seeds, digital pictures, and blog entries.

The sunflower club is a simple yet powerful concept that begins with growing sunflowers and passing on the seeds, but goes on to explore social ancestry and weaving a local social network. The idea for developing the project further is to take the central concept, and make an open source software tool that allows local residents to collaboratively create a social family tree. The tool will allow people to trace their sunflowers back to the original generation, and at the same time, to explore the blogs of their fellow local residents. People have responded positively, on Facebook and elsewhere, and shown enthusiasm as the club has grown from year to year. What is needed is a tool to help draw it all together, to capture the magic of the collective story, in a way that makes it easier for other residents to explore, through a social family tree, which celebrates the web of relationships.

How will the project improve communities?

The sunflower club provides thought-provoking motivation to join in the fun, and a variety of opportunities for people to participate, regardless of their age or level of technical knowledge. Members have included children as well as senior citizens. Some people have blogged, whereas those with technical expertise have helped others to capture their sunflower story. This has resulted in an organic way to draw people into involvement with the skills and platform needed to engage in civic journalism. The popularity of dispersed social networks prove that people want to hear from each other, and this project provides a way to engage people in local, physical, in-person communication and cooperation, supplemented by learning blogging.

How is the idea innovative?

The central innovation is a 3-dimensional ancestry—organic, digital, and social. There is a dimension of organic ancestry (the flowers), digital ancestry (blogs leading to other blogs and sites), and social ancestry (the people who pass on the concept to each other). The club ties together citizen journalism, sustainability (both technological and environmental), and intergenerational cooperation. The concept itself is extremely sustainable, as inexpensive as sharing a bag of seeds with someone and accessing free software tools. It also provides a proven, effective motivation for participation and people to have fun. See http://www.sunflowerclub.net for more information.

Thinkwriter

An open-source, thought-controlled typewriter.

Thinkwriter is thought-controlled software that leverages the new Emotiv brain-machine interface, originally developed for controlling videogames. Thinkwriter takes this consumer electronics device and provides a way for people without muscular ability to type and participate in citizen journalism, based on Emotiv's open source Linux software development kit. The Thinkwriter project also proposes plug-ins called Thinkpaint and Thinkmusic to help enable the creation of multimedia elements for news stories based on thought control.

How will the project improve communities?

It will enable someone without muscular control to participate in citizen journalism, at a significantly reduced cost, with new potential for creativity.

How is the idea innovative?

It takes the advances of brain-machine interfaces and brings them into the domain of journalism and represents a paradigm shift that can also be taken advantage of by non-disabled people, opening up new forms of creativity in written, visual, and auditory realms, with the combination of thinkwriter, thinkpaint, and thinkmusic. See thinkwriter.com for more information.

Funvelope

A physical, low-tech envelope with a digital counterpart.

The original funvelope design was a decidedly low-tech, non-digital design for a new kind of envelope that conveys a sense of fun and whimsy. The central principle of the funvelope is fun, to be different. The digital funvelope takes this principle and provides a way for people to pass news, information, and local shopping referrals, through a system of digital gifting. Word of mouth referral is the single strongest form of marketing, whether the object of referral is news, information, or product testimonials. The funvelope is one part social bookmarking, one part whimsy, one part open source software, and one part fun. The digital funvelope can be Drupal module that can be added to a local community site. The physical funvelope can be a gift item which could be set up with local manufacturing to provide employment.

How will the project improve communities?

By providing a unique way of gifting information through a simple visual user experience, to help support people exchanging local news and information, by wrapping it in the strength of local word of mouth and testimonial. What one user deems fun and recommends becomes a gift that is wrapped in a virtual funvelope. When it is opened, it can be shared. The original idea was also organic, local merchants, newspapers, businesses, and other institutions can also offer organic funvelopes to extend the system into physical space, either for the novelty (for example, parties and celebrations), or for extending some offers and exchanges of information to people without computers. See funvelope.com for more information.

The "physical" funvelope is featured in the following images:

It's a parallelogram-shaped envelope. Different, whimsical, fun. Perfect for gift giving at parties. Kids like whimsy.   *Take the paper out. It's a parallelogram too.*

This is what the paper looks like when it is unfolded.

When you fold the paper back, it becomes a parallelogram and can fit in the funvelope.

Digital Archaeology for Libraries

Empowering libraries to become sustainable hubs for collective curation using Drupal.

In the extreme pressures of an evolving economy, community institutions such as newspapers cut staff, coverage, and some even go out of business. A library may be the last community resource to fall back on. However, libraries everywhere are facing the perfect storm of declining budgets, an increased demand for supporting their communities and the challenge of continuing to provide services that are relevant in an atmosphere of rapidly changing Web technology. Drupal has been used by CFTW members over the last year to provide a series of local libraries (in hard hit areas such as the Bloomfield Library District in the Detroit area), with a sustainable alternative to their previous web sites, reducing costs and complexity while simultaneously opening the doors for their communities to take advantage of all the Drupal platform offers. The DAFL project seeks to build on this foundation to draw upon acquired expertise and innovations in developing library sites and seeks to refine a turnkey platform that can use a variety of modules to add plug and play services for these local communities.

How will the project improve communities?

DAFL empowers libraries to be the central repository for digital artifacts associated with their communities, as a supplement to the role that newspapers have played and continue to play. By providing a sustainable platform, DAFL empowers libraries expanding their capability to offer traditional information services to their local communities, including tools for learning new skills, engaging in citizen journalism, capturing digital artifacts, and establishing a sustainable community archive (for example: capturing photographs, videos, articles, and clippings from local events, both past and present).

How is the idea innovative?

DAFL allows libraries in the pilot areas to respond dynamically to community interest and needs as simply as installing and enabling modules in Drupal, which include innovating open source learning curriculums that allow library administrators to easily add (and customize) learning material oriented to local residents. Furthermore, DAFL will leverage and extend the multilingual capability of Drupal to enable communities with diverse multilingual constituencies to provide a way for bilingual residents to extend both news and learning material to additional community residents.
See digitalarchaeology.org. (Also, check out libraryhub.org, an interesting project that has a goal of empowering libraries to help communities.)

NewsAid

A turnkey collection of Drupal modules to help sustain newspapers and local communities. NewsAid proposes a series of Drupal modules based on validated concepts that have the potential to extend the role of local newspapers, based on emerging technology.

- *NewsAdAgency*: Resources to help newspaper staff essentially become a local online ad agency, approaching local businesses and helping them to leverage Google AdWords and related low-cost/free tools such as Google Analytics, Google Docs, and Google Sites to create landing pages. The suite of materials will help a newspaper to focus on making it easy for local merchants to take advantage of these technologies and to explore how online advertising can result in exactly trackable return on investment, and safely manage their limited ad budgets (as opposed to guessing on traditional, diminishing forms such as display advertising). The NewsAdAgency kit will provide an open source curriculum that is delivered through a Drupal module.

- *NewsCard (ReGiftCard)*: The NewsCard is based on the ReGiftCard platform, and provides a turnkey customer loyalty program, where a newspaper, local merchants, and local organizations can offer virtual (and physical) gift cards, and where local residents can also accumulate community points, much like uPromise, which can be directed towards the benefit of charities or redeemed for physical items or premium news items. See regiftcard.net.

- *xCredits*: The xCredits module provides a simple system to enable a newspaper and other local businesses (with the newspaper as the hub), to offer xCredits as part of a shopping cart purchase. The xCredits can be accumulated in a local resident's account and then directed towards a local charity. See xcredits.net.

- *NpoEx*: NpoEx provides a simulated local stock market, allowing residents to rate local businesses and organizations for their local impact, thereby affecting share price. See npoex.com.

- *FrameAds*: Frameads leverages a combination of a drupal module and WiFi-enabled digital photoframes to create a valuable local advertising network in local stores (which can then be brokered to big fish). It is managed by the local newspaper and also delivers Amber alerts. See frameads.org.

- *1dworld*: Text-based virtual world is a module/virtual space for both sighted and visually-impaired people to interact, create new places, and go on adventures or create new ones. Like Second Life, but with text, including a connection to Twitter, for PCs or mobile devices. The vision includes providing translation between various languages. See 1dworld.com.

- *JobLife*: Using xCredits, full virtual employment is offered for any resident, after skills training is taken. Virtual employment is apprenticeship, using skills such as online advertising on behalf of local non-profits. Residents earn virtual currency, which rises in value. See joblife.org.

- *Twinklepixel*: A module providing an extremely powerful way for local residents to have a visual representation of Twitter data from their local community. See twinklepixel.com.

- *Kahonua*: Accessible, local virtual park for kids. Module provides a simple interface that allows disabled kids and others to join a game environment like club penguin (but open source). See kahonua.com.

How will the project improve communities?

It helps to sustain newspapers by providing them with a way to generate additional revenue, support local business, and engage residents.

How is the idea innovative?

The modules provide new sustainability paradigms.

ShopLocal TLD

A system to help empower local economies.

A TLD is a top-level domain (see http://en.wikipedia.org/wiki/GTLD). For example, .com is a top-level domain and any web site that is created with this dimension is like a piece of virtual real estate. The ShopLocal TLD project proposes a set of underlying open source software that provides local newspapers or other businesses with a means to register local web site names for the purposes of generating revenue to sustain their operations, and a way to help support and sustain local business and news, including citizen journalism. The newspaper or community shop is a local hub in effect and becomes a registrar. CFTW owns sl.vu, and it can be used to facilitate a new series of web address. For example, Chicago could use chi.sl.vu and register web site names such as news.chi.sl.vu. The organization ICANN has recently allowed individual companies and organizations to propose so-called gTLDs, but the costs are enormous (the application fee is 200k USD) and the technical hurdles are significant. However, using a new open source framework called Agile PHP, as well as a suite of modular open source tools such as JHosting, ShopLocal proposes to place the ability to register (as well as sell and manage) web site names in local hands, based on the sl.vu name, which can be used as a web site extension.

How will the project improve communities?

By empowering a local entity to register local web site names, an emphasis on local business and news is generated. It provides a newspaper or other community institution with a unique source of revenue, and provides residents with a way to connect and express their local identities and presence, for the purpose of having a site for local online shopping, a local blog, etc. By providing a local organization for the registration of names, this system makes it significantly easier to browse, group, and gather locally-connected web sites. Instead of having every possible word in the English language between www. and .com, the local community can have a clear coherent set of local web sites, which reinforces a sense of community.

How is the idea innovative?

ShopLocal TLD seeks to take the power of controlling a TLD (top-level domain) and places it in the hands of a local community, by providing powerful open source software that makes it vastly easier and less costly to manage the registration and management of web site names. The precedent would be something like a country-level domain such as .cc, which has been used around the world after it was opened up for registration. But this system takes the domain sl.vu (owned by CFTW), and places it into the local public domain, so that local and regional communities can then create entirely new local spaces, such as chi.sl.vu, opening up new possibilities for the exchange of information and commerce.

Index

You Need the Companion eBook

Your purchase of this book entitles you to buy the companion PDF-version eBook for only $10. Take the weightless companion with you anywhere.

We believe this Apress title will prove so indispensable that you'll want to carry it with you everywhere, which is why we are offering the companion eBook (in PDF format) for $10 to customers who purchase this book now. Convenient and fully searchable, the PDF version of any content-rich, page-heavy Apress book makes a valuable addition to your programming library. You can easily find and copy code—or perform examples by quickly toggling between instructions and the application. Even simultaneously tackling a donut, diet soda, and complex code becomes simplified with hands-free eBooks!

Once you purchase your book, getting the $10 companion eBook is simple:

❶ Visit **www.apress.com/promo/tendollars/**.

❷ Complete a basic registration form to receive a randomly generated question about this title.

❸ Answer the question correctly in 60 seconds, and you will receive a promotional code to redeem for the $10.00 eBook.

233 Spring Street, New York, NY 10013

Offer valid through 8/10.